WHEN THE
WORLD STOPPED
TO LISTEN

WHEN THE
WORLD STOPPED
TO LISTEN

Van Cliburn's Cold War Triumph

and Its Aftermath

STUART ISACOFF

ALFRED A. KNOPF · NEW YORK · 2017

Library of Congress Cataloging-in-Publication Data
Names: Isacoff, Stuart, author.
Title: When the world stopped to listen : Van Cliburn's Cold War triumph
and its aftermath / by Stuart Isacoff.
Description: New York : Alfred A. Knopf, 2017. | Includes bibliographical
references and index.
Identifiers: LCCN 2016032873 | ISBN 9780385352185 (hardcover) |
ISBN 9780451494030 (eBook)
Subjects: LCSH: Cliburn, Van, 1934–2013. | Pianists—United States—Biography.
| International Tchaikovsky Competition (1st : 1958 : Moscow, Russia) | Music—
Competitions—Russia (Federation)—Moscow.
Classification: LCC ML417.C67 I83 2017 | DDC 786.2092 [B] —dc23 LC record available at
https://lccn.loc.gov/2016032873

Jacket image: Van Cliburn during the Tchaikovsky Competition, Moscow,
April 1958. Courtesy of the Van Cliburn Foundation.
Jacket design by Peter Mendelsund

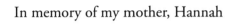

In memory of my mother, Hannah

The changing wisdom of successive generations discards ideas, questions facts, demolishes theories. But the artist appeals to that part of our being which is not dependent on wisdom; to that in us which is a gift and not an acquisition—and, therefore, more permanently enduring. He speaks to our capacity for delight and wonder, to the sense of mystery surrounding our lives; to our sense of pity, and beauty, and pain; to the latent feeling of fellowship with all creation—and to the subtle but invincible conviction of solidarity that knits together the loneliness of innumerable hearts, to the solidarity in dreams, in joy, in sorrow, in aspirations, in illusions, in hope, in fear, which binds men to each other, which binds together all humanity—the dead to the living and the living to the unborn.

—JOSEPH CONRAD

Contents

WHEN THE
WORLD STOPPED
TO LISTEN

Crowds in the Streets

THE CROWDS GREW DAILY in front of the Moscow Conservatory of Music: workmen in their fur hats; matriarchs draped in black coats and scarves; teenage girls clutching bundles of flowers and shivering in the crisp air. A haze of chilled breath covered those who gathered, like fine dust. Clouds hovered overhead, lending a bleak cast to the setting. It was April, when the patches of ice on Moscow's streets usually give way to the spring sun, as tender blades rise up from beneath the ground's frozen surface. In 1958, though, the ghost of winter lingered on. And people still continued to congregate.

They clustered around the monument of Tchaikovsky at the perimeter of the school—a restructured eighteenth-century manor house, once occupied by royalty—and spilled out into the snow-covered courtyard. As they reached a wall of militiamen blocking the entrance, their unsynchronized parade congealed into a serried mass before falling into disarray.

In a city where people often queued up even without knowing what they might find—fish? bananas? concert tickets?—long lines were a way of life. Writer Igor Efimov invented a character who secretly loved these assemblages: "She felt peaceful in them, as if contained in a safe shell composed of the people in front of and behind her." Most Muscovites simply resigned themselves to the situation. In this crowd, though, people were fired up.

They were there hopefully to see the talk of the town: a long-legged young Texan whose soaring pianism had for days been enthralling audiences at the first-ever Tchaikovsky International Piano Competition, a high-culture version of the World Cup pitting musical talents from around the globe against one another. The contest had been designed to bolster Soviet pride by anointing a hometown winner. Yet all attention was now focused on the uncanny American whose musical talent stunned the judges and drove mobs of ordinary citizens into a frenzy.

The buzz about him began in the Conservatory's Great Hall during the contest's opening round, and soon floated through the city like a vapor. As newspaper editors and broadcasters fanned the excitement, tickets became as rare as the Romanov crown jewels. Van Cliburn, from Kilgore, Texas, was all the rage. Workers with little education began to stalk certain streets hoping for a glimpse of him. When pianist Lev Vlassenko, the Soviet Union's top contender in the competition—and the Kremlin's presumptive winner—took a taxi to the conservatory, the driver asked him, "And how is the tall one doing?"

It was a stunning turn of events. Tension between the United

States and the Soviet Union had been steadily rising since the launch in 1957 of the first *Sputnik* space satellite. By the time of the Tchaikovsky Competition, the West was collectively holding its breath out of fear that bombs would soon be falling from the skies; American children regularly practiced diving under their desks in school in preparation for the coming disaster.

With such pervasive antipathy between the nations, no one could have predicted that by the end of the first two series of eliminations an American would be poised to reach the top rung in this Soviet contest. In a culture where nearly everything was based on political calculation, Van's advance toward a possible victory was big news. Yet, to nearly everyone who heard him, it seemed inevitable.

He was six foot four and capped by bushy blond hair (the American ambassador's wife dubbed him "Brillo Top"). His face had an Irish lilt, with its finely sculpted jaw and cheekbones; thin, sensual lips; and cornflower-blue eyes. And he was oh, so thin! When seated at the piano he looked like "a peapod with great Jack the Giant Killer hands," said one of his managers, Schuyler Chapin. Critic Winthrop Sargeant described the pianist's fingers as a "bunch of asparagus." Neither image sounded especially lovely, though each framed him as a force of nature.

Nevertheless, remembered Max Frankel, then in Moscow as a correspondent for *The New York Times,* young Russian girls were swooning. Women of a certain age wanted to adopt him. Their daughters had other designs.

His admirers in the concert hall and those who heard him over the radio or saw him on television were hooked almost from the moment the twenty-three-year-old first appeared on the stage. But it wasn't the music alone that drew them. His Southern charm was as thick as gravy on fresh biscuits as he greeted his new fans with the prim decorousness of a proper East Texas gentleman, unfailingly gracious at every turn. The Russian public had embraced virtuosos before, but Van was a different sort. He showed none of the brooding intensity of Sviatoslav Richter, or the demonic sparks of Vladimir Horowitz; the ground and the walls didn't shake when he performed, as they had seemed to for Anton Rubinstein. He simply played like an angel. Muscovites surrendered their hearts to him.

Even his odd mannerisms were inexplicably endearing, like the way he casually furrowed his brow when speaking, suggesting a sort of backwoods Clark Gable, or his habit of looking upward when he played, as if communing with the heavens whenever the music reached an emotional peak, while his lips formed a nearly perpetual pucker from the Life Savers he routinely kept in his mouth. Two of the competition's most celebrated jury members, pianists Lev Oborin and Heinrich Neuhaus, debated those head motions. "Why does he do that?" asked Oborin, disapprovingly. "He's conversing with God," replied Neuhaus. "That was [a gift] not given to us."

Broadcasts of the competition were so popular that the streets were often empty when the pianists were performing. Listening became a collective rite, binding enthusiasts together into what one prominent Russian music critic called a national *veche*, the equivalent of a medieval popular assembly. Those admirers created so strong a ballast against possible Kremlin tampering with the jury vote that it was said years later by critic Tamara Grum-Grzhimailo that the seeds of perestroika were first planted in this moment, during the Tchaikovsky Competition. Some in the Kremlin, of course, resisted the American's coronation, dreading a Cold War defeat. Yet Van's appeal was hardly political. It was personal. He had the uncanny ability to melt nearly anyone's self-reserve. He had always worn his heart on his sleeve, and though hard-nosed friends in New York often snickered at his overwrought sentimentality, the Russians responded in kind. Van's deep-seated humility made his magnetism, even his exaggerated emotions, feel trustworthy.

Below the surface, a more complex dynamic was in play. Raised in the genteel hothouse of an East Texas culture where people are taught to keep their inner demons well buried, Cliburn was less simple than he seemed, yet he projected a kind of spiritual purity: not in the sense of his having rejected earthly temptation—far from it—but through an aura of plain, unsullied decency.

His pianism shared many of the same qualities. He sat regally erect at the instrument, like a king on his throne (not unlike the great nineteenth-century pianist Sigismond Thalberg, who had allegedly developed his posture by smoking a Turkish pipe while practicing); but his tone, like his character, was warm and entrancing, a "magnolia blossom" sound, as one Texas patron described it. His hands could swallow large portions of the keyboard in a single swoop, and through them the music flowed as naturally as a spring breeze, its surges and taperings artfully measured, gently gusting with a pulse that was both sure-footed and elastic.

And somehow, it all sounded confessional. Whether he was performing Bach or Rachmaninoff, the piano seemed to be sharing intimate secrets. His unique sound—the glowing tone and gentle earnestness, the way the music's dynamics under his fingertips rose and fell like sighs as he shaped a melody—collapsed the distance between himself and his listeners, so that as he played, Chopin's heart seemed to beat within their own chests.

Though his rivals at the competition were well trained, there was something different about Van's art. For many in the audience it represented the face of freedom. Performing under the auspices of a repressive regime and before an intimidating jury of some of the world's greatest musicians, he seemed to answer to no authority other than the shifting tides of his own soul. The mere act of hearing him became liberating.

When the American took home the gold, it set off a commotion around the world, opening diplomatic doors and launching one of music's most remarkable careers. Van Cliburn's story has the outlines of a Homeric epic, with great forces arrayed against each other like deities on a great battlefield; challenges that tested the strength of individual souls; and a hero who rose to mythical heights in an extraordinary victory that proved only fleeting, before the gods of fortune exacted their price.

Much of what happened has remained untold: It's a dramatic mix of political intrigue and private struggle; of blossoming artistry and the pitfalls of celebrity; of small glimmers of hope that thrived in the midst of a terrifying clash of global powers. It is above all a tale of the ability of an artist to touch and transform others, but also a caution about art's limitations. For Van Cliburn—as well as for other top winners of the first Tchaikovsky Competition—triumph and decline were inextricably joined.

CHAPTER I

Van

I N THE BEGINNING were Mommy, Daddy, and Steinway
no. 157754. They formed the fabric of Van Cliburn's world
from his very first moments.

When Van was born, in Shreveport, Louisiana, on July 12,
1934, the ebony concert grand was already an entrenched member of the household. It inhabited the Cliburns' music room like
a sleeping giant, an imposing presence, noble and inert. When
his mother pressed its keys, stirring it to life, he was completely
entranced. The instrument cast a spell over him even before he
could speak.

It had journeyed over 1,600 miles west during Christmastime
of 1915, from the instrument maker's factory in Queens, New
York, looping its way south of Shreveport to reach Galveston,
Texas, a temporary home, before settling in Dallas. That's where

Van's father, Harvey Lavan Cliburn, acquired it secondhand. For a family of limited means, it was a luxurious item, even at something less than the original list price of $1,600.

But his wife, Rildia Bee O'Bryan Cliburn, a local piano teacher with a brood of young talents in her charge, considered it worth every penny, and not only because of the income she brought in from lessons to help make ends meet. She simply couldn't live without a piano in the house. Rildia Bee had once entertained serious ambitions as a pupil of renowned pianist Arthur Friedheim, a former disciple of two titans of Romantic music, Anton Rubinstein and Franz Liszt. Friedheim was musical royalty, described by fabled pianist Vladimir de Pachmann as both "inspired by God" and "a pupil of the devil," which befitted a student of Liszt, the classical superstar whose demonic energy drove women into a frenzy even as he undertook religious vows.

Some pianists are able to charm us through poetry, impress us with brilliant technique, or seduce us through exquisite tone production, noted one observer, but Friedheim possessed the complete package. And Rildia Bee was said to have been his favorite student. The two grew extremely close (his family even heard rumors of a romance), and he was clearly preparing her for an important musical career. That, however, would not have been a fitting occupation for a Southern belle. Under the weight of parental pressure Rildia Bee resigned herself to a life away from the concert stage. Still, with the insights she gained from Friedheim she had a precious legacy to impart, and it took just a short while for her to discover that the best candidate for that inheritance was living under her own roof.

Young Van showed the right signs early on. He often crouched in a corner to listen as his mother gave instruction to an endless stream of youngsters. After hours, when she practiced her own repertoire, he sat mesmerized. He once made note of her "perfect" hands and powerful presence. There was much else to admire: her refined exuberance, the beatific smile and devout air—like a Madonna of the Red River country.

She introduced her son to the instrument's physical allure. Well before Van could walk, his mother would playfully suspend him over the keys of the piano and watch as he'd reach down and touch them, never succumbing to the normal childish urge to bang out a sound. She took this as a sign of unusual sensitivity. One day, after ending a lesson with a young student named Sammy Talbot and sending him on his way, Rildia Bee continued to hear one of the boy's pieces—"Arpeggio Waltz" by Caroline Crawford—being played. She called out to Sammy to hurry along before his mother became worried. Sammy, though, had already left the premises: Van was sitting at the piano. At the age of three he had picked up the music simply by listening and observing.

Many musical legends boasted similar starts. Mozart began playing a keyboard at age three after watching his sister take her lessons. He toured Europe professionally before most children learn to ride a bicycle. Aware of his own unusual abilities, he touted his gifts brazenly. He was so self-confident that at age six he blithely informed Marie Antoinette—later to be queen of France—that he intended to marry her. She was charmed. Even then his charisma could light up a room.

Rildia Bee was mindful of the possibilities. "She asked if I wanted to study the piano," Van recalled. "I said yes. She said, 'Well, you're not going to play by ear . . . you're going to know what you're doing.' And she started teaching me the language of music." She composed little pieces for him to learn.

His mother and the Steinway filled his life with order and romance. Rildia Bee—who had a hint of the martinet in her— was often more teacher than nurturer, bringing discipline and structure to his days. Van would later lament that he never had a real childhood, but there were compensations. The piano provided emotional succor, especially as he progressed from soothing childhood lullabies to rapturous fantasies. Music fed the emotional core of his being, and from the start, the sonority of the piano was entwined with his feelings for his mother. Little wonder his every performance sounded like a valentine.

The training was a family affair. "My father made a blackboard with lines and spaces for my theory lessons," Van said. "It was a vivid, interesting, wonderful experience." Rildia Bee's lessons went beyond the common "little fingers learn to play" approach, with its emphasis on the mere mechanics of piano technique. She understood the importance of using varieties of touch and phrasing to suggest the sound of the very first instrument, the human voice. It was a secret shared by all the great virtuosos. Even Anton Rubinstein, with a reputation for bombastic fireworks at the piano, sat in his youth for hours trying to imitate on the keyboard the singing of Giovanni Battista Rubini, the Enrico Caruso of his day.

So among Mrs. Cliburn's instructions to her son was the admonition to vocalize everything—Mozart, Beethoven, Liszt, Rachmaninoff. When she assigned him a Bach two-part invention, Van recalled, "she had me sight-sing it before I played it." He quickly discovered that bringing each part of the melodic line into independent relief before it was absorbed into the musical whole made for a more rewarding interpretation.

There were practical reasons. The physical separation that exists between the pianist and the piano's strings also reflects a psychological distance, a gap that leads inartful musicians into the trap of simply moving fingers reflexively, without giving proper attention to the tonal shapes being generated. The result can be as coldly mechanical as the clicks of a computer keyboard. In contrast, the human voice box produces a more visceral experience: By singing the tones, a player becomes mindful of where to breathe, which notes to emphasize, how to shade the music's dynamics to illuminate a phrase's emotional intent. Taking that extra step also impacts the speed at which things will be played. "If you are singing, you have to gauge the tempo and judge the comprehension of sound by the audience," explained Van. "So, because of my mother, I can't really play much faster than I can sing the notes."

He was already strongly inclined toward a songful approach. From the time he was taken to the opera to see *Carmen* at the age of four (he saw it four times, he said, three evening performances and a dress rehearsal), he considered the human voice to be the greatest of all instruments. Late in life he confessed that he would much rather have been a singer than a pianist, but simply didn't have the equipment for it. Once he began to perform publicly, the memory of that early operatic experience became central to his uniquely beautiful sound.

His parents used other types of training to mold the future star, bringing the attentiveness they had devoted to his piano lessons to the task of building his character. If Mozart's father sometimes abided his son's self-indulgent, even vulgar, behavior, the Cliburns would have none of that; they were determined to instill deeper values in their offspring. When Van was four, they compelled him to wait on them at the dinner table as if they were guests, and then to do the same for neighbors. The exercise was designed to inculcate a sense of humility, a counterbalance against the danger of feeling too special. Their admonitions that he behave deferentially toward others left a lasting imprint.

Indeed, serving graciously became a life refrain, an eleventh commandment. Even as the accolades mounted and his fame and stature grew, he would find it difficult to say no to anyone (at least directly). As an adult he would reflexively leap to his feet like a startled gazelle at the arrival of strangers, rushing to greet them as if they were close family members he hadn't seen in years. Courteousness would become a trademark. Perversely, it was a quality that would also bring him anguish.

This was especially true in the concert hall, where he came to view the audience as guests to be served, a notion that brought such attendant pressures it could turn routine musical occasions into ordeals. That relationship with his listeners was fraught from the beginning, even in his debut at Dodd College in Shreveport at the age of four. "I was absolutely as nervous about going before the public as I am today," he would recall.

Cliburn linked his agitation on stage to those early parental lessons. "Even at the age of four I knew that I was not there for myself, but for someone else," he explained. "When you have to serve . . . you're more interested in the experience of your guests than in partaking of the food." Worrying about pleasing those guests, a tremble could course involuntarily through his hands. He usually managed to shake it off; but over the years there would be moments when his fingers wriggled helplessly like the glowing filaments in a candle's wick. As a musician, he decided, "only 50 percent of you can really be there, because half of you must be in the audience. It is for the audience that you are performing. That is your reason for being, and your responsibility . . . And that's how I have felt all my life."

Young Van couldn't have understood the hurdles that had been placed in his way. No artist can afford to be uncaring about an audience. Some, like pianist Arthur Rubinstein, became known for radiating a palpable energy that made individual listeners believe he was playing for them alone. Rubinstein's daughter Alina, whose relationship with her father was troubled, reported that when she wanted to feel his warmth she simply attended one of his recitals.

But achieving a kind of spiritual communion with listeners is not the same as becoming their emotional prisoner. Fulfilling the task set out by the composer is challenge enough. Van's job became doubly difficult: wrestling with the demands of the music while also worrying about gratifying his fans. "Heaven cannot brook two suns, nor earth two masters," as Alexander the Great's adage says. The strain of that divided self fueled a pattern of performance anxiety from which he would never really escape. Nevertheless, his course was set. By the time the family moved to Kilgore, Texas, where the Magnolia Oil Company relocated his father, he was, at six, already becoming an active public performer.

Kilgore is one terrifying hour east of Dallas by small commuter plane, a white-knuckle ride as the craft continually swoops, banks, and shakes—a jaunt befitting the rough-and-tumble legacy of the territory it traverses. The place was once home to "the world's richest acre," the field that transformed a depressed cotton-based economy into a wealthy boomtown in 1930, after wildcatter Columbus M. "Dad" Joiner struck it rich with an oil well called Daisy Bradford no. 3. There are still derricks in town—adorned with colored lights at Christmas—and, scattered here and there, oil pumps, surging and clanging as their heads incessantly rise up and dip back into the ground, looking for all the world like thirsty prehistoric creatures. But the oil rush has long been over, and the rickety shacks and gambling joints that once dotted the landscape are just faded memories.

Today, the place is notable mostly for the Kilgore College Rangerettes—often seen performing their dance routines at Dallas Cowboys football games—and as Van Cliburn's boyhood home. During his childhood, oil still lubricated the local economy, the water tasted of sulfur, and the nighttime sky gave way to a pervasive orange glow. But Kilgore had many winning aspects, including a small-town ambience; everyone knew everyone else, and social life was a well-ordered mix of church functions and double features at the local movie theaters.

Though Van was born in Shreveport, he never considered himself to be anything but a Texan, through and through—it was an article of faith, like the idea he formed early on that he would one day be a concert pianist. The family tree boasted generations of Texas preachers and politicians. Rildia Bee's grandfather, Dr. S. G. O'Bryan, was a Baptist minister and a personal pastor to Sam Houston, the president of Texas before it became a state. The Cliburns took up residence in a tiny white frame house just in back of a public school, where students could easily walk from class to the wooden fence behind the Cliburns' back porch, scoot through a well-worn opening, and scurry on into the dining room, which served as Rildia Bee's studio. She added a second piano, an 1869 Bechstein upright, to the furnishings sometime in the 1940s.

She was a typical East Texas matriarch, a picture of Southern politesse, with heavily rouged cheeks and her trademark lavish hats. She taught Sunday school, sang in the choir, and, as the town's most prominent keyboardist, played organ both in the local Baptist church and for the small Lutheran congregation. Her position helped ensure that her son would be featured prominently wherever music recitals were a possibility, whether in school or at meetings of Kilgore's social clubs.

Playing the piano put Van in good stead with neighbors and teachers. Though he wanted to please his mother most of all, she was always his toughest critic. "He's lucky he didn't fall off the bench," was her familiar refrain as he rose in prominence. It just made him work harder; on the hottest days of summer he would practice for hours on end with the doors and windows of the house thrown wide open.

Van's finger choreography and keyboard leaps became studies in poise. His mother imbued his hand motions with a Russian pedigree, teaching him tricks like the technique of stroking rather than striking the keys—drawing his fingers in toward the palms as they caressed the ivory surfaces—in order to create a sweeter sound.

Her lessons always went beyond physical drills. Playing an instrument is more art than science, demanding not merely accuracy but the ability to create a sense of enchantment. Arthur Friedheim reportedly could play some passages with a sound that was not merely soft, but "eerie and fantastic: like a thing disembodied, afloat in the air between daylight and darkness." There are physical tricks to such an effect, which is accomplished partly through subtle control of the piano's pedals, the devices that can sustain the instrument's tones in midair once they are struck, or soften their volume to a muted whisper.

Yet technical mastery is merely a starting point. Friedheim told the story of how he was preparing to play Liszt's *Harmonies du soir* for the composer when Liszt called him to a window. "The slanting rays of the declining sun . . . were mellowing the landscape with the delicate glamour of approaching twilight," he remembered. " 'Play that,' [Liszt] said. 'There are your evening harmonies.' " No amount of uninspired, repetitive practice could make it happen. Van understood much of this instinctually. He had a natural ability to grasp and convey the meaning of the music, to animate the virtual world that arises through the art's subtle symbolic gestures. It set him apart.

But the piano is a demanding master, and he missed out on many life lessons. His mother nixed the idea of any recreational activities that might endanger his hands. Basketball was forbidden. So was riding a bicycle. He never learned to swim. He did manage to expand his horizons in other ways—for example, through weekly drama lessons from a local graduate of Northwestern University's School of Speech, Mrs. Leo Satterwhite Allen. Rildia Bee made the arrangements. In exchange, she gave piano lessons to Mrs. Allen's child.

Beginning at age seven, Allen taught him to shape his spoken phrases into "Oxfordian"—or, as he called it, "*English* English"— which he learned to deliver with oratorical flair. By the time he reached high school, these skills brought him the presidency of the dramatics club, the Thespians. Acting was an art impervious to the nervous tics that had gripped him at piano recitals, perhaps because it allowed him temporarily to become someone else. Learning to role-play onstage became his saving grace.

He absorbed Allen's lessons and gradually folded them into his public persona. When Soviet pianist Nina Lelchuk met Van in Texas in 1962, she assumed his clarity of speech reflected a special effort made for her sake; he informed her that it was simply a result of those boyhood lessons with Allen. They would serve him well throughout his career.

Life in Kilgore wasn't all practice and study, of course, though Van's occasional bouts of mischief—like the time he and his friend Lottie Lou Lipscomb took some of his father's adding-machine paper, twisted it into a roll, and lit up—were tame. "We were brought up not to do anything bad," said Texas-raised pianist Jeaneane Dowis, Van's close friend during his Juilliard days, "and we felt bad even if we just thought about it."

It was a more innocent time. Kilgore was typical of hundreds of small towns where people congregated at church and at local hot spots like, in this case, Jay's Café in nearby Henderson. Van always felt at home among people for whom warm rolls at a favorite truck stop could spark heartfelt reveries. That he would spend special occasions, like Christmas Eve, gathered at a place like Jay's with friends was emblematic of what set the pianist apart from the northeastern sophisticates whose domain he would soon be entering. He never left his childhood world behind.

Van was fairly timid around girls, especially after his skin erupted during his teenage years. Yet he still stirred their interest. Rosemary Butts, his junior by two grades, accepted his last-minute invitation to the school prom, acceding to his request for a dance lesson beforehand. They went out again on his eighteenth birthday, to a drive-in, where he finally found the courage to steal a kiss. The experience left him so flummoxed that when the movie ended he drove off with the theater's loudspeaker still hanging inside his car window. His romantic inclinations seemed on safer grounds with Schumann's reveries.

Each of life's little dramas deepened the well of experience from which he could draw on to recognize the emotional language of music's masterworks: the way Tchaikovsky conveyed the gracefulness of a human sigh or the poignancy of unrequited love, for example, using subtle dynamic shifts and plangent harmonies. Van brought out the heartbreak and loneliness in romantic piano works like Frank Sinatra plumbing the depths of a torch song.

All the while, his local reputation as a pianist continued to grow. He began attending every major musical event and competition within driving distance, often sleeping under a blanket in the back of his parents' car. "I sometimes say I grew up on Highway 80, because we were always rushing up and down to Dallas or San Antonio or wherever a wonderful performer was playing," he would later explain. When notable artists, including José Iturbi, Arthur Rubinstein, and Risë Stevens, came through the area, his mother brought him backstage to meet them.

By the age of twelve he had won the 1946 Texas Gulf Sulphur Company contest, playing the Tchaikovsky First Piano Concerto (the piece would become his musical signature), which led to a performance with the Houston Symphony on the radio. Despite his intense stage nerves, the next year he triumphed over sixteen other pianists in Dallas for a Carnegie Hall date. He cut his musical eyeteeth on those local contests, which became his training grounds for bigger things. As time went on, the awards proliferated.

Ardent supporters in Texas, like Mildred Foster, the grande dame of Dallas music society, flocked to him. The competitions brought him face-to-face with other young Texans who were treading the road to musical fame. He met his close friend Jimmy Mathis at one such match. Mathis remembered when he first set eyes on the Cliburns. "Van came piling out, playing the concerto, with Rildia Bee performing the orchestra part on the second piano," he recalls. "I was twelve and Van was eleven. They were both terribly sloppy. But he still showed enormous talent."

The two became friends, says Mathis, because he was the only pianist Van knew within a thousand miles. Whenever the Cliburns went to Dallas on a shopping spree, they would drop by to see the Mathises. "My parents were not so religious, so they got tired of Rildia Bee talking about Van's God-given talent," says

Mathis. "My mother would say, 'Where in hell does she think yours comes from?'" Nevertheless, the two boys grew close, leaving "tire tracks all over East Texas," says Mathis, even before they were of legal age.

Like a fidgety Huck Finn slipping out the window to escape the Widow Douglas, the woman whose ways Huck found too "dismal regular and decent" for comfort, Van let loose from the confines of his sheltered routine through roadside adventures along Kilgore's plains and pine forests. In high school, he would take his friend Lottie Lou's black Buick for a ride at lunchtime. "Rural areas were not so far away, and he wanted to go where he could drive fast," she said. "We'd head out for about thirty minutes, and get back in time for class."

Once he took Bill Morton, a childhood friend with whom Van often sat on a kitchen floor and played board games, home in the family car, along with a girl from their Latin class. It scared the daylights out of both passengers. "Van was usually shy, and somewhat under his mother's shadow," remembered Morton. "But when he got in the driver's seat he was a totally different personality. It was like he was at the keyboard, playing as hard and as fast as he could. I think it was the first and last time I ever rode with him."

There were few such opportunities to break free of parental restraints. Over time, Harvey Lavan Cliburn faded into the background. As Van's Juilliard piano teacher, Rosina Lhévinne, would say of his father, "He was a piece of furniture, dear." Rildia Bee, indifferent to the call of youth, continued to cast a veto whenever her son expressed interest in anything that would distract from her rigorous program. It only solidified their bond. Despite small signs of teenage waywardness, when it came to his mother, Van was forever smitten.

"Once in church, during our high-school years," remembered Lottie Lou, "Mrs. Cliburn sang a solo and one of the parishioners made a disparaging remark about her voice. Van reared up, filled with passion, and forcefully chastised the offender. 'You are speaking of the woman I love!'" he declared.

Rildia Bee's summer treks with Van to the Juilliard School of Music in New York introduced him for the first time to other piano teachers. While she attended master classes, he took private lessons from two of the school's most important faculty members: composer and pianist Ernest Hutcheson, in 1948, and, in 1951, Carl Friedberg, a former student of Clara Schumann. Friedberg had valuable insights and historical tales to share, especially about Clara, who as a young girl gained the admiration of Chopin, Liszt, and Mendelssohn. Hutcheson had also rubbed elbows with many illustrious music figures; he became the dean of the school in 1926, and then its president from 1937 to 1945. But Van didn't speak of either man; for him, there was really only one piano teacher, and she lived in Kilgore.

Rildia Bee, though, understood the need to find her own replacement, and she was intrigued to learn that Mathis was studying with the legendary Juilliard teacher Olga Samaroff. Samaroff's exotic moniker was counterfeit: for career purposes she had wisely discarded her far less scintillating given name, Lucy Hickenlooper, and also disguised the fact that she had been born in Texas. Yet in other respects she was the real thing—the first woman to debut at Carnegie Hall (in 1905). However, she could be indelicate in dealing with students, and with the Texas matrons who watched over them.

Mrs. Mathis's air of gentility, like Mrs. Cliburn's, masked a core of hard steel. Both were take-charge personalities who scrutinized the musical progress of their sons with the vigilance of mama bears guarding their cubs. Neither would brook any sign of laxity. One day Samaroff reported to Jimmy's mother: "Mrs. Mathis, your son is very talented, but he does need to play with more expression." Later, while eating at a restaurant, Jimmy suddenly felt sharp kicks under the table. "*When* are you *going* to *play* with *more* expression?" demanded his mother.

Rildia Bee was keenly aware that it was helpful to be associated with a teacher of high repute like Samaroff, who held concerts at Town Hall every month. And there were other practical advantages, remembered Mathis: "she got me a scholarship and support. And I reported it all to the Cliburns." Rildia Bee took it all in. Jimmy encouraged Van to study with his teacher. Introductions were made. Then, at the end of 1948, the venerable Samaroff died.

As Rildia Bee searched for a suitable alternative, she learned that Mathis had moved on to a new mentor at Juilliard: a gold-medal graduate of the Moscow Conservatory, Rosina Lhévinne. Her late husband, Josef, had been considered one of the world's greatest pianists. By the time Van was ready to enter the school, in 1951, Lhévinne's students included not only Mathis but also Dowis and the formidable John Browning, a contingent that would form a tight network of friends for the remainder of Van's school years.

The diminutive Lhévinne was not yet the shining star of the Juilliard piano faculty. She had, in fact, spent years in Samaroff's shadow. When Olga was giving music courses for laymen at Town Hall, "Rosina sat in a back seat, like a little mouse, trying to catch some of the gold dust that Samaroff was spreading," recounted Juilliard teacher Joseph Bloch. Once Samaroff was gone, Lhévinne came into her own.

That competitive dynamic was not atypical at Juilliard. The

school's rarefied atmosphere was like an intrigue-ridden imperial court where music's royalty, an assortment of truly oddball characters with bloated egos, vied incessantly for position. Sascha Gorodnitzki reportedly walked the long way around in school to avoid seeing a rival, Adele Marcus; Irwin Freundlich notoriously set out to steal everyone else's students, so other piano teachers refused to speak to him for years.

Aside from the infighting, behavior at the school could often verge on the bizarre. "A teacher named Bernard Taylor," reported Bloch, "was once discovered sitting on a nun. He claimed he was teaching her breath control, but they fired him anyway." Strangest of all was Alexander Siloti, an exemplar of music's golden age who had studied with Tchaikovsky, Nikolai Rubinstein, and Liszt. Siloti claimed that the long-deceased Liszt actually visited him in the evenings. He and his wife kept an extra setting at the dinner table for the late composer. Bloch performed a Liszt piece at one of Samaroff's soirées once, and Siloti told him that Liszt had objected that the performance was too fast. Samaroff intervened: "'Mr. Siloti,' she said, 'would you please explain to Liszt that Mr. Bloch is very busy, so he had to hurry?'"

Samaroff now out of the picture, Rildia Bee decided that Lhévinne would make the best mentor for Van. Yet it wasn't immediately clear to the teacher that the two were meant for each other. At his audition, says Lhévinne's assistant, Martin Canin, she turned to another student, Shirley Aronoff, and asked, "'Do you think I should take him?' 'Of course,' Shirley replied, 'he's wonderful.'" Apparently, additional arm twisting was needed.

"Van's family had driven him to Juilliard, and he played a good audition," says Mathis. "But they assigned him to Josef Raieff. That was clearly not what the Cliburns, who were waiting downstairs, had come all the way from Kilgore for. They said,

'If he can't study with Mrs. Lhévinne, we will take him home.'"
Mathis went upstairs to speak to her. He was pushy, he says, in
the way only a seventeen-year-old can be, telling her that if she
didn't take him, she would be making a big mistake. Finally, he
begged. Lhévinne hemmed and hawed, then finally told him to
tell the Cliburns she would take Van.

It was the kind of moment on which the wheels of history
turn. "Thank you so very much for the inspiration and encouragement you are lending him," Rildia Bee wrote in a note to
Lhévinne. "He would have been terribly disappointed had you
not 'squeezed' him into your class." But the transition to New
York was traumatic for the young Texan. In those first days he
wrote home to his high-school dancing partner, Rosemary Butts,
that he never felt so alone in his life. "When my parents drove off
and left me here, I went down to get a haircut, just so I could be
with somebody," he confessed. It wouldn't be long before things
began to look up.

CHAPTER 2

From Juilliard to the Big Time

J UST STEPS BEYOND Juilliard's doors on Claremont Avenue and 122nd Street in Manhattan awaited the city that never sleeps, a dizzying amalgam of bright lights, bustling traffic, glittery theaters, and extravagant shops. New York was never a single town, but a puzzle of ethnic neighborhoods, each crammed with unique colors, aromas, and sounds. Just to the north of the school sat Langston Hughes's Harlem, the heart of black New York, with its legacy of "dreams deferred," where improvised music blazed from a string of raucous nightclubs, all teeming with the pulse of life. Downtown in artsy Greenwich Village, the dreams wafted like sweet incense through streets prowled by Allen Ginsberg's feverish "angelheaded hipsters"—outcasts "burning for the ancient heavenly connection to the starry dynamo in the machinery of night."

These were new vistas for Van, each with the promise of expanded horizons. Texas had given him a solid foundation, both musically and spiritually. New York was a bolder playground: vivid, tempting, bewildering, and often scandalous. The city was an intoxicant, as powerful in its effects on Juilliard's young musicians as wine-and-opium-doused Paris was on Baudelaire and his circle. Van held fast to his roots, yet he couldn't help being lured from his Texas moorings—at least a little.

Soon after settling into his room in the nearby apartment of Allen and Hazel Spicer on Claremont Avenue, an accommodation arranged by Rildia Bee, Van was ready to explore these new frontiers with the members of the little clique formed from among Lhévinne's students. Their piano teacher's idea of a fun outing was a trip to Long Island's Jones Beach or to Bear Mountain up the Hudson River, where she regularly organized picnics. On their own, these students made excursions of a very different sort to the seedier parts of town, with Mathis as the impish ringleader.

Within a couple of years they were frequenting the newly opened Club 82, a cabaret situated near Second Avenue, in the old Yiddish theater district. "It was kind of wild for Texas boys and girls," remembers Mathis: The performers were men dressed as women, and the waiters were women dressed as men.

That kind of cross-gender clowning could be found even in the Juilliard practice rooms, where pianist Herbert Rogers, another of Cliburn's Texas friends, could be discovered dressed up as the famed British pianist Dame Myra Hess. "He used to do her all the time, and he had every gesture down," said Mathis, "except that he had a cigar in his mouth. Another time we heard a rumor that a new Hungarian pianist had come to the school, and that she played louder and faster and cleaner than anyone in the world. It turned out to be Alexis ['Ziggy'] Weissenberg in drag."

At Club 82, said Mathis, the atmosphere was more burlesque theatrics than titillating, comedic rather than sexually charged. The fact that the men in the Juilliard group were all homosexual was only tangentially relevant. "It might have been considered risqué that we were there, but sexual preference really never came into it," he explained. It was the artistic crowd's equivalent of a frat party. The group would soften up with rum punches, then take the ferry to the Palisades, on the New Jersey side of the Hudson. Van maintained a public image of avoiding liquor (what would Mother have thought?), but that pretense dissolved in the company of friends, where he would match his companions glass for glass. As he explored his new turf, the strict boundaries of Van's early upbringing yielded to other immoderate conduct. He became a habitual smoker. "Sometimes I think it's my only friend," he once said of his pack of cigarettes.

"Van and I would go to a bar near 112th Street," said Mathis. "I got him to be a lounge pianist, and he was great, a fabulous improviser. He had a marvelous ear, like Cy Walter's"—the elegant café-society pianist who was labeled "the Art Tatum of Park Avenue." "And he also performed opera roles—he was wonderful in *Samson and Delilah*. He could sing all the parts." Pianist Glenn Mack recalled another bar in that uptown neighborhood, where "Van would get tanked up, put a napkin on his head like a babushka, pick up a flower, and do his impersonation of *Carmen*—and everybody would get a free drink."

Life became one long party. "We would meet at ten, go to a movie, get out at one, and go have a beer. And then do it again the next night. Or go dancing. That was just the way we lived," Jeaneane Dowis remembered. "I got to know every drag club in New York—I was the only girl, so the MC's would pick on me."

At church, Van would still hear the usual pronouncements about sinful behavior, but by now he could regard the direst warnings with whimsical detachment. "Van belonged to Calvary Baptist Church on Fifty-Seventh Street," said Mathis, "where the senior pastor was John Summerfield Wimbish. I went with him to a service once after we had been out cavorting, and we got very silly. The sermon was 'Where Is My Wandering Boy Tonight?' and Van doubled up with laughter. Of course, on another level he took it very seriously, and prided himself on double-tithing to the church—he gave 20 percent."

Cliburn was developing the ability to slip easily in and out of personas as the circumstances required: He could be the Southern gentleman one moment, the playful free spirit the next; alternately a debonair showman, a panicky pianist, an irresistible charmer, a happy lounge singer, a reckless roadster, a drunken reveler, or a devout believer. These roles not only reflected the many sides of a complex artist, they also became extremely useful. Both the crooner and the opera star facades, for example, offered him the chance to assume a character of extravagant emotion, whether inhabiting the identity of a melodramatic diva in a biblical narrative or of a pop singer gushing about lost love. Sinking into either frame, he was free to deliver earnest performances, unrestrained by concerns about the need for classical moderation or the fear of critical scrutiny.

Opera provided a musical model for both his exquisite pianism and the joys of high camp—like those evenings at Club 82, where audaciousness and theatricality were the rule. Van and his friends went to the La Puma Opera Workshop in New York City to see performances by Olive Middleton, an over-the-hill singer who had once performed leading roles at Covent Garden under Sir Thomas Beecham. She had by now become a caricature of her former self. But her appeal was not lost on "opera queens"—avid opera fans in the gay community—who flocked to her appearances, cheered her on, and carried her out on their shoulders afterward.

Contradiction was simply built into his nature. Pianist Ivan Davis remembered the day Van brought his friends to the basement of Calvary Baptist Church, where he performed the final scene from Richard Strauss's decadent opera *Salome*. In the oddest of contexts, he did it very well.

Yet, he continued to regard some behavior as off limits. Van and his colleagues once attended a performance at Carnegie Hall by an elderly woman who composed piano works for the black keys alone. "At the concert, we were in hysterics," says Davis. "She would do things like *The Sports Suite*, imitating the sounds of golf and tennis, with the music going back and forth between her hands. *The Weather Suite* had raindrops on petals—it was very atmospheric. 'The Storm' was for the left hand alone. People were putting handkerchiefs in their mouths to stop themselves from laughing. I said to Van, 'Have you ever heard anything like this?' And he became very serious. 'I can't laugh at a white-haired old lady,' he responded."

Van said once he was not really a Baptist so much as simply a Christian. He valued the tradition's foundational rules, including the admonition to show respect toward one's elders. Even while he caroused in the heart of cynical New York, his childhood lessons were never entirely forgotten, and one role trumped all the others: in some ways, he would always be Rildia Bee's little boy.

Life at Juilliard could seem at times like an extension of those late-night sorties, given the institution's idiosyncratic inhabitants. Dowis described Rosina Lhévinne as combining "the merriness of a teddy bear with the majesty of a czarina." Her malapropisms and mispronunciations were notorious. "Lo and behold!" said Dowis, became in Rosina-speak "Hold and below!" Lhévinne once said to the elevator operator at Juilliard, "Darling, I'm exhausted. I had *sex* lessons today." "Well," he answered, "you wouldn't do it if you didn't love it."

Those who spread these tales did so with affection. As a mentor, Lhévinne drew on a deep reservoir of piano knowledge, covering everything from the correct rhythmic feel in a Chopin mazurka to "the technique of the toe," the proper positioning of parts of the foot to control the speed of the piano pedals. If Rosina really cared for you, Dowis explained, she would constantly make constructive comments even about your manners, your dress, your friends.

Lhévinne's student Gladys Stein said her teacher could be "in turn . . . loving, irascible, cruel, kind, petulant and altogether totally unpredictable." A remembrance in the *Los Angeles Times* after her passing in 1976 recalled her reaction to meddling parents. "One set of ambitious parents, worried about their son's indifferent progress, asked her if she was preparing him to be an accompanist rather than a solo performer. 'No,' she replied a bit acidly. 'He doesn't have the musicianship.'"

Lhévinne certainly had her darker side. She was often depressed. It might last for two days or for a week. When it hit, numerology and various superstitions would rise up, absorbing all of her attention. But when she wasn't moping around in a funk, she would be an attentive caretaker.

Within her flock, "Van was first," explained Dowis. "Maybe we were all close seconds, but he was always first." This was a particularly difficult pill to swallow for John Browning, who seemed to work harder, play more meticulously, and learn more repertoire than anyone else. According to Dowis, he "gobbled up" the music he was given while Van "learned primarily by ear and rote, so he covered much less." Browning was painstakingly disciplined and possessed a voracious intellect. In contrast, Van didn't crack a book unless he had a quiz, so the more academic courses in his schedule, such as piano literature and theory, became real challenges. But Browning's impressive artistry, carefully calculated and honed through lengthy practice, somehow paled beside Van's natural ease in making music. It really seemed unfair.

History is replete with such rivalries. Mozart and Clementi, pianists who dominated the field just as the instrument began to take hold in Europe, were thrown together in an impromptu contest set up by Emperor Joseph II in Vienna—they were ambushed, in fact, at a reception in 1781 and placed into battle without warning. The two strutted their musical wares, and the emperor declared the pair evenly matched. In truth Clementi was all flash and no substance; Mozart called him a mere "robot" who performed without feeling. (Clementi more generously found in Mozart's playing "spirit and grace.") It mattered little to Joseph, who simply enjoyed the show.

Similarly, Franz Liszt, electrifying on stage, was pitted against the note-perfect but boring Sigismond Thalberg; the analytic Artur Schnabel was a persnickety foil to wild-haired Ignacy Jan Paderewski. Vladimir Horowitz's pianistic lightning bolts earned him the reputation of a musical Zeus—the opposite of Arthur Rubinstein, whose tender persona and human warmth permeated a concert hall; they were at one time considered the two greatest living pianists.

So it was with the Juilliard rivals. Van didn't have to think about what he was doing, said Dowis. "He was unafraid to pick up his hands and drop them from two feet in the air . . . For him it came from the birds and the bees and the trees and the air." Like Browning, Van practiced a lot (though he hated it); no one could play the piano that well without investing many hours daily at the keyboard. But these two pianists were shaped by vastly different temperaments, reflecting an artistic tension that was elucidated in another artistic realm by Henri Matisse.

Matisse revealed that while gathering flowers during a walk in the garden, his choices prompted simply by momentary pleasures, he produced a beautiful assemblage. But when he carefully considered their arrangement in preparation for a painting, his deliberateness seemed to rob the collection of its charm. The more effort he invested, the less artful was his bouquet. (Pierre-Auguste Renoir told Matisse that in order to counteract that loss of spontaneity when painting a bouquet, he simply walked around to the side he had not seen before.)

In music, willful, single-minded practice—drilling down into a piece over and over until it nearly plays itself, with the aim of avoiding unexpected pitfalls—can be a thief, draining an interpretation of freshness. The magic often occurs in the flash of the unforeseen. Van's approach left room for that contingency, though it also opened the door to potential inconsistencies. "I don't know anyone who wasn't bowled over [at times] by Van," recalled pianist Glenn Mack. "The kids stood up and cheered. It was staggering." His natural pianistic brilliance emerged when he was feeling emotionally solid and in the right frame of mind. When he wasn't, things could quickly go awry. Sometimes nature cooperated, and sometimes it didn't.

Van recognized the disadvantage he was working under. At his fourth-year Juilliard theory exam, a jury member asked him to play the final movement of a piece he knew well—Prokofiev's Seventh Piano Sonata—starting from a spot in the middle instead of at the beginning. Cliburn moved his fingers silently for a moment and then gave up, murmuring, "And this is my whole problem!" His musical memory might have been made more secure through greater attention to theory and analysis, but these were disciplines he tended to shun, because for him music was visceral, not abstract or academic. He played the way he did because he felt it in the core of his being.

Lhévinne also avoided rigid principles. She taught instinctually, with an inborn sense of what worked. This was better suited to Van's disposition than the methods of interpreters who argued their cases like Talmudic scholars, swamping a composer's original text with finicky commentary. Such practitioners could often be found exaggerating a pause here or a dynamic shift there to underline a work's navigable markers until, burdened with layer upon layer of interpretation, what was once a delicate musical soufflé had become a clotted fruitcake. Lhévinne simply wouldn't do that.

Neither would Rildia Bee, whose general guidance helped mold Van's sound into something both plush and unique. Her advice was, however, built on consistent principles. He still turned to her, even after beginning studies with Lhévinne. Continuing the idea she conveyed in urging him to sing the music before playing it, she told him to be sure to listen for the "eye" of the sound—the kernel at the center of each tone—thus compelling him to regard every note as not merely carrying the music along but shining in its own light. Thus immersing himself in the essence of each vibration, Van gained a special awareness of the individual building blocks of a musical piece, and he learned to bring them to life. When other students asked him how he got his enormous, full-bodied sound, Van said he didn't know. But this was likely an important clue.

Though Lhévinne was straightforward in her teaching, she wasn't above a little Machiavellian gamesmanship. She subtly egged on the competition between Cliburn and Browning. "At the beginning, Rosina had wanted us all to love each other," Dowis explained. "But Jimmy, Van, and I were all from Texas and close. And the first impression we had of John was not good. He was conceited, and difficult—sometimes insulting. On the other hand, he was extremely good-looking, and my friends were attracted to him."

So was she. Browning's dark complexion and bedroom eyes held an allure for her. For a brief time she and Browning were engaged. "But his sexual preference was a hindrance," she said. Browning thought they could work it out: the temptation to adopt a "normal" life style—at least in appearance—was compelling to many homosexual men in his situation. "He said to me, 'Look at Lenny [Bernstein] and Felicia [Montealegre, his wife]. Everybody's got problems.' But I couldn't see it, even though we were immensely close." (Bernstein had been advised by conductor Dimitri Mitropoulos, his mentor and lover, that to improve his chance of leading a major symphony orchestra he should marry. He did. Bernstein succeeded Mitropoulos as music director of the New York Philharmonic.)

Van experienced similar emotional tugs. In the early years of his Juilliard stay, his friendship with Mathis had blossomed into romance. He told a friend that their relationship was like that of David and Jonathan—biblical heroes whose souls, according to the Good Book, were "knit" together in a loving covenant. Later, Van considered becoming engaged to a woman. He had a heart-to-heart talk with Dowis about it. "She was a singer. They were together a lot. It was the most intimate conversation Van and I ever had," Dowis recalled. The idea was wisely put to rest.

Musically, Van continued to move forward. There were endless master classes and competitions—in school and out—and he accumulated more wins: the G. B. Dealey Memorial Award in Dallas and the Kosciuszko Foundation's Chopin Scholarship Award (both in 1952)—along with invitations to perform in Shreveport; Chautauqua, New York; and elsewhere. His only setback came in Chicago in 1953, at the Michaels Memorial Award competition, which was open to all instrumentalists and vocalists. He came in second to veteran cellist Paul Olefsky, and was obviously wounded by the loss. "Each day I keep thinking I will receive a letter of 'condolence' from you, my beloved teacher," he wrote to Lhévinne. "Mother was very proud of me the way I took it on the chin."

Nonetheless, his professional life was taking off in earnest, boosted by the efforts of Juilliard's dean of students, Mark Schubart. In 1953, Schubart called professional artist manager William Judd and said, " 'You've got to hear this kid.' And once he did, Bill signed him," recalled Gary Graffman.

Judd worked for Arthur Judson, music's power broker nonpareil, a man whose fingers seemed to be in every pie—the radio network he started that grew into the Columbia Broadcasting System; Columbia Concerts (later Columbia Artist Management Inc.), with a roster of 125 performers and organizations, where he became president; head of both the Philadelphia Orchestra and the New York Philharmonic. His web of "Community Concerts" stretched across the nation, making it possible for small municipalities to import high-quality artists without much financial risk. Many budding musicians relied on these concerts to sustain their fledgling careers. Judd placed Van in that program, with a fee structure of $300 per concert; $450 for a concerto; and $600 for two concertos.

Judd had descended from American musical blue bloods. His father had been a distinguished manager of the Boston Symphony, and his brother served as manager of the New York Philharmonic. Naomi Graffman, Gary's wife, who worked as Judd's assistant, described her boss as "kind, decent, intelligent, sophisticated, and high-class, with one problem—he was an alcoholic." Despite that, he managed to maintain a strong roster of artists for many years. People around him could count on having a good time. And that included the Graffmans.

"We all went together with Van to see Liberace at Madison Square Garden [in 1954]—loaded up with martinis," Naomi reports. "We had a dozen at Bill's apartment and staggered over to the show, where Gary accidentally stepped on the foot of [television personality] Faye Emerson, bandleader Skitch Henderson's wife." It could have been a consequential gaffe: Henderson, music director of television's *Tonight Show* with Steve Allen, would soon prove important to Cliburn's career. Luckily, no one seemed to notice.

Thanks to a wealthy socialite named Rosalie Leventritt, all of musical New York began to notice when Van was around. "Winnie" to her friends, the Jewish, Alabama-born New Yorker quietly subsidized such cultural institutions as the Casals Festival in Prades, France, and pianist Rudolf Serkin's Marlboro Festival in Vermont. When she decided to create a music competition in memory of her late husband, Edgar, an eminent lawyer, she leaned on those relationships, ensuring that the Leventritt Competition would be unparalleled in stature and influence. The finals were held in New York's Town Hall, with only a smattering of onlookers.

The jurors in 1954 included pianists Serkin, Nadia Reisenberg, Leopold Mannes, and Eugene Istomin; conductors George Szell and Leonard Bernstein; and violinists Alexander Schneider and Lillian Fuchs—along with Arthur Judson and author and broadcaster Abram Chasins. It was a formidable group.

Many competitions feel the compulsion to award a prize, but this jury was encouraged to be more selective. No award had been granted at the Leventritt since 1949, when Graffman won, in a victory for the Curtis Institute in Philadelphia, a school known as "the St. Petersburg Conservatory in exile," where Lhévinne's greatest competitor, Isabelle Vengerova, held court. This time around, the sheer number of Juilliard students in the running made it likely that the triumphant contestant would be a Lhévinne protégé.

The finalists were Browning, Claude Frank, Van, and Dowis—all but Frank Lhévinne students, and all exceptionally strong. "Probably John Browning and Claude Frank were on a higher level even than the second prize winners in Moscow," says Gary Graffman, referring to the competition that would make Van's name. Dowis was not quite of the same rank, but she captured the judge's hearts in another way early on: "She was playing the Rachmaninoff *Rhapsody* and hit an obvious clinker," remembers Naomi Graffman. "And very loudly blurted out, 'Shit!' And because of that, it was said, she got put into the next round."

Naomi worked with Mrs. Leventritt's daughter, Rosalie Berner, to organize the proceedings. "We had a game going," she reports, "guessing who would be a winner. Van's application was a [thick] directory with a picture on the cover of him as a little boy, and an announcement that he had won the G. B. Dealey Award in Dallas. We had never heard of this award, and we were hysterical."

As usual, Van stood out. Gary Graffman was sitting at home on Eighty-sixth Street when Serkin called. "It was just before the Leventritt finals. 'You really should come,' he said, 'there is a fantastic talent, a major talent—you should hear him.' I said, 'What did he play?' He said, 'The Chopin was so beautiful, and Rachmaninoff and Tchaikovsky and Liszt.' And I said, 'Yes, but did he also play Mozart and Beethoven?'"

It was a natural question. Serkin's aesthetic was wedded to the Germanic repertoire—music requiring a more sober, analytical approach than that suited to Van's emotionally gushing showpieces—and he could have been expected to reject the Texan outright. "'Oh,' Serkin said in response, 'it was terrible. But he's such a major talent!' It was actually the only reasonable response," explains Graffman. "You didn't judge Serkin by the way he played Rachmaninoff."

Cliburn's Leventritt performance was capped by a coruscating Liszt *Twelfth Hungarian Rhapsody*—a work he always kept in reserve, ready to use whenever he needed to win over an audience. The jury had actually requested the final movement of the Brahms Second Piano Concerto. Van told them he had not been feeling well and wasn't quite up to it; could he offer the rhapsody instead? he wondered. His Liszt performance settled matters. "John [Browning] played marvelously, but it just didn't matter," said Dowis. "It all flowed out of Van."

The Leventritt award brought him a performance at one of the New York Philharmonic's Sunday-afternoon concerts. (Thanks to Leventritt's connections, it also included concerts with the orchestras of Cleveland, Pittsburgh, Buffalo, and Denver.) "Carnegie Hall looked like the Alamo," reported Graffman. "Planeloads of Texans had come up for the launching. Van played Tchaikovsky, and the place went wild. After the smoke had cleared, we fought our way backstage, bearing with us Rosalie Leventritt. . . . He grabbed fragile Mrs. Leventritt in an enormous bear hug, and would have swept her off her feet if there had been room. 'Honey,' he drawled, 'see all these people?' She nodded. 'Well, they all comin' to yo' party,' he announced. Mrs. Leventritt gulped."

When he arrived with his entourage at the Leventritt apartment, he began devouring everything in sight. "Van," asked Mrs. Leventritt, "didn't you have dinner?" The invitation was for a party long past mealtime. "I thought you fancy people in New York might eat late," he replied.

Despite the popular wisdom that classical music did not work well on commercial television, Skitch Henderson agreed to book Van on Steve Allen's *Tonight Show* for January 19, 1955. Playing the Toccata from Ravel's *Tombeau de Couperin* and a Chopin étude, he was a hit, and they signed him for a return appearance in April. His blossoming concert opportunities helped the pianist sustain his penchant for stylish clothes, and allowed him to secure an apartment at the elegant Osborne building on West Fifty-seventh Street, diagonally across from Carnegie Hall, where Bill Judd lived.

Rudolf Serkin remained a supporter, and invited him to attend the Marlboro Festival in the summer of 1956. The festival was founded in 1951, in a farmlike setting designed to cultivate a sense of community, "like an Israeli kibbutz or perhaps like a Soviet commune as they would like it to be," said Serkin. Its laureates, who tended to rise to the top of the field, remained devoted advocates long after their tenures in Vermont.

Van expressed some trepidation about going to Marlboro to

Jimmy Mathis, since the emphasis there was on collaborative performance and musical classicism—not his strongest suits. Chamber music is an exercise in musical democracy, where grandstanding is ethically proscribed—a gentleman's game in which restraint is prized. Van was cut out more for the grand romantic blockbusters—edge-of-your-seat exploits that put him in the spotlight—where his emotionality and charisma could shine.

From the start, he and Serkin were on very different wavelengths. In Isaiah Berlin's famous formulation, both men were "hedgehogs," not "foxes"—their sensibilities embraced a single central vision rather than a liberal plethora of styles. For Serkin, that meant a dedication to the core Germanic repertoire, with its structural intricacies and philosophical gravitas. Van lived on the other side of the musical spectrum, where the head is expected to give way to the heart.

"You don't really *like* the late Beethoven sonatas, *do* you?" Van asked David Buechner (later Sara Davis Buechner) years later, when the younger pianist held the Cliburn Scholarship at Juilliard. Without waiting for a reply, he answered his own question: "They're for those *Schnabel people*." Beethoven's late, intellectually rigorous music, beloved by the Marlboro crowd, seemed to him the province of an odd cabal of specialists like Schnabel and Serkin, performers with academic dust in their eyes.

Yet Van was now temporarily a resident in Serkin's territory. Perhaps the older man had hopes of reshaping him into his kind of pianist, with a more classical sensibility; or else he felt that, two years after the Leventritt, the prototypical romanticist might have developed in other, less familiar directions. In any case, he was disappointed. One of Van's roommates at Marlboro, pianist and school administrator Robert Freeman, recalls a discussion with Serkin that summer in which the venerable pianist and teacher declared, "Nothing will ever become of poor Van."

"It was because Van spent the summer playing Rachmaninoff and Tchaikovsky," says Freeman. "Serkin had difficulty with his resistance to the Marlboro regimen." It was an odd fit in other ways as well. Freeman found Van "nice but kooky." Every time his mother came for weekends he had his hair done, said Freeman. He naturally became the butt of pranks.

Van's roommates set up a clanging contraption in the crawl space behind his bed, waited for him to go to sleep, and caused a loud commotion as soon as he closed his eyes. "I'd pull a rope and there would be an uproar," said Freeman. Surprisingly, such mischief was spurred on by the antics of the venerable Serkin, who, against his public image, turned out to be an inveterate practical joker, employing hand buzzers to shock unaware victims, and throwing paper napkins at people during dinner and pretending he hadn't.

That summer Van studied the Dvořák Piano Quintet in A Major, and performed it along with an illustrious ensemble of Alexander Schneider and Felix Galimir on violins, Lotte Bamberger-Hammerschlag on viola, and Hermann Busch on cello. But he spent most of his time learning the Rachmaninoff Second Piano Concerto for an upcoming performance with the Cleveland Orchestra—no small feat—rehearsing it at Marlboro with thirteen-year-old pianist James Levine, who would later become music director of the Metropolitan Opera, on the second piano. Despite pressure from Serkin, Van's heart was more focused on the steppes of Russia than on the stone palaces of Vienna. And that turned out to be the key to one of music's most extraordinary careers.

As Van was studying Rachmaninoff, at the Russian frontier events were taking place that would have a huge impact on the Texan's life. Mikhail Tikhonravov, a shy scientist who had for years been obsessed with the idea of mechanically replicating the flight of birds and insects, was close to fulfilling a dream. The scientist had lived and worked in Yubileiny, a Moscow suburb that was so secret it didn't appear on any maps, and now, together with his colleague Sergei Korolev, he was in Tyuratam (later named the Baikonur Cosmodrome), hoping to fulfill his fantasy of launching an engineered bird that would soar into space.

He finally succeeded on October 4, 1957, when the Soviets announced that the *Sputnik* satellite was circling the earth. America reacted with shock and despair. Scientist Edward Teller, the "father of the hydrogen bomb," compared the news to the disastrous World War II attack by Japan on Pearl Harbor. Asked what we would likely find on the moon, he answered, "Russians."

Paranoia about a Soviet nuclear threat had already become a part of the American fabric. The 1951 film *Duck and Cover* taught a generation of schoolchildren that "when there's a flash, duck and cover!" Three years later, on June 14, 1954, emergency sirens were sounded in twenty cities as part of "Operation Alert." It took less than two minutes after the "take cover" signal for Times Square in New York to become deserted as President Dwight D. Eisenhower was helicoptered to a secret mountaintop location.

Now that the Soviet space program had achieved a milestone, the Cold War's ideological battles for hearts and minds took on even greater impetus. *Sputnik*'s itinerary, as it circled the earth every ninety-six minutes, was designed to include a pass over the American city of Little Rock, Arkansas, where the National Guard had to be sent to force racial integration at Central High School. It was an easy political target for Soviet propagandists.

Aside from such petty political point scoring, though, the Soviets had truly gripped the world's imagination.

Sputnik toys, postage stamps, magazine covers, and perfume bottles were soon in huge demand, and not just in Moscow: *Life* reported that bartenders in America were making *Sputnik* cocktails (with vodka as the main ingredient, of course) and that toys, shirts, jackets, hats, and balloons with a *Sputnik* motif were popping up around the country. Nikita Khrushchev was chosen for the cover of *Time* as "Man of the Year" for 1957; he appeared crowned by the Kremlin and holding *Sputnik* in his hands.

The American retort to *Sputnik*—an attempt on December 6 to launch a satellite called *Vanguard*—turned into a further embarrassment. The rocket simply fizzled, and its cargo "rolled into hiding at [Cape Canaveral's] palmetto and scrub brush." The front-page headlines in the United Kingdom were "Stay Putnik!" and "Oh, What a Flopnik!" American scientists were finally relieved when the small *Explorer I* was successfully launched on January 31, 1958. But the Russians merely gloated over the diminutive American satellite, the size of a grapefruit (though the Explorer program ultimately produced significant results for researchers). America strained to celebrate its belated triumph with forgettable songs like, "I'm Going to Build Me a Satellite."

Of course, Americans could trumpet other scientific triumphs—notably, a cure for polio in 1955. Just a year before, 38,741 new polio cases had arisen in the United States. At the announcement of the successful testing of the polio vaccine, church bells rang, car horns beeped, and storekeepers painted "Thank You, Dr. Salk" on their windows, in praise of the man who had spearheaded the effort. But the public's focus on such breakthroughs was fickle. Now, just two years later, the marvel of the moment was no longer medicine, but space technology.

Ironically, the scientific advance, wrote Leonid Vladimirov, an engineer and author imprisoned by Stalin, "suddenly imposed on the Soviet Union . . . the heavy [financial] burden of being a power in space." *Pravda* could brag that *Sputnik* had "broken through the American dollar curtain" and contend that the Soviet Union was ahead scientifically because America stood on a "rotten capitalist foundation," but the Soviets were in desperate need of some of that capital. Their citizens were measuring official boasts against the failings of the Communist system to fill everyday needs, and they found their government wanting. After the Soviet launch of "cosmonaut" Yuri Gagarin into space, the cynical remark heard on queues in Soviet-controlled East Germany was "There'll be butter again soon—Gagarin is already on his way to the Milky Way." In Eastern Europe, they joked that the most important postwar Soviet invention was the crossbreeding of a giraffe with a cow. "The new animal," went the jest, "eats in the fraternal countries and is milked in the Soviet Union."

To remedy the situation, trade and tourism were needed, and the Tchaikovsky Competition, which might serve that end, became the nation's next important launch. For that reason, though Van's Rachmaninoff and Tikhonravov's satellite could have seemed unrelated in 1956, they would soon become twin cogs in the gears of history. When the Tchaikovsky Competition got under way in the spring of 1958, observers in both the Soviet Union and the United States would begin to refer to Van Cliburn as the "American Sputnik." It's a role he never expected or wished for. But it changed his life, and the course of history.

CHAPTER 3

The Big Decision

T HAT MOMENTOUS EVENT was still in the future; for the present, there were still hurdles to overcome. A pattern of lateness that had surfaced in Kilgore and grown worse during his student years at Juilliard continued to be a problem. He seldom arrived anywhere on time. He was perpetually absent from his piano literature class taught by Joseph Bloch. As Van routinely told Bloch's wife, Dana, in morning phone calls to his teacher's Westchester home, "Please apologize to Professor Bloch. I just couldn't get out of bed." Classmates chipped in to buy him an alarm clock. It didn't help. He received an F in piano literature. The classroom bored him, but he'd show up late even to his own performances.

This behavioral glitch gave birth to a new keyboard ritual. Abram Chasins traced it to a specific date—April 9, 1953—

when the pianist, arriving very late to give a concert in Kilgore, found 1,500 Texans "squirming in their seats." Embarrassed, Van panicked, claimed Chasins, bolted to the stage, sat down at the piano, and began playing "The Star-Spangled Banner." Everyone in the audience promptly stood. And when they regained their seats, the air had been cleared for the programmed music to start.

From then on Van began his recitals with the national anthem. It gave him extra time in which to calm his nerves, while lending a touch of grandeur to the proceedings; it also helped ease the attendees into the concert. There were precedents for that: Liszt claimed to have written the opening page of his Fantasy on Bellini's *La sonnambula* to give audience members a moment to "assemble and blow their noses" before they had to settle down to listen. But bringing patriotic fervor into the mix—a practice usually reserved for sports events—was a new angle.

Friends debated the roots of the lateness problem. Pianist Jerome Lowenthal had a simple explanation. Van, he said, was a man of extraordinary gifts, "and besides that he was the nicest person in the world. There seemed to be no exceptions to his generosity." Yet, he mused, no person can be completely free of dark impulses, resentments, even touches of cruelty—it's the human condition. "So where does the human side find an outlet?" asked Lowenthal. "The answer is, he made everybody wait for him. Even when he was the guest of honor."

Was it really a streak of mischievousness, or, as publicist Mary Lou Falcone, a close friend, believed, a matter of Van's "ferocious nerves"? In her view it was merely a self-defense mechanism: being late, he had to rush from the car to the stage door and then right onto the stage. "Once he was seated at the piano, his fragility didn't show. But then the pattern became chronic."

The behavior grew progressively more extreme, even after his standing in the music world had been solidly established. Falcone cites as an example a scheduled 8 p.m. recital in Buffalo, New York, during the winter of 1977. She was with Van all afternoon in New York City, as he dawdled the hours away. At a certain point she informed him that there was no longer any possibility of finding a commercial flight that would get him to Buffalo on time. "He said, 'Don't worry—we'll just charter a flight.' And he did. But we didn't get out to the airport until seven-thirty. And there was a blizzard in Buffalo," she said. They arrived at the hall at nine-thirty and the audience was still sitting there, waiting. He walked out on stage and apologized, saying that he had gotten stuck in the snowstorm. "It was only partially true. He condensed the program, so that everyone was out by ten-thirty or eleven o'clock. Then we boarded the plane in the blizzard to go back to New York."

To avoid such situations as his career began to flourish, Naomi Graffman was assigned to handle the logistics of his daily life. Every morning at around ten, she would call the switchboard at the Osborne and speak to Mrs. Hughes, who manned the desk. Hughes would keep ringing until Van got out of bed, and usually by twelve-forty-five he would pop his head into Graffman's office and announce, " 'Honey, I'm hungry.' We'd go downstairs to Beefburger Hall . . . and we'd have a beef burger for thirty-five cents. I always paid," said Graffman, and if I was feeling rich, I'd have a cheeseburger for forty-five cents."

Over the years, Van's nocturnal predilections would grow even more pronounced. When he occasionally startled his friend Jack Romann, who was head of artist relations for the Baldwin Piano Company in New York, out of sleep with a three a.m. phone call, Jack would wearily lift the phone off its hook and answer,

"Hello, Van." "How did you know it was me?" asked the pianist innocently, as if night had become day for everyone.

Inevitably, his career began to slow. "I used to beat around the countryside getting him dates," remembered Schuyler Chapin. "But after a brilliant beginning he hit a bad patch." Sustaining a classical piano career in America has never been easy. Presenters tend to clamor for the next new thing, and Van was running out of competitions through which he could get yet another shot of instant celebrity.

"It is a myth that if you play somewhere and they like you, you will be re-engaged," says Lowenthal. "The way Community Concerts worked was that if they were interested in an artist, they would book him for sixty dates. The next year, he would get eight. The year after that, one." The object was to give new people a chance. Musicians who were in the program often believed they were building a career, but a letdown was sure to come.

In 1957, Van received notice he was to be drafted into the United States Army. He told Judd to stop booking dates. He readied himself for a new phase—as a musician in the Army Band, headed for a tour of Africa. Then he failed the Army physical, apparently a result of continuing nosebleeds he had faced since childhood. Meanwhile, his mother fell and injured her back, and his father was involved in a bus collision. The pianist headed back to Kilgore to help out. "Cliburn called the summer of 1957 the lowest and most disheartening period in his life," reported *The Dallas Morning News*.

By the fall, though, his teachers and colleagues at Juilliard were humming with news of an intriguing development. Pianist Olegna Fuschi, a Lhévinne student, had been in Brazil and happened to meet Pavel Serebryakov, director of the Leningrad (now St. Petersburg) Conservatory. He told her that he was going to be on the jury of a new competition in Moscow, and handed her an official announcement. Fuschi brought it back to New York and gave it to Lhévinne. "She stood by the window," remembers Fuschi, "read it silently, and softly uttered a single word: 'Van.'"

She wasn't the only one with that thought. Over at Steinway Hall, the elegant piano showroom with an exalted history—a gathering place for the world's great pianists, its basement the spot where Vladimir Horowitz and Sergei Rachmaninoff met for an exchange of piano fireworks—Alexander Greiner, a German-Latvian refugee and former student at the Moscow Conservatory, saw the competition notice and had exactly the same reaction. Greiner had worked for Steinway & Sons (or, as Van liked to call it, "the House of Steinway") since 1926, when he was hired primarily to coddle an egoistic, demanding, and often petulant Horowitz. Within two years he was director of concerts and artists, pampering myriad other star performers who were crucial to Steinway's reputation. "If Rachmaninoff had a birthday party, Greiner would be there," wrote Theodore Steinway, president of the firm from 1927 to 1955. "If [Josef] Hofmann needed him, there would be a telegram sent instantly to soothe him."

Like Lhévinne, Greiner was deeply interested in Russia's musical life, and he found the competition exciting news, instantly deciding that Van was a perfect candidate. It took several lunches and all of his persuasive powers to win the pianist over to the idea. Van had never been out of the country, and traversing such a long distance to compete in a foreign environment filled him with apprehension. It didn't help that Judd had advised Van against going. After all, he explained, the pianist had already won the Leventritt. What could be more prestigious than that?

Rosina Lhévinne countered with an outline of her reasons Van should go.

POINT 1: You will have to work with great intensity, and this will be good for you, regardless of the contest.

POINT 2: You will have to learn a great deal of new material.

POINT 3: You will meet the elite of the young pianists from other parts of the world.

POINT 4: Last, but not least—I believe you will win.

Van relented, and "Rosina gave up her Sundays—usually devoted to rest and trips to the country—entirely to Van," recalled Jeaneane Dowis. "The repertoire requirements for the competition were immense, and she spent three to five hours every week working with him." Participants had to play a Bach prelude and fugue, a Mozart sonata, four études (either by Chopin, Liszt, Scriabin, or Rachmaninoff), and Tchaikovsky's Theme and Variations, op. 19, no. 6, in the first round; four works selected from a list of technically daunting music by Russian and romantic composers, a movement from Tchaikovsky's Sonata in G Major, and a contemporary piece by a composer from the pianist's own country, in the second round; and two large concertos (including either Tchaikovsky's First or Second), plus a specially commissioned solo work by Dmitri Kabalevsky, for those who made it to the third round.

Meanwhile, there remained the crucial issue of finding the financial means to get there. The Soviets would take care of all expenses except for the flight over. Juilliard's dean, Mark Schubart, was enlisted to solicit funds to enable as many Juilliard musicians as possible to purchase plane tickets. It also fell to him to "persuade our most successful young soloists to participate," according to an internal Juilliard memo. This was not a simple matter: for musicians already out on the concert circuit, the idea of entering a competition smacked of amateurism.

The State Department gave a positive response to the idea of American musicians participating, but offered no monetary support. Schubart found a sympathetic ear in César Saerchinger of the Martha Baird Rockefeller Aid to Music program, and reported to his superiors that it was likely that money would be found to send "a reasonable number of contestants. Three was the number discussed."

Juilliard did not want its official fingerprints on the endeavor, so Schubart decided to recuse himself from the workings of the Rockefeller committee. Remaining concerned about the selection process, though, he offered the school advice about how to proceed. "In my view [the choice of candidates] should be made on an invitation basis and without any publicity whatsoever," he said. The only possibility of a good result, he believed, "devolves upon our being able to send to Moscow not students, but young professionals, preferably with a good deal of concert experience."

In December, the Rockefeller Foundation decided it would fund travel for two musicians. Since the Tchaikovsky Competition was being held in two sections, one for violin and the other for piano, Juilliard determined that it would send one performer for each: Joyce Flissler and Van Cliburn. Van was the only pianist at the school capable of receiving an unqualified endorsement. Other Juilliard pianists who decided to enter—Daniel Pollack, Jerome Lowenthal, and Norman Shetler—would get to Moscow on their own steam.

Given the Cold War tensions, American officials were understandably nervous about how things would unfold in Moscow for the American competitors. Schubart was told by the State Department that the government would pay his travel expenses

Young Van Cliburn at age nine surrounded by fans. Just three when he began piano lessons with his mother, he debuted in his hometown of Shreveport, Louisiana, at four.

Twelve-year-old Van is declared winner of the 1946 Texas Gulf Sulphur Competition. The prize included a performance on the radio with the Houston Symphony.

LEFT Van's parents delivered him to the Juilliard School of Music in New York in 1951 to study with Russian-born piano master Rosina Lhévinne. She became his only trusted piano teacher, after his mother. Lhévinne convinced him to enter the Tchaikovsky Competition.

RIGHT The Marlboro Festival in Vermont, a high-level summer chamber-music school founded by Rudolf Serkin and his colleagues, invited Van to study there in 1956. Among the other students was thirteen-year-old James Levine, who would later become music director of the Metropolitan Opera. The two rehearsed the Rachmaninoff Second Piano Concerto together that summer.

RIGHT Russians demonstrate at the US embassy in Moscow in 1956 in retaliation for Western protests against the execution of leaders of the Hungarian revolt. The tense political climate made Van Cliburn's achievement at Moscow's Tchaikovsky Competition all the more remarkable.

BELOW Before the Cold War put an end to friendly relations between the US and the USSR, Russians had long embraced aspects of American culture, including Hollywood films, especially comedies and adventure stories. This Russian poster announces Paramount-Artcraft Pictures' *The Silent Man* (1917). Russian title, when it was screened in 1927: *The Chinaman from Florida*.

BELOW The Boston Symphony, appearing in the Soviet Union in 1956, astonished Moscow's musicians with its high level of performance, and overturned the commonly held belief that Americans were talentless. It paved the way for Van's acceptance.

It was Van's childhood dream, spurred by a picture book, to see the magnificent St. Basil's Cathedral on Red Square. When he arrived in Moscow, this striking architectural wonder created by Ivan the Terrible was the very first place he visited.

The Hotel Peking (originally the Hotel Pekin), shown in 1956, was home to the Tchaikovsky competitors during their stay in Moscow. It was also known as "the KGB hotel," a moniker borne out by the electronic bugs pianists found hidden in the rooms. French pianist Evelyne Crochet stumbled across one while trying to plug a hair dryer into the wall.

Van and the Soviet pianist Lev Vlassenko in the 1950s. Vlassenko was the presumptive winner of the competition until Van showed up. The two battled for first place, yet remained close friends for the rest of their lives.

Dmitri Shostakovich, the chairman of the competition, was heralded all over the world for his gifts as a composer. Nevertheless, he was constantly hounded by iron-fisted Soviet authorities, who alternately praised him and subjected him to disgrace.

Sviatoslav Richter, broad-shouldered, gloomy, and fierce, caused trouble in the jury room when he felt that Van Cliburn was being treated unfairly. The Soviet pianist gave especially low grades to most of the competitors, even winners of other international competitions, while rewarding the American with the highest ranking, and was criticized by Soviet authorities for it. "For me," he said, "either you make music or you don't."

Emil Gilels, the jury chairman, took personal risks to remain an honest broker. Those in power shamed and threatened him during the competition for his unbending impartiality. Gilels strongly influenced Nikita Khrushchev's decision to allow Van to receive the award for first place.

LEFT Van in rehearsal with Kirill Kondrashin. Under Kondrashin's impeccable conducting, the pianist and orchestra sounded like a single entity, helping Cliburn's performance achieve the highest artistic level. The conductor would later travel to the United States to conduct Van's victory concerts.

RIGHT During a rehearsal for the final round, Kondrashin (*left*) and Cliburn (*right*) confer over a musical detail.

Behind the scenes at the Tchaikovsky Competition, Lev Vlassenko (*left*) and Van with his obligatory cigarette, share a casual moment with Emil Gilels. Political mistrust between the United States and the Soviet Union melted away in the genuine affection these musicians held for each other.v

The moment of truth, as Van performs at the third and final round of the Tchaikovsky Competition in the Moscow Conservatory's Great Hall. Tchaikovsky's portrait hangs in the background. Van's interpretations of concertos by Tchaikovsky and Rachmaninoff clinched the prize for him.

МЕЖДУНАРОДНЫЙ КОНКУРС ПИАНИСТОВ И СКРИПАЧЕЙ имени П. И. ЧАЙКОВСКОГО

ОБЩИЙ СПИСОК ПО ОЧКАМ

I ТУР

КОНКУРС ПИАНИСТОВ

The official first-round scorecard. Judges gave each participant's performance a value from 0 to 25. Van's scores are listed in the twelfth column from the left (ВАН КЛИБЕРН). At the end of this initial round, seventeen pianists were eliminated, and Van was tied for first place with Chinese pianist Liu Shikun. Two more rounds would follow.

ABOVE The official second-round scorecard. Based on these results, the competitors were now narrowed down to a field of nine, and it was still anyone's game. The favored candidates at this point were Liu Shikun, listed in the fifth column (ЛЮ ШИ-КУНЬ); Van, listed in the sixth column (ВАН КЛИБЕРН); and Lev Vlassenko, listed in the fifteenth column (Л. ВЛАСЕНКО).

LEFT A rare look at handwritten jury notes made at the end of the second round. These calculations were compiled in the jury room and passed on through official channels. At this point, Lev Vlassenko was in first place (referenced here with the number 24.18), and Liu Shikun was in second.

if he agreed to observe the event and file regular reports. Juilliard's president, composer William Schuman, found the situation ironic: The school had asked the State Department for moderate funding to send Van to the 1958 Brussels World's Fair with the Juilliard Orchestra, and the answer had been a resounding no; now money could be found to pay for Schubart's trip—as long as he engaged in intelligence gathering. Schubart agreed, and promised Lhévinne to photograph the plaque in the Moscow Conservatory that listed her name as a recipient of a first prize in piano during her student days.

Van's misgivings were at least partly dispelled by a prediction made by a clairvoyant who was living in his building. He would visit an agrarian country and win a gold medal, he was told. After his victory, Van developed an enduring fascination with psychic phenomena and astrology that eventually grew into an obsession. The world of stargazing became a vital part of his life. "He was compulsive about it," remembers Falcone. "Eventually, he did not make a move without consulting an astrologer. And he learned more about the subject than most experts." Like his smoking and his intense need to please, it became a psychological tic from which he never managed to escape.

Before embarking, Van sought coaching from Dimitri Mitropoulos, the conductor with whom he had played the Tchaikovsky First Concerto at his New York Philharmonic debut in 1954. Mitropoulos, who had once conducted the great Rachmaninoff, was happy to oblige. He selected the repertoire Van would play, including the Prelude and Fugue by Sergei Taneyev, who had taught harmony at the Moscow Conservatory and was a trusted friend of Tchaikovsky's. "It's very difficult, but you can do it," he said. He also found for Van a copy of the music for the required Tchaikovsky Sonata in G Major.

How might the conductor have affected Van's playing? Though Mitropoulos's approach tended to be quixotic, he was particularly skillful in shaping large-scale works. One Mitropoulos student, American composer Otto Luening, described his teacher's focus as "projecting the form of each piece . . . His sense of phrase affected his tempi, so he never played a piece fast just to dazzle listeners." It was the kind of interpretation for which Cliburn, with his narrative-like piano style, became celebrated. Mitropoulos's inclinations, though, differed from some of the guidance Van had been receiving.

His mother, and then Lhévinne, had focused on technical finesse and beauty of sound rather than on musical structure. Van's best qualities as a pianist rested on surface polish and emotional persuasiveness. At Marlboro, he was to have added a sense of architecture. But that analytical aspect of music didn't much interest him. If it had, he might have more thoroughly investigated the theories of the high priest of Germanic classical theory, Heinrich Schenker, who laid out a system of hierarchies within a musical piece, describing tones as "creatures" that obey natural urges, just like living organisms. Schenker and his followers sought to analyze and illuminate the subtle internal forces that animate a work. In comparison, Lhévinne's teaching style could be a blunt instrument. Dowis's written recollections of her first Juilliard lessons, in which Lhévinne urged her to "sink," are typical.

"I obligingly sank toward the piano, but she kept bellowing, 'No, no!' It was only when she began to sing the melody in a dreadfully out-of-tune way that I realized that she was saying 'Sing!'—with the hand, not the voice. Quickly adjusting my stance and touch, we went on, but soon the outcries of 'Sink!' again rent the air. I was nonplussed; we were in the middle of a very fast staccato passage, but I tried valiantly to sing. Again, 'No! No!' This time she took my hands off the keyboard and pointed to my head. 'Sink!' now appeared to mean 'Think!' After a while I intuited what she wanted, and off we went. A third time came the dreaded 'Sink! Sink!' I tried my best to look cerebral but nearly fell off the bench as she suddenly leaned her entire upper body weight on my hands and arms. Finally, it seemed, 'Sink!' really meant 'Sink!'"

Lhévinne's ideas in such matters complemented Rildia Bee's exhortations to her son about sound production. "Rosina hated above all else a harsh sound (even when it might have benefited the music), and if someone played with a hard, loud tone, she would shriek at the top of her voice, 'Nails in the wall, nails in the wall!'"

Because of his lack of interest in the more cerebral side of things, some felt that Van's pianism was less than complete. Even Dowis confessed that though she appreciated Van's talent, she was never an all-out fan. "His playing struck me as without finesse and real depth, bordering (dare I say it) on the cheap thrills side," she wrote.

Mitropoulos's analytical acumen surely brought a bit more depth to Van's performance. And there was another aspect of the conductor's style that likely made a difference: he was known for orchestral performances of explosive power—a freewheeling approach that might have served as a counterweight to Lhévinne's moderating influence, perhaps sharpening the pianist's expressive edge. When, as a young student, Mitropoulos played for his teacher Ferruccio Busoni, he was castigated for a lack of restraint. "Too much passion! Go back to Mozart in order to learn purity of form!" he was told. It was his nature to go all out when it came to music—even in his manner of conducting, which, wrote the *New Yorker* critic Winthrop Sargeant, resembled "a Greek bartender vigorously shaking cocktails." Yet, Sargeant reported, "electricity crackles in the air" when he was on the podium.

Van's inborn tendencies toward exaggeration—the "cheap thrills" that concerned Dowis—were usually held in check by Lhévinne. "In a way, Van was the godson of Rosina's late husband, the elegant and tame Josef," remembers Juilliard teacher David Dubal. Like Josef's, his playing was never volcanic, but leisurely, with a golden sound beautifully tempered. Without Rosina's stringent guidance, Van might have dripped sentimentality, deteriorating into the pianistic mannerisms of a high romantic. Lhévinne tamped down those inclinations. Mitropoulos could have edged him toward a more dramatic reading of the repertoire, pushing the emotional temperature ever so slightly toward the hotter side, infusing his Tchaikovsky and Rachmaninoff with just enough extra sizzle to make a difference.

In fact, Van's playing seemed to achieve a new level of brilliance as the date of the competition approached. In March of 1958 Rosina invited several people to the Leventritt apartment to hear Van play all the pieces he had prepared for the competition, just before he left for Moscow. "He played simply magnificently," recalled Dowis. "Every piece, every style was perfect—the timing, the balance, the tone, the technique—all unbelievable. I was entirely, albeit initially unwillingly, seduced by his playing, and it seemed impossible that anyone could have beaten him."

The paper trail of Van's urgent letters and telegrams to Moscow traces a state of continued nervous ambivalence about the whole affair. "HAVE JUST MAILED MY APPLICATION TONIGHT DECEMBER TWENTIETH HOPING IT REACHES YOU IN TIME," read one early wire. At the beginning of February, only twenty-three years old, he was still writing to competition chairman Dmitri

Shostakovich about changing the repertoire, following this up with another telegram after receiving a well-meaning but confusing reply. It was all done with his usual charm, of course. "May I extend my congratulations to you on your Eleventh Symphony, and its great success at the premiere performance in Leningrad?" he wrote to Shostakovich at the end of his repertoire inquiry. "I was so interested to read Marietta Shaginyan's glowing tribute to you as it appeared in the magazine *USSR*. I am most eager to hear it." By its casual tone, it could have been a note to a classmate rather than a letter to one of the world's most revered composers.

Just days before he left for Russia, Van stopped by to see Lucy Mann at the Juilliard School's concert department. She had a small office by the elevator, where students came to pick up concert tickets. "Van wandered in and he sat down next to my desk," Mann recalled. "His mood was gloomy. I said, 'Van, what's the problem?' And he said, 'Lucy, first my mother didn't like my playing; and now they want me to go to Moscow.'" There was little she could offer him, other than a piece of practical advice. Noticing that a button on his coat was hanging by a thread, she told him, "If you do go to Russia, you'd better sew that button on." No doubt he did.

Van would soon be facing a formidable array of competitors. Soviet musicians who wanted to enter the competition first had to pass daunting tests along the way—musical and political— and then underwent more intensive training as the date drew near. They knew that at every contest, the grim reaper was waiting expectantly in the wings, ready to end their careers if a performance went poorly.

As a wave of foreign competitors was making its way toward

Russian soil, the event's organizers made note of those musicians they considered particularly strong—the ones to beat. These included Lowenthal and Pollack from the United States (Van was not on their radar) and Roger Boutry and Annie Marchand (later Annie Marchand Sherter) from France. Those in charge of the Soviet contingent, just like Schubart at the Juilliard School, had to muster their arguments to win over the best, albeit reluctant, artists. So the Central Committee of the Communist Party ordered the creation of a list of potential candidates, and pianist Lazar Berman was on it. *The New York Times*'s chief music critic, Harold C. Schonberg, wrote in 1961, after hearing Berman in Moscow, that the man had twenty fingers and breathed fire.

Berman had been through the routine before, and he was at this point less than excited about yet another competition. Like Van, he had been taught first by his overbearing mother, before studying with the important pedagogue Alexander Goldenweiser. He certainly bore the scars of his encounters with a thoroughly capricious system. After first being invited and then disinvited by Soviet authorities to the Youth and Student International Festival in 1949, he was put through the same emotional roller coaster again at the Concours Long-Thibaud in Paris in 1955. What's more, Berman's record at those events in which he actually competed was decidedly mixed. He had won a 1951 contest in Berlin, then struggled at both the 1956 Queen Elisabeth Competition in Brussels—he blamed his loss on his mother, "a woman with a wild imagination and dictatorial behavior," who insisted that he change his repertoire at the last moment—and the 1956 Liszt Competition in Budapest. As he later explained in his memoirs, he found the process psychologically grueling. "I felt that my every show was like an execution, so my life turned into an incessant tragedy," he wrote.

Now, the Tchaikovsky Competition would exert even greater pressure. "It was clear that a Soviet musician had to win it," he said. His account of being summoned, along with several other of the best pianists of the nation, to a meeting at which the minister of culture, Nikolai Mikhailov, spoke, gives a sense of the stakes. "Imagine what a shame it would be if the first Tchaikovsky prize went to a foreigner!" Mikhailov said. "It would be a greater shame than our national football team's loss to Poland in Warsaw!" The Soviets were still licking their wounds over that embarrassment.

It turned out that almost none of Moscow's preeminent pianists on the verge of a major career were willing to step up to bat. Each had a specific reason, along with a general reluctance to become embroiled in the political machinations of the event; and of course they all feared the chilling possibility of a humiliating loss. Hoping to twist some arms, the authorities brought the greatest Soviet musicians of the day to act as cheerleaders for their cause. Pianists Lev Oborin, Goldenweiser, and Sviatoslav Richter, violinist David Oistrakh, and composers Shostakovich and Kabalevsky all urged the generation of emerging piano stars to enter the contest.

The meeting was filled with high drama. According to Berman's account, first in the spotlight was Vladimir Ashkenazy, "who said he was not a big Tchaikovsky fan." In truth, he didn't feel particularly well suited to the composer's style. Ashkenazy had been first-prize winner of the 1956 Queen Elisabeth Competition, and he was among the most formidable talents of the day, so he was naturally a strong candidate for the Moscow contest. He would eventually succumb to Soviet strong-arm tactics to sign up for the next Tchaikovsky Competition, held four years later. But this time around, he was let off the hook.

Next came Georgian-born Dmitri Bashkirov, who explained that he had never played Tchaikovsky's First or Second Piano Concerto (finalists were required to perform one or the other), and there was too little time left to master either. He was also excused.

Berman himself hesitated when asked. "I had been thinking that if I got the first prize, nobody would be surprised. But if the opposite occurred, everyone would say, 'How could that happen?'" he reported. He tried to leverage his acceptance of the invitation. At that time he was living in a very small apartment without decent conditions for practicing. "I explained that if I had a better place I could spend all my energy and time getting ready for the competition." The ploy wasn't successful. "They just ignored me," he complained. He, too, bowed out.

Yevgeny Malinin, a disciple of the legendary Heinrich Neuhaus, also declined, citing his psoriasis, which became acute when he was anxious. He was, he said, "medically prohibited" from such situations. To prove the seriousness of his skin condition, Malinin began to undress in front of the judges, wrote Berman, at which point "the minister screamed, 'Do not play if you do not want to—just stop taking off your pants!'"

Finally, it was Lev Vlassenko's turn. He agreed to compete. At that moment, this solid, well-respected pianist seemed clearly destined to win.

Berman's version of events is not totally reliable, however. The two pianists he refers to who are still living—Ashkenazy and Bashkirov—both refute at least some of the details. In Ashkenazy's case, Berman may simply have confused the first competition with the one that followed, since the authorities tried to induce him to enter both (and succeeded the second time). Ashkenazy says he was actually never at the gathering Berman describes.

"The First Piano Concerto was not—and is not—one of my favorite Tchaikovsky pieces," explains Ashkenazy, "[though] I love his symphonies, *Romeo and Juliet, Sleeping Beauty,* and more." Ashkenazy is temperamentally a classicist, attracted to music of symmetry, transparency, and elegance, like that of Mozart: "a composer with whom many Russians have a lot of difficulties." The mismatch, he explains, is due to Mozart's "impeccable sense of form, which one could describe as the practical gift of putting your material in an ideally communicative shape—the very thing which is probably most foreign to a chaotic, emotional Russian."

When the authorities pressed Ashkenazy to enter the second Tchaikovsky Competition in 1962, he could not refuse, because he was in a delicate political situation, having married a foreigner. "Plus, after my first successful US tour, I was downgraded career-wise, because I had not 'behaved as a good Soviet citizen should behave abroad,'" he says. He had read a banned book, for example, and his official "minder" (who had actually read the same book) reported him. "I am mystified by Berman's statement," says Ashkenazy. "Had I been asked I would have remembered it."

Dmitri Bashkirov also denies having attended the get-together between pianists and authorities cited by Berman, though he says Soviet officials did try, unsuccessfully, to pressure him into participating. "I played in just one competition in my life," he said. "I won the 1955 Marguerite Long competition [Concours Long-Thibaud] in Paris, and it turned out that I was not a 'competitive' pianist. I told myself afterward that I would never go to another competition. And that was that—I never did."

CHAPTER 4

A Tale of Two Nations

THE TCHAIKOVSKY COMPETITION, created in part with the hope of prompting an economic windfall for the Soviet Union, was also a propagandist's dream. Still basking in its scientific glory in the space race, the USSR would now be propelled to impressive artistic heights as it assumed the mantle of arbiter of musical greatness. What's more, the winners of the new competition for violinists and pianists would undoubtedly be Soviet citizens. Success seemed historically inevitable. America was a society wealthy beyond measure, but it was also, in the Kremlin's view, brutish and empty. The capitalist system cultivated "stupid and greedy animals," in Maxim Gorky's phrase. How could such crass, materialistic people know anything about art?

Such was the familiar refrain, and it was not restricted to the Soviet Union. Anti-Americanism was widely spread among

European intellectuals, a 1955 cable from the American embassy in Brussels said, because of the "impression that in America the artist and the thinker is of no real importance, in comparison with the engineer and the businessman." What little art it produced extolled "formalist vices"—the term Communists used to label a work as too abstract or antisocial. The charge was easily leveled at many classical composers—including Soviets—whose works were complex or discordant. Even populist art in America came under attack. Jazz, the country's leading musical export, was "devoid of soul," claimed renowned Soviet composer Dmitri Kabalevsky, in a phrase rich with unintended irony.

At least that was the official stance. Sergei Khrushchev, son of Soviet premier Nikita, asserted that by the late fifties among the intellectual elite, no one believed such things. Those who did were in for a rude awakening when, in the years leading up to the Tchaikovsky Competition, Muscovites began to experience firsthand what the West had to offer.

Pianist Bella Davidovich was in the hall when the Boston Symphony came to Moscow to perform in 1956. Many in attendance had low expectations, she says, and were prepared to mock the visitors. "Slava [cellist Mstislav] Rostropovich was there," says Davidovich. As the American players casually walked onstage, "someone whispered to him, 'Look at how they come out, just wandering around willy-nilly, not at all together.'" Their deportment suggested a lack of discipline, especially in contrast to the soldierlike demeanor of Russian orchestra members. "After the concert began, though," remembers Davidovich, "Rostropovich whispered back: 'But they sure do play together!'"

Indeed, the high caliber exhibited by these Bostonians sent shock waves through Moscow's professional music community. *New York Times* critic Harold C. Schonberg was told by a Moscow musician, "It was a blow to our pride . . . The difference between Boston and our orchestra was so great it was insulting. We had meetings and decided to do something about it, about the caliber of playing, about the caliber of the instruments themselves."

Today, explains Vladimir Ashkenazy, "out-of-tune playing is a fairly grave crime, but in my day it was the norm." Even the best Soviet orchestras were subject to continual brass cracks and untuned woodwind chords. "Then . . . the Boston Symphony came—the first foreign orchestra to visit since the war—and we all heard what an orchestra really could and should sound like."

The easy informality displayed by the Bostonians was already seeping into the Soviet culture at large. Three years after Stalin's death the lid was slowly being lifted from his tyrannical pressure cooker of a society. Elements of westernization were catching on, especially among young people. The trend was another impetus for establishing the Tchaikovsky Competition: The idea of creating an international meet represented a pushback against the political undertow that seemed endlessly to drag the governments of East and West ever closer to confrontation. Isabella Rafaelovna, widow of Alexey Skavronsky, a Soviet pianist who participated in the competition, says the idea of the contest wasn't about international brinksmanship at all.

"We didn't want war again," she said. World War II—the terrible scourge from which the Soviet people had not completely recovered—was still on everyone's mind. It was important, she says, to have a way to meet people from different countries, to share culture and knowledge. "Also, to show people in the West that in Moscow there were no bears in the streets, and that people didn't drink only vodka."

The timing was right. Actually, a proposal to create what became the Tchaikovsky Competition had been made long before the *Sputnik* era, though it was initially rejected because of the anticipated expense. By 1958 a perfect storm of motivations had set in to resurrect the idea.

Named "Moscow Musical Holiday," the ambitious project, conceived by Nikolai Bespalov in 1951, just three months after he became chairman of the Soviet Committee on Artistic Affairs, was intended to make the case for Moscow as the capital of global musical culture. "The objective of the festival," he wrote, "is to show the indisputable superiority of socialist culture." Bespalov presented a vision in which established talent and young artists were to be invited from all over the world—musicians, dancers, conductors, and composers. Visiting participants would make trips to Moscow's museums and tourist attractions. There would be three or four concerts each day, performed by Soviet and foreign participants together; the Bolshoi Theater would give six operas or ballets; Moscow's leading orchestras and choirs would all participate; and an international piano and violin competition would be launched in honor of Tchaikovsky. Of course, Russian and Soviet music would be featured, but also other "Slavic composers," like Chopin, Smetana, and Dvořák. Meanwhile Soviet performers would demonstrate their superior mastery by playing works by Beethoven, Bach, Mozart, and others even better than the Westerners could do it.

Bespalov imagined inviting nearly one thousand participants, including, for the competition part of the event, fifty to sixty-five contestants and seventy to eighty jury members. The organizational committee for the competition would be chaired, as the Tchaikovsky Competition eventually was, by Dmitri Shostakovich. When asked what the price would be for all of this, Bispalov gave a calculation that staggered the authorities: more than twenty million rubles. That put an end to it.

But in June 1956, Minister of Culture Nikolai Mikhailov wrote to the Central Committee to bring a scaled-down version of the idea back to life—as the Tchaikovsky International Music Competition. An Organizational Committee (Orgkom) was formed, chaired by Shostakovich, with pianist Emil Gilels and violinist David Oistrakh on board, and the group began work in earnest in August of that year. From the beginning, Gilels displayed the kind of moral leadership that would become his hallmark as head of the 1958 piano jury. Tossing aside political considerations, he wanted the first round to contain a polyphonic composition, linking Soviet efforts to the greatest technical accomplishments of Western music. And he openly worried that including Scriabin and Rachmaninoff on the mandatory program might disadvantage competitors from abroad. After all, the Soviet desire to come out on top was fine, but not if it meant tipping the scales of justice. Many of the committee's other decisions, such as the choosing of jury members and some ancillary activities, were similarly approached with Gilels's impressive determination to guide the new ship in the right way.

"Five years before," wrote Sergei Khrushchev, perhaps unaware of Bespalov's suggestions, "no one would have even thought of such a thing. And no one would have come here." Heavy-handed interference from government overseers, ballerina Maya Plisetskaya wrote, made fair competition impossible. In Prague and Budapest, juries behaved as though "only envoys from the land of the Soviets could dance, sing, play the piano, or walk the circus tightrope well."

Even then, winning often required the right kind of pedigree. Sviatoslav Richter, though heralded as one of the country's greatest pianists, was nonetheless prevented from being crowned the sole winner of the 1945 All-Union Piano Competition because of his German ancestry. Similar attitudes prevailed in dance or sports, with little pretense of impartiality. American choreographer Jerome Robbins, invited to be on one jury, refused to vote, finding the judges' behavior inexplicable. Sports contests were especially tainted. At women's events, the winners were often clandestine hermaphrodites, claimed Plisetskaya: "They looked like women, with mounds on their chests, but if you looked more closely—these were regular bruisers."

The dishonesty was an open secret. A US State Department memo from Warsaw in 1955 described the voting at the Chopin Piano Competition as affiliating "along national political, rather than strictly musically technical lines." The formidable Italian pianist Arturo Benedetti Michelangeli, seen emerging from the competition's jury room after midnight looking "gloomy and dismal," sat at a remote table with a glass of wine and his pack of cigarettes, and refused to sign the official document, so offended was he by the politicization of the process.

At a certain point, wrote Plisetskaya, foreign competitors simply stopped showing up. That wasn't the only impediment to holding a successful international competition in the Soviet Union. The country was also ill prepared to host visitors who made the effort. Soviet hotels were notoriously abysmal: Touring dance companies would discover that warm water was available for only two hours a day. "It was always so rust-red that you couldn't wash it off when you got home," lamented Plisetskaya. "We brought our own soap. And stuck in a corner: boiling water in a rusty wooden tub, with a bashed-up cup fastened to it with a chain. This depressing setup was the hotel snack bar." (The American company of *Porgy and Bess* discovered much the same during their 1955 visit to Leningrad: "The bathroom . . . had peeling sulfur walls, a cold radiator, and a broken toilet that rumbled like a mountain brook," remembered Truman Capote, who accompanied the troupe.)

Still, staging an international musical competition on home turf was tempting. In the years leading up to the first Tchaikovsky Competition, young pianists at the Moscow Conservatory were a force to be reckoned with. Ashkenazy brought home prizes in 1955 from the Chopin Competition in Warsaw and in 1956 from the Queen Elisabeth Competition in Brussels; his friend Lev Vlassenko won the Liszt Competition in Budapest in 1956 (though Vlassenko's rival Liu Shikun claimed that he was unfairly disadvantaged simply for being Chinese rather than Russian). Naum Shtarkman, another Moscow student, won the first Vianna da Motta International Music Competition in Lisbon in 1957. It was an impressive record.

Soviet authorities had prevailed in a string of victories against the West in other forums, like the long-distance chess match between New York and Moscow initiated by New York mayor Fiorello La Guardia in 1945, just after the defeat of the Nazis, when the Soviets won by a score of 15½–4½. That same year, the Moscow Dynamo soccer team went to England and played Chelsea for a surprising 3–3 draw. Unfortunately, propaganda-minded Soviets used the visit to undermine the British with baseless stories of English war veterans with barrel organs begging for bread in the streets, and children being kept on leashes.

Still, exhibition sports were a natural way to facilitate contact, and in the mid-fifties many such exchanges were actively promoted. An American weightlifting team visited Moscow and Leningrad in 1955, while Soviet weightlifters flaunted their prowess in Chicago, Detroit, and New York. In 1958, Soviet wrestlers would travel to the United States as American basketball players set out to tour the Soviet Union.

Of course, in 1957 most of the world was transfixed by a very different kind of Soviet demonstration—its extraordinary breakthrough in rocket technology. Ironically, the launch of *Sputnik* and the reaction it generated set in motion new efforts at cultural diplomacy. The success allowed Soviet leaders to stand tall on the world stage and confidently address their Western counterparts as true equals. By the beginning of 1958, the two world powers were agreeing to an exchange of artists and citizens. The Tchaikovsky Competition became one more step in that expansive program.

Despite the ongoing rivalry between the United States and the USSR, the historical trend was not entirely grim. After Stalin's demise in 1953, "the Thaw"—an easing of political hostilities, named after the 1954 novel by Ilya Ehrenburg—opened the door wider between the two nations, though the Soviet transition to a new worldview required tremendous boldness. "Right up until his death," remembered Khrushchev, "Stalin used to tell us, 'You'll see, when I'm gone the imperialistic powers will wring your necks like chickens.' "

Up close, Stalin wasn't physically imposing: "An ordinary, shabby little man, short, fat, with reddish hair," wrote Shostakovich. "His face was covered with pockmarks and his right hand was noticeably thinner than his left. He kept hiding his right hand . . ." But looks can be deceiving. The dictator's reign of terror resulted in between 17 and 22 million deaths before World War II—more than twice the number of Hitler's victims in the Holocaust.

Khrushchev's courageous seven-hour speech in February of 1956 denouncing Stalin and his "cult of personality" precipitated the release of millions of prisoners from labor camps. "We arranged for a special closed session of the Congress," Khrushchev recalled, "and I delivered my speech. The delegates listened in absolute silence. It was so quiet in the hall you could hear a fly buzzing." As the delegates left the hall, they were heard uttering "*Da-a, da-a, da-a*" ("Yes, yes, yes") in stunned recognition of what had occurred. A very nervous Khrushchev still wondered to himself, "What if a flood resulted from the thaw, one that would overwhelm us and that we would find it difficult to cope with?"

He needn't have worried. Even in an atmosphere of liberalization much remained the same, including the unpredictability of which creative artists might next receive official approval or scorn. A 1940s cartoon appearing in the Russian periodical *Krokodil* (Crocodile) accurately depicted the continuing situation: A young couple sits on a bench and listens to a bird singing. She: "Don't you love the song of the nightingale?" He: "I dare not say before I know who wrote the song."

Entire catalogs of art were subjected to capricious judgments that could turn composers overnight from national treasures into enemies of the state. Dmitri Shostakovich, Aram Khachaturian, and Sergei Prokofiev all suffered that indignity for violating the tenets of "socialist realism"—a catchphrase for works deemed politically correct and easily understood by the masses. In music, that meant compositions filled with old-fashioned melody, free of jarring dissonances and untraditional forms.

Lurking in the background, though, was a notion that had been circulating for over a decade: that wealthy visitors from abroad could solve the nation's financial problems. An international piano competition was just the thing to generate the kind of positive publicity needed to make Moscow a more desirable destination for money-bearing visitors.

The tourism idea was floated in the press as early as 1945, but it really took hold in 1955, as the Kremlin began cultivating a relationship with New York City's Cosmos travel bureau. When the "tourist ruble" was introduced in 1957, making travel more affordable for foreigners, the Soviet Intourist agency reported five times the number of visitors as in the prewar period. Between 1957 and 1965 it would double to one million.

Nineteen fifty-five was also a banner year for artistic export. The Soviets shipped out pianist Emil Gilels, cellist Mstislav Rostropovich, and violinist David Oistrakh. They also imported *Porgy and Bess*. In return, America dispatched violinist Isaac Stern and tenor Jan Peerce to the Soviet Union. Stern explained: "We send them our Jewish violinists from Odessa and they send us their Jewish violinists from Odessa." The magazine *USSR* (called *Soviet Life* after 1964) was distributed in the United States, and its counterpart, *Amerika,* hit the streets in the Soviet Union.

The seeds of such exchanges were planted long before, at the Potsdam Conference in 1945, as Stalin, Winston Churchill, and Harry Truman met to negotiate terms for the end of World War II. Truman had summoned two American soldiers, pianist Eugene List and violinist Stuart Canin, to play for the assembled leaders at a dinner at which the president himself led off with a performance of Paderewski's Minuet in G (as a young boy, he had received a backstage demonstration of how to play the piece from the composer, who was visiting Kansas City on tour).

In response, Stalin sent to Moscow for some of his finest musicians—including pianists Gilels and Vladimir Sofronitsky and violinist Galina Barinova—who gave their performances at a Soviet-sponsored affair. Stalin's party was the more lavish, remembered Truman, starting with caviar and vodka and winding up with "watermelon and champagne, with smoked fish, fresh fish, venison, chicken, duck and all sorts of vegetables in between. There was a toast every five minutes until at least 25 had been drunk." Churchill, not much of a music aficionado, told Truman he was bored to tears, and shuffled off to a corner where he "glowered, growled, and grumbled" until the concert ended. National pride was somehow preserved on all sides.

Now, as the Thaw began to take hold, such gestures were occurring on a large scale, culminating in the first US-Soviet cultural agreement, signed in January of 1958. Although the nations had long engaged in cultural outreach, it had always taken the form of proxy wars, where each side tried to outdo the other. (It was a more subtle approach than the street demonstrations and counterdemonstrations, often held in front of embassies, like those that took place in New York and Moscow in response to the Soviet invasion of Hungary in 1956.)

The competition could be intense. The Soviets invested in cultural conferences "for peace" in East Berlin and Wrocław, Poland, Paris, and, eventually, New York City. The Americans countered with programs like Masterpieces of the Twentieth Century, a musical and literary avant-garde festival in Paris, meant to demonstrate the openness of the United States to radically modernist works (but they were apparently so off-putting that the *New Yorker*'s Janet Flanner, writing under her pseudonym, Genêt, called the festival a "fiasco"). These cultural crusades for the hearts and souls of cultivated audiences would never completely subside, yet on the surface at least, a sense of mutual understanding seemed finally to be growing.

Relations between the two powers had not always been so barbed. Ivan Turgenev, Russia's great nineteenth-century novelist, earned the nickname "the American" in his student days because of his enthusiasm for the young nation. In that early era, popular works by François-René de Chateaubriand and James Fenimore Cooper depicted the United States as a natural paradise blessed with lavish technological conveniences, and America's War of Independence and its ensuing democracy served as powerful inspirations for Russia's intelligentsia.

Nevertheless, conflicts were inescapable, and chronic tensions developed. Russian settlements in Alaska stirred American concerns about losing Oregon and California, helping to spur the creation of the protectionist Monroe Doctrine. Russia's Czar Nicholas I, facing an uprising at home and fearing the influence of American revolutionary ideals, began to censor information about the United States. At the same time, the institution of slavery tarnished America's utopian image in the eyes of many Russians. Ironically, it ended with the Emancipation Proclamation two years after a similar proclamation freed Russian serfs.

Maxim Gorky fanned the embers of those disaffections when he visited the United States in 1906, hoping to skew opinion against American loans to Russia's czarist government and toward the Bolshevik Party. Gorky's dystopian picture of America was breathtakingly disingenuous: "No inner freedom, no freedom of the spirit, shines in people's eyes. And this energy without freedom reminds you of the cold gleam of the knife that has not yet been dulled. It is the freedom of blind instruments in the hands of the Yellow Devil—Gold." Gorky had personal as well as political reasons to vilify America. When American newspapers learned, thanks to a tip from the Russian ambassador, that his companion, Maria Andreeva, was not his wife, the couple was abruptly evicted from their New York hotel and faced the wrath of an unforgiving press.

His description of the United States nevertheless became entrenched in the Russian worldview. Futurist poet Vladimir Mayakovsky continued the onslaught: the two great nations, he wrote, represented an "opposition between the materially poor but spiritually dynamic Soviet Union and the rich but spiritually poor United States."

More moderate voices offered a more positive view. As poet Sergei Esenin (who was married for a time to dancer Isadora Duncan) acknowledged in 1923, an undeniable dynamism had taken root on American soil: "Europe smokes and throws away the butts; America picks up the butts, but out of them something magnificent is growing." The allure of that spirit of enterprise and creativity was difficult to resist, and one inescapable influence was American film.

Adventure movies, detective stories, and zany comedies were more popular in Moscow than Soviet films, especially when they featured Douglas Fairbanks, Harold Lloyd, Charlie Chaplin, or Mary Pickford. Bolshevik Russia eagerly embraced silent Westerns during the late teens and the twenties, a peak period for Russian avant-garde film-poster production, when anonymous, highly artistic posters drew on American publicity materials featuring cowboy stars like William S. Hart, as in the 1917 film *The Silent Man,* screened and promoted in Russia in 1927 as *Khishchniki Floridy* (The Chinaman from Florida). A decade later, singers Deanna Durbin and Jeanette MacDonald were the idols of a generation of Russian girls. Even Stalin adored an American film, *The Great Waltz* (1938), about the life of Johann Strauss II, and gave orders to have it distributed to Soviet screens. The Soviet leader, reported Maya Plisetskaya, "had a soft spot for plump singing women" like the film's star, soprano Miliza Korjus.

The Hollywood aesthetic spawned homegrown hits on the Soviet side. Grigori Aleksandrov, who had worked with legend-

74

ary film director Sergei Eisenstein, created the blockbuster movie *Circus* (1936)—a spectacular musical melodrama in which a circus star bears a black child and is driven out of a Kansas town by white racists—and started a sensation with a song used in the production. In the film, the heroine falls in love with a Russian acrobat who, wearing a white peasant tunic, sings "Song of the Motherland" to her while at a white piano in the Hotel Moskva, overlooking the Kremlin. The melody became so popular it was played on the Kremlin's chimes for many years, and adopted as the station signal of Radio Moscow (replaced only in 1956 by "Moscow Nights").

Soviet authorities found they could endow Hollywood movies with social legitimacy through ideological reinterpretation. John Ford's *Stagecoach* (1939), starring John Wayne, was retitled *The Journey Will Be Dangerous* and described as a movie about the Indians' struggle against white imperialists. *The Roaring Twenties* (1939), a gangster film set in the days of Prohibition and featuring the song "My Melancholy Baby"—which became a big hit in Russia—was renamed *A Soldier's Fate in America*, to highlight the heartlessness of capitalists toward veterans.

Young audiences, though, more interested in human characters and entertaining plots than in any political arguments, eagerly memorized lines, imitated gestures, and reenacted scenes from their favorite films. *Tarzan* movies starring Johnny Weissmuller were shown in the Moscow University dorms, where fellow students of Mikhail Gorbachev filled the corridors at night with apelike howling. In 1954, reported *The New York Times*, people lined up for blocks to see *Tarzan,* and teenage boys began to wear "Tarzan" haircuts—described as "a horrible kind of long bob." *The Times*'s Harrison E. Salisbury reported hearing boys on Gorky Street on summer evenings calling to girls, "Hey, Jane!"

In America people were watching films with a more pointed

political message. *The Iron Curtain* (1948), *The Red Menace* (1949), and *The Woman on Pier 13* (1949; originally titled *I Married a Communist*) provided a backdrop for the nation's emotional agitation over their Red counterparts. In earlier times, when the Soviets were still seen as World War allies, they were more favorably depicted in *Mission to Moscow* (1943) and *Song of Russia* (1944). But as a conspiratorial imagination gripped the nation, dozens of filmmakers found success by promoting xenophobia and patriotic fervor—sometimes with a little armchair Freudianism thrown in. *My Son John* (1952), about a Communist, suggested that the main character was turned to the political dark side because of liberal ideas and the sexual looseness of his mother. As full-blown hysteria over the Red Scare swept the country, the 1951 alien-intruder film *The Thing* and the 1956 *Invasion of the Body Snatchers* reflected an agitated national psyche.

Consumer magazines like *The Saturday Evening Post* also offered constant reminders of the Soviet threat with alarmist headlines like "Communist Wreckers in American Labor" (1939), "Case History of College Communism" (1950), and "The GI's Who Fell for the Reds" (1954) splashed on its covers beside painter Norman Rockwell's artful depiction of American life at its most wholesome.

The head of the Motion Picture Association of America, Eric Johnston, revealed a protectionist reflex as ill conceived as that of the Soviets. "We'll have no more *Grapes of Wrath*, we'll have no more *Tobacco Road*s," he announced in 1946, "we'll have no more films that deal with the seamy side of American life. We'll have no more films that treat the banker as a villain."

Ironically, the power exercised by American popular culture on the Russians had come from its dissident spirit—the antiestablishment stance Johnston tried to quash at home. At parties in the years just before the Tchaikovsky Competition, young Russians embraced that revolutionary zeal, disregarding their leaders and listening to banned music—including Bing Crosby, Louis Armstrong, and Peggy Lee—dancing the jitterbug, smoking Camels and Pall Malls, and addressing each other as "darling" and "baby," while they self-identified as *shtatniki* (Americans). Despite governmental displeasure, such music was sold on the black market through "X-ray editions," crude recordings made from used X-ray plates. Purveyors of the practice called the process "recording on the bone." In that post-Stalin climate, the working class revolutionary fashions of leather jacket, military boots, and worker's cap also gave way to Western accouterments: girls turned to bright-red lipstick, bobbed hair, and short skirts.

The trend culminated at the 1957 World Festival of Youth and Students in Gorky Park. For two weeks in July and August, over thirty thousand foreign students descended on Moscow for what *The New York Times*'s Max Frankel described as "a dizzying round of games, conferences, parties, and carnivals." American ambassador Llewellyn Thompson's wife and two daughters, newly arrived in Moscow, were lost in the vast, three-hundred-acre park. While searching for an exit with growing apprehension, the trio was finally accosted by the KGB agents who had been assigned to follow them. "Would you like help getting back home?" they asked gently.

Rock 'n' roll songs that had previously been prohibited had become the anthems of a new generation. Teens at the event began bidding each other goodbye with, "See you later, alligator" (from the Bill Haley song), and trading black-market copies of Western recordings, while Western gear assumed prominence as the latest fashion statements. According to a State Department intelligence report, there was also "genuine jazz as performed by

Western experts." United States agencies tried to discourage participation by American citizens, though 160 showed up.

The music was a thorn in the side of Soviet officialdom. A year earlier, in 1956, an American journalist in Tashkent witnessed young people dancing to "Stompin' at the Savoy" played by a live combo, when a security officer lectured the gathering: "All this energy could be invested in building a hydroelectric power station, rather than wasted here on a dance floor." Even as late as 1960, government youth patrols were trained to distinguish between acceptable music and *bugi-vugi*.

The 1958 International Tchaikovsky Competition was floated partly on the perceived success of that World Festival of Youth. The competition would in itself spur even greater cultural activities, such as the 1959 American National Exhibition in Moscow, where United States fashions, appliances, and cars were displayed as proof of the advantages of capitalism. It drew huge crowds.

American music, fashions, and films fed the growing youth movement, with zoot-suited hipsters called *stilyagi* (the ones "with style") leading the way. As writer Vasily Aksyonov put it: "It was amazing. We were being brought up as robots, but we began to listen to jazz." The music represented a breakaway from the strictures of state domination.

There had once been a "Red jazz age"—from 1932 to 1936— when beloved Soviet bandleaders like Alexander Tsfasman and Leonid Utesov regularly played American hits like "The Man I Love." Utesov fashioned his stage presence after the American bandleader Ted Lewis ("Is Everybody Happy?"), and became a personal favorite of Stalin. But during World War II a national retrenchment rendered the American art poisoned fruit.

Now this music was staging a comeback. (Official policy was still another matter. The 1952 edition of *The Great Soviet*

Encyclopedia quoted Gorky's essay "Music for the Gross," which lamented "the evolution from beautiful minuets and lively passionate waltzes to the cynicism of the foxtrot and the convulsions of the Charleston." Gorky preposterously claimed that "Negro jazz bands" were "secretly laughing, because their white masters are evolving into the kind of barbarians that the Negroes have long left behind.") The trend had the power of a tidal wave. The most popular American in Moscow before the ascendance of Van Cliburn was Willis Conover, whose jazz program on the Voice of America garnered an audience estimated at 30 million in the Soviet Union and Eastern Europe, and up to 100 million worldwide. His programs featured what he called "the music of freedom." (Not surprisingly, he had to struggle against significant congressional opposition to the idea of spending money on "frivolous music.") Yet Conover, wrote *The New York Times* in his obituary, "proved more effective [in the struggle between communism and democracy] than a fleet of B-29's." The Soviets had opened the door for him by marketing 5 million shortwave radios to their citizens—with a much different agenda in mind. They couldn't put the genie back in the bottle. (Attempts at jamming VOA signals were mostly ineffective. The high-pitched squealing created by sending out a signal with a slightly different wavelength was described as the "buzzing of a gigantic electric razor, mixed with a scraping noise and the roar of a squadron of B-24s." The United States simply shifted signals to escape the problem.) By the mid-1950s jazz ambassadors like Louis Armstrong became part of the program of cultural exchange. Soviet officials, still fighting the trend at the end of the decade, unsuccessfully tried to promote the *Lipsi*, a fast waltz invented in East Germany, as an antidote to decadent Western music and dance. They had already lost the battle.

The defiant youth phenomenon was not restricted geographi-
cally, and Americans similarly had their hands full of unruly
teenagers. Rock 'n' roll music in the United States blossomed in
an atmosphere of rebellion against parents and other authority
figures. Its first big hit, "Rock Around the Clock" by Bill Haley
and His Comets, rose to the top of the charts after appearing on
the sound track of the 1955 film *Blackboard Jungle*, about teen
angst and juvenile delinquency—any parent's nightmare. (The
disc of "Rock Around the Clock" was issued with a B-side of
"Thirteen Women [and Only One Man in Town]," about the
aftermath of a hydrogen bomb detonation. There was plenty of
anxiety to go around.)

US officials attempted, in an echo of Soviet policy, to ban
provocative materials as a way of keeping a wrap on those roiling emotions. In a 1954 book by Fredric Wertham called *Seduction of the Innocent*, comic books were singled out as a source of
the problem. By 1955, thirteen states had passed laws regulating
them. That year, *Time* published a special issue with the title
"Teenagers on the Rampage." Who could blame adults for over-
reacting? According to psychologist Robert Lindner "the youth
of the world today is touched with madness, literally sick with an
aberrant condition of mind."

It was hardly the only American effort to revoke access to
provocative materials. As Senator Joseph McCarthy and his
House Un-American Activities Committee railed against imagined Communist conspiracies, United States postal authorities
blocked Americans from receiving certain foreign publications,
and the government's overseas libraries set about to remove books
written by Communists or "any controversial persons."

Nevertheless, the antiestablishment train was unstoppable. In September of 1957 Jack Kerouac's *On the Road* launched the "Beat" writer to stardom, giving romantic luster to a lifestyle that celebrated provocation and controversy. Norman Podhoretz, in *Esquire*, compared the Beats to juvenile delinquents. "We are witnessing a revolt of all the forces hostile to civilization itself," he wrote, "a movement of brute stupidity and know-nothingism."

Meanwhile, in Moscow, a black market for Western goods flourished. Soviets who bought and sold whiskey (*viski drink*), blue jeans (*dzhinsi*), and other items through foreign tourists became known as *fartsovshiki*, and developed their own special argot. When a *fartzman* said, "He treats me in an American way," for example, it meant, "He treats me well." An excellent meal became "an *Amerkanski* supper." The sentence "Because of a lack of money I cannot go looking for foreigners who would like to exchange their dollars for rubles" became "No cabbage [rubles] no grin [dollars] bombing [seeking out foreigners for trade]."

Soviets increasingly embraced these colorful elements of Western society, yet fundamental differences remained at the roots of the two cultures. A comparison of proverbs from each side illustrates the point. The Western phrase "Out of sight, out of mind" became, in its Russian version, "Out of sight, out of heart." It highlights the difference between America's purported cold rationalism and Russia's tendency toward teeming emotionality, which continued to define the nation's character. This divergence goes a long way toward explaining why Van Cliburn's triumph seemed written in the stars.

CHAPTER 5

The Great Convergence

A S WORD OF THE FORTHCOMING Tchaikovsky Competition spread, an army of musical gladiators prepared to descend on Moscow. There were myriad motivations spurring them on. Some, like America's Jerome Lowenthal, were merely fascinated by the prospect of going to "that forbidden area, filled with mystery." Having been brought up in a leftist family environment, he says, "I was intrigued." Others hoped to be propelled to new career heights.

Thorunn "Dodi" Johannsdottir traveled from Iceland to meet her two favorite Soviet pianists, Sviatoslav Richter and Emil Gilels. For Bulgarian Milena Mollova, the impetus was true desperation. "Back home I was called a wunderkind," she says, after beginning piano at age four, and giving her first recital at six. At nine she won a Bulgarian music competition. But it did her little good. Living in that Eastern Bloc nation was an artistic dead end; the society was so closed and devoid of opportunity that even her successes felt bitter. She was, she relates, a virtual prisoner, unable to explore possibilities elsewhere. "It wasn't my idea to enter, but my teacher's," she said of the Tchaikovsky. "I was a little afraid in fact, because the Tchaikovsky concerto is difficult. I agreed to do it because taking part in the competition was the only way I could get permission to go anywhere." Moscow offered her a rare chance for escape into the greater world, if only temporarily.

The stakes were especially high in Russia, where musicians were placed in the position of having to defend national honor. Lev Vlassenko practiced the Tchaikovsky First Piano Concerto day in and day out in the apartment of his teacher, Yakov Flier. He played the piece so incessantly, recalls Bella Davidovich, that Flier's dog, Athos (named after one of Dumas's three musketeers), began to howl every time he heard the opening strains.

The government set up an arduous training regimen for the entire Soviet contingent—as pressure-filled as that of athletes preparing for the Olympics. Contestants were watched over like hatchlings in a nursery. When Vlassenko occasionally slacked off, Flier was there to prod him. Once, the pianist was tardy getting out of bed in the morning, so his teacher roused him with the news that another pianist, on the floor above, had already begun to practice. "The enemy doesn't sleep," announced Flier, quoting an old Russian saying.

Vlassenko seemed to be the hands-down favorite. In Warsaw, his performance of Liszt's First Piano Concerto led a reviewer to comment that he had "the best octaves of the socialist camp"—a reference to the technique of playing double streams of notes an octave apart in rapid succession, a feat of no minor accomplishment. Like the other Soviet contenders who eventually consented to join in the contest, he was provided with special living conditions in which to sharpen his gifts.

"The time period proved to be very short: from January to April," Vlassenko remembered. Each of the pianists studied at the Composers' House of Creativity in Ruza, a musicians' colony outside Moscow, occupying separate wooden houses—little dachas—for several weeks. Then they were taken to Malakhovka, a well-known resort. "Yakov Vladimirovich [Flier] also took up residence at Malakhovka," Vlassenko confided. "That is when the competition drudgery began."

Things went fairly smoothly for him, but they didn't work out well for all of the players. Pianist Alexey Skavronsky was so cold in his dacha, remembers his widow, that "he got sick, and developed terrible muscle cramps, in his shoulder and arm. During the competition, he performed in a lot of pain."

For Vlassenko, preparing for the Tchaikovsky was the final lap of a musical journey that had begun in Tbilisi, in the Caucasus Mountains, where he was born in 1928. Like Van, his first teacher had been his mother, a member of a family of musicians, the Benditskys, who were significant enough to be mentioned in a story by Sholem Aleichem. His grandfather, a self-taught trombonist, was a member of the Tiflis opera house orchestra, and their home environment was a fertile atmosphere, invigorated by regular visits from influential cultural figures.

Heinrich Neuhaus, the venerable Moscow Conservatory teacher who would be a judge at the 1958 Tchaikovsky contest, was often there. "In the morning he used to go out onto the veranda and sit in the wicker chair, having endless discussions with my grandfather, mainly on philosophical topics," Vlassenko remembered. In the evening, there would be visits by musician friends, like the Kuftins—she was a professor at the conservatory and he an academician and archaeologist.

In those early years Neuhaus was not yet the intimidating Tchaikovsky juror, but an avuncular presence, listening attentively as the youngster performed. "I don't think I played very successfully," admitted Vlassenko, "although I have remembered Neuhaus's words ever since: 'One should sit quietly at the piano.' I was swinging from side to side, trying to produce a stronger emotional impression."

Evidently, he was expressive enough to earn a place in the special music school for gifted children. He was called "the Bachist" because of his affinity for Bach and Beethoven. Then, as he came under the influence of Flier, "the last chevalier of romanticism, with his blood boiling all the time," said Vlassenko, the young student inclined less toward the architectural gracefulness of Bach and more toward the fire-eating virtuosity of Vladimir Horowitz.

He had to work hard for technical mastery. His first two years at the Moscow Conservatory were particularly challenging. He was forced to live in a rented room without a piano, and went without a bed as well, sleeping instead in a big chair. He quickly solved the piano problem: as a student at the Institute of Foreign Languages, his second, parallel course of study, he simply showed up at seven a.m. each day to use that institution's piano, and returned to it again in the evening.

His interest in language was serious, even passionate, and it was an avocation that in the end offered him unusual opportunities. While traveling in Israel with violinist Mikhail Vaiman, for instance, he was invited to give a speech in Hebrew at the Knesset; at a competition in Japan he surprised jury members by perfectly enunciating complicated Japanese phrases. Because of those talents, Soviet authorities prevented him from going abroad for several years out of concern that they couldn't control his communication with foreigners. In 1957, though, those unusual linguistic gifts placed him at the center of a ground-breaking event in the musical life of Moscow.

That was the year Glenn Gould, the quirky Canadian pianist whose kaleidoscopic 1955 rendition of Bach's *Goldberg Variations* had set the world on its ear, decided to perform in Russia. Gould had already made history by taking Bach's intricate webs of crisscrossing musical lines, long regarded as austere and academic, and turning them into something spellbinding, imbuing the music's straightforward baroque melodies with qualities like nobility, heartbreak, joy, and jauntiness. His recording was a revelation, though news of it evidently hadn't yet reached Russia. So at Gould's Moscow recital, the hall was half-empty until intermission—at which point the city's most prominent pianists rushed out to call their colleagues, telling them the event was not to be missed. The venue quickly filled for the second half.

Gould never reached a large Russian public, nor did he melt his listener's hearts, as Van Cliburn would. His impact on the musicians who heard him, however, transformed their understanding of what piano playing could be. In a way, Moscow's two most famous visiting pianists from North America sparked equally powerful but radically different reactions. They were in fact opposites: Gould's playing caused you to hold your breath. Cliburn's made you sigh.

"Gould was such a sensation that the Moscow Conservatory invited him to meet with students," said Ella Vlassenko, Lev's widow. The pianist had come with his own professional interpreter—he wanted not only to play Bach, but also to perform and talk about twentieth-century music. So he included on his program Alban Berg's Sonata and atonal music by Anton Webern and Ernst Krenek, works unfamiliar to the Soviets and anathema to the political authorities. In truth, even Bach was considered risky at this time; the composer was practically banned because of his association with religious themes. Gould's biggest challenge, though, arose when he began to talk about the music, and it became apparent that the interpreter was lost.

The crowd shouted out for Vlassenko to do the translating. "Believe me, it was not easy," he remembered. "Gould sat at the piano in his habitual manner [on a short, rickety chair], bending his head very low to the keyboard." His fingers possessed "great intensity, along with unusual sensitivity. It was striking how independent and differentiated was the sounding of each finger." The overall effect, he said, was hypnotic. Lev's spontaneous translation saved the day.

That visit was yet another step in the slow political thaw that allowed the Communist nation to embrace a greater world of ideas and inspirations. There was a backlash in the official press, which accused Gould of serving as a representative of bourgeois values. Yet because of his efforts, the doors to the West had opened just a bit wider.

The non-Soviet performers also endured circuitous paths and psychological trials on their way to the competition's stage. For Liu Shikun, Vlassenko's Chinese rival from the 1956 Liszt Competition in Budapest, the Tchaikovsky contest was more than a mere test of musical skill; it was his road to redemption. He regarded his third-place finish behind Vlassenko at that earlier competition as a travesty of justice. This was going to be his opportunity to even the score.

To prepare, Liu moved to Moscow and into a hotel on Gorky Street in the bleak November of 1957, and took lessons twice a week from Moscow Conservatory teacher Samuil Feinberg. Practicing eleven or twelve hours a day, he did little else. He never left the room, he said, not even to eat. It was a bitter winter. The windows had double panes of glass, so he put his food between them to keep it cold.

Reflecting on that time almost six decades later, Liu still exuded an aura of inner strength. His body was tall and sleek, his posture as erect as a bamboo stalk. During his childhood years in the port city of Tianjin, where he was born in 1939, he said, life was easy. His father, a baritone, graduated from the Shanghai Music College (now the Shanghai Conservatory), went into business, and became rich. Few people in China played the piano at that time, Liu explained, but his family's wealth made it possible, and his home environment encouraged that pursuit. "We had four pianos at home—one grand and three uprights, along with ten thousand records," he said.

Like Cliburn's, Liu's affinity for music emerged early. When he was just two years old he began to exhibit unusual behavior, crying unexpectedly at odd times, and his father realized that whenever it happened, a Mozart piece had been playing on the phonograph. He later revealed that Mozart's sounds had conjured an image in his mind of a mother singing to her children, and he wondered what would befall them if she were tragically lost. Clearly, he was a born romantic.

His music lessons began in earnest before he was three, though he couldn't seem to stay still, and practiced while sitting on his father's lap. His father and his first teacher, Liu Jin Din, together focused mostly on developing his musical ear. "My father wanted me to have perfect pitch," he said. "He would play a cluster of ten notes and ask me what they were. And eventually I could answer him." Liu began to compose at the age of seven, because the harmonies were so clear in his mind.

When the family moved to Shanghai, Liu began to work with a graduate of the St. Petersburg Conservatory, a man from Belarus named Lazarov, whose teacher had been a student of Liszt. Liu won first prize in a national competition for children in 1949, and entered the Beijing Conservatory in 1951. In the ensuing decade China and the USSR grew closer, and the Soviets began sending more teachers to China. That's when he came under the tutelage of Aram Tatulian from Moscow's Gnessin School of Music.

Tatulian trained Liu for the 1956 Liszt Competition. Since the minimum age was eighteen, an exception had to be made for the seventeen-year-old pianist. He at first feared the contest would be on too high a level; nevertheless, he asserted, the jury, which included Emil Gilels, Alexander Goldenweiser, and the Hungarian pianist Annie Fischer, wanted to award him first prize. "They stood up after each of my performances," Liu recalled. However, politics made his win impossible.

"I got third prize, in a tie with Lazar Berman," he said. "But this was a shock for the audience." At that time, explained Liu, contest officials felt they had to give Vlassenko, a Soviet, first prize. And naturally they had to give the second prize to a Hungarian. After the announcement, the government, in an effort to calm the public and the press, gave Liu a special award: a lock of Liszt's hair. "I got home just as a revolution was breaking out in Hungary." The Soviets quickly put down that revolt, creating an additional layer of tension with the West.

Liu was steadfast in the face of the Liszt Competition setback. When he met Feinberg for the first time, however, he discovered that the repertoire requirements for the contest were more demanding than he had expected. And, he remembered, "the competition was just around the corner." Feinberg asked him if he played various pieces, and he answered no each time. "You play nothing!" the teacher said, and sighed. But neither of them was ready to give up. Assigned a Bach prelude and fugue on a Monday, Liu demonstrated that he could play it by the time of their next meeting on Thursday. Little by little, Feinberg gained confidence in his young pupil. "Still, I knew that if I were going to have a chance I would have to work at the piano all day, every day," Liu explained. Amazingly, by the time of the opening round, he was ready.

Other contenders made their way from Hungary, Poland, Japan, Bulgaria, the Federal Republic of Germany, Canada, Portugal, Ecuador, Mexico, Argentina, the People's Republic of China, and elsewhere. In all there were thirty-six pianists from thirteen countries. Most had been accepted with little vetting of their abilities. Sometimes factors other than technical accomplishment came into play, however, as in the case of American musician Neil Sedaka, a budding pop music icon.

The fact that Sedaka even considered entering would have shocked most of his fans. His love of the piano had begun, in fact, in elementary school, at PS 253 in Brighton Beach, Brooklyn, where his teacher, Evelyn Glantz, singled him out and sent a note home urging his parents to buy a piano. They didn't have much money, but his mother bought a used piano for four hundred dollars and arranged for lessons.

At thirteen, Sedaka began crafting songs with a sixteen-year-old friend, Howie Greenfield, his eventual longtime writing partner. Shy and conscious of how high his voice was, Sedaka gravitated toward being the pianist in the high-school orchestra rather than a member of the chorus. Then a teacher at his school, Ben Goldman, suggested one day in 1956 that he try out for a talent competition in New York sponsored by classical radio station WQXR.

He was one of seven winners, chosen as a finalist by Arthur Rubinstein, who liked his interpretation of Chopin's G Minor Ballade. "But my life took another course," said Sedaka. When he learned that Goldman had submitted an application to the Tchaikovsky Competition on his behalf—with a tape of Sedaka's performances of the Bartók Third Piano Concerto and Prokofiev's Third Sonata—he felt unsettled. He needn't have worried. At first, the Soviets were receptive, but when they realized that his name was linked with American rock 'n' roll, it made him unacceptable. With a string of hits soon to come, beginning with "Stupid Cupid," recorded by Connie Francis just as the Tchaikovsky Competition had ended, he had no reason for regrets.

Other Americans, including Jerome Lowenthal and Daniel Pollack, faced their own hurdles. Lowenthal, studying in Paris as a Fulbright Scholar, learned of the contest—and of Van Cliburn's intention to enter it—and quickly sent off his inquiry. He was already a fairly seasoned performer, having debuted with the Philadelphia Orchestra at the age of thirteen, before studying with Olga Samaroff, American piano phenomenon William Kapell, and Eduard Steuermann, a Juilliard teacher celebrated as much for his Beethoven as for his ventures into the modernist music of Arnold Schoenberg. By 1958, Lowenthal had garnered prizes in international competitions in Bolzano (the Busoni Competition) and Darmstadt. The purpose of his sojourn to Paris was to study with French piano great Alfred Cortot.

Once he was there, though, things did not shape up as he had hoped. He was unhappily taking lessons from Cortot's assistant, Jules Gentil, when news of the Tchaikovsky presented him with a dilemma. The competition was to be given over a six-week period, he recalled, which meant he had to obtain permission from his teacher to take the necessary time off. It should not have been a great obstacle.

He asked Gentil to send a letter to the commission, and began working on a program for Moscow. Then the Fulbright Commission turned down his request. "I asked them if they had received the letter from Gentil," Lowenthal recalled, "and they replied, 'Yes. He asked us *not* to give you permission to go.'" The reason became clear. If Lowenthal competed, it would have meant lost income for his teacher. Infuriated, he decided to go even if it meant giving up the fellowship. "The Fulbright Commission was always tense about someone like me anyway, whom they suspected of being more of a performer than a scholar," he remembered.

"It all seemed very heroic at that moment. I didn't have a penny," he said, but he was ready to assert his artistic independence against the power brokers. Desperate, he wrote to a friend and patron in America, Fredric R. Mann, for financial support. At that point he couldn't even have purchased his plane ticket. The money finally arrived at the last possible moment. In the interim a second package from Moscow helped solve his problems. The piano section of the event, it turned out, would last only two weeks, and those weeks coincided exactly with the spring school break in Paris. He didn't need permission to leave after all. The news, he says, "felt like a miracle," and off he went.

On the plane from Paris Lowenthal met the French contingent of applicants, most of whom later became friends. Among them, the best recognized today is Roger Boutry, better known now as a composer than as a pianist. The group also included pianists Annie Marchand, Evelyne Crochet, Annie Petit, and Blandine

Crosti, a woman from a wealthy, quasi-aristocratic French-Italian family who had fallen in love with Lazar Berman at the Liszt Competition in Budapest in 1956. They were covertly engaged.

Crosti fared poorly in the competition. At a reception in the Kremlin Khrushchev went to her and said through an interpreter, "I understand that you want to get married." She practically fainted, recalled Lowenthal—it was supposed to be a secret. She and Berman did marry, and then divorced after a very brief time.

The trip for the French group started out badly. The route to Moscow was meandering, and the experience extremely uncomfortable. At a stopover in Prague, Lowenthal and Marchand took a late-night walk before boarding another small Russian plane heading to their final destination. "It was the worst flight I've ever had," Marchand remembered. "The plane was badly pressurized, so our ears were in torment. The pilot would dive down and climb back up, and all the pianists were suffering. Then we landed somewhere in the middle of the steppes. At every airport, they were playing a recording of the Tchaikovsky [First] Piano Concerto. It was the last thing we wanted to hear."

When they finally arrived, the pianists were delivered to the Pekin (later changed to "Peking") Hotel. Lowenthal's initial impression of his new environment was that it was "like being on the moon." Officials were "pushing us around, taking us to the Kremlin, not letting us go to the sites we wanted to see," he said. "But gradually the realization came upon me that I was involved in something more than just a musical contest." His resentment toward his minders was tempered by the understanding that he and his colleagues were making history.

Daniel Pollack faced his own very personal set of difficulties. After working with Lhévinne at Juilliard, he was studying abroad on a Fulbright, in Vienna, at the Hochschule für Musik.

His teacher, Bruno Seidlhofer, saw the Tchaikovsky notice and shared it with him in December of 1957, translating the German text on the spot. Intrigued, Pollack contacted American officials to test the political waters.

"BEING URGED BY TEACHER TO ENTER INTERNATIONAL TCHAIKOVSKY PIANO CONTEST MOSCOW MARCH-APRIL, 1958," read the wire from the embassy in Vienna to the secretary of state in Washington, DC. "POLLACK ANXIOUS TO COMPETE BUT ASKS EMBASSY ADVICE. PLEASE ADVISE SOONEST DEPARTMENT POSITION SINCE CLOSING DATE FOR ENTRANCE DECEMBER 21, 1957."

A reply came two days later: The U.S. government favored the involvement of its citizens in the Soviet competition—with one caveat. "DESIRABLE OF COURSE THAT AMERICAN PARTICIPANTS BE WELL PREPARED AND OF HIGHEST POSSIBLE CALIBER."

With two and a half months to go, being well prepared was going to be a challenge. Pollack had come to understand that the required repertoire consisted mostly of unfamiliar music by Soviet and Russian composers. He set out to learn the new works, practicing nine or ten hours a day, and then continued to absorb some of them as he and his new wife headed from Vienna to Moscow. Their train crossed into Czechoslovakia, Poland, and Belarus during a trip that took two days. All the while the pianist was busy studying and memorizing. Arriving in Moscow and seeing the snowdrifts, he thought "it was like a fairyland."

But all was not wonderful. When Pollack came down for dinner at the Pekin Hotel, all the tables were arranged with the flags of the participating countries. He sat next to pianist Sérgio Varella-Cid from Portugal, who asked him what he was playing. "I said, 'Myaskovsky and Medtner and Shostakovich,'" he recalled. "Then he asked me why I was doing all of those Russian pieces. 'I thought that's what was required,' I replied, and he told me no, you only had to play one of them. I quickly realized that I had prepared the wrong repertoire."

His teacher in Vienna somehow having led him astray, Pollack offered the Soviets a letter of withdrawal. Dmitri Shostakovich, the chairman of the competition, was reluctant to accept it, and he asked the jury to deliberate over the matter. Initially, the Soviets thought it had been a political ploy for Pollack to offer music solely by Soviet composers. "You can imagine my feeling. I was horrified," he said.

The official jury protocol issued on April 2 included among the typed entries one handwritten note: "Provide pianist D. Pollack (USA) the option to choose a piece for performance from the four sonatas from Soviet composers named in his program, with the required performance of Barber's Sonata, op. 26." That decision was more than fair. Every competitor was already required to play one work from his or her own country in the second round, and Pollack had listed the Barber in his application. He had, in fact, played the work (written in 1949) at his 1956 Town Hall debut in New York, as winner of the Concert Artists Guild Competition.

Since he was a prizewinner in a previous international competition, he was allowed to skip the first round of the Tchaikovsky entirely. Now that things were settled, he was able to reflect on his situation, inspired by thoughts of his ancestry—his parents were originally from czarist Russia. His mother escaped with her family from the Ukraine and traveled to Palestine at the age of three. His father, from Belarus, came to America after World War I. Of course, he was also keenly aware that Rosina Lhévinne had graduated from the Moscow Conservatory. His spirits were lifted by those historical connections.

All the practicing had paid off. He made it through the second round and was chosen to move on to the third and final round. However, next on the program would be the Tchaikovsky First Concerto, and he wasn't quite ready. He had just five days left to prepare for it. "Looking back, I don't know where I got the nerve," he said. The field had been narrowed, and the players who remained—including Vlassenko and Liu—would be hard to beat.

And then there was Van—a challenger like no other. When the Texan alighted on Russian soil, Henrietta Belyaeva, his official translator, spotted him in an instant. The American seemed as tall as a Moscow poplar, with a curly mop of blond hair. As he walked, his eyes darted furtively around the airport, seeking signs of a welcome. "Is this Van *Klee*-burn?" asked Belyaeva, stepping up to him. He didn't bother to correct her. The mispronunciation was somehow fitting, amplifying the strangeness of the setting and solidifying his special place in it. From that moment on he was *Klee*-burn.

He loved this new version of his name. The elimination of the sharp-edged i gave it a softer, more musical cast, and offered a subtle advantage over the American version: shifting physically from an open-mouthed i to a sustained ee engaged the facial muscles so that the cheeks were pushed outward and the corners of the mouth lifted upward. You couldn't say "*Klee*-burn" without smiling. Van began to insist on the new variation whenever Russians were around.

Standing nearby Belyaeva at the airport was an old acquaintance from Juilliard, pianist Harriet Wingreen, in town to accompany violinist Joyce Flissler in the earlier violin portion of the event. She had come to reassure the apprehensive Cliburn that all was well. Indeed, things couldn't have been better. If the prediction by his New York psychic helped spur him to board the plane, any misgivings that remained were quickly dispelled in those first hours. Since childhood he had harbored the desire to see St. Basil's Cathedral, the architectural marvel on Red Square created by Ivan the Terrible, with its birthday-cake façade and colorful swirls representing a bonfire rising into the sky. Van had first learned of it in a picture book he received as a Christmas present when he was only five, and the image still entranced him. Belyaeva agreed to take him there on the way to his hotel. What he encountered was even more beautiful than he had imagined: a wintery dreamscape reminiscent of Nikolai Gogol's "mysterious time when lamps endow everything with some enticing, wondrous light."

Snow was falling and strings of electric bulbs hung in the air. "I've told every one of their heads of state [since then] that the lighting that night was so breathtaking," Van remembered. "[There were] streams of light. It was so cold and so snowy. It looked like diamonds stretching toward the church. It will never be more beautiful than it was to me that night." That inspirational moment buoyed his spirits as he considered the task ahead. His next stop was the Pekin Hotel.

CHAPTER 6

_____

The Land of Snow and Spies

O PENED IN 1956 as a symbol of friendship between the
Soviet Union and China, the Pekin Hotel—"heavily ocher
in color, both the stone outside and the pillared lobby, and used
to house privileged, usually Communist visitors," remembered
New York Times correspondent Max Frankel—featured high
ceilings and spacious rooms, stucco moldings, and wood-and-
marble interiors (but surprisingly tiny, cramped elevators). The
Pekin quickly became one of the city's most elite locations. It also
garnered a reputation as "the KGB hotel," a tag borne out by the
hall monitors who took notes on everyone's comings and goings,
along with the listening devices people were forever uncovering
in their quarters.

Pianist Evelyne Crochet stumbled across one while trying to
use a hair dryer. "I had trouble plugging it into the wall," she
explained, "so I opened the electrical panel and found a micro-

phone hidden there. I started saying really silly things, bad words, like 'shit' in Russian. And I announced loudly, 'Look at this . . . a microphone!' My roommate, another French girl, was laughing uncontrollably." She was not alone. At the Hotel Metropol, which housed the jurors, the French judge, Armand de Gontaut-Biron, stood on a chair nightly and cursed at the chandelier after recognizing a microphone hidden among the glistening crystals. How well the Russian eavesdroppers understood his colloquial French is another question.

Some Westerners took the intense scrutiny of their Soviet hosts as a call to action. "As a young girl, I was very playful and made a game of losing my minders," says Crochet. As she walked from the hotel to the conservatory to practice, she noticed several little alleys along the way. One day she ducked into one, entered a bicycle store, and left through a different exit, losing the man who was following her. When she arrived back at the hotel that night, an official contingent was waiting.

"'You cannot do that,' I was told. 'It's dangerous.' I countered with, 'Is it dangerous to live in Russia? What's so dangerous about it?'" Nothing much happened as a result, she says. But there was a feeling of secrecy everywhere, "and a lot of suspicion between people."

Participants from free societies found themselves herded, scrutinized, and sometimes tricked by a shadow force, like ancient Athenians in the grip of their invisible gods. If the inhabitants of that long-ago empire felt bludgeoned by mighty Poseidon or roiled by mischievous Erinyes, here the ever-present agents of influence resided not on Mount Olympus but in the Kremlin.

Crochet received special attention. "We all had an assigned 'translator,'" she recalls. "I knew a little Russian, so they were suspicious of me immediately. They thought it was strange that I had a good accent, so I was always followed." For the Soviet authorities, not a thing went unnoticed. At a Kremlin reception, Khrushchev stopped in front of her and asked why she spoke Russian. She was flabbergasted that he knew. "Then he asked me for the name of the French woman who had a friendship with Lazar Berman—the one he would later marry." Khrushchev often overstepped personal boundaries in a way that verged on rudeness, even with people he liked. The rotund Soviet leader grilled jury member Sequeira Costa about his slight build—"Tell me," he demanded, "do you suffer from hunger in Portugal?"— just as he would later grill Van about his height.

Annie Marchand had an even more troubling experience. She met and became friends with a violist in Moscow who spoke French. They went out a lot. He took her to the Bolshoi Theater and they visited his friends. The Soviets reached out to the French government and asked them to put an end to the relationship. Soon she got a phone call from the secretary of the French ambassador asking about her intentions. Her friend was from a very prominent Communist family, she was told, and the Soviets would be very upset if they chose to marry.

Journalists, keenly aware of being followed, sometimes engaged in games like Crochet's hide-and-seek. From the files of the American embassy a report from August 1958 tells of a correspondent with a reputation as a man-about-town who often managed to shake the surveillance team that followed him on his social escapades. "On one occasion he returned to his car with his date to find the tires riddled with nails," it said. The man hailed a taxi and offered the driver one hundred rubles to elude the car that was following them, which, he claimed, was being driven by the lady's husband. After the driver had successfully lost the tail, the newsman paid him and offered thanks for sparing them the husband's wrath. "The driver retorted with a smile, 'You mean all three of them.'"

As the pianists settled in to their hotels, frustration mounted. "People were nice, but the service was lousy," said Costa of the Metropol's restaurant. He sat at a table in the dining room for no less than forty minutes, waiting for a waiter to show up. He knew a little Russian at the time, and asked what was going on. "Oh, this table doesn't work," was the reply. He later learned there was a special dining room for the jury—huge and noisy, with a band playing fox-trots and tangos, where "everyone was smoking terrible cigarettes. And it took more than two hours for the food to arrive."

Truman Capote had a similar experience in a Leningrad hotel three years earlier, when he was traveling with the American company of *Porgy and Bess*. The service was minimal, he found, and the ambience strange: on the dance floor were couples who seemed gripped by fantasies of a forbidden world brought on by the strains of the American jazz being played. "Madame Nervitsky danced well," Capote wrote of one patron, "but her body was tense, her hands icy. '*J'adore la musique des Nègres*. It's so wicked. So vile.'"

The Pekin's attractiveness rested partly on the professed availability of the traditional flavors of China in its dining room (a later incarnation of the place announced such delicacies as "jugged hare," and "braised pig's trotters in pimiento sauce"), but none of the Tchaikovsky pianists ever got a whiff of such culinary exotica. "The food was mediocre," noted Marchand, "and there was little to be had, except for plenty of caviar and black bread." She would often sit for twenty minutes before a waiter peeled himself away from the wall and started ladling some kind of cabbage soup. Even the seemingly endless mounds of caviar were not to everyone's liking. "I didn't care for it," recalls Dodi Ashkenazy, the Icelandic competitor who later married Vladimir. "So I gave all of my caviar to Van."

In fact, Western visitors found the hotels seriously wanting. When first opened in 1907, the luxurious Metropol was the only lodging in Moscow to offer hot water, refrigerators, and elevators. It served for a while as an official residence of the All-Russian Central Executive Committee after the Revolution of 1917. By the 1930s, it was again attracting sophisticated guests, including such luminaries as George Bernard Shaw and Bertolt Brecht. But by 1958, things had deteriorated dramatically—even the plumbing had become a serious issue.

Costa's wife was shocked by the condition of things. The tub in the bathroom was almost black, so she filled it with alcohol as a disinfectant, and then lit it all on fire. "The people from the floor—on each floor they had special KGB people taking care of things—came running," says Costa. "The Russians weren't crazy about this, and not just because of the danger of fire. There was a lot of cueing up for goods, with long lines everywhere. They were upset that we lit the alcohol on fire instead of drinking it. In their view, my wife was wasting a valuable asset."

Some pianists began to make close observations on their own of the dynamics of everyday life in Moscow. Crochet was shocked to see, on the streets, that most of the heavy work—fixing the pavement, driving trucks—was done by women. "Where else did that happen?" she asked. "It was a sight to see." In that respect at least, the culture seemed more advanced than that in the West. But they were way behind in so many other ways, she noted. Soviet architecture was ugly, "as if deliberately meant to depress people, though the monuments—and historic places like Lenin's Tomb, and Red Square—were beautiful."

She found that people hungered for something better. "Someone approached me and asked, 'Will you sell me your coat?' But

I didn't have a fancy coat—my sister had lent it to me for the trip. It was very light, and the climate was so cold—when I went outside, ice formed in my nose." Roger Boutry also attracted attention with his garment. "Nearly everyone wore a black overcoat," he remembers, "and I had one of camel hair. People thought it was quite special, and they wanted to touch it."

The interest in Western clothing was telling. Marchand recalled going to Moscow's biggest department store, GUM, in search of a souvenir, and finding nothing there except shoes made in Bulgaria that seemed to be constructed of cardboard. Yet in the special section reserved for important Party members, the shelves were full. "The people at the top had absolutely everything they wanted," she noted.

Officials hewed to the Party line, consistently asserting Soviet superiority. Crochet was taken out to a Georgian restaurant and presented with a glass of champagne—as if she'd never heard of the refreshment before. She pointed out that it came from France. "They had no idea, and thought it was a Russian term." That was a logical assumption when the official position was that all good things had to have come from the homeland.

However, the warmth and the yearning of the Russians were palpable, remembered Crochet. "They were easily moved, and cried a lot [at musical performances]. You had to take that with a grain of salt—it was their character. I came from France, where we analyze our thoughts." For Paris-raised Crochet, life was a rational argument. In Russia, where strong emotions were the coin of the realm, life was a broken heart.

Nevertheless, laughter could bubble up from beneath the surface. A standing joke in Odessa involved a barber who was asked why he always talked politics. "Because," came the answer, "it is easier to cut your hair when it's standing on end."

American pianist Misha Dichter, who nearly won the Tchaikovsky Piano Competition in 1966, was at a party with his pianist wife, Cipa, at Lev Vlassenko's Moscow apartment in 1969 or 1970. On the piano was a special commemorative edition of Beethoven's "Appassionata" Sonata, which was known to be Lenin's favorite piece. "I looked at the music and saw that the fingerings"—editorial markings indicating which finger to use on particular notes—"were so perverse that a pianist would have to play the music by positioning himself upside down," remembers Dichter. " 'Maybe they were Lenin's fingerings,' Cipa commented, in full hearing of the crowd. Some muffled laughter erupted at the remark, but the partygoers all held themselves in check," recalls Dichter. "Afterward, though, people would come up to us on the street, giggling and saying, 'We heard about Cipa's comment on Lenin's fingering!' Then they would burst into laughter. It went on for days."

Like the Cathedral of St. Basil, the Moscow Conservatory seemed enchanted—it was itself an ancient shrine where the ghosts of Russia's musical past still inhabited the halls and classrooms. Late one night, as his turn arrived to try out the pianos in the Great Hall, Van climbed "an endless, humongous marble staircase to the anteroom of the hall," then paced back and forth waiting for French pianist Nadia Gedda-Nova to finish practicing a Rachmaninoff Étude-tableau in E-flat Minor, a darkly passionate work filled with unrelieved longing.

He was awestruck. "It is impossible to imagine all the beauty and grandeur of that spacious room with its marble columns and marvelous luxurious rugs that descend down the large stairways," he said. "I was remembering famous people, and it was as if their music was still sounding in those walls: Rachmaninoff, Tchaikovsky, Scriabin, Glinka, Mussorgsky—those who founded Russian music, bestowing it with a national originality." Cliburn continued to suffer from stage fright, and here in Moscow, he admitted, he especially felt "like a small boy, scared at finding myself where Rachmaninoff studied and Tchaikovsky taught."

Happily, the piano sounds churning in that corridor lifted him, just as his eyes fixed on a pin light that fell on a statue of the great Modest Mussorgsky—one of the group of "Mighty Five" composers who had laid the foundations of Russian musical style. It seemed as if an angel were illuminating his path forward. "It was the most magical, overwhelming thing I had ever experienced," he said of that moment. "It's something that I still can't believe. It's hallowed ground. So much famous music had been performed and written there."

A feeling of peace suddenly descended. The images of all the greats coalesced in his mind, a chorus of kindred spirits, allowing him "to forget about myself to such a degree that I overcame my fear and was no longer nervous." He was in that moment not a solitary performer facing a terrifying spotlight, but a songful starling comfortably nestled deep within its flock.

For a musician so sensitive to his surroundings, whose playing was subject to pronounced peaks and valleys, Van found these Moscow experiences—and the wild support he would soon receive from the populace—a tonic to the nerves. As he demonstrated at home, once his anxieties abated, there was almost nothing he couldn't do.

The preparations had been extensive, the ceremonies artfully arranged, and the jurors selected and prepped as a publicity campaign for the competition began to permeate Moscow. On opening day, *Pravda* carried an article about the event by Khacha-turian, *Izvestia* published one by Shostakovich, and *Literaturnaya Gazeta* ran a discussion with both participants and members of the jury. Radio broadcasts had begun promoting the activities weeks before, and once the contest was under way a "Compe-tition Diary," featuring interviews and musical highlights, was added to the schedule. As soon as the music began, people around the city became glued to their radios and televisions. It was as if the world had suddenly stopped spinning and the Mos-cow Conservatory had become the new epicenter around which all things converged.

At the opening ceremony on March 18, the stage of the Great Hall overflowed with flowers as members of the organizing com-mittee, the jury, and prominent figures in the arts took to the stage. After the minister of culture, Nikolai Mikhailov, offered a predictably officious greeting, children scampered onstage to deliver bouquets to the honored guests, then a flock of young violinists gently sawed away at the bright, dance-inflected music of Antonio Vivaldi.

The long speeches continued: there were greetings from N. I. Bobrovnikov, chairman of the executive committee of the Mos-cow City Council of People's Deputies; from Shostakovich; and from violin jury members Efrem Zimbalist of the United States and Sasha Popov of Bulgaria. Just as the eyes of attendees were ready to glaze over, as an antidote to the musty torpor of offi-cial logorrhea, there came a whole evening's worth of beautiful Tchaikovsky. The USSR State Symphony Orchestra, under the direction of Konstantin Ivanov, played a program that included the composer's sumptuous Fifth Symphony and the *Capriccio Italien,* with its imperious fanfares evoking stately grandeur. Also on the bill were the First Piano Concerto, featuring Emil Gilels as soloist, Joan's aria from *The Maid of Orleans*, and Prince Gremin's aria from *Eugene Onegin*.

A week earlier, when the program was first announced, there had been no mention of the piano concerto; instead, cellist Sviatoslav Knushevitsky was scheduled to play Tchaikovsky's *Variations on a Rococo Theme*. Whatever the reason, the change was certainly for the better. Presenting the renowned chairman of the piano jury in the signature work of the competition conveyed a double message to those assembled. First, it offered an official welcome to Moscow from an envoy of the highest musical echelon to all who had made the journey. But it was a challenge to them as well: "You call yourself a virtuoso," Gilels seemed to be saying to the arriving pianists. "Let's see how you measure up to *this*." In the audience, spirits were buoyed; and hearts sank.

"The conservatory's Great Hall is a beautiful place with perfect acoustics," says Sequeira Costa, who had a ringside view as a jury member. "Our seats were reserved, and it was an unbelievable sight, packed with people. I still remember the way Gilels performed—truly great music making. The orchestra players seemed to know the music from memory, without even looking at their parts." Then, once the ceremonial requirements were fulfilled, the trials began—for the violinists. The pianists would not take to the stage until April 4.

Costa's inclusion as a member of the jury seemed curious; it was out of keeping with the luminous reputations enjoyed by most of his colleagues. The pianist himself recognized that his invitation was largely a matter of politics. He had first met Emil Gilels in 1956 or 1957 when the Russian gave concerts in Paris. "He saw me in two ways: as a young, accomplished pianist, and as a representative of Angola, where I had been born," he said. At the time, the Soviets had their eyes on that Portuguese settlement, where civil unrest had sown the seeds of a colonial war. In 1956 the National Front for the Liberation of Angola had emerged from the conflict, and the Kremlin felt it had a stake in the outcome. There was an additional reason: Costa had founded the Vianna da Motta International Piano Competition in Lisbon, named after his teacher. At its launch in 1957, two judges for the 1958 competition, Lev Oborin and Armand de Gontaut-Biron, were on the jury, and the top three prizes went to two Soviets and a Pole. Naum Shtarkman, now a contestant at the Tchaikovsky, was the winner. In a way, they were all part of the same big musical family.

The jury largely represented serious star power, which made it fertile ground for the emergence of personal rivalries and a whir of rumors. A rhyme in Russian that circulated about jury member Pavel Serebryakov, director of the Leningrad Conservatory, for example, pegged him as the "best pianist in the KGB"—aligning him with the Kremlin's most conservative forces. His voting at the Tchaikovsky event would show no evidence of this. Yet he could truly be a difficult customer. Pianist Dmitry Paperno recalled seeing Serebryakov on the jury of the first Enescu Competition in Bucharest in September 1958, where he once again sat in judgment of pianist Jerome Lowenthal. As Lowenthal performed, recalled Paperno, "Serebryakov's behavior in the jury was almost obscene: he nudged his colleagues at the table, pointing at the young American." It wasn't necessarily a sign of anti-American bias, however.

Gossip also rose up about Richter, Gilels, and even Neuhaus, musicians who ordinarily held a special status in the music community. Most competition officials, like Costa, were content simply to take on the task at hand and mind their own business. However, others, among them Shostakovich, who remained a significant presence despite his nonvoting status, were uneasily caught up in the political winds as the proceedings progressed.

Shostakovich was the saddest case of all. In many ways he seemed a broken man. "Awkward, tetchy, nervous, [and] fearful," is how Richter saw him, noting "the suspicious, nearsighted look behind thick glasses; the narrow, tight, rarely smiling mouth, strained at the edges; the tormented boyish features; the haunted expression; the pallid face." Vying with Sergei Prokofiev (who died in 1953) for the title of greatest living Soviet composer, Shostakovich spent years caught like an orb in a cultural pinball machine, with official pronouncements routinely flinging him from the most exalted heights to the depths of crushing disgrace. The two most famous composers handled the political pressures very differently. "Prokofiev was violent," claimed Richter. "Shostakovich was always mumbling 'Sorry.'"

Igor Stravinsky's assistant, Robert Craft, completed Richter's sketch of a man besieged, after meeting Shostakovich in 1962: "He chews not merely his nails but his fingers, twitches his pouty mouth and chin, chain smokes, wiggles his nose in constant adjustment of his spectacles, looks querulous one moment and ready to cry the next. . . . There is no betrayal of the thoughts behind those frightened, very intelligent eyes."

Shostakovich's demeanor was no surprise, after the many assaults and excruciating upheavals in his career. The most notorious example was his opera *Lady Macbeth of the Mtsensk District*. It premiered in 1934 with a flood of favorable reviews even though the work reflected everything the defenders of "socialist realism" detested, with a narrative built around corruption, violence, and sex and with music that was often raw, sensuous, and immodest. As late as January 20, 1936, the opera was still being described in *Izvestia* as "the most brilliant Soviet production in music." But eight days later, undoubtedly at the behest of Stalin, *Pravda* reversed the positive judgment with an attack on the work and its composer entitled "Muddle Instead of Music."

"The music quacks, grunts, growls and suffocates itself in order to paint the love scenes as realistically as possible," claimed the review, with some accuracy. Sadly, nearly all of Shostakovich's fellow musicians immediately turned against him, including Dmitri Kabalevsky, who sat on the Tchaikovsky jury in 1958. It was par for the course. "Why do Soviet doctors remove tonsils through the anus?" went a popular riddle. "Because nobody dares open his mouth." And so the schizophrenia began. Ilya Ehrenburg reported in his memoirs that after Shostakovich was dethroned, "no one in my circle felt secure the next day; many had a small, packed trunk ready."

In 1948 the Party Central Committee branded Shostakovich, Prokofiev, Khachaturian, and others as "formalists" and "cosmopolitans," and banned many of their works. Shostakovich, in an attempt to placate his critics, produced compositions like *The Sun Shines Over the Motherland*—efforts that earned him occasional reprieves. But he was robbed of all dignity, and in the face of brute force, he always caved. In 1949 Shostakovich found himself in a particularly agonizing situation: His tormentors demanded that he represent them at the Cultural and Scientific Conference for World Peace, held in the Waldorf Astoria Hotel in New York. The appearance was an opportunity for the American opposition to score big points. A counterassault was spearheaded by Nicolas Nabokov, a White Russian émigré who had defected to the United States in 1933. Nabokov, who worked for the CIA, publicly confronted Shostakovich for supporting the official Soviet portrayal of composers like Hindemith, Schoenberg, and Stravinsky as "decadent bourgeois formalists" and "lackeys of imperialist capitalism." With his minders looking on, Shostakovich had to reiterate that stance. Shostakovich himself later explained in his memoirs, as purportedly dictated to Solomon Volkov: "People sometimes say it must have been an interesting trip; look at the way I'm smiling in the photographs. That was the smile of a condemned man. I felt like a dead man."

Perhaps Shostakovich would have been happier pursuing his original intentions of becoming a pianist. His experience as an entrant in the First International Chopin Competition in Warsaw in 1927, though, revealed a modernist approach out of step with the mainstream: "He never allowed himself the slightest hint of 'Chopinesque' sentiments," said Soviet pianist Nathan Perelman. "It was an 'antisentimental' approach to playing which showed incredible clarity of thought." Shostakovich won no prize, and found the outcome upsetting. But his playing, like his compositions, was too stern and individualistic to win favor.

At the time of the first Tchaikovsky Competition, however, Soviet officials realized that the world-famous Shostakovich was the perfect standard bearer for the event—in the words of soprano Galina Vishnevskaya, he was a figure who "young foreigners [became] delirious with joy to see . . . in the flesh and to have the honor of shaking hands with . . ." For the sake of appearances, it became important that the composer be brought back into the fold. And so one morning, Vishnevskaya recalled, the newspaper carried a government decree entitled "On Correcting Mistakes Made in Evaluating the Work of Leading Soviet Composers."

"If it had not been for the Tchaikovsky Competition, I am convinced that the decree would never have been issued," she declared. As soon as Shostakovich got wind of it, he called the singer and her husband, Mstislav Rostropovich. "We rushed to his place on Kutuzovsky Prospekt," she wrote.

He was incredibly overwrought and ran about the apartment. We had scarcely managed to take off our coats as he ushered us into the dining room.

" 'You read it?' we asked.

" 'I read it. Oh yes, I read it . . .'

"He poured vodka into the tumblers, and all but shouted, 'Well, Slava and Galya, let's drink to the great historical decree "On Abrogating the Great Historical Decree." '

"We spent the whole evening trying to talk only about other subjects, but he would come back to it suddenly: 'A historical, don't you know, decree on abrogating the historical decree . . . It's really so simple, so very *simple* . . .' "

Sviatoslav Richter was as far temperamentally from Shostakovich as anyone could possibly be. The broad-shouldered, gloomy, impenetrable Richter was autonomous and fierce, a warrior for art who cared little about anything else—least of all the social niceties. He seemed to embody a line from Pushkin's "Elegia": "I want to live to think and to suffer." A Parisian critic once described his stage presence "as if he'd been sentenced for a crime." When French pianist Philippe Cassard turned pages for him during a performance, Richter announced, "If you move at all, I will kill you."

Richter's occasional run-ins with Soviet authorities merely strengthened his resolve. During the war, he'd been accused of pessimism for playing Schubert's "Wanderer" Fantasy. " 'When you play this work,' I'd been told, 'there's nothing left but to throw yourself in the Moskva [River],' " he said. At the time of the Tchaikovsky Competition, Kabalevsky added another charge. He accused the pianist of "individualism."

Naturally, Richter was unmoved by such criticism, especially from a mediocre talent like Kabalevsky. "Neuhaus summed him up rather well when he called [Kabalevsky] the poor man's Prokofiev or Shostakovich," he said. "I knew him, but it would never have occurred to me to play his threadbare music." Similarly, no amount of editorial pressure could ever bully Richter into submission. "I never read the papers," he told filmmaker Bruno Monsaingeon. "In my view, they only serve to dirty the fingers."

Somehow, he remained supported despite all the provocations. At least part of the reason for Richter's unique, protected status in later years was the fact that he was in demand all over the world. Of course, even those open arms didn't temper Richter's growl. Invited to the United States in 1960 as part of the growing cultural exchange program, he almost missed his connection, and then remarked, "No such luck!" The visit wasn't entirely terrible; he found American orchestras to be of the first rank. But he complained that the rest of the culture was "cheap."

He had been essentially self-taught before showing up on Neuhaus's doorstep at the Moscow Conservatory. But as soon as the venerable teacher heard him, he declared the pianist a genius. "When Richter began to play Schumann after playing Haydn," wrote Neuhaus, "everything changed—it was a different piano, a different tone, a different rhythm, a different character or expression, and the change was so easy to understand: that was Haydn, and this was Schumann . . . His singular ability to grasp the whole and at the same time miss none of the smallest details of a composition suggests a comparison with an eagle who, from his great height, can see as far as the horizon and yet single out the tiniest detail of the landscape."

Nevertheless, Richter was twice expelled from the Moscow Conservatory in his first year. "I was admitted without any examination or competition, on the one condition that I would attend the mandatory courses," he revealed. "These courses, however, had nothing to do with music but were a half-baked political and philosophical shambles that I could not bring myself to attend." The late, eminent Moscow piano teacher Vera Gornostaeva told a similar story about her school experience, though her rebellion was subtler. Her relatives were "people of the church," she related. She grew up in a religious family, with lots of icons at home. And she read forbidden literature, like Orwell and Solzhenitsyn. The people at the top knew about these things, she said, but when she entered school she was given a Stalin Scholarship, because she was first in the entrance exams. "To keep the scholarship I had to pass all my exams in every subject with distinction," she explained. "And I did. But then I did a risky thing. When I finished my test on the history of the Communist Party, I went with my friend to the toilet and burned the book that I had been studying from. My friend said, 'What are you doing? What if someone comes in?'" Luckily, no one did.

Richter, on the other hand, made a public display of his disrespect. Despite the political operatives who pressured and punished him, his relationship with his teacher remained steadfast. Neuhaus once wrote that "when it comes to talents like Richter, it really does not matter with whom they study." Richter had a different take on their relationship. It was through Neuhaus, he explained, that he found "a singing tone, the tone I'd always dreamed of."

Naturally, Richter was drawn to the sumptuous sound of Van Cliburn, so much so that he was willing to create a serious ruckus when he felt that the deck was being stacked against the American. As the competition progressed, his fireworks in the jury room would be every bit the equal of the ones onstage. The jury was anything but one big happy family, and each member was unhappy in his own way.

CHAPTER 7

Some Wins, Some Losses

THE CROWDS WERE UNRELENTING. Vladimir Zakharov, director of the conservatory's Great Hall, remembers many who were rushing the portico as "old Arbat ladies"—cultured women of the intelligentsia who had consolidated into a social group before the war, some "even before the October Revolution." After living in the old Arbat Street neighborhood for decades, they were relocated to accommodate the "new Arbat"—a reconstructed area filled with big office buildings and prestigious stores—making it more difficult for them to attend concerts. Even so, the hall remained their special destination, as a venue that hosted only serious classical music. "Even folk-instrument orchestras supported by the Communist regime would not be invited," explained Zakharov. Artists loved it. "[Composer-conductor] Igor Markevitch once said that in this hall, you had 'an impression of playing inside a Stradivari violin.'"

Once Van arrived on the scene, getting a ticket for one of the 1,700-odd seats became increasingly difficult even for the Arbat regulars, who implored Zakharov for permission to bring "Van Klee-burn" a present. "What do you think they brought? A basket of strawberries! These were people who lived modestly on a very limited pension. Art was as vital for them as bread." He decided to make it easier for them to get inside by assigning two or three people to each ticket; once past the doors, they simply looked for free places to sit or crammed onto steps. "For most others, getting into the Great Hall was nearly impossible," recounted Zakharov, "though some very brave students managed to enter through the roof!"

Young people who attended classes there were used to getting in by dodging the ushers, "or, as the Russians say, *'biler-*ing'— running like a hare," reported Dmitry Paperno. That wasn't possible now: the potential audience had turned into a mob. Victor Bunin, later a professor at the conservatory, was one of those enterprising students who managed to circumvent the throng by using alternate entrances known only to insiders. "But," he says, "it meant arriving six hours early. We snuck in and brought along playing cards to stay occupied."

Inside, a lone piano sat on the stage in front of the glistening pipes of the conservatory's organ. A huge portrait of Tchaikovsky hung in the background, his eyes overlooking the scene with a gaze that seemed "benign" to composer Sir Arthur Bliss, a member of the jury. Nevertheless, Sir Arthur explained, the situation was certainly "an ordeal for these young players." As they walked to take their place at the piano, the hall was ablaze with television lights. Directly facing them were "the seventeen members of the jury . . . Behind the jury [sat] the public, rows and rows of them."

It was an ordeal for the judges as well. With so many competitors, it quickly turned into a long slog. "The organizers had accepted everybody—top, medium, and poor," remembers Sequeira Costa. The opening round seemed to go on forever, as each contestant ran through his or her pieces.

At any competition, the intense scrutiny required for judging takes its toll. The process is less like a beauty contest than like a round of speed dating, where the sensitive antennae of the panelists hone in on the character traits of each candidate. One may be too held back, another too impetuous, while a third may be superficially attractive but lacking in the deeper, engrossing qualities that grow from the hard work of penetrating the music's structural sinews. There is no magical formula for choosing a winner; in the end, the decision is usually distilled down to a basic overriding question: Do I want to hear this performer again? As the hours tick by, there is a danger of it all becoming a blur, the pianists beginning to seem like mechanical figures on an endless carousel.

Controlling the monotony was one of the organizers' tasks. "We had breaks for tea in the jury room," says Costa, "with sandwiches and, always, caviar—red and black. There was no alcohol, but the tea was extremely strong, served in a glass with a silver holder. This would go on until eight-thirty or nine in the evening." The refreshment break was when he first met other jury members, including Richter and Poland's Henryk Sztompka.

There was good reason for Costa to be awed by the members of the panel he was joining, which also included pianists Lev Oborin, Heinrich Neuhaus, and Pavel Serebryakov—formidable talents with strong personalities. Dmitri Kabalevsky, who created the required piece for the competition finalists, held a jury chair; so did several foreign dignitaries, including Romanian conduc-

tor George Georgescu and Brazilian composer Camargo Guarnieri. Costa was inured to feelings of beguilement in the presence
of these artists because of his long association with Vianna da
Motta, already an old master when Costa began lessons with him
as a youngster.

For the contestants, however, it was easy to be overwhelmed.
American Norman Shetler arrived with low expectations to begin
with, though he experienced a moment of panic when his lot for
the order of performances turned out to be slot number one. He
began at ten a.m. on the opening day—"scared shitless. Luckily,
Richter didn't arrive until that evening, so he didn't hear me."

The pianist knew he was underprepared. "Are you crazy?"
asked his friend the Austrian pianist Jörg Demus when he
learned that Shetler had entered. "You don't even play the Tchaikovsky concerto." He responded that he was, in fact, learning the
first movement. "Jörg told me, 'You can't win.' I said, 'I'm sure
I won't.'"

Shetler had been studying unhappily in Vienna when he
heard about the contest, and decided to go partly because the
flight from Vienna cost only $120, and partly because there was
one building in the world that he really wanted to see: the Cathedral of St. Basil. "It is music captured in architecture," he states.
Besides, Moscow in 1958 had a special allure: "No one had been
there since the war, and it still had the old mystique of imperial
Russia," he says. With virtually no hope of winning, the competition itself became for him just another travel experience. As
predicted, he didn't advance.

Another early casualty was Ecuador's José Eduardo Alvarado,
who ended up receiving the lowest marks of the competition.
Most of the panel gave him 0, 1, or 4 out of a possible 25 points.
Marchand explained why: "He had taken so many tranquilizers

that he sat staring at the piano and had to be removed." As he sat motionless, a jury member rang a bell and he was escorted out. The next day, Alvarado walked around the hotel muttering, "Too many pills. Too many pills."

They kept coming—pianists from twenty-two different countries—rushing in like waves at high tide. Melita Edith Bán from Hungary did her best with Bach, Mozart, Chopin, and Scriabin, but it wasn't enough. Hungary's Klára Bella, Czechoslovakia's Alex Biel, and France's Blandine Crosti also failed to make the grade. Annie Marchand was eliminated despite delivering a delicate Bach partita and a heartfelt Rachmaninoff étude-tableau. The jury also quickly dispensed with Iceland's Thorunn Johannsdottir. The repertoire was repetitive enough from player to player to dull a listener's senses: for most, Bach was followed by Mozart, then Chopin, with selections by Liszt, Scriabin, or Rachmaninoff filling out the bill, along with Tchaikovsky's difficult Theme and Variations, op. 19, no. 6. On and on they went.

Drawing number 15 in the playing order, Van had to appear on stage at nine-thirty in the morning—closer to his bedtime than to the normal start of his day. But he made it on time, playing Bach, Mozart, Chopin, Scriabin, Rachmaninoff, Liszt, and Tchaikovsky. The program booklet announced Liszt's difficult "La campanella," one of the composer's Paganini Études, as part of his program, but earlier in March Van had written to Shostakovich asking if he could substitute Liszt's Transcendental Étude "Mazeppa" instead—an even more challenging work, inspired by Victor Hugo's poem in which a page named Mazeppa is strapped onto a wildly galloping horse. Shostakovich consented to the change. The audience vociferously applauded his efforts, especially the Mozart, for which the pianist rose and bowed three times before the clamor died down.

Not everyone on the jury was bowled over. Costa, for one, was unhappy—especially with the Mozart. "Being guided by teachers like Vianna da Motta and Edwin Fischer, both players of the Germanic school, I couldn't swallow a romantic performance of a great classical sonata," he said. In the view of Costa—who might be regarded by Van as one of "those Schnabel people"—the American's Mozart went stylistically too far afield. Like Serkin at the Leventritt, Costa nevertheless found the pianist's Tchaikovsky and Rachmaninoff "out of this world." Yet Costa just couldn't give the American a very high mark. Emil Gilels, who tried to police the voting process, afterward confronted him about his grading.

Heinrich Neuhaus also had reservations. "I don't particularly like his Chopin," he said later. "But I like him." Everyone did. One reason Van's pianism did not always comport with Neuhaus's ideals was that the Moscow professor disdained pianists with an excessive admiration of a beautiful sound. "The concept of beauty in tone," he wrote in his book on playing the piano, "is not sensuously static but dialectic; the best tone, and consequently the most beautiful, is the one that renders a particular meaning in the best possible manner." For Van, beautiful tone was everything—the beginning and end of pianistic performance—and he used it unsparingly to imbue everything he played with a soft musical glow.

Neuhaus was also wary of performances filled with too many personal liberties—pushing and pulling the music to suit the emotions of the moment. "Someone once said to me of an extremely egocentric performer," he said, " 'He puts so much of himself into the music.' 'Quite right,' I said, 'and takes so much of what the composer put in out of it.' " Though Van had learned through Lhévinne to moderate his interpretive flourishes, his overriding personality—emotionally exuberant, and unshakably sentimental—was still present in every bar.

The general public had no such hesitations. Other pianists in the contest, though highly accomplished, too often resembled the French waiter who served Jean-Paul Sartre at Les Deux Magots. The man, said Sartre, had "an exaggerated manner, a little too precise, a little too fast." He thus resembled a robot, carrying "his tray with the temerity of a tightrope walker." Van's approach was more natural, ruminative and free of brashness. The crowds went wholeheartedly for his luxurious sound, and for the gentle affection with which he induced every score to sing. They swooned at the crooner in him. "That was the great paradox of the competition," Jerome Lowenthal recalled. "The Russians had convinced themselves that they knew the heart of this repertoire. But the heart had just gone out of it, and it had become really quite routine. When they heard Van, they suddenly remembered how beautiful this music was." Some said they discerned in his playing a "Russian soul." That stirred a debate among aficionados.

In truth, there wasn't anything particularly Russian about it, according to pianist Dmitri Bashkirov. "It wasn't a Russian soul, or French, English, or American. It was the soul of Van Cliburn. God gave him that kind of soul and it had a rare romanticism and charisma," he said.

In any case, Russian musical style was not a singular thing: it reflected a wide range of influences, including the electrifying Hungarian Franz Liszt and the dreamy Irishman John Field, inventor of the nocturne—wistful music evocative of the night. Liszt was the model for the tempestuous romantic virtuoso, the kind of performer who was, as James Huneker said of Anton Rubinstein, "torrid as midday in the tropics." (When he performed in the United States, Rubinstein was described by one critic as like a cyclone: "The house trembled, the lights danced, the walls [shook], the sky split, the ground rocked.") Without Rubinstein's precedent, there would have been no possibility of Cliburn mania. But Field was also important to the tradition, as the teacher of Mikhail Glinka, the founder of Russian classical music. Field, Glinka said, "did not seem to strike the keys; instead, his fingers fell on them like large drops of rain scattered like pearls on velvet." The description brings to mind Van's playing.

Nevertheless, the term "Russian" pianism is most often used to describe Anton's potent legacy, as descended through his student Felix Blumenfeld, which emphasized not a patina of beauty—as in Van's sound—but subtle changes for each tone, eliciting a narrative roiling with emotion. Neuhaus was strongly influenced by Blumenfeld. So was the incendiary Vladimir Horowitz. Their playing teemed with sexual tension, soaring ecstasy, exuberance, bitterness, and the laughter of the gods. Van was never a part of that tradition.

In the wake of Van's spectacular showing, though, some Russians defended national pride by pointing to his Juilliard mentor, Rosina Lhévinne, as a product of the Moscow Conservatory. (So, of course, were some of the other Moscow contestants who fared less well.) They failed to notice that the Lhévinne approach was less about instilling a strong national character than about reaching a stylistic middle ground of refined musicianship. American critic B. H. Haggin, realizing this, chastised his colleague Winthrop Sargeant for asserting that Cliburn's "tasteful and assured use of *rubato*"—the technique of stretching and contracting time—was "in the style of the distinguished virtuosos of the past." Nonsense, wrote Haggin. "What distinguished Cliburn from those virtuosos is precisely his tasteful use of the *rubato* which they used tastelessly." Van stood out mostly for his sense of balance.

In an introspective moment, Van described Lhévinne's teaching as "geared to following my personality. My mother and she were both interested in good taste," he said—that is, in playing that reined in extremes of emotional expression. "Each of us has pain and sorrow," he explained. "We have to be careful not to let that [over]influence us." Van's temperate approach affected many of the Russian musicians at the competition. Something new started to emerge in their playing after they heard him, Dmitry Paperno explained, especially as a result of his "drawling," more leisurely, tempos.

But ask any Russian about what made Van's playing stand out and there would be a singular response: a hand placed palm-down over the heart. This was a quality that transcended geographical boundaries. In fact, the American said that he found Muscovites to be very much like Texans. What they had in common, he suggested, were heart and pluck. That explains why Vlassenko called him "the most Russian of us all."

In the hall, no one was splitting hairs over style. When Van played, they were gripped by what they heard. In all, seventeen pianists were eliminated at the end of the first round, and Liu and Van were now tied for the highest score. It was still anyone's game.

Many competitors studiously avoided listening to their rivals' performances, but a spirit of shared adventure pervaded the group, especially in chance meetings that occurred when pianists bumped into one another at practice sessions. Van spotted Liu and followed him into his rehearsal room, asking if he could listen. The Chinese pianist played Chopin's A-flat Polonaise, op. 53. "Van applauded," he reported, "so I asked him to perform. He played Liszt's 'Liebestraum.' I also applauded."

Officials did their best to cultivate that sense of camaraderie, arranging activities for the pianists in their off time, like visits to landmarks such as Tchaikovsky's home. "We were taken to the Kremlin," says Lowenthal, "supposedly to see the great cathedrals. So for an hour or two we stood outside while they took pictures of us. I said, 'When are we going to see the cathedrals?' 'Oh,' they replied, 'what do you want to see those old churches for?'" He didn't react well to what he regarded as insensitive bullying. "I was a bad boy," he says with a mischievous smile. He left to explore on his own. "They went crazy," he reports. "It was an hour before they found me. It could have been a big scandal."

At Tchaikovsky's home in Klin, where the composer had once taken quiet garden walks and proofread his scores, a celebration of his music was under way. Lowenthal, invited to play on Tchaikovsky's piano, began with some Chopin. But he was not yet ready to be the obedient guest. "Really intending to be subversive, I started to play the Webern Variations, which of course were verboten," he remembered. "And the woman who was running things said, 'Tchaikovsky, please, Tchaikovsky!'" (Years later, Lowenthal would return as a member of the Tchaikovsky jury and was once again invited to play the composer's instrument. By virtue of his having been in the 1958 competition, he was now considered a "historical personage.") At around this time, conductor Leopold Stokowski planted an oak tree at Klin as a "gift of love" on behalf of the musicians of the world. It became an ongoing tradition to mark subsequent stagings of the competition.

Back in Moscow, more tributes to Tchaikovsky were taking place, including an exhibition about his life and works in the foyer of the Great Hall, organized by the Glinka Central State Museum of Musical Culture. Around town, there were performances of Tchaikovsky ballets; touring musicians from Tbilisi presented his opera *The Maid of Orleans*; and concerts of his music were staged by a variety of orchestras and brass bands, featuring such stellar piano soloists as Richter, Ashkenazy, and Malinin (who had declined to enter the competition because of his troublesome skin condition).

As the second round was set to begin, Roger Boutry, who had fallen ill on his arrival and remained confined to his room for the opening activities, joined up with other previous prizewinners of international competitions who had been allowed to skip the first round. That contingent included Americans Lowenthal and Pollack, Frenchwoman Crochet, Soviets Vlassenko, Shtarkman, Skavronsky, and Inna Malinina, and Japanese Toyoaki Matsuura. Van had not been given that privilege, because the Soviets did not recognize the Leventritt as an international competition, despite its prestige in America. Indeed, both before and after the competition they failed to recognize any of Van's past achievements.

Soviet Eduard Miansarov and Parisian Annie Petit advanced from round one, but she soon suffered a setback. "I was just a kid," she said of her time in Moscow, "very interested in eating caviar." Her main ambition was to find a way eventually to get to the United States. Musically, she was doomed from the start— her dislike of the required movement of the Tchaikovsky Sonata was so intense that she found it impossible to memorize. "So when the time came to perform it," she remembered, "I made a fool of myself, playing the big chords with just one finger—in front of the royalty of the piano world."

Others took their turns and were duly dispatched, including the rebellious Lowenthal, who had decided to offer what he called an "un–socialist realist" program. It included Beethoven's difficult "Hammerklavier" Sonata, but also the *Out of Doors* suite by Bartók—music that was abrasive and percussive enough to make a conservative juror's teeth chatter. Writing back home to his colleague Lhévinne, Mark Schubart described Lowenthal's performance as "stunning." The pianist, however, had clearly chosen the wrong repertoire.

"They didn't know the Bartók at all," Lowenthal remembered. "I mean, this was 1958 and the Bartók had been written in 1926. But for the Soviet Union it hadn't been written yet." He was treated with respect by Richter and Neuhaus, but after receiving scores in the mid-to-high teens, there was no way he could move on to the third round.

Lowenthal nevertheless lingered in Moscow for a while, performing on the radio, at the Scriabin Museum, and at a school, where, he says, "I got a penciled note: 'Our students, our teachers, we all beg you, please play pieces of Bartók.' There was such emotion in that. I played [them] and they loaded me up with oranges—filling my coat with them—because they were so scarce in Russia."

Some musical variety was introduced into the proceedings when the second-round pianists presented little-known compositions from their native lands. Japan's Matsuura played a sonata by Yoshinao Nakada; Bulgaria's Milena Mollova a piece by Pancho Vladigerov; Liu Shikun a suite by a Chinese compatriot; France's Roger Boutry highlighted an original composition of his own. Now the field was narrowing rapidly.

Evelyne Crochet, who failed to make it past the second round, was among a handful given "honorary diplomas" for receiving a score of 15 or higher. But she soon ran into difficulties of a new sort. As an award recipient, she received some money. It marked the beginning of her troubles. There was a man at the competition named Tolstoy, an American who spoke fluent Russian and seemed to know a lot about music. "He wanted to give me dollars for my rubles," she recounts. "I agreed. Suddenly I was called into the ministry to speak with [Ekaterina] Furtseva," a scary and powerful member of the Central Committee.

Maya Plisetskaya described her own encounter with Furtseva: "a pretty, stately woman . . . middle-aged, with a weary, crooked smile, neatly coifed, with a tight blond knot at her nape, in a severe gray suit . . . 'Did you say that people join the Party to further their careers and not out of conviction?' she asked. 'I don't remember,'" replied Plisetskaya. "'But if that's what it says in [Ivan] Serov's files . . .' Furtseva shuddered. My mention of the omnipotent name [of the head of the KGB] was not pleasant. She quickly looked around her office. Could it be bugged, too?"

Furtseva asked Crochet why she was so close with Tolstoy, noting that the two had taken the same train to Leningrad. Crochet didn't want to make waves, since she was hoping to return to Moscow to study with Richter. Now, though, she was under suspicion. Worse, Tolstoy never paid her for the rubles. "When I got back to France, I called him and he was extremely rude," she says. "I threatened to call the embassy. He came to my house and threw a few dollars in my face. He didn't give me half of what he owed."

Soviet critic Tamara Grum-Grzhimailo had assessed the performances throughout. In the first round, she found in Shtarkman's playing "that enchantingly poetic imagery and tonal fantasy that are accessible only to the mature artist." She named Liu as a serious rival for first prize. She also noted Vlassenko's "bright, monumental, and expressive execution of Liszt's B Minor Sonata."

That was after the first round, before the audience—"holding its breath," she wrote—began to follow the next phase. There, she found Matsuura "impetuous, enchanting, at times paradoxical," and Mollova "heartfelt and noble." Pollack, she said, was "stunning with his phenomenal technique and rhythmic elasticity." Then, at last, she heard "our beloved Van, our inspired minstrel, all-powerful pianist of spontaneous force, creator of heavenly beautiful sound paintings, the 'Raphael of the piano.'" What he offered, she suggested, was almost an embarrassment of riches.

Pollack had indeed been impressive with Prokofiev's Seventh Sonata, a robust work guaranteed to rev up an audience with a final movement in agitated "perpetual motion." The American let loose with savage velocity, like a rocket with the afterburners flipped on. He was determined that nothing would stand in his way. The rest of his program was similarly brilliant, including Kabalevsky's Third Sonata; a sonata by Nikolai Myaskovsky, who had taught at the Moscow Conservatory and was known as "the father of the Soviet symphony"; a work by the lyrical romanticist Nikolai Medtner; and the required Tchaikovsky Sonata movement. He ended with the Barber Sonata, yet another tour de force. The performance was blazing, with not a speck of sentimentality.

Things had gone exceptionally well for him. Pollack's wife, Noemi, recalled that her husband started practicing every day at noon, ate lunch at three-thirty, practiced again until eleven, and then returned to the hotel for dinner. The hotel kept the dining room open for competitors until twelve-thirty a.m., and the conservatory remained open twenty-four hours a day for the contestants. He had not a minute to waste.

The stakes had risen, and every subtle inflection by a player was noted by the jury. Lev Vlassenko was solid as well as fiery, and he shaped Chopin with exquisite dynamics. Yet, like most of the competitors, he couldn't match the sense of simple inevitability in Van's playing. Naum Shtarkman's approach was often straightforward but rhythmically stiff; Eduard Miansarov's Beethoven was polite rather than stormy. On the other hand, Miansarov's performance of Prokofiev's acidic *Sarcasms* made the piano grunt and sneer; when this piece is properly performed, listeners can almost taste the bile on their tongues. Roger Boutry was typically French: fleet, insouciant, and energetic—and in comparison with some of the others, underwhelming. Liu was simply brilliant—he seemed, said Costa, to have been preparing twenty-five hours a day.

Van played Taneyev's Prelude and Fugue in G-sharp Minor and the Tchaikovsky Sonata movement, along with Prokofiev's bitingly acerbic Sixth Sonata (the first of the composer's three "War Sonatas"). To those he added Beethoven's tempestuous "Appassionata" Sonata. It was gravid with emotion, yet this was Beethoven not as a warrior battling his darkest demons but as a lovelorn poet, the strident German undercurrent softened with traces of Chopin's Polish accent. He unfurled everything else with impeccable style: Chopin's mysterious Fantasy in F Minor crept in on little cat feet, while Brahms's Variations and Fugue on a Theme of Handel was rigorous and majestic. Liszt's Hungarian Rhapsody no. 12—the showpiece that had clinched the Leventritt for him—again stunned his listeners. He capped it all off with the tricky fugue from Barber's Sonata.

Van's program was designed to show range. Beethoven, Chopin, and Brahms were the meat and potatoes of the romantic repertoire. The Prokofiev Sixth, on the other hand, was a modernist piece that reflected political tensions and fears growing in Russia as the winds of war were bearing down in 1940. Richter described it as a work in which "with wild audacity the composer broke with the ideals of Romanticism and introduced into his music the terrifying pulse of twentieth-century music." Van played it all marvelously, though in the view of some his American colleague Pollack was hot on his heels in the race for the prize.

"Danny would have thrilled you," wrote Schubart to Lhévinne. Noting the pianist's progress, he hazarded the view that the improvement was actually in spite of his Fulbright studies rather than because of them. As for Van, wrote Schubart, he was turning out to be the sensation everyone at Juilliard had expected. "I only hope Van keeps his head," he warned. "I'm worried about this aspect." The piano star's emotional solidity was, he implied, less than reliable.

During the proceedings, Norman Shetler had diligently checked out the performances of his colleagues and, says, Lowenthal, "he was coming to me every day with hysterical reports that made me nervous. I was practicing and he had nothing to do but gossip. He told me that Danny Pollack's Prokofiev Seventh Sonata had been amazing, but that Van's Tchaikovsky had arches and tunnels and a very beautiful evocation," says Lowenthal, who really didn't want to hear anything about it.

With approbation building around Van, there was bound to be pushback. When Paperno returned to Moscow after a trip to the Ukraine, he got a full report from musician friends on what had transpired. They said of Van that "there was something in his Mozart sonata and the etudes of Chopin, Liszt, and Rachmaninoff that compensated for his relatively unfortunate Tchaikovsky Sonata." That Tchaikovsky piece is an obstacle course for the fingers, with wild leaps and pounding chords that charge up and down the keyboard like cannon fire. Bringing out its lyrical core presents a real challenge, and perhaps Van was not quite up to it.

Paperno found his teacher, Alexander Goldenweiser, in the crowd strolling up and down the foyer on the main floor of the Great Hall. He asked the older pianist to rank the competitors. " 'Pollack first, Cliburn second,' he replied."

As the pressure intensified, more rumors sprouted about the boy wonder from Texas. Annie Marchand contended that although Van was a strong player, he was "less than stellar" in some of the repertoire. For that reason, she found it suspicious that newspapermen were already following him around. Was the outcome already decided? "I won a silver medal in Geneva and there were no correspondents there," she commented, adding that in her opinion, Vlassenko was actually the best all-around musician.

She wasn't the only wary one. Rumors of a conspiracy to rig the competition were brewing on all sides of the Cliburn/Vlassenko/Pollack divide. Marchand's roommate, Thorunn Johannsdottir, suggested that officials had prevented her future husband, Ashkenazy, from participating in order to make way for an American. That was clearly untrue; Ashkenazy reiterated more than once that he simply had no desire to be a contestant. (At one point during the competition Cliburn happened upon a practice room from which he heard extraordinary playing; he knocked on the door and found Ashkenazy at the piano. "Boy, am I glad you are not competing!" said Van.)

Emotions often run high at music contests, and accusations of corruption are simply a fact of life. At Tchaikovsky Competitions following this first venture, Gilels would be pelted with tomatoes and find his car tires slashed. According to Ivan Davis, such riotous behavior was not uncommon at music contests around the world. When Davis entered the first Vianna da Motta Competition in Lisbon in 1957, he was a popular favorite, but received only fifth place. "The audience," he says, "began to throw things at the jury."

At the first Tchaikovsky Competition, some believed that the fix was in for Van. On the other hand, plenty of others feared that the odds were actually being stacked against him. One of these was Richter. Typically, he decided to foment a ruckus over it.

The violin phase of the competition had come off smoothly, with Valery Klimov, a student of David Oistrakh's, crowned winner. American Joyce Flissler placed seventh. She was disappointed, but one of the judges, British violinist Philip Newman, announced, "I have never known a jury to be so united and fair." The panel assembled to decide the piano phase was another story: It became a study in turmoil, especially as the hulking, fiercely independent Richter expressed himself.

He hadn't bothered to show up for the first round, but as the jury set about to cast its second-round votes he made everyone keenly aware of his presence. Standing apart from the seated group and leaning up against a piano, he surveyed the list of contestants and—according to his own account, as well as an official report by the Central Committee of the Communist Party—he placed a zero next to nearly every name on his sheet. Only a few received a respectable showing: the top grade of twenty-five went to Van, twenty-four to Vlassenko, and twenty-three to Liu.

"It was the first international competition to be held in Moscow, and it was vital that it should be won by a Soviet pianist," Richter told Bruno Monsaingeon. "But during the preliminary rounds it was Van Cliburn who played best. He was miles better than any of the others. He was talented, [and] he played with sincerity, even if he swamped Prokofiev's Sixth Sonata with too much pedal." Richter's own rendition of the Prokofiev Sixth Sonata was considered definitive.

"By giving a zero mark to all but three of the other candidates (one of these three, Lev Vlassenko, had played the Liszt Sonata superbly, rather in the manner of Gilels)," Richter claimed, and giving Van the highest possible mark, he had sufficiently skewed the results to put the American on top. "The public had in any case fallen madly in love with Van Cliburn."

Despite Richter's assertion, that is not how the second round scorecard reads. The official paperwork shows Richter's tabulations containing a large smattering of low and medium scores—several threes and four fifteens—in addition to the three higher marks. Yet, even if his account were true, the size of the jury would have made Richter's impact fairly insignificant. As a lone voter he could neither significantly elevate Cliburn nor lower the status of others. Indeed, calculating the total scores at the end of the second round with and without Richter's numbers, the result turns out the same. (In the Appendix I have corrected minor mathematical mistakes in the tabulations for Boutry and Petit.) In the actual vote, Vlassenko was ranked first, Liu was second, and Shtarkman was tied with Cliburn for third. When Richter's vote is not counted and the scores are adjusted to reflect one less judge, Vlassenko is first, Liu is second, Shtarkman is third, and Cliburn is fourth. All of the eventual top prizewinners would have gone on to the final round in any case.

Nevertheless, Soviet officials were outraged. The Central Committee issued a memo castigating the "poor behavior of one of the members of the jury, S. Richter, who placed himself opposite all other members of the jury in the piano competition . . . It caused bewilderment and protest from the other members of the jury. S. Richter tried to conduct the 3rd round similarly, although after strong protests from the members of the jury he was forced to apply a normal method of voting."

What could account for the discrepancy between Richter's purported zeros and the written record? Costa provides an answer. Gilels confronted Richter, Costa remembers, arguing that some of the recipients of Richter's zeros were prizewinners of other competitions. "It's really not done, and we can't accept it," he declared. "Why did you do this?

"Richter looked up at the ceiling in silence, then said, 'Well, for me, either you make music or you don't. You can be a first-prize winner of the best competition, but if you don't make music, it's a zero.' But Gilels begged him to make changes. So he thought it over and revised the zeros to threes."

It is impossible to document exactly what actually happened, says Costa, because there was no transparency in the voting process. "We gave our marks to a secretary," he said. "But we never saw how our colleagues voted. We were free to talk, but it made no difference. The 'presidium'—Gilels and a few others—simply told us what the final outcome was, and never revealed what each of us had decided."

The crowd in the hall had already chosen a winner. "At the end of his second round, people were afraid Van might be denied the first prize, so they gave him a standing ovation for fifteen minutes," recounted Victor Bunin. "It was a message to the jury." As it turned out, there was really no need.

After deciding who would move on to the final round, a few details remained for the judges to discuss. They gave honorary diplomas to five pianists with sufficiently high scores (a proposal to further divide these into first and second levels was rejected) and issued certificates to the others who had made it to the second round. Then Soviet juror Boris Lyatoshynsky suggested a substantive change: increasing the number of finalists from eight to nine, in order to allow French pianist Nadia Gedda-Nova into the third round.

Gedda-Nova had made a big impression. Born in France to Russian parents, she attended the Paris Conservatory and graduated with a first prize in piano, then took a position at the Paris Opéra rehearsing singers, and married the great tenor Nicolai Gedda. Soviet publicity materials produced for the Tchaikovsky featured her testimonial, comparing "the bright classes" of the Moscow Conservatory with "the gloomy halls of the Paris Conservatory." Her exuberance for the Soviets was lavish. "In the Moscow building," she claimed, "it is just unforgivable to play badly." Many French musicians, she asserted, could only dream about the opportunities open to graduates of the Moscow Conservatory. This was far from true, but it certainly cheered the competition's organizers.

Yet the decision to bend the rules on her behalf was not really political: her numerical ranking was off by only a fraction from those who had advanced. The jury was unanimous in its agreement with Lyatoshynsky's proposal. "I have listened to many competitions and this, perhaps, was one of the more remarkable," said Sir Arthur Bliss, "and therefore I fully support this proposal and even insist that the French candidate be allowed into the third round." The French judge, Armand de Gontaut-Biron, was touched by the jury's "manifestation of friendly relations and . . . delicate feelings." The matter was settled, and nine pianists were advanced into the last round.

The scoring is a bit confusing, because the cumulative figures received by each pianist were modified in the end by the number of judges contributing to the tally. Not every judge voted each time. Oborin, for example, gave no score in two cases. So, although Gedda-Nova received a higher arithmetical score than Miansarov (a total of 328 for her and only 283 for him), her cumulative number was divided by 17 (the number of judges submitting marks for her), while his was divided by 16. With a final average of 17.35, Gedda-Nova just missed matching Miansarov's average of 17.69. Thus, the impetus for a special vote to allow her in was understandable. Because Liu was feeling ill, he was scheduled to play on the very last day of the event. The rest of the lineup was announced: April 10, Gedda-Nova and Mollova; April 11, Cliburn and Miansarov; April 12, Shtarkman, Vlassenko, and Matsuura; April 13, Pollack and Liu. Each would have to play two large concertos (including one by Tchaikovsky), and the specially commissioned solo piano piece, Kabalevsky's Rondo. Passions were running high.

CHAPTER 8

The Storm Before the Calm

V AN WAS LOSING WEIGHT. Though already razor-thin when he arrived in Moscow, the pounds just kept melting away. "My stomach is my Achilles heel," he told Jerome Lowenthal, who was startled to see the pianist routinely swallow raw eggs. Aside from the caviar he delightedly scooped up, little else seemed to agree with him.

He always had a delicate constitution, and it made him eager to try any treatment for it, no matter how exotic. His suitcase for the Moscow trip had been filled with an assortment of vitamins and elixirs, and while he was there an additional package of remedies arrived for him at the American embassy. It was possibly sent by a favorite snake-oil salesman named Dr. Max Jacobson, a New York health guru otherwise known by the nickname "Dr. Feelgood." Jacobson's patients included, at one time or another,

Anthony Quinn, Ingrid Bergman, and Marilyn Monroe; Truman Capote and Tennessee Williams; Leonard Bernstein, Maria Callas, and Leontyne Price; New York governor Nelson Rockefeller, Senator Claude Pepper of Florida, and JFK.

Singer Eddie Fisher described the effect of Jacobson's formula as like being lit from within. "You feel like Superman. You're flying," is how Capote put it. Inevitably, though, "you crash—it's like falling down a well, like parachuting without a parachute." United States Attorney General Bobby Kennedy, who was also a patient, asked federal drug-enforcement experts to test the doctor's "miracle tissue regeneration" recipe, and they found a blend of amphetamines, vitamins, painkillers, steroids, and human placenta. Those powerful amphetamines were responsible for that sense of soaring—and they posed the most serious dangers.

Jacobson's assistant, Harvey Mann, began receiving his own treatments at the age of fourteen. Once he started working for the doctor, Mann's assignments included self-experimentation with substances like the glands of an electric eel and beef bone marrow. He was charged with the preparation of a hand-cream concoction made of vitamins and "leftovers of whatever was injected into patients that day, including hormones." This remedy was sold to eager customers at "forty dollars a throw . . . We used to call it Max's chicken fat," he said.

Van was introduced into the doctor's circle through a Juilliard friend, Royal Marks. The pianist was quickly welcomed into the fold, and Jacobson "shot up Van and started him coming on a regular basis," remembered Mann. "He charged him little or nothing during those years when Van was a student at Juilliard . . . By the time he made it big with his Russian performance, Max really had him hooked." Like most of Jacobson's patients, the pianist had no inkling of the deleterious effects of the doctor's potions, or of its addictive properties.

Searching for health and inspiration through better chemistry was not unusual when it came to the arts crowd. Jacobson became a celebrity. "Everybody went to him," explained Jimmy Mathis. "Jeaneane and I had another 'Dr. Feelgood,' Dr. Amos Cobert, who was Martha Graham's doctor. You didn't go to Amos every week, but if you practiced too much and you were bored and depressed, you saw him and came out feeling like dynamite. I went once every two months. On the other hand, Jacobson really got people hooked on this stuff. John F. Kennedy was more hooked than Van. We didn't know about drugs, and the harm they could cause." Jacobson's biological bag of tricks helped steady Van's nerves and calm his stomach—for a time.

Van's challenges in Moscow were as much emotional as physical. Outwardly, the pianist was the picture of self-possession. To the young among his admirers, he was the fresh face of an emerging, better world; to the old, a balm for the pain of lost youth and the bitterness of mortality—a bright spot in a dreary world still pulling itself up out of the gray muck of war. But the pressures and unusual atmosphere of the competition helped expose cracks in the pianist's character.

His corniness and high-flown rhetoric, though authentically homegrown, also served as a kind of camouflage—a metaphorical wall meant to keep emotional discomfort at arm's length. It was no more unusual than any number of ways in which public figures protect themselves. Yet, to the extent his perfectly held-together outer image covered deeply rooted frailties, red flags were bound to appear, and the intense scrutiny he received made that even more likely.

Van's lack of sophistication wasn't always a bad thing. "He has the psychology of a fourteen-year-old boy," Richter said. "And thank God," Neuhaus agreed, pointing to the positive aspects of Van's naïveté by framing it as typical of what many regard as a "classic" artistic personality. Van was childlike and playful, often embarrassingly earnest, and subject to moments of intense religiosity. In Neuhaus's view, this linked him with the sensibilities of Goethe, Tolstoy, Schubert, Tchaikovsky, Grieg, and Rachmaninoff. The artlessness of the man, he asserted, was the bedrock of his art.

Still, it created missteps and vulnerabilities. The journalist from *Time* who wrote a cover story on Van at the competition's conclusion reduced the pianist to a cliché, presenting him as an unworldly hillbilly. More gravely, there lurked beneath the glamorous façade character failings that created a diplomatic minefield for American ambassador Llewellyn "Tommy" Thompson.

The ambassador was a seasoned professional, "lean and elegant, a tall man with a benign but aristocratic bearing, soft spoken, given to well-tailored suits obtained from a tailor named Silhavy in Vienna, where Thompson had been posted before Moscow," remembers Max Frankel. Anatoly Dobrynin, the Soviet ambassador to the United States from 1962 to 1986, found him to be "the best American ambassador in Moscow during the entire period of the Cold War." But in some ways Van challenged his skills. During the competition, Thompson's duties came to include reassuring his bosses in Washington—repeatedly—that the pianist was not a threat to American interests.

Among other things, that meant defusing rumors that the American from Texas was having an affair with another male pianist, a possible catastrophe in an environment where homosexuality was a criminal offense. The perception was fueled by his apparent lack of caution, as if he recognized no real distinctions between the freewheeling atmosphere at Juilliard and the heavily monitored halls of the Pekin Hotel.

Years later, President Lyndon Johnson asked FBI director J. Edgar Hoover if there was any reason Van should not play at the White House, and Hoover—a closet cross-dresser—advised him that the pianist was a homosexual. "The President remarked," wrote Hoover in an FBI report, "that most musicians probably are homosexuals and I told him a great many are. I further advised the President that, while he was in Russia, Khrushchev gave Van Cliburn a great deal of publicity but he is a great pianist and I would see no reason why he should not be used for the White House entertainment."

In the Soviet Union, where eyes and ears were everywhere, sexual orientation was a trickier matter. Naum Shtarkman, though managing to finish the Tchaikovsky Competition without incident, would be arrested and jailed in the Ukraine soon after for the crime of homosexuality. Thompson got wind of the gossip about Van, says one pianist who was there, probably because the Russians themselves were becoming concerned. The ambassador searched for an American competitor who might discreetly suggest to Van that he exercise restraint, but it was difficult to find anyone willing to become embroiled in the situation.

Norman Shetler, the man alleged to have been Cliburn's love interest, recently declared unambiguously that the rumor was untrue. Nevertheless, it was a universal perception. "We were aware that these two guys were looking into each other's eyes," reported one member of the French contingent, "and that something was happening there. They seemed in love."

"It's amazing what people will say about other people," comments Shetler incredulously, maintaining that there was nothing between them beyond friendship. "I'm bisexual and always have been," he says, but that was no reason to jump to conclusions. "I was a great friend of Van, and it turned out I could be there for him as a kind of moral support." At the time, he recalls, he especially resented critics who were anxiously picking apart Cliburn's performances, and he felt very protective of his colleague.

If there was a misreading of the nature of that relationship, it was no doubt due to optics. Van wanted someone to shield him against the crowds, and Shetler happily took on the role of gate-keeper. "Everybody had to go through Shetler to get to Van. The Russians didn't like it at all," said one competitor. "He behaved like Van's wife-manager, and once, when he accompanied Van to the Kremlin, the Russians barred his entrance."

The *Time* cover story about Van, published on the heels of the competition, offers more clues about the nature of the relationship. In it, Van is painted as a person who "can be considerate to a fault." As a result, the magazine reported, "in Moscow one of his American friends had to lock him into his hotel room before he dropped from exhaustion receiving the glad-handers and autograph seekers who streamed in all through the night." Shetler claims responsibility for much that was in the article, so the description—pegging him as a young Cerberus, guarding the fragile, good-natured pianist who simply couldn't say no—is no doubt of his own making. That social dynamic—in which Van found someone to act as armor against the world—would become routine as Royal Marks took on the role of "personal representative" after Van's return to the United States. It would continue for years after, with an ever-changing roster of assistants.

The bond between Van and Shetler wasn't, as so many had assumed, physical, said Shetler. On the other hand, he did have an ongoing affair with Richter. "Of course, Richter was homosexual," Shetler noted, "as was Shtarkman." As was Tchaikovsky, for that matter, though the Russians are loath to admit it.

If, in the end, the ambassador was mollified about the so-called affair, Van presented Thompson with other headaches to resolve, such as the pianist's love fest with the Russian people and their leaders, a cause of worry for American officials. Van praised

the Russians as connoisseurs of music, and declared of Muscovites that "the benevolence of the public inspires, and it seems,
even to oneself, that you play better than normal." That set off
alarm bells in Washington. When Van embraced the Russians
as "my people" and said he had never felt so at home anywhere
else, this verged on treason in the eyes of the State Department.
Thompson was ordered to discuss the matter with Cliburn. He
did so and reported back that there was really no need for concern. Nevertheless, as Van ascended closer and closer to the winner's circle, Washington became increasingly agitated.

Thompson wasn't the only official in Moscow feeling the
heat at this time. The chairman of the piano jury, Gilels, also
found himself at the center of a political storm. "I'm familiar
with the behind-the-scenes battles Emil Gilels had," wrote Maya
Plisetskaya, "because we lived in the same cooperative building
on Gorky Street for many years and would discuss the latest
news in the courtyard. He was summoned to speak to the minister, accused of a lack of patriotism, shamed, and threatened. If
you're not smart enough [he was told], then at least have [Cli-
burn] share first place with our Soviet pianist. Explanations that
Cliburn's talent was head and shoulders above the rest were not
taken into account."

The harassment was intense. As the Tchaikovsky Competition began to draw to a close, however, Gilels never wavered.
He was passionately determined to protect the integrity of the
fledgling enterprise he had been asked to guide.

Over 5,700 miles away, in Kilgore, Texas, a small contingent
was doing its best to bolster his efforts. Jessie Armstrong, who
had been one of Van's elementary-school teachers, remembered

receiving a phone call from the pianist's father. "Mrs. Armstrong, I'm getting a little nervous," he told her. "I'm afraid things won't turn out the way we thought."

Armstrong thought it over and came up with a plan. "I said, 'Mr. Cliburn, let's quit praying for Van, and start spending our prayer time on those judges, that they will see in Van the ability that is there, and that they will be honest and fair,'" she recalled. "And he said, 'Let's start.'"

If competitions are, as composer Béla Bartók said, for horses, the Tchaikovsky final round was a race fit for thoroughbreds. Liu had played well, as had Vlassenko. Two of the Americans were shining. After the second round, Sviatoslav Richter gave a press conference, claims Pollack—though jury members were actually forbidden to make public statements about the pianists—"and he spoke about my performance of the Prokofiev Seventh Sonata, a piece he had premiered, as being inspired by the devil!" Indeed, it seemed in that moment that Pollack was ahead by a nose.

Then came the third round, where all depended on the two concertos that had to be performed. Gedda-Nova, Mollova, and Miansarov acquitted themselves with respectable performances, but none of them swept the judges off their feet. It was a different story for Van. According to Annie Marchand, "he wouldn't have won except for that third round." The critic of *Sovetskaya Kultura* agreed with her: "Generally speaking, Van Cliburn, like many highly emotional musicians, plays unevenly." Yet, in the final round, "the young American instrumentalist literally staggered both the jury and the audience with his phenomenal gift."

At the crucial moment he was at the peak of his form. He began with the Tchaikovsky First Piano Concerto, the sprawling romantic blockbuster, performed with the Moscow State Symphony under the baton of conductor Kirill Kondrashin. Among those in the packed house was Queen Elisabeth of Belgium, perhaps Europe's greatest patron of the arts. Her presence added even more glamour to the proceedings.

Few noticed that one of Cliburn's fingers was bandaged—he had cut it, he said, while practicing. He was nonetheless prepared to unleash all the weapons in his arsenal. The music gave him ample opportunities. Concertos revel in the theatrics—and inherent violence—of a musical battle. This is perhaps nowhere truer than among the Russians. When Anton Rubinstein performed a Mozart piano concerto in 1858, one critic reported that "he seized it, shook it, worried it, tore it to pieces, and then devoured it, limb by limb." (And that was in music by Mozart, the elegant classicist!)

Tchaikovsky's concerto, as the composer explained to his patron, Nadezhda von Meck, was intended as a confrontation between two forces: "the powerful, inexhaustibly richly colored orchestra, with which there struggles and over which there triumphs (given a talented performer) a small, insignificant, but strong-minded rival."

The work had its own history of struggle. Originally intended as a showpiece for pianist Nikolai Rubinstein, it was dismissed by that renowned pianist as "worthless, absolutely unplayable." His critical attack was stinging. "An outsider, dropping into the room," claimed Tchaikovsky, "would have thought me a madman, without talent, ignorant, a worthless writer who had come to annoy a famous musician with his rubbish." After Rubinstein bowed out, the music was premiered instead in Boston by Hans von Bülow.

Rubinstein was too quick to reject the work, though Tchaikovsky eventually did reconsider aspects of the music, changing certain passages after admitting that "my seams show." But history was largely on his side. Russian composer Sergei Taneyev called the piece "the first truly Russian piano concerto." Audiences today still clamor for it. In fact, in the West it spurred a double hit on the pop charts for bandleader Freddy Martin in 1941, first as an instrumental with Jack Fina on piano and soon after, with lyrics added, as "Tonight We Love," with vocalist Clyde Rogers.

The Moscow audience had of course heard it many times before, but Van's interpretation was extraordinary. The work's thundering octaves and delicate filigree were perfectly rendered. Musical lines soared and swooped and darted swiftly to and fro, unfolding a narrative that sounded both noble and ardent, majestic fanfares alternating with lovelorn airs. From the concerto's opening piano chords, which pealed like colossal church bells, to its dark bass rumblings and songful melodies, every tone was imbued with an inner glow, with long phrases concluding in an emphatic, edgy pounce. The effect was simply breathtaking.

Nina Lelchuk, then a fifteen-year-old teaching assistant to Yakov Flier at the conservatory, found a school janitor weeping during Van's performance after the lilting serenade of Tchaikovsky's second movement. "He said he never listened to classical music," she reported, "but that he was so struck by the tenderness he heard in the lullaby-like slow movement of the Tchaikovsky that he couldn't control himself. The man cradled his arms and gently swung them from side to side. 'It felt like he was rocking a baby,' he said, with tears in his eyes."

The performance was perfect. Pianist and conductor performed as if of one mind. Though Richter later took issue with some of Van's tempos, he declared the Texan one of only two competitors who actually understood the Tchaikovsky work (the other, he said, was Miansarov).

Next Van played Kabelevsky's solo-piano Rondo. During the performance, one of the piano's strings snapped. A piano technician was called in to repair the problem while everyone waited. And then the ensemble was poised to play Rachmaninoff's treacherously difficult Piano Concerto no. 3.

Its dedicatee, pianist Josef Hofmann, whose small hands made the task especially hard, never attempted to pull it off. By 1958 it had been little performed in Russia—"too many notes," was the feeling, and even Rachmaninoff seemed to agree. It was regarded as merely a flashy platform for show-off virtuosos. Van's performance not only changed minds, but also made the choice of a winner other than the American almost impossible.

"His Tchaikovsky made me fall in love with him," remembered Vera Gornostaeva, a revered member of the Moscow Conservatory piano faculty. Yet, she recalled, his Rachmaninoff was even more powerful: It changed history. After Van, people would never again hear this music the same way. Dmitry Paperno was also in the audience, and remembers the warm applause that greeted Van as he appeared onstage. But with the short, soft orchestral introduction and the piano's first motif, he began to wonder, "Isn't it a little too slow?"

"There are not many such openings," he says, "where the piano captures the audience from the first note with its disarming sincerity." That theme, reminiscent of a Russian chant, "Thy Tomb, O Savior," sets a plaintive mood. Deceptively simple yet gripping, the music soon builds into a cascade of rapid, technically daunting keyboard figures.

Van's leisurely tempo was a surprise. Yet, paradoxically, his slower pace made the time seem to go by faster. "A highly technical pianist playing it fast will create the opposite perception," explained Sergei Urivaev of the St. Petersburg Conservatory. "It will seem to take longer, because the message of the music, the inner content, is missing." As Van played, Paperno spotted an elderly woman who brought a handkerchief up to her eyes to wipe away the tears.

There is no simple explanation for why in that moment Van played perhaps the best concert of his life. Sometimes a performer experiences an instant of artistic grace, when heaven seems to open up and hold him in the palm of its hand—when the swirl of worldly sensations gives way to a pervasive, knowing stillness, and he feels connected to life's unbroken dance. If that was not exactly Van's experience when playing Rachmaninoff Concerto no. 3, it must have come close. He and Kondrashin became a single entity, shadowing each other as together they brought the music to luminous completion.

All the details fell into place. When Rachmaninoff reiterated a specific tone, the pianist would imbue it with a different nuance each time. Musical phrases were spaced like pauses in a natural conversation; thematic sequences were varied in inflection, with iterations alternating in emphasis, like "end-stopped" lines and "run-ons" in a poem. The pulse slowed or moved forward to allow the music to grow heavier or to break out in small dramatic bursts, but everything was in service to the ongoing story.

Van offered other surprises. Few who played the concerto took on the option of the more elaborate, and perilous, cadenza, the place in the piece where the orchestra stops and the pianist takes the audience on a spectacular solo journey. Rachmaninoff, who offered a choice of two different cadenzas to performers, had always used the simpler one himself. In Russia, said Vlassenko, Van was the first to perform the "big" cadenza. Even Yakov Flier and Emil Gilels played the easier one.

After his win, Van gave encore performances throughout the Soviet Union. The reaction shown here, in Moscow, was typical, the auditorium filled with swooning fans and bouquets of flowers.

The competition's three top winners during the days following the event: (*left to right*) Van (first place) and (tied for second) Liu Shikun and Lev Vlassenko, now cheerful comrades. Cliburn's spontaneity and heart won out over Vlassenko's technical brilliance and Liu's fire.

Van with Soviet premier Nikita Khrushchev at the end of the Tchaikovsky event. Van and Khrushchev genuinely liked each other, and their friendship continued for years afterward.

Following Van's victory and subsequent performances around the country, his translator, Henrietta Belyaeva, and hundreds of Moscow fans on the Moscow airport rooftop bid him farewell.

Van blows kisses to bystanders at the ticker-tape parade for him held along Broadway in New York City on May 20, 1958, in celebration of his victory at the Tchaikovsky Competition. The crowd was estimated at 100,000. It was the first and only time that a classical musician was feted in this way by the city of New York.

Van plays piano for New York's Mayor Robert Wagner at the reception in the Waldorf Astoria Hotel following the parade. The parade and the reception were just the first signs of the new status the Moscow event had bestowed on Cliburn.

Left to right: Van Cliburn; President Dwight D. Eisenhower; Van's parents, Harvey Lavan Cliburn Sr. and Rildia Bee Cliburn; and conductor Kirill Kondrashin meet at the White House, May 23, 1958.

Pianist Ivan Davis (*right*), one of Van Cliburn's close friends during his Juilliard years, was another brilliant young American, here being honored as winner of the 1960 Liszt Competition in New York. The presenter is Mrs. Arthur Friedheim (*center*), widow of Rildia Bee Cliburn's piano teacher, who was a Liszt disciple.

LEFT Whenever he returned to the Soviet Union, Van's spirits were lifted by the continuing embrace of the Russian people. He used the occasions—this one in 1960 or 1962—to visit with friends as well as to perform. The love for him was unflagging, though Moscow's musicians felt less happy with his playing as time went on.

ABOVE The daughter-in-law of Soviet statesman Anastas Mikoyan, Eleonora, took Van under her wing, and he felt completely at home in the Mikoyan household. He was especially fond of singing both opera and (as here) popular love songs. The act of singing strongly influenced his approach to the piano, a percussion instrument that must be made to sound like the human voice.

LEFT Van plays "Moscow Nights" for the American embassy staff, as Ambassador Llewellyn Thompson (*behind him and slightly to the left*) sings along, July 4, 1960. Performing the sentimental Russian favorite became Van's way of showing gratitude to his Moscow audiences.

LEFT Van's mother and father, with Cliburn's manager Schuyler Chapin (*standing right*) at a reception in 1964 honoring the tenth anniversary of Van's New York debut.

BELOW At the same event, impresario Sol Hurok (*left*) with Van and Henry Z. Steinway, president of the piano maker. Hurok, who represented Van after his Tchaikovsky win, became a powerful ally.

LEFT American pianist Misha Dichter almost garnered first place in the 1966 Tchaikovsky Competition, duplicating Van's achievement, but this time the jury ruled against the audience's wishes. Here, Misha sits next to his wife, Cipa, as Aschen Mikoyan, granddaughter of Soviet statesman Anastas Mikoyan, holds their son Sasha on her lap.

LEFT The Van Cliburn International Piano Competition, begun in Texas in 1962, continues to this day, though it never managed to re-create the success experienced by its namesake. Here Van poses with the 1985 Cliburn Competition finalists in Fort Worth. Photograph by Ken Howard

BELOW Van visits Lev Vlassenko's grave in Moscow, accompanied by Eleonora Mikoyan, the daughter-in-law of Soviet official Anastas Mikoyan.

LEFT Moscow Conservatory teacher Vera Gornostaeva indicates what distinguished Van's playing by placing her hand over her heart. She was bowled over, along with so many other Moscow musicians, by Cliburn's gorgeous tone, ability to make the music flow naturally, and mastery of music's emotional undercurrents.

RIGHT Liu Shikun, Van's competitor in 1958, hearing that Cliburn was ill, traveled to Texas in 2012 to see him. It was a year before Van's death from bone cancer. Here Liu performs "Moscow Nights" for an audience of one in Van's home at the time of the Cliburn Competition's Silver Anniversary Gala.

Even after Van had retired from the stage, he visited Moscow regularly. Here he is at the Kremlin with Tommy Smith, his partner for the last two decades of his life. With Smith, Cliburn achieved an elusive happiness at last. Van died on February 27, 2013.

Critic W. J. Henderson, reviewing Rachmaninoff's performance of this piece, wrote that it exhibited "honesty and simplicity and the single pursuit of musical beauty, without desire to baffle or astonish." That was exactly the way Moscow's musical elite perceived Van's rendition.

By the third round, wrote Paperno, "Goldenweiser had fallen in love with Cliburn's playing unconditionally ('the brightest performance of the Third Concerto after Rachmaninoff himself!' he said)." His colleagues were equally smitten. When it ended, the whole jury rose to its feet, remembers Sequeira Costa. Richter was crying. The crowd—"so vibrant, it was terrifying really," remembered Mark Schubart—broke into bedlam, then settled down into synchronized rhythmic clapping and stomping. Though the contest was not yet over—six more pianists were still to come—unison shouts of "First prize!" rang out. Gilels then broke the rules by going backstage and escorting Van out again for additional bows, something that was strictly forbidden. And then he did something utterly remarkable.

"That's true," Cliburn remembered. "I was not supposed to go back onstage after I had bowed, and the jury was not supposed to come backstage, but Gilels came and pulled me out in front of the audience again—and kissed me. That was a moment I cannot begin to describe."

Neuhaus later wrote that Cliburn's performances were "the most phenomenal events since the October Revolution, eclipsing such masters as Schnabel, Cortot, Rubinstein, and Petri." Two rivals on the jury who until that moment were not on speaking terms—Neuhaus and Goldenweiser—now turned and faced each other as if for the first time. There had been a long-running history of antagonism between them. How it started was a faded memory, though Vera Gornostaeva pointed to one incident that lingered painfully. "Once, when Goldenweiser performed Liszt's "Mephisto" Waltz [no. 1, a piece that ordinarily takes eleven or twelve minutes], the playing was so slow that when a woman asked Neuhaus afterward how he liked the interpretation, he remarked, 'It was the best half hour of my life.' Word of this got back to Goldenweiser."

By the time of the Tchaikovsky Competition, the two men had already taken first steps toward a personal détente, through an exchange of letters. Still, they continued to treat each other with reserve. Neuhaus had made the first move. "About 16–17 years ago something went astray inside me (personal adversities, the incurable illness and death of my son)," he wrote to Goldenweiser. "I struggle against the tireless desire for putting an end to my life, even though I love life, but not myself in it. I have an almost pathological striving to be offensive to people . . . Forgive me this incoherent letter. Maybe you will feel that I deserve compassion rather than anger. Your old and ill-fated colleague, HN."

"Dear Heinrich Gustavovich," replied Goldenweiser, "your letter affected me deeply enough to make me cry. Thank you for the moral trust, without which you would not write me this way . . . I embrace you as my friend, and wish wholeheartedly you may free yourself from the heavy burden that poisons your life physically and morally." Caught up in the excitement of Van's achievement, their own Iron Curtain crumbled, and they finally embraced.

Of the remaining competitors, two made serious strategic blunders. Shtarkman's good friend Maria Greenberg advised him to perform a concerto by Chopin. "She said that everyone [else] would be playing loud and fast," explains the pianist's son, Alexander, who is also a formidable pianist, "and that [with Chopin] he would distance himself [from the crowd] and show the jury the refinement and lyricism of his playing." The older Shtarkman later realized that he should have chosen Rachmaninoff's Second Piano Concerto instead.

Then, Daniel Pollack's unfamiliarity with the Tchaikovsky concerto caught up with him. After a brilliant beginning in the second round, the pianist's final performance was lackluster. If only he had spent his time preparing the Tchaikovsky instead of learning all the Russian repertoire that he really didn't need, the outcome might have been different. One of his colleagues called his Tchaikovsky concerto the most mediocre performance of the work he had ever heard. The other pianists in the competition all did well enough, but Van's extraordinary performance was in a class by itself.

Many young, aspiring pianists, like Moscow-born Dmitri Alexeev, were profoundly moved by Van's playing. The ten-year-old found it to be "like fresh air, like spring." Years later, in 1975, Alexeev would win the prestigious Leeds Piano Competition in England. Recalling the impression Van made on him in 1958, he pointed to "a sense of 'freedom.' The Soviet performers felt that every note had to be strictly controlled. They had excellent training, but the result lacked freshness and poetry." That word, "freedom," was secretly on the lips of many. In that sense, Van's message became unintentionally political.

Still, the jury did not have an easy time of it. After the final performances, they spent two hours trying to make a decision. As Costa remembered it, the final vote was made vocally by each judge, not written down, and "there was this wish that Vlassenko would win. An idea—probably mandated—came from the Russian members to work it out so that Cliburn and Vlassenko would both get first prizes. But Gilels and Richter felt that Cliburn should have a unique standing." Despite Costa's recollection, final ballots held in the Tchaikovsky House Museum in Kiln show Van the winner, with an initial tally for second place of six for Liu, four for Vlassenko, and six to split the prize between them. An additional vote taken to resolve the matter affirmed that both men would get the second prize. Richter again grumbled and balked, then caved in. But only one man in the country had the authority to decide the outcome: the clever but uneducated leader of the Soviet Union, Premier Nikita Khrushchev.

He admittedly knew nothing about the arts. "After a year or two of school, I had learned how to count to thirty and my father decided that was enough," Khrushchev recalled in his memoirs. "He said that all I needed was to be able to count money, and I would never have more than rubles to count anyway." He never pursued further academic studies, though he developed keen political instincts, and had an innate intelligence for which he was seldom given credit. Partly as a defense against the dread of Soviet power, many Westerners depicted him as a clown. Writer Saul Bellow, for one, found it "hard to believe that this bald, round, gesticulating, loud man may be capable of overcoming, of ruining, perhaps of destroying us." Bellow saw Khrushchev as having been "inspired by the Russian comic tradition," as exemplified by Gogol's *Dead Souls*. Khrushchev, he wrote, took elements of Gogol's "grotesquely thickheaded" provincial autocrats, gluttons, gamblers, and drunkards. "He is one of Gogol's stout men who 'know better than thin men how to manage their affairs.'"

The Soviet leader, in fact, was no fool. In matters of culture, he relied on experts like Vladimir Lebedev, an aide on the staff of the Council of Ministers. The two first met because of the premier's habit of having literary works read to him aloud. That became Lebedev's job. And it was through Lebedev's influence, in fact, that Solzhenitsyn's *One Day in the Life of Ivan Denisovich* received permission to be published.

That Lebedev could push Khrushchev toward Solzhenitsyn's side was impressive, and the Tchaikovsky situation quickly became a similar game of influence exercised at the highest levels. Sources close to Gilels reported that he called Lebedev about Van, hoping to influence the situation through a back channel before reaching out to Furtseva, who would be speaking with the premier. Operatives in the Kremlin were each beginning to choose sides.

Vera Gornostaeva, who had been giving piano lessons to Gilels's daughter, Elena, was later invited to meet with Khrushchev, and he told her that Gilels had argued on behalf of giving the prize to Van, asserting that "it could end the Cold War, and there will be peace." The Soviet leader seemed to believe it, though he was not about to rush into a decision. Instead, he decided to discuss the matter with a small group of advisors, including Furtseva, who agreed with Gilels, and, in opposition, Mikhail Suslov, a conservative politician and Stalin protégé with nationalist leanings. Suslov was known to his enemies as "the Black Cardinal."

Khrushchev certainly liked Van, who subsequently made much of Khrushchev's remark to him at a post-competition reception that he regretted missing the radio broadcast of the pianist's Chopin F Minor Fantasy. (Over time, the story evolved, so that in later tellings Khrushchev actually heard the performance, and enthused, "I loved the way you played the F Minor Fantasy." That never happened.) Khrushchev had surely been prompted by experts to say something nice about Van's Chopin, possibly because that performance bore traces of Anton Rubinstein's interpretive approach, which were likely handed down from Rubinstein to Friedheim to Rildia Bee. But in the end, Khrushchev's decision about who would win the First Tchaikovsky Competition could not be based on subtleties of high art. There were political dimensions to consider.

"In the Ministry of Culture they were worried," wrote Khrushchev's son, Sergei. An idea arose in the Central Committee to split the first prize between Van and Vlassenko. But First Deputy Minister of Culture Sergei Kaftanov "carefully warned that that ploy would bring nothing but harm and shame, and the authority of the Moscow competition would be buried forever."

On April 12, 1958, the brewing scandal was reported to the secretary of the Central Committee, Furtseva. The arguments were now placed before her. Ideologists, including Suslov, considered the victory of an American to be an ideological defeat. Furtseva tested the idea of a split decision, unofficially chatting with two Soviet members of the jury, Gilels and Kabalevsky, but she met with a resolute refusal. Kabalevsky, following Kaftanov, announced that such a decision would be a death sentence for the competition and that without a written order from the Central Committee he refused to vote that way.

In fact, a Cliburn victory was actually a welcome idea in some quarters, especially because the end of the violin phase generated some embarrassment over the overwhelming dominance of Soviet winners. Ultimately, it seemed to give the wrong impression. Minister of Culture Mikhailov even passed along suggestions made by several participants that in the future more Western music should be added to the requirements, and that the number of Soviet contestants should actually be decreased. In

retrospect, the appearance of fairness seemed increasingly important to the prestige of the enterprise. But not everyone was on
board with that idea.

Suslov ran to Khrushchev, but Furtseva was ahead of him; she
didn't want to take responsibility for such a final decision. When
Suslov entered the office, Khrushchev was reading Kaftanov's
official note about the situation and Furtseva was next to him.
Suslov sat down across from her at the other side of the table. He
didn't like Furtseva and considered her recent transition to the
Central Committee as undermining his position. "After reading,
my father looked at Suslov," Sergei Khrushchev wrote.

" 'The jury is insisting on Cliburn, but . . .' began Michael
Andreevich [Suslov].

" 'Kaftanov is right, if we try to pressure the jury there
will be a catastrophe, the foreign members will just turn
around and leave Moscow,' Furtseva interrupted him.

" 'But he's an American!' Suslov was not giving up.

" 'But his style of playing is ours, Russian; Cliburn studied in the U.S. under Professor Lhévinne and she, in turn,
came from the Safonov school,' Furtseva intervened again.
She had come well prepared to the discussion.

"Suslov tried to continue, but my father had already
made a decision.

" 'As the jury is insisting on it, we do not need to interfere. They are professionals. And having an American win
is even good, we will show the world our impartiality,' my
father concluded and smiled.

"Suslov was dejectedly silent.

" 'Is that all you have?' my father said dryly. The visitors
nodded."

In the end, it all came down to a comment Khrushchev made to Gornostaeva: "The future success of this competition lies in one thing: the justice that the jury gives," she remembered him saying. "I don't know who told him that," she added, assuming that he couldn't have reached that conclusion alone. It was likely Gilels, and it was a smart move.

In the official story released to the press, Khrushchev acted instantaneously and decisively: "Was he the best? Then give him the prize."

The verdict was made official to the world on April 14. There is little doubt that the pressure exerted by Max Frankel of *The New York Times* had contributed to the final decision. Frankel had sensed a good story during the piano phase of the Tchaikovsky. All those screaming girls were a tipoff—bobby-soxers, he called them, like the ones back home who went into hysterics over Elvis. Besides, the dean of Juilliard had been lobbying him for coverage.

At one point Schubart told him that not only was Van doing extremely well, but the public was taking to him in an extraordinary way. Frankel went to see him perform. "The place went wild," he remembers. "I ran into people carrying bunches of flowers to throw at this kid. And afterward there were no longer any tickets available for his next round. Schubart said he would be surprised if they let Van win, but that by all rights he should. That informed my first story. Much to my shock, [the editors] put it on page one. It never occurred to me that they would. It added to the excitement at home, and, in a way, to the pressure on the Russians."

"A boyish-looking, curly-haired young man from Kilgore, Tx., took musical Moscow by storm tonight," the article began. Yet, it warned, "it is far from certain that Mr. Cliburn will win first prize in the competition. The nine finalists are all first rate and include another American, Daniel Pollack of Los Angeles. But Mr. Cliburn is clearly the popular favorite and all Moscow is wondering whether an American will walk off with top honors."

Frankel had laid out the issue: Would the Soviets have the courage to give Van the prize? The placement of his article made it impossible to ignore. The entire world began to pay attention to the event. Frankel soon realized that in addition to giving a push to the Soviets, his reportage also offered a personal career opportunity.

"You want to know how journalism works?" he asked in an interview. "I was the number-two man in Moscow. My boss, [Moscow bureau chief] William Jorden, at first deferred to me on coverage of the competition. But when I landed on page one, he announced that he thought *he* would cover the final judgments. I went into a rage, but not openly.

"At the final performance they did not announce the winners. But then I hung around, and when they brought Van back after midnight to record the music, I asked what was happening— and learned that he had won. They hadn't yet announced it. Jorden had gone to bed. So I filed the article myself. It was a delicious way to slap this guy who was going to steal the story. The next day he was furious." Frankel's savvy reporting would one day gain him the position of executive editor at the *Times*, as well as a Pulitzer Prize.

In New York, plans were quickly set in motion for a ticker-tape parade—the first ever for a classical musician. (As it turned out, *The New York Times* secretly had a hand in that decision as well.) Cliburn's career took off like a rocket.

Beyond the political context, there was actually little reason for all the excitement. The Tchaikovsky Competition was young and without a track record. Many Americans had previously reached the top tier in other, highly prestigious competitions both at home and abroad—some, as music critic Paul Henry Lang contended in the *New York Herald Tribune* just days after the Tchaikovsky event, "with requirements far higher than those stipulated for the Moscow meet." Perhaps Lang revealed a chauvinist streak with his claim that the Russians were actually less serious for being too enamored of "thunder, brimstone, and saccharine—Tchaikovsky, Rachmaninoff, Kabalevsky." Yet it was true that Cliburn's prestigious Leventritt award in New York, judged by some of the finest musicians in the world, had received comparatively little attention.

The same was true of American violinist Berl Senofsky's win at the Queen Elisabeth Competition in Brussels in 1955—the first time that a Russian violinist had not placed first. "On the evening of the final decision, over two thousand persons remained in the Grande Salle of the Palais des Beaux-Arts in Brussels until 2:00 in the morning to learn the name of the winner. Queen Elisabeth was among this number," noted a State Department memo about the Brussels contest, adding, "American participation in international artistic events of this sort has major importance in promoting our national prestige abroad."

Even earlier, in 1952, American Leon Fleisher had won the Queen Elisabeth Competition in the piano division. Where, some wondered, was *The New York Times* then? But in 1958, as Van triumphed over the Soviets, the paper became a major player in the event, helping to create an international sensation.

Once the top prize had been decided, everything else fell into line without much controversy. Vlassenko and Liu shared second place. Shtarkman took third place, followed by Miansarov, Mollova, Gedda-Nova, Matsuura, and Pollack, who, says Frankel, "was very bitter."

"The Japanese pianist had played the most brutal Schumann Concerto imaginable," remembers Lowenthal. "Danny [Pollack] and his wife were sitting at a table, literally crying. Danny was saying, 'Worse than the Japanese pianist!' They were tearing their hair out." Giving a pianist last place in a competition is often a message from the jury—an intentional snub. Pollack seemed devastated.

As the announcement was made, legions of flashbulbs went off and reporters descended like birds of prey. Pundits dubbed Cliburn the "American *Sputnik*," and fired off rapid questions. Van, startled, made for his hotel as soon as he could escape, to phone home. A noisy horde, complete with hysterical, star-struck girls, followed him. Now Cliburn began to experience a new phase of his career—being pummeled by good fortune. Harriet Wingreen stopped by his room to offer her congratulations. Norman Shetler opened the door a crack to see who it was, ushered her in, and quickly closed it again. She spent just a few moments with her old friend and left. Later that night, Wingreen was in her own room at the Pekin Hotel when she heard loud pounding on the door. She opened it to find a very agitated Van, with a look of fear in his eyes.

"Van, what's the trouble?" she asked, suddenly concerned. "The girls are after me!" he blurted out in a panic.

She invited him in, and quietly closed the door. "He was so tall that I let him have the bed and I slept on the couch that night," she remembers. If only, like the Greek mythological character Autolycus, he had the gift of invisibility. But Wingreen was happy to provide at least temporary safe haven.

CHAPTER 9

Hurt Feelings

FLURRIES OF CABLES crisscrossed the globe, raining down on Moscow, Washington, and New York. Juilliard's Mark Schubart received Max Frankel's call at four o'clock in the morning in Moscow with the news that Van had won, and promptly sent off an exultant cable to the school's president, William Schuman, in New York: "WE ARE IN ORBIT."

Schuman wired Cliburn:

ALL OF US AT THE SCHOOL ARE GLOWING WITH PRIDE . . .
AND LOOK FORWARD TO YOUR TRIUMPHANT RETURN.

Gilels sent one to Schuman:

GORACO POZDRAVLIAU BLESTIACHIM UPECHOM VAN
CLIBURNA VOSPITANNIKA VASCHEI SCHKOLI ZELAJU

DALNEISCHICH USPECHOV. (I WARMLY CONGRATULATE
THE MAGNIFICENT SUCCESS OF VAN CLIBURN, STUDENT
OF YOUR SCHOOL, AND WISH FURTHER SUCCESS.)

The U.S. government agency most closely involved with the day-to-day workings of the event, the State Department, fired off a message to the American embassy in Moscow on April 15:

PLEASE DELIVER FOLLOWING TO PIANIST VAN CLIBURN:
HEARTIEST CONGRATULATIONS. SPLENDID PERFORMANCE.
SIGNED WILLIAM S. B. LACY, SPECIAL ASSISTANT TO THE
SECRETARY OF STATE.

That official response presented a positive face. But as the Kremlin prepared for a series of glamorous gatherings, and Khrushchev's warm embrace of Van gained increasing media attention, newspaper correspondents got wind of a less happy undercurrent and began to inquire whether President Eisenhower or Secretary of State John Foster Dulles had sent congratulatory messages. They hadn't. In a confidential report, Richard H. Davis of the American embassy voiced consternation about it. "Even Van Cliburn," he wrote, "expressed privately to an Embassy officer his disappointment."

On the date of a Kremlin celebration capping the event, the White House belatedly sent a telegram, but Ambassador Thompson intercepted it. The April 16 laudatory cable, inviting Van to visit the president on his return, ended with best wishes to Pollack but failed to mention Joyce Flissler, who had gained a medal in the violin competition. Thompson wouldn't deliver it, and asked for a revision. The new version finally went out two days later, and on April 19 Cliburn sent Eisenhower an acknowledgment. An embarrassing amount of time had elapsed, and feelings had been bruised.

Van wasn't the only one fostering resentment. Pollack, says Frankel, was bitter over a perceived lack of attention. What followed made it worse. Looking for a scrap of recognition from his native land, the pianist sent a letter entreating the White House for his own personal invitation to meet with the president. He had, after all, reached the Tchaikovsky finals, which was no small feat. But a White House staff member merely scribbled a note on Pollack's letter before filing it away, noting, with a dismissive air, that it had come from the "boy" who got eighth place in the competition that Cliburn had won—and leaving instructions to ignore the request.

Perhaps little more could be expected from the office of a president who would tell Leonard Bernstein that he liked a good tune but disliked "all them arias and barcarolles." Khrushchev's enthusiasm about Cliburn's Chopin, even though calculated for show, presented a marked contrast.

The White House kerfuffle was just the first sign of friction following the remarkable outcome. Behind the scenes, ego wars had begun, even among Cliburn's purported allies. Schuman, it turns out, was less than fully supportive of his star. Like many music professionals, he found all the sensationalism—the frantic scrambling for the limelight, as well as the political posturing—odious. Receiving a request from a congressman for ideas about how music could overcome "the barrier of the Iron Curtain," he saw it, cynically, as a plea for "ways in which music can be used as an international weapon." And he wanted no part of it.

Meanwhile, in a letter to Schubart, he reported that Lhévinne was busy having her picture taken with students for *Life* magazine. "The room is, of course, the very room in which she taught the great Van Cliburn," he remarked with a touch of sourness, adding facetiously that he was searching for good rates in Europe for Van Cliburn plaques. "I am planning several for the outside of the building and am even thinking of taking one home to New Rochelle." His typical Juilliard day, carped Schuman, now included telephone calls from Lhévinne, the writing of reports, visits "to the office of newborn babes," and many other things, "but somehow always returning to Van." Part of his challenge, he said, was "to keep Rosina on the ground." She was crushed by the fact that Van had not been in touch with her since the contest.

In fact, he noted, Schuman and Lhévinne had tried to reach the pianist by phone, to forestall his making any commitments before returning home, and learned that already "he has made some foolish moves." Among them, Van was planning performances in New York, Philadelphia, and Washington, and a television appearance on *The Steve Allen Show*. Meanwhile, much to Schuman's chagrin, a groundswell was building to bring the pianist to Brussels for Juilliard's planned performances there. The school's president didn't want to ask Van for anything. "This is a bandwagon of our making," he said, "and we don't have to jump on it."

Whatever the intricacies of the rift between Van and his teacher, Lhévinne was clearly out of sorts. She reached out for consolation to the Rosboroughs, friends of hers in Aspen, Colorado, where she traveled to teach in the summer. "John has a wonderful spirit, and a heart full of tenderness," she wrote to Schubart in French. "I spoke to [him] about our disappointment with Van in a totally frank manner and I am happy I did so, because he made some very wise comments." Schubart convinced her that the important thing is that Van won the first prize, and that "you and I know that Van would never have accomplished this with-

out our counsel and our interest and you should have great satisfaction from that." Instead of making Van her principal focus,
he advised, concentrate instead on other successful students, like
Pollack and John Browning.

When Schubart next communicated with Lhévinne, he was
glad she was "at peace with the Van situation," and he reported
that he was able to say the same, "though the number of people
'getting into the act' increases daily." There was, he said, a growing group of hangers-on who were attempting to steal the thunder. "I was pleased to learn through an article in *The Reporter*," he
wrote incredulously, "that [musician and writer] Abram Chasins
was really the man responsible for it all. I guess he needs the
publicity very badly!" (Chasins, whose short biography of Van
was churned out at record speed after the Moscow win, had a
reputation for being less than fully truthful. He later admitted
to having made up aspects of the book for the sake of creating a
more interesting story.)

Wounded by the perceived slights from Van, Schubart and
Lhévinne moved quickly to forge new allegiances. Pollack, noted
Schubart, was doing well, and seemed to be "going about things
in a mature way and I hope that when he returns in the fall you
will give him some further guidance." The Soviets were actively
giving him performance dates all over the country.

Ironically, it was Van's success that propelled Lhévinne to the
height of fame once enjoyed by her rival Samaroff. Overnight
she became the most important piano teacher in the world. Van's
tide was lifting all boats, though Lhévinne's allies maintained a
vigilant overprotectiveness on her behalf against any perceived
affront by the pianist. This scrutiny went on for years: when the
television program *Portrait of Van Cliburn* was aired in 1966,
Helen Coates—Leonard Bernstein's childhood piano teacher
and later his personal secretary—wrote a stinging letter to Van,

"shocked over the fact that there was not one mention of your wonderful teacher, Mme. Rosina Lhévinne." It spoke to her of the lack of gratitude toward someone who had nurtured and inspired him. Of course, Van very likely had nothing at all to do with the editorial decisions made by the program's producers.

However, his mind-set after the win quickly became a topic of concern for a number of people. Schubart had earlier expressed doubts about the pianist's ability to handle the acclaim, and Thompson raised a similar warning on April 16, following the Kremlin reception. "Because of his immaturity and some personality traits there is some danger that public and official adulation will go to his head," he reported, "and I took [the] occasion of [a] luncheon which I gave for contestants to give him some friendly advice." Afterward, things seemed to have settled down.

But only until May 9, when Richard Davis of the American embassy received word that Van's manager and a friend "are concerned over what they consider to be [a] decided change in [the] attitude of [the] young pianist." For one thing, Van was reportedly planning to return to Moscow for a long vacation. And in one conversation, he had supposedly said, in regard to a possible visit to Washington, that if the president wanted to see him the White House could get in touch with him.

"Under [the] circumstances, [the manager and friend] are particularly apprehensive as to what might happen when Cliburn first returns to the U.S. and meets [the] press. They believe he is likely to make some very unwise statements if queried on political matters about which he knows very little, particularly in view of his reported change in attitude. They speculate in this regard that Cliburn may have been 'approached' by [the] Soviets."

Three days later, Davis had lunch with Van and baritone Leonard Warren, one of the few American artists in 1958 invited to give concerts in the USSR. "Considering his age and emotional temperament," and that he received international recognition and the traditional warm overhospitality of the Russians, Davis wrote afterward, it would be strange if Van had not been affected by his experiences. "However, he has so far kept away from any political comment . . . While undoubtedly naive and politically unsophisticated, I would doubt that he has been 'approached' by [the] Soviets."

Van was in fact planning to return, with his mother and father, for a vacation in Sochi during July and August. But at the moment, explained Davis, he was engaged in a strenuous schedule of recording ("The Russians kept him at the piano from 11:00 PM to 5:00 in the morning last night"), for which he would be paid approximately twenty-five thousand rubles (a little more than $6,000 in 1958). Most of that currency had to stay in the country. "He thus has an inducement and reason for [a] return to Russia with his parents," Davis commented, "though he mentioned vaguely to [the] Embassy staff members an idea to establish a scholarship fund for American musicians to study in the Soviet Union."

From all appearances, Van was actually handling the situation far better than his nervous manager, his Juilliard teachers, or the bureaucrats in Washington. One sore point remained, however. Davis asked him if he had been in touch with anyone regarding the president's invitation to the White House. "He replied in [the] negative. I asked him what he had in mind about this. He said he was eagerly looking forward to being received but expressed his personal wish that it might be arranged while he would be in Washington since he wanted to try to get some rest immediately upon his return to U.S."

In Moscow, the exuberance of the moment placed political considerations on the back burner. The Kremlin gave two receptions in two days, one of them in honor of Queen Elisabeth of Belgium. That great walled city within a city that served as the seat of government was resplendent, remembered Annie Marchand, with "immense tables groaning with food—every delicacy you could imagine: fresh fruit, vegetables, caviar, Russian champagne." Van was first introduced to Khrushchev at that party, and the photograph of their bear hug of a greeting made its way quickly around the world. With a surprisingly avuncular air, the Soviet leader asked him why he was so tall. "Because I'm from Texas," the pianist replied.

"You must have lots of yeast in Texas."

"No," replied Van, "it's vitamin pills." He later regretted not coming up with the line "I'm from Yeast Texas."

An evening concert was held to showcase the top winners, and Van warmed up by singing some Richard Rodgers, George Gershwin, and Cole Porter. "A-a-ah've got you un-day mah skin!" is how *Time* depicted the "long-legged, tousled" Texan's crooning of the familiar standard as he offered a lighthearted musical aperitif before the first movement of the Tchaikovsky concerto. Shostakovich presented the competition medals, Khrushchev settled into his box, and the music began. "He was called back for three encores, and finally retired to shouts of 'more' in English," the magazine reported. At last a tired but exhilarated Cliburn looked up at the premier's box. It was empty.

The biggest thing that ever hit Moscow, reported *Time*, Van was "trailed by adoring crowds that recognized him on sight. His arrivals and departures at the conservatory set off small riots. Girls sent fresh blossoms to his practice room, and when word got around that he had lost weight and that he suffers from colitis, platoons of females turned up with bags of oranges. One determined girl even popped up in his room at the Hotel Pekin in the middle of the night." He attempted to address his ongoing medical woes by seeing a well-known blood specialist in Moscow named Dr. Sikirsky. But the physical ailments, which accounted in part for his thinness, would continue to plague him all his life.

At a second Kremlin reception in honor of the contestants, Van addressed former Soviet premier Nikolai Bulganin as Vyacheslav Molotov—Stalin's henchman. It turned out to be only a minor mishap. Khrushchev introduced him to his son, daughter, and granddaughter, and Van forever cemented their relationship with the kind of startling innocence that had already won the hearts of Muscovites all across the city. Jerome Lowenthal overheard the comments as they were recounted to the American ambassador. "I said to Mr. Khrushchev," reported Van, "that in this post-Sputnik age we all have to love one another. And I want to be the first pianist on the moon."

In response to the celebrations at the Kremlin, the American ambassador also held two receptions. First, there was a lunch in honor of the American participants. Then, at Van's request, he arranged a special light dinner following the pianist's recital in the Great Hall on April 18. Van's guest list was a challenge. He had asked permission to invite the top three winners of the violin and piano competitions to Spaso House (the neoclassical mansion once owned by textile industrialist Nikolay Vtorov, now the U.S. ambassador's residence), along with several Soviet friends associated with the competition "such as Gilels, Shostakovitch [sic] and conductor Kondrashin." Thompson explained in a cable to Washington, "I consented, but pointed out [the] difficulty of including [the] Chinese winner, Liu Shi-Kun."

Van had spoken to Gilels, who expressed agreement to the invitation for an after-concert buffet supper at Spaso House on the basis that it was an informal social affair. But certain reassurances were required. "No correspondent would be invited and only one or two officers from [the] embassy would be present in addition [to] Soviet guests," explained Thompson. That was easy in contrast to finding a way to tender an official American embassy invitation to an artist from Communist China. It just wasn't done. The solution? Magically, Liu was made un-Chinese.

"[The] Counselor [of the] Indonesian Embassy informs us that [the] Chinese student was in reality up to four years ago an Indonesian citizen but exercised [an] option [to] take Chinese citizenship," asserted the ambassador. This ridiculous claim was bolstered by the Indonesian's eyewitness testimony. "[He] asserts that Liu speaks fluent Indonesian and Dutch but rather bad Chinese."

It was all nonsense, of course. But it was a way out of the predicament. Secretary of State Dulles went along: "In light [of] circumstances outlined . . . Department concurs . . ." Liu, who never showed up, doesn't recall ever having received the invitation, but he now says there was no way he would have been allowed to accept. Van's starry-eyed plan to turn the disparate nationals into one big circle of friends was bound to run into a wall. In the end, the only foreign winner to attend was Romanian violinist Stefan Ruche, along with his accompanist. However, the Moscow contingent—Shostakovich, Kabalevsky, and Kondrashin (with their wives), Richter, and Shostakovich's son, Maxim—all came. Only Gilels failed to appear. Even Van's charm wasn't enough to rescue his attempt at international conciliation.

Spaso House, with its elegant domed ceiling and enormous bronze-and-crystal chandelier (the largest in Moscow), was nevertheless the scene of important moments of relief from the political fray. It had a fantastically storied history. There was the Christmas party in 1934 at which three trained seals from the Moscow Circus went berserk in the ballroom when their trainer fainted from too much champagne. A year later, the American consul general's wife, Irena Wiley, clearly having failed to learn a lesson from that fiasco, decided to bring in more animals, using a barnyard motif. Hundreds of finches noisily hovered around the high-ceilinged rooms over the four hundred guests, some mountain goats, a baby bear, and a dozen white roosters and filled the space with droppings. A member of the editorial board of *Izvestia* substituted champagne for the milk being fed to the bear, and the unfortunate creature vomited on the uniform of a Soviet general.

Mikhail Bulgakov attended a spring ball in the residence, which inspired a scene in his classic novel *The Master and Margarita*. Relations with the Soviets remained amicable even after listening devices were discovered all through the building in the 1930s. "We found them in the fireplaces, we found them in the little vents, in the inner walls," revealed Ambassador Joseph E. Davies. Decades later, during Khrushchev's reign, one was even uncovered in the replica of the Great Seal of the United States that had been a gift from the Soviet government, and the culprit behind this was revealed to be a telephone operator at Spaso House. He was discovered because he wore the same color lipstick as that found on cigarette butts left at the scene of an attempted bugging in the attic. Ambassador George Kennan "preferred not to inquire into" why the man was wearing lipstick.

Spaso House became a comfortable and familiar place for Van, who sometimes performed for Ambassador Thompson's two young daughters, Sherry and Jenny. "Van put me on his lap and played the piano," says Sherry. "Even though I was only five, I remember being taken to another world. He closed his eyes and shook his head when he played. I never saw that anywhere else until I went to a Stevie Wonder concert."

Such was Van in the company of children, as carefree and open as when he would lie on the floor and play board games with his Kilgore neighbor Bill Morton, or take a spin in the family car, or laugh himself silly with his Juilliard pals. On his return trips to Moscow, as the family of Stepan Mikoyan, son of Anastas Mikoyan, first deputy premier of the Soviet Union, extended their hospitality, he spent time frolicking and giggling with Aschen, their young daughter, and played and sang American pop standards at the family piano for hours. (Aschen has the home recordings to prove it.) There was something about singing those popular songs that was, for Van, the emotional equivalent of comfort food. His singing wasn't merely a lark, but a sentimental journey into a fantasy world of longing, romance, and the mysterious pleasures of heartbreak.

The Thompson girls were in a position to observe and overhear a great deal, and the impressions of those days remain. "When Khrushchev said yes to giving Van first prize there were implications," said Jenny. "It was a signal, not only toward détente but toward fair play. They were just coming out of Stalinism. Here was tangible proof that things had changed." It was an opportunity for the American government to wind down its defensive posture, but "the State Department made it difficult for Americans to participate" in Soviet-sponsored activities. "This is one of the things my father fought against," explained Jenny. "He said, 'They can't hurt us—exchanges work in our favor.'"

Of course, even when agreements were made there were always misinterpretations to iron out. "The Russians complained: why were things taking so long?" In part, confusion arose over an inability to fathom the differences in the two nations' economic systems. "They could send the Bolshoi to New York, and their government would pay," Jenny explained. "But if you wanted to send the New York City Ballet to Moscow, you had to raise the money. They didn't understand. That's where Hurok came in."

American impresario Sol Hurok, born Solomon Izrailevich Gurkov in Russia, was, remembered Jenny, a "rotund man, baldish, always laughing and jolly," who managed some of the greatest names in the performing arts, including Marian Anderson, Margot Fonteyn, and Arthur Rubinstein. He had a crafty ability to facilitate trade deals between the two superpowers.

Hurok's fictionalized film biography, *Tonight We Sing*, debuted in 1953; Van had gone to a showing and, awestruck, dreamed of seeing his name featured under the manager's famous logo, "S. Hurok Presents." Ironically, during the competition, Hurok sent a telegram to Frankel: "Get a message to Van," he wrote, "that I'd like to sign him up." The pianist laughed when he heard it, recalls Frankel, "and said, 'I tried to sign with him years ago.'" Within a year, they would forge an agreement.

Hurok "took me to dinner, bribed the guys in the Ministry of Culture, brought presents to the Bolshoi Ballet dancers," says Frankel. He was a smooth operator. It was Hurok who had sent Isaac Stern and Jan Peerce to Russia in 1956, paying their fees out of his own pocket to make the trip possible. Now, with new cracks in the Iron Curtain, enticing opportunities were arising, and he seized them. He arranged for the Moiseyev Dance Company to tour America in April, just as the Moscow competition was coming to a close, and they were featured at New York's Metropolitan Opera House. The Russian folk-dance ensemble sold out the house and garnered rave reviews, and Hurok hurriedly arranged for four more dates at the much larger Madison Square Garden.

It was tangible evidence that diplomacy was working. The Metropolitan Opera performance opened with an American orchestra under Russian conductor Samson Galperin, playing both "The Star-Spangled Banner" and the Soviet national anthem, "Unbreakable Union of Freeborn Republics." The audience stood for both. According to writer Harlow Robinson, there were seven curtain calls. "A crowd estimated at fifteen hundred then gathered around the stage door to catch a glimpse of (and perhaps even to touch) the exotic visitors as they left the theater," wrote Robinson. "That night at the Met, a new era in Soviet-American relations (and therefore in international relations) began."

Newspapers wrote editorials celebrating "The Arts as Bridges": "The world cannot fail to applaud the spirit that led [the Russians] to honor an American artist," announced *The Washington Post,* in a nod to the Tchaikovsky Competition. "It is gratifying to be able to report that the same spirit was manifested in New York on Monday evening at the American debut of the Moiseyev Dance Company from Moscow."

The *Post* even laid out the argument for a new era built on this foundation. "Perhaps the world's best hope today," it said, "is to be found in the understanding which art affords between peoples whose official spokesmen seem incapable of communication." Hard-bitten newspaper columnist Drew Pearson of the *New York Mirror*, ordinarily on the attack, marveled that "events which five years ago would have been considered unbelievable occurred in Moscow and New York this week, illustrating the new look in American-Russian relations."

It all was made possible not by political scheming but by very human interactions. Marketing whiz Martin Feinstein, understanding the implications, instructed Igor Moiseyev on how to prepare for a press conference. "I want three or four of your most beautiful girls," he ordered. "I want someone who's a mother, who's left a child behind in the Soviet Union, in the care of a grandma; I want a beautiful girl who has a boyfriend she's left behind; I want someone who's a newlywed, and so on and so forth, and I'm going with this to the editors of the women's pages." Hurok objected: they're going to ask political questions, he asserted. They won't, replied Feinstein. He was right.

Most observers were truly elated, though critic Walter Terry of the *New York Herald Tribune* raised a worry that gnawed at American officials as well: the United States could offer Russia no folk-dance company on the same artistic level as the Moiseyev in exchange. The challenge of finding suitable talent to send to Russia was a real problem. "Harold Prince wanted to bring *West Side Story*," remembers Frankel. "I know a guy who translated it into Russian. Yet the State Department rejected it, because it was about gangs."

Yet the prospects were too inviting to let pass. Days after he agreed to organize a New York ticker-tape parade for Van, American real-estate mogul and Broadway producer Robert W. Dowling flew to Moscow to push for more exchanges. He found Khrushchev warmly amenable. "Khrushchev expressed his approval," reported Thompson, and even commented that the Soviet and American people had no problems with each other. "He implied that it was only the American Government that prevented closer relations." In the glow of Van's win, the two countries agreed to host each other's major exhibitions in the summer of 1959. It started to seem that after years of protracted wrangling, a period of true détente might actually be dawning.

The choice of talent for an international road show still

remained a delicate matter. The State Department floated the idea of sending the Mormon Tabernacle Choir. Thompson balked. Even if they were to present only secular music, he wrote, the "religious angle would make the group unwelcome to Soviets." On the other hand, he noted, it would be worthwhile to "consider instead [a] high-quality vaudeville performance which would permit use [of a] good jazz orchestra without labeling it as such."

The Soviets were not willing to accept a name jazz orchestra because of their long-standing antipathy to the art form, but a way to promote this classic genre of American music would be to embed one surreptitiously within a wide-ranging, comprehensive entertainment package. Thompson pointed to the popularity of Russia's *estradny* theaters—"variety or vaudeville shows"—in the summer, when "people are tired of the winter diet of serious drama, ballet, opera and symphony . . ." The United States, he thought, could build on that model.

Talking acts were of limited appeal because of the language barrier, explained Thompson, but "pantomime comedy, high-quality vocalists, acrobats," would be suitable. "If a magician is included, he must be first-class as the Soviet magicians are of high quality. Americana should also be considered, such as rope twirling."

At that point no one dreamed of the success that would soon be achieved by Leonard Bernstein, who rode into Moscow with the New York Philharmonic and delivered a riveting concert and lecture aired in the United States on October 25 by the CBS television network. "During our three-week stay in the Soviet Union, we not only played for thousands of warm, wonderful Russians, but we talked to them, touched them, argued, fought and laughed with them," announced Bernstein to the cameras.

"On this, our final day in Moscow, I am about to speak to students . . . about the similarities of our two great peoples as seen through our music."

It was an easy sell. The conductor reminded the audience of "how you Russians loved *Porgy and Bess* . . . There is something in this Gershwin music of a tragic beauty, of an unashamed emotional candor that is as typically Russian as it is American," he asserted, noting also the popularity in America of Tchaikovsky's *Nutcracker* Suite.

With Soviet musicians integrated into the New York ensemble as a token of mutual cooperation, he led the orchestra in examples from Shostakovich's Seventh Symphony and Aaron Copland's beloved ballet *Billy the Kid*, which, he claimed, "describes the opening of new Western frontiers . . . A pioneering strength that could [also] describe the opening of your Siberian frontiers." Then, after introducing Shostakovich—who rose from his seat in the audience and walked to the stage sheepishly to shake hands and take bows, but only after several moments of prodding by the audience—Bernstein conducted the entire long first movement of the Seventh Symphony. It was a brilliant example of what could be accomplished with the right artist and forum.

It was a brilliant beginning. Cultural inroads were also made at the American National Exhibition in July of 1959, as washing machines, cars, samples of Pepsi-Cola (Coca-Cola foolishly refused to participate), Polaroid cameras, and model homes were viewed by more than 2 million people, and where an impromptu "kitchen debate" between Khrushchev and Vice President Richard Nixon over the practical results of their ideological positions brought their simmering disagreements out into plain view. (While Coca-Cola caved in to routine Cold War fears and pressures, Donald Kendall, head of Pepsi-Cola, scored a publicity coup when Khrushchev happily handed out cups of the soda as part of a taste test between American and Russian brands. "Our advertising at the time was 'Be Sociable, Have a Pepsi,'" remembered Kendall, "and there were pictures all over the world of Khrushchev handing out Pepsis and the headline was 'Khrushchev Learns to Be Sociable.'")

The two sides, edging toward a new relationship, were still feeling each other out. Despite the sparring, everyone wanted to move toward an easing of tensions.

"It all served Khrushchev's purpose," says Frankel about the opening to the West. If there were any political calculations behind the decision to allow Van to win, they were indeed paying off. Almost immediately the frigid relations with America began to melt at a swifter pace. Khrushchev would travel to the United States the following year—a visit capped by talks with President Eisenhower at Camp David. He was able to use the political ammunition he gained from that show of respect to further his own programs.

"When he came back from America, he started an economic campaign that by Russian standards was inconceivable," says Frankel. Khrushchev wanted his country to gear up to beat American production, and the new policy was a way for him to admit that the Soviets were behind. It gave him a starting point. "Catch Up with America" became the new slogan. "Far from seeing America as the enemy," said Frankel, "he was trying to move his country closer to what America was accomplishing."

The impact of Van's win had other serious consequences behind Soviet doors, where cultural authorities began to devote more of an effort to picking over what had transpired at the event.

In truth, they regarded the outcome as a defeat, and naturally they wanted to avoid a repetition. At the same time, Moscow's leading musical figures continued to reflect a genuine appreciation for Van's talents.

Richter praised Cliburn, Pollack, and Lowenthal in glowing terms in *Sovetskaya Kultura*. Both he and Kabalevsky, writing in the same magazine, expressed regret that Pollack's concerto performances had fallen short of what he had accomplished in earlier rounds. But Shostakovich—or what was portrayed as having been written by Shostakovich—didn't pass up the opportunity to pour cold water on the warming atmosphere. He declared most of America's musical accomplishments as having come not from artists born in America but rather from "countries of the European continent," rendering Van's achievement as a fluke. In a similar vein, the publication *Soviet Russia* continued to insist that Van was a Soviet discovery, and set him up as an exception against the "abstract, ultra-modern bourgeois" fare that usually came from the United States. The theme of America's cultural backwardness continued.

Surprisingly, in a serious post-competition autopsy, the Central Committee of the Communist Party turned its attention to the deficits on the Soviet side. It was "worth noting that, in the end, Van Cliburn is also a pupil of the Russian piano school as he studied under Professor Lhévinne, who in her own time graduated from the Moscow Conservatory in the class of Professor [Vasily] Safonov," noted its report. Nonetheless, it continued, the foreign performances made necessary a close examination of the young Soviet players, as well as of their preparation and training. It was not the first time the Central Committee had gone through such an exercise. In 1955, with Soviet musicians turning in disappointing showings in several international competitions, the same call was raised for an inspection of the training methods used to prepare them. The conclusions were twofold and contradictory: juries were biased against Soviet performers; but the conservatories also had become sloppy and lazy. (There was always someone to blame for every problem.)

The postmortem on the Tchaikovsky was equally dour. Even at their best, the majority of Soviet musicians "turned out to be extremely similar to each other with only one difference, that some were more technically spotless, while others less. The biggest flaw of many Soviet performers at the competition was the absence of an individual creative image." This may explain, said the committee, why the jury preferred French pianist Gedda-Nova and the Japanese Matsuura—"always unique but far from flawless"—to the large group of more technically accomplished Soviets who lacked "bright, original performance traits."

The analysis stopped short of considering how the Soviet political culture and its overwhelming pressures to conform—its insistence that individuality was a crime against the revered spirit of collectivism—might contribute to this state of affairs. It pointed instead to ostensible faults in Soviet musical training, "where the most attention is given to the development of [the players'] technical skills and not 'creative individualism,'" and called for a return to the "pre-revolutionary" practice of limiting the number of students admitted to programs, so that each could work with a top professor. It complained of an attitude of complacency in the conservatories. It recommended a retreat on the world stage—pulling back for a retrenchment—by limiting the foreign tours of young Soviets, who had developed an attitude of "conceit" and "neglect," as well as curtailing their participation in international competitions.

Did that report have an effect? In the years following that first competition, the Russians produced important, unique voices in the piano world. Still, when asked if any changes were actually made in the way conservatory students were taught at that time, Vera Gornostaeva smiled with a hint of condescension. "It's a very naive question," she said. In her view, the report itself was political nonsense.

Each teacher in the school has always been an individual, she claimed. "You can't say our country has been very free." So why, she asks, do Russian pianists today play with such freedom? Why do the French on the other hand play with so much pressure? Her answer is that artistic sensibilities transcend politics. The training at the Moscow Conservatory is the best in the world, insisted Gornostaeva. What the Central Committee misunderstood is that talent can't be manufactured: "It is given by God. Van Cliburn," she explained, "had something that couldn't be taught."

CHAPTER 10

Red, White, and Blues

THOUGH IT HAD ALL BEEN EXHAUSTING, Van's pace in Moscow never slowed. He managed to keep going through sheer exuberance, though he lost a great deal of weight.

The pianist's features were immortalized in a "life mask," to be preserved at the Moscow Conservatory. He was taken to Tchaikovsky's home, where he spent an entire day under the glare of klieg lights, being photographed while playing the composer's piano. A victory lap of performances brought him to Leningrad; Kiev in the Ukraine; Minsk, Byelorussia; and Riga, Latvia. In Latvia, musicologist Solomon Volkov, author of the notorious Shostakovich "memoir," was moved to tears by Van's playing. "Riga was off limits to most foreigners," says Volkov, so the very fact of the pianist's appearance carried special significance. Van's artistry, though, is what made the day so memorable. "It was the first time I ever cried on hearing the Rachmaninoff Third Concerto," he confessed.

In Leningrad, Van visited Tchaikovsky's grave at the Tikhvin Cemetery and scooped up some soil to bring to Rachmaninoff's grave in Valhalla, New York, along with a lilac bush he had received from fans to plant there. During that visit to Valhalla, in the company of Kirill Kondrashin, the conductor would take a handful of soil from Rachmaninoff's grave to bring back to Tchaikovsky's resting place—completing a symbolic circle across the great US–USSR divide.

Just before heading home, the Tchaikovsky winner gave a valedictory concert in Moscow. "I can still remember the details about how he played," said Vera Gornostaeva, pointing to a small, unexpected moment as evidence of Van's love for the people who came to see him. "He had just finished the Tchaikovsky, and already the audience members were 'on their heads,' and applauding for a long time. Kondrashin picked up his baton, but a young girl had given Van a note." A video of the performance shows the pianist holding the folded note and using it to scrape away the tiny blossoms and twigs from tossed bouquets that had fallen between the cracks of the piano keys. Kondrashin was ready to begin the Rachmaninoff Third Concerto. But Van couldn't wait to read what he had been handed—which was probably a fan letter. "He had such a strong relationship with the audience that he picked it up and started to read it at the piano, while Kondrashin continued to stand and wait," said Gornostaeva. "Everyone laughed. Finally, he put it on the floor and nodded to the conductor. When he began to play it was pure genius from the first to the last. The whole audience sat hypnotized."

That act was a key to understanding Van's nature. As Mary Lou Falcone explains it, "For Van, it wasn't about playing the piano. I think the piano was merely his vehicle for communicating. It could have been anything." His interest was less in the instrument than in the gratification he felt from touching people, and being touched in turn. "His fragility didn't show," says Falcone. "Yet his heart was the biggest heart I've ever encountered. The spirit of generosity, the loving—it was more than in anyone else I've ever known."

After the Rachmaninoff, as applause and shouts of "Bravo!" filled the hall, a bouquet of flowers appeared, and the pianist handed it to Kondrashin. The audience stood, clapped rhythmically, and rushed to the stage to shower him with gifts: first flowers, a balalaika—which he received with giddy excitement, his lips forming a rubbery oval in a gesture of exaggerated surprise—and then more flowers. They would join a growing stockpile of other items that he had been given: a landscape painting from a professor in Leningrad; a huge porcelain plate; a treasured family photograph; a leather-bound volume of Shakespeare sonnets; amber and silver jewelry; a satin evening bag with matching gloves for his mother; bottles of perfume; ceramics and antique enamels.

His encores that day included a Rachmaninoff prelude and his ever-ready sentimental favorite, the Schumann-Liszt "Widmung" (Dedication), from the poem by Friedrich Rückert: "You my soul, you my heart, you my bliss . . ." But it was the final encore that drew gasps. "He was a big child, really, and that's what made him so charismatic," explained Gornostaeva. "He came out and he was crying and blowing kisses, and said, 'I have fallen in love with you.' Then he sat down and played 'Evenings Outside Moscow' ['Podmoskovnye Vechera,' more familiar as 'Moscow Nights'] with his own improvised accompaniment. The audience started crying. It was so naive and beautiful." The scene in the concert hall couldn't have been more uplifting. With his parting gesture, Van hit a home run.

Hundreds of fans showed up at the Moscow airfield for his return home, many standing on the roof of a building to wave goodbye. On the flight, as he stared through the window at the clouds below, he finally had time to think. In the frantic hubbub of the competition and its aftermath, with one surprise following another, he could hardly digest what had happened. Now his parents would be meeting him in New York in anticipation of the historic ticker-tape parade to be held in his honor.

The official account of the event appeared in the *New York Herald Tribune*. "I was in Mayor [Robert] Wagner's office about the time the news of Van Cliburn's winning of the prize reached New York," parade organizer Robert W. Dowling told reporter Robert S. Bird. "The Mayor turned to me and said, 'This is a wonderful thing. Van Cliburn's winning the Russian prize. We ought to give him a great reception here.' I heartily agreed and the Mayor asked me if I would take charge as chairman."

That wasn't the full story. *The New York Times* had been lobbying city hall to create the event. After turning Van's Moscow win into headline news around the world, the paper was doing its best to continue the story's forward momentum. As soon as the results in Moscow were released on April 13, Michael Caracappa of *The New York Times International Edition* sent a telegram to Mayor Wagner, urging him to stage a parade. "Since our city takes pride in being [the] cultural center of the world," it read, "it would be, I respectfully submit, a heartwarming gesture to greet Van Cliburn, U.S. winner of Soviet piano contest, with [a] Broadway ticker parade as an incentive to American youths everywhere." Within days a hastily assembled organizing committee was at work.

No one realized that the music world would be reluctant to join in. Even Juilliard at first resisted the idea of giving students time off from classes to participate in the parade, though it did eventually come around. "All we're trying to prove is that there are thousands of potential Van Cliburns and that every music teacher is doing a job that we respect and admire," said Dowling. Yet responses to invitations by Richard C. Patterson Jr., commissioner of the Department of Commerce and Public Events, were lamentable. Many institutions claimed their music departments were simply not set up for "marching" or for supplying bands. Even the First Army declined to furnish its usual ticker-tape band, "because somebody in the military brass decided the celebration was 'too commercial,'" it was reported.

Apparently, wrote the *Herald Tribune,* there was a backlash in some quarters, with some voicing resentment that "American winners of top music prizes offered in this country are never publicly feted"—an odd argument at a time when one of the nation's top musicians was being praised—and bitterness that American contestants had to turn "to private philanthropy rather than to [enjoy] government or municipal support." Why any of that should stand in the way of celebrating Van's achievement, or of recognizing the potential for musicians to have a dramatic impact on the world, is unclear. There seemed to be a good deal of petty jealousy at work, along with some anticommunist jitters.

Cold War worries were still in the air, of course. Juilliard dean Mark Schubart received letters objecting to the entire enterprise. One correspondent likened Van to a Trojan horse: "It is a pity to see an artist become embroiled in politics when he doesn't know what the score is . . ." Most unfortunate, claimed the writer, was that this pianist accepted the patronage "of people who have stunned the civilized world with their unabating and wholesale criminal acts."

The mayor was also subject to angry missives: "Comrade Wagner, What the hell did Cliburn the pianist do for America USA to deserve a parade at the taxpayers' expense? Cultural relations or exchanges with our no. 1 enemy the Moscow Butchers? Is this it? We demand a stop to Red dancers here and parades to those that go to Russia. Let the red traitors here go there and stay there. P.S. We want no unionized cops either. This is the U.S.A."

The disappointing response on the part of institutions forced the city to change its concept. Instead of a parade of college-level musicians, it would settle for nine hundred junior-high-school pupils marching to a dozen bands, "including high school [bands], [and] Boy Scout and Girl Scout bands." The celebration would also include a folk-dancing contingent from Yeshiva College, plus a chorus of three thousand high-school music students. Despite the critics, it promised to be fun.

Cliburn's plane touched down at New York's Idlewild Airport at 9:45 in the morning on May 16, where he was met by a gaggle of reporters ready to pounce. Why did he call Khrushchev a nice man? Why did he call the Russians "my" people? "You must think you're a big success," came one accusatory lob. "Oh no, I'm not a success. I'm just a sensation," he replied.

Flanked by his parents, and wearing his typical black jacket and dark, thin tie, he responded to a question about what the Russians were like. Haltingly, as if deep in thought, lips pursed and eyebrows arched, the pianist doled out his response at the leisurely pace of a Texas turtle on a hot afternoon, emphasizing each salient point with a variety of head shakes and eye rolls. "They . . . are very *warm* individuals," he stated. "They *love* . . . very *strongly*. And yet they are very sincere as people. As a matter of fact, I . . . couldn't refrain from telling them that they are much like Texans," he confided with a small chuckle. This last revelation, delivered with a hiccup of a shrug, as if he had just told himself a secret joke, led to his folksy conclusion. "If a Texan likes something, he'll tell you. And if he doesn't, he'll certainly let you know."

Hours later, "after he had left a gift lilac bush at the terminal for clearance by plant quarantine authorities," reported *The New York Times*, Cliburn arrived at a twenty-second-floor suite at the Pierre Hotel, accompanied by seventeen suitcases filled with gifts. The room featured a piano, reported the *Times*, which was soon "piled high, not with sheet music but with souvenirs. So was most of the furniture in the room." Over time, he would amass many roomfuls of odd, emotionally piquant objects— not only antiques, but old wilted and crumbled flowers, saved as sentimental keepsakes. Among the items he displayed at the hotel were "several sets of silver cups and a miniature of the Czar Kolokol, a famous Russian bell from which a wedge was cracked when its scaffolding burned and collapsed in 1737. The [original] unrung 200-pound bell is now a showpiece within the Kremlin."

At Van's insistence, and through the exertions of both the American embassy and official agencies in Moscow, Kondrashin was also on his way to serve as conductor for the pianist's planned concerts. On Monday, May 19, they made their highly anticipated American debut together at Carnegie Hall, where, noted the *New York World-Telegram* about Cliburn, "the boy is so tall and thin, he had the appearance of a rope hanging from the ceiling, until he bowed and smiled." Van was only slightly late this time, arriving backstage five minutes after Kondrashin had started the concert with a performance of Prokofiev's "Classical" Symphony.

"He played with such bravura and nuance," reported *Time*, "that the audience paid him the rare tribute of thunderous applause between movements." The *Times* noted that out of the entire hall only two people seemed to refrain from joining in the ovation after each of Van's two featured concertos (naturally, he played the Tchaikovsky and Rachmaninoff works with which he had won the contest). "Every time waves of applause swept the house," came the report, "a man and a woman, seated in the center of the first-tier boxes, sat stiffly, with folded hands.

"They were Harvey Lavan Cliburn, Sr., and his wife, the former Rildia Bee O'Bryan. They seemed not so much bursting with pride—and perhaps disbelief—as transfixed by it." Or, more likely, they were vigilantly keeping watch against the sin of vanity.

For Kondrashin, the trip to America was like winning the lottery. Most Russian artists had to turn over almost all of their foreign earnings; he was allowed to keep 50 percent of the fee. Van had wanted to give the conductor a car as a sign of his gratitude, but now that Kondrashin was flush with cash, he bought himself a Czech Koda. He quickly learned to play the Western game of free agent: When his fee was delayed, he simply threatened to speak to the press, and the problem disappeared. At the end of his tour he craftily left his hotel with the bill unpaid, and Van's manager, Bill Judd, had to settle his expenses.

Who could blame him for making the most of his luck? The conductor had certainly witnessed life's inconstancies. His teacher, composer Nikolai Zhilyaev, a respected associate of Scriabin and Rachmaninoff, had been denounced as an enemy of the people and sent to an internment camp, where he died during the war. And life for Kondrashin had not always been easy. He developed his skills in the lion's den of the Leningrad Philharmonic, with its long-standing reputation for destroying even the finest conductors. (During the 1920s, one of the ensemble's senior musicians, Ilya Brik, would routinely undermine guest maestros by removing his handkerchief as a signal for the orchestra to follow him, not the conductor. The musicians were proud to uphold that legacy.) What's more, the critics were not always kind. When Kondrashin had collaborated with Isaac Stern during the violinist's visit in 1956, a review in *Soviet Life* claimed that the Mendelssohn concerto would have gone better without a conductor. But at the Tchaikovsky Competition, his every moment with Van was pure magic. Now he was reaping the rewards.

Performing with Van was its own prize in a way. Though the pianist's "old-fashioned bravura" was alien to him, Kondrashin found the American's "liberated playing" and the sound he achieved "remarkable." Their concerts and the best-selling recording they would make together were tremendous successes. The conductor would travel with Van and his parents to meet the president of the United States.

The two artists did not see eye to eye on everything, of course. Kondrashin was privately concerned about his young colleague, wrote the conductor's biographer, Gregor Tassie. "Why do you play only two works in concert?" he asked. "In America, there are two hundred orchestras and it will take up a lot of time to tour all of them, but what else are you going to play afterwards?" Van contended that a new generation would grow up and they would want to hear him play Rachmaninoff and Tchaikovsky.

"You will earn enough money and you can go abroad, you can even come to the Soviet Union," Kondrashin said. "Just sit in on rehearsals, go to concerts, listen to opera and assimilate musical life, identify with true academicism, your music needs this." It was the kind of advice he had already received from other quarters, including Rudolf Serkin. "No, Kirill," he replied. "You don't understand that if I don't play in the States someone else will take my place and no one will want to hear me anymore."

The issue truly weighed on him. Abram Chasins asked Van during an interview how he planned "to read, to study, to consider and reconsider new works and try them out in unexposed places, to find leisure for the absorption and reflection which alone can bring maturity. Before answering, he took a deep drag at the cigarette that never leaves his hand except when he is playing," reported Chasins. "Then he said, 'That's exactly what worries me.' He spoke not with the air of a wonder boy with the world before him, but like one whose time is running out."

In public, Van drew on a stock of lofty aphorisms in defense of sticking with the tried and true. "Choose carefully which works to learn, and never let them go; they will always be your friends," he told a *Time* correspondent. After coming under increasing fire for playing the same repertoire over and over, he would contend that "in classical music, there is no such thing as a twice-told tale." The young pianist wasn't entirely closed to the idea of expanding his repertoire, or of getting help from others, however. He'd soon travel to Los Angeles to study the Brahms Second Piano Concerto with conductor Bruno Walter. Yet Kondrashin's warning and Van's responses explain a good deal about the difficulties the pianist would encounter as time rolled on.

For the moment, the money and the concert dates were pouring in. On that front, the Tchaikovsky win had changed everything.

"Bill Judd was in our apartment on Fifty-fifth Street," remembers Gary Graffman, "when the results were announced. We were all sitting on the floor, on a rug that Schuyler Chapin had given us. In no time, Bill was on the phone talking to his brother, George." The New York Philharmonic had been booking young artists for a series on Saturday mornings and Sunday afternoons for a fee of $500, and Van was one of them. But now Judd got on the phone and said, " 'Georgie, we're going to have to review this contract,' and he got it up to $2,000, which was phenomenal at that time." Indeed, the highest-paid instrumentalist then was violinist Jascha Heifetz, whose fee was $3,500, according to Naomi Graffman. After the renegotiation, the Philharmonic announced that Van would now play four concerts with the ensemble instead of one.

Cliburn's rising fee affected the entire industry; and as his compensation increased, the trend continued. When Van's charge for a performance eventually reached $5,000, Arthur Rubinstein began to insist on $6,000. Before long, the economics of musical performance were universally reconfigured. *Time* predicted that Van would earn $125,000 in the first year after his gold medal performance. It was only one sign of success. Another was the ticker-tape parade, planned for the day after his Carnegie Hall performance. It proved to be spectacular.

All the resistance to that event mattered not a whit. Juilliard's William Schuman accepted chairmanship of the parade. The date, May 20, was named "American Music Day." As the pianist and his parents rode in an open car along lower Broadway, "as far as you could see both ways, there were people," reported the Associated Press. "People crowded a dozen deep on the sidewalks. People on tops of cars. People hanging out of windows 30 to 40 stories high, tossing out coils and scraps of paper." Estimates put the size of the crowd at 100,000. Cliburn blew kisses to all of them. Mayor Wagner's official proclamation urged "New Yorkers, young and old alike, to show their appreciation of this great talent and those who brought it to fruition . . ." The entire parade was broadcast live on New York's municipal radio station, WNYC.

The pianist repaid the city with a check for $1,250, taken from his Tchaikovsky prize money. He had offered to give it to the Rockefeller Foundation in gratitude for their funding of his plane ride to Moscow. They demurred. He specified only that the money be used "on behalf of creative artists and cultural welfare."

His performing tour gained steam, taking him to a host of cities, both domestically and abroad, including Washington, DC, on May 23, where he finally met with President Eisenhower. The president and his wife opted to skip his concert that evening. The only people in Washington who thought to celebrate his arrival with the proper amount of fanfare, noted *The Washington Post*, were members of the Soviet embassy, who hosted a dinner in his honor.

The tour was tiring, but he kept going. "Van and Kondrashin performed the Tchaikovsky and Rachmaninoff at Symphony Hall in Newark [New Jersey]," recalls Gary Graffman. "I went in a limo with [soprano] Renata Tebaldi, and Van and his mother were in another limo. At the concert, I sat next to Rildia Bee. Afterward, it was pandemonium, and he came out again and played 'Dedication.' I said to his mother, 'I don't know how he can do that after playing two concertos, as if it was nothing.' And she looked at me and said, 'Honey, that's where God comes in.'"

"Right around that time," remembered Schuyler Chapin, "everywhere he went it was hysteria." Walking down the street, he would find people reaching out to touch him and tearing at his clothes. Then, one night he telephoned Chapin from his doctor's office and asked if he could come over. "He was strung out," remembered Chapin. "He walked in, and looked sort of messianic, and stunk of medicine—you know, that odd odor of pills or [castor] oil—and he was exhausted. He spent that night on the sofa in our living room. The next morning the phone started to ring—people were looking for him. He had been seeing the infamous Dr. Jacobson, who was pumping him full of amphetamines."

It was a warning of worse things to come. Soon after, as he rehearsed for an appearance on *The Steve Allen Show*, the pianist finally came apart. "When Van got back," explained Chapin, "the two engagements he wanted to fulfill immediately were with Skitch Henderson on *The Steve Allen Show* . . . and a lady in South Bend, Indiana, who had been a supporter. I had the pleasure of calling her and saying, 'Mr. Cliburn would like to play for you.'"

Chapin remembered the appearance on the television show clearly because, he contended, it was the only time jazz trumpeter Louis Armstrong had ever been upstaged. "They were rehearsing," he said, "and Steve Allen had a record cover from RCA [of Van's impending album]. Van looked at it and blew up—something I had never seen before. He took it and tore it up into pieces, and stomped off to his dressing room in the old Century Theater. Bill Judd called Dr. Jacobson, who came down."

The doctor—"a hulking, disheveled figure," according to Marilyn Monroe biographer Barbara Leaming, who wore "large horn-rimmed glasses with thick lenses [that] magnified roaming, unsettled eyes"—brought along a little black bag. He turned to Van, said Chapin, and murmured, "'Now Van, what is this all about?' There was a period of half an hour, and Steve Allen was very concerned. Van came down and he was calm." With a fresh injection, the emotional storm was over.

Jacobson's assistant, Harvey Mann, remembered Van's first visit to the doctor. "He was suffering badly from colitis. Max, in that godlike way of his, took him over. No matter what a patient had when he came to Max, hangnails to cancer, Max was confident he could cure it. And his cure for all of them was injections that had speed in the mix." The effects inevitably included severe mood swings.

"It was sad," remarked Chapin. "Perhaps his treatments were gentle at first. Van kept saying he was being injected with 'oxygen' and vitamins. If I had had any real prescience, I would have shot Dr. Jacobson right there in the Century Theater." The incident instead remained a secret. In a *New York Times* review at the time by Jack Gould, Van was praised as "not only a virtuoso but a personality," fascinating to watch and notable for "his meticulous good manners." It was the sanitized face of the Cliburn persona. A scandal had been narrowly averted.

The touring continued. In Chicago's Grant Park, the crowds stretched as far as the eye could see for both of his concerts. After the first night's performance, Van came down with a fever of 103 degrees; a doctor told him to cancel, but he refused to disappoint the people who had come out to hear him. Next came the Hollywood Bowl and New York's Lewisohn Stadium.

The grueling schedule was unlike anything he had ever faced before. By August, he was already talking to journalists about a time when he might find relief from the demands of his new high-pressure career. "I'm going to build a house . . . someday," he said. "It will be comfortable, old-fashioned . . . but always warm and sincere. Each night has to be a new experience, because if it becomes an old experience, then the audience knows it. When it fails to be new, I'll quit."

He finally announced a sorely needed vacation, but quickly cancelled it to play at the Brussels World's Fair with a Russian orchestra. Then, like a beneficent parent avoiding a show of favoritism toward his children, he flew to Heidelberg to perform for United States Army servicemen and their families. The pace continued.

Cliburn's appearance in Brussels with the Russians was a nod toward the political thaw that had now blossomed. Nevertheless, the propaganda machines of both nations were still firing away at full throttle, and the World's Fair became a battleground for each side as it tried to entice potential converts to its cause. In the Soviet pavilion, which stood under the gaze of a fifty-foot-tall bronze statue of Lenin, an aura of technological brilliance and cultural richness was carefully projected. Visiting artists included the Bolshoi Ballet and the Moscow Circus.

It was up to the Americans to find a suitable counterargument. In considering what theme would best represent America, the State Department had initially rejected "life, liberty, and the pursuit of happiness" as too "corny." A three-day symposium to find a fitting alternative took place in March 1957 with the participation of psychological-warfare veterans from MIT, including Walt W. Rostow. The conclusion? "The dominant theme should be, simply stated, that the United States constitutes a society in ferment." From a marketing standpoint, the suggestion was a disaster.

The MIT experts thought the best course of action was for America openly to admit its social problems. The group quickly hit sour notes with a newspaper montage showing police violence against blacks. The State Department was proven wise in its perennial mistrust of well-meaning academics. On the positive side, the American pavilion also offered a range of sunny entertainments, with fashion shows, jukeboxes, a hot-dog stand,

and a 360-degree motion-picture tour of the United States produced by Disney. These were seen as more attractive than the
Soviet Union's machine tools, reported one American journalist.

President Eisenhower had insisted on the inclusion of voting machines at the exhibit—as a reminder of the joys of a free
society—allowing visitors to choose their favorite presidents,
movie stars, and musicians by registering their preferences from
behind a curtain. Anastas Mikoyan showed up and chose Abra-
ham Lincoln, Kim Novak, and Louis Armstrong (when he was
told that Shostakovich was not an option). Boris Agapov, a member of the board of the Soviet magazine *Novy Mir*, dismissed the
show of American opulence and political openness as a pack of
lies. This was one event, however, in which the Soviet side clearly
came up short.

While Cliburn shared the stage with Soviet musicians in a
show of cultural cooperation, the CIA was funneling Russian-
language copies of *Doctor Zhivago*—a book banned by the
Kremlin—to Soviet visitors. Taking to heart Maxim Gorky's
1934 statement that books are "the most important and powerful weapons in socialist culture," the American spy organization
arranged for Boris Pasternak's novel to be secretly distributed
through the Vatican pavilion.

What especially vexed the Soviets about Pasternak's work were
lines like these, spoken by the title character: "Revolutions are
made by fanatical men of action with one-track minds, men who
are narrow-minded to the point of genius. They overturn the old
order in a few hours or days . . . but for decades thereafter, for
centuries, the spirit of narrowness which led to the upheaval is
worshipped as holy."

Distributing the banned book was a way of contrasting
freedom-loving America with the restrictive Soviet apparatus. In

truth, America was also experienced at playing the censorship game. At the beginning of the decade, the FBI had worked to stifle the publication in the United States of Howard Fast's novel *Spartacus*. The author spent three months in prison for refusing to answer questions posed by a congressional committee as part of the Communist witch hunt. Eight major publishers went along with J. Edgar Hoover, and the author was forced to self-publish in 1951.

However, the Pasternak ploy at the fair proved startlingly effective. "Soon the book's blue linen covers were found littering the fairgrounds," wrote Peter Finn and Petra Couvée, authors of *The Zhivago Affair*. "Some who got the novel were ripping off the cover, dividing the pages, and stuffing them in their pockets to make the book easier to hide." No doubt, as he performed, Van was blissfully unaware of the underground battle of ideas taking place all around him.

As the year came to a close, Van's feverish schedule, his fame, and his album sales all continued to grow. In February he was hospitalized after experiencing unbearable pain in one of his fingers during a performance at a convention in Atlantic City. In some ways it was actually a lucky turn of events. His long-anticipated rest was about to be imposed. As the headline in the *New York Herald Tribune* proclaimed: "Van Cliburn Has Surgery on Hand; His Concerts Off." Following the emergency procedure, announced the paper, he would cancel "his concerts of the next few months, including one for 18,000 students at Madison Square Garden on March 16"—a special benefit he was to do for public, private, and parochial schools within the five New York City boroughs.

Again, Dr. Jacobson's "miracle" treatments had nearly fomented a disaster. Chapin said he suspected something was awry when he noticed that Van seemed exhausted, and that, strangely, "one finger was bandaged and the others were filthy dirty. I thought, Why doesn't someone take care of that?" The bandage displayed the kind of unhygienic state that visitors to Jacobson's office would find familiar.

One of his nurses described the place as grimy, an unsanitary mess, with used hypodermic syringes, a jumble of unmarked bottles, and the evidence of bodily fluids everywhere. It seems that Van had become another item among Jacobson's tainted detritus. In a way, the situation was a metaphor for the emotional chaos that was slowly enveloping the pianist's life.

The finger episode began with an infection in a cuticle, which Van went to Jacobson to have treated. "Max put a needle into the infection and injected it, then coated the finger with . . . a substance like airplane glue," reported Harvey Mann. "Van got through the concert all right, but by the time he got to his dressing room that finger, which had been puffy to begin with, was now the size of his wrist. It was a frightening sight, this sausage-like finger on the hand of this great young pianist. Van's manager rushed him to the Hospital [for Special Surgery] where an emergency team of surgeons went to work on his finger. Later on, Van told me that the head surgeon had said that another hour or so [and] they might have been forced to amputate the finger. But you know something?" Mann recounted. "A week later Van was back in Max's office, getting his regular shots."

Chapin never had to carry through with his threat of shooting Jacobson. The doctor's practice was exposed in the press in 1969, when Kennedy photographer Mark Shaw died at the age of forty-seven after receiving treatments, and by 1975 Jacobson's office was closed down by government officials. The doctor was charged with forty-eight counts of unprofessional conduct, and his license was forever revoked.

In 1959 big changes were afoot in the pianist's life. By the end of the year Bill Judd would be dropped in favor of Sol Hurok. Cliburn's contract with him included a clause naming Rildia Bee as his road manager; her job was apparently to keep him in line, and onstage. RCA producer Max Wilcox recalled a line that Mrs. Cliburn used constantly about her son: "Well, he's a nice boy," she would say, "but sometimes I could just wring his neck." When it came to Van, she would tolerate no breach of professional decorum.

Jascha Heifetz once declared that to lead the life of a virtuoso, "it takes the nerves of a bullfighter, the digestion of a peasant, the vitality of a nightclub hostess, the tact of a diplomat, and the concentration of a Tibetan monk." Van had some of those qualities, but not the required nerves or healthy digestion. The professional commitments began to take their toll.

Just a year after the phenomenal Moscow win, critic Paul Henry Lang was writing about the pianist's being "hounded and clobbered by the public and entrepreneurs." Now, if anyone was to do the clobbering, it would be his mother, who had always been his harshest critic. That suited Hurok and Rildia Bee. However, at this point Van could occasionally be seen moping despondently around Beefburger Hall.

There were, of course, some bright spots. A Soviet youth delegation visiting the United States—an outcome of the softening relations Cliburn had helped foster—brought his competition friend Lev Vlassenko to New York as one of twenty-four actors, musicians, scientists, and, as Vlassenko wrote in his diary of the 1959 trip, "KGB people masked as students." His main interest in coming to the United States, he wrote, was to see "Vanya."

The diary records Vlassenko's reactions in detail while he waits for his friend at a concert in Carnegie Hall. The concert starts—a Haydn symphony under the direction of Thomas Schippers. "Magnificent orchestra!" he says. But predictably, there is still no Van. The group decides to step outside, into the street. "Suddenly a familiar lanky figure in [an] English coat with the familiar mane of ripe rye appears," writes the Soviet pianist. They run towards each other and hug. Van has gained some weight, notices Vlassenko, though his skin color is off due to some substance or other he has taken. They return together to the concert, taking box seats. The conductor, he decides, is mediocre.

At the intermission they want to leave, but stay out of politeness. Afterward, as they go backstage to congratulate the conductor and the soloist, pianist Jascha Spivakovsky, people ask for Van's autograph, which he gives—"even on dollar bills. He is charming, as always."

Together they visit a friend who has a bottle of Armenian three-star cognac, but Van's health is spotty, as usual, and he explains that he is allowed neither liquor nor sweets. They sing. Vlassenko conducts. Van cries. Then it's off to Van's apartment. It's a gorgeous building, notes Vlassenko, though the place has only two rooms—a bedroom and a studio—with "a little kitchen and a little foyer. Paintings are piled up in the foyer." The bedroom is filled with curios and antiques. There is a Bible in a black cover near the bed. A "wonderful" concert piano takes up nearly the whole studio. While food is being prepared, Vlassenko plays—Scarlatti, Mozart, Beethoven's "Tempest" Sonata—and Van listens from his position on the floor. Then it's the American's turn: He performs "Widmung," of course, and a little of Chopin's Concerto in E Minor.

"He seems a little out of shape," remarks Vlassenko of his friend's technique, and Van tells him that he doesn't practice, and has stopped playing in public. But conductor Bruno Walter has invited him to record concertos by Brahms and Chopin. (The resistance to practice was not unusual for him after his student days, but it placed Van in stark contrast to others at the top of the field. Cellist Pablo Casals was asked, at the age of eighty, why he continued to practice four or five hours a day. "Because," he replied, "I think I am making progress.")

After their chat, reports Vlassenko, Van plays "Moscow Nights," and they sing. "I promise to write down the words in transliteration," says the Georgian. They drink beer out of cans, and Van produces a huge tin of black caviar, which they eat with spoons. Afterward, they drive to a jam session led by Willie Ruff, the jazz horn and bass player, who had just recently performed in the Soviet Union with pianist Dwike Mitchell.

Finally, back at Van's apartment, they talk until three a.m. Van gives him a score of the Barber Sonata. Vlassenko writes out the words to "Moscow Nights." But Vlassenko is not entirely comfortable with their interactions, which seem awkward. Van, he says, is very "nicey-nice" and tries to please everyone. Vlassenko tells him that all of Moscow is waiting for his return, but he learns that the pianist is a little afraid of revisiting the site of his victory—who could measure up to that previous success? They drink tea with lemon. Van puts on a recording of Barber's opera *Vanessa*—his "favorite"; he wants it to be produced in Russia.

"It seems to me that he is not very well read, but there is so much nobility in him," reports Vlassenko, attempting to understand his companion more deeply. Van gets easily carried away, he says, but regards Moscow as something unrepeatable. He looks young and fresh, yet "there is an impression, confirmed by Madame Lhévinne, that he is in crisis, depression. I am afraid that they can destroy him here!"

The next morning, Vlassenko further reflects on the visit. It was his best time in America, he declares, but he was also a little disappointed. "Van is very nice to me and even tender," he reveals, but there seems to be some kind of restraint or mistrust. He knows that Van was warmer toward Shtarkman. "I just want us to be cordially closer," he confesses. Could Vlassenko have been unaware that Cliburn and Shtarkman shared a sexual orientation (a dangerous one) that might have led to a more sympathetic understanding between them, an easing of normal personal defenses? In any event, his sentiments are touching. Like almost everyone else, Vlassenko wanted something more from the acclaimed pianist. But Van was a difficult man to get close to, perhaps now more than ever.

CHAPTER II

The Van Effect

K HRUSHCHEV WAS INVITED to the White House, and Van wasn't. A year after the Moscow competition, it would have seemed natural to reunite the celebrated American pianist with his Soviet aficionados through a piano recital.

"Eisenhower chose to book pop music instead," explained Ambassador Thompson's daughter Sherry, "so Van told Khrushchev about this great piano at the White House, and how he wanted to play for him on this wonderful instrument. Thompson was not happy that he was trying to get that gig through Khrushchev." His attempt came to nothing.

Van accepted instead an invitation from the Soviet ambassador in Washington, Mikhail Menshikov, to a reception honoring Soviet First Deputy Premier Mikoyan. As *The New York Times* reported, the pianist was led to the Soviet embassy's grand piano, where he began playing "Moscow Nights." Mikoyan "and other Russians joined in the chorus." The Soviets met him once again with open arms.

Van extended his in return, offering gestures of goodwill to the Russians and the Americans in equal measure. On a trip to Russia in July 1960, he managed to stir Thompson and others present into a rousing rendition of "Moscow Nights" as part of a celebration of American Independence Day. The song had by now become a Cliburn standard, though Rildia Bee wasn't happy about that. She wished he would keep to the great classical works instead. He donated his earnings from a performance in Moscow during that trip—80,000 rubles (about $20,000)—to the city's sole, run-down Baptist church.

His relationship with Khrushchev had continued to deepen beyond the initial rush of publicity, and the premier's private home movies in 1962 include footage of the pianist visiting his country home. In a lengthy segment, Cliburn, wearing his traditional white shirt and dark tie, mingles with Khrushchev and guests as if part of his extended family. He sits with them while stroking a small dog in his lap (the pianist told the TASS News Agency that the trainers of Belka and Strelka, the Soviet dogs sent into space, had gifted him with a canine of his own); picks berries; plays the piano; and takes a motorboat ride on the Moscow River—a lit cigarette held casually in his fingers—as Khrushchev, in a wide-brimmed summer hat, relaxes beside him. The seeds of friendship he had planted in 1958 had truly taken root.

Van's bond with Russian people was equally strong. It did not automatically smooth the way for other Americans who wanted to gain their affections, especially when external events conspired to scuttle the diplomatic progress that had already been achieved.

American pianist Byron Janis made his Moscow debut through an artistic exchange program in 1960, but at the time the two superpowers were in the midst of heightened tension over the Soviet downing of an American U-2 spy plane over its territory. Janis recalled stepping onstage to shouts of "U-2! U-2!" followed by chants of "Klee-burn, Klee-burn!"

"For one frozen moment," wrote Janis, "I felt the ugly shock of being utterly alone, despite the presence of our ambassador, Llewellyn Thompson, and the entire U.S. Embassy staff." As he played, however, he could feel their hostility melting away as they listened. Music again worked its wonders. "When I first walked onto that stage I was literally the enemy," he wrote. "Now they saw I was just a human being, like them, who could please their deep musical spirit."

A second tour in 1962 brought Janis together with jazz clarinetist Benny Goodman in a performance of Gershwin's *Rhapsody in Blue*. "The Ministry of Culture tried to stop me," he wrote, "asking, 'How can you want to play such inferior music?' I stood up to them, saying Gershwin was one of our great composers . . . When I played the *Rhapsody* with Benny, it was not just the first live performance but the first time this music was heard in Russia at all." It was the sound of yet another bridge being built.

A decade earlier, merely showing respect toward American or European culture could be grounds for arrest. Even before Van Cliburn's appearance, things had already begun to change. When Isaiah Berlin, the Oxford don, visited a Russian writers' colony in 1956, the scholar reported that it was "like speaking to the victims of a shipwreck on a desert island, cut off for decades from civilization—all they heard they received as new, exciting and delightful." Khrushchev was responsible for much of this shift, despite his avowed hostility to the United States.

American cultural attaché Hans Tuch described the impact on Moscow of visiting artists like Isaac Stern and soprano Roberta Peters: "It is one of the strange contradictions of Soviet society that at the same time when Premier Khrushchev wrecks the Summit Meeting, when he heaps invective on the President of the United States and the American Government, and when the press is full of anti-American propaganda, the Soviet public can react so enthusiastically and genuinely to these artists." The schizophrenia reflected a widening gap between private attitudes and public policy. Van had encouraged that dissonance. The pianist, wrote Tuch, became "a symbol of the unifying friendship that overcomes old rivalries. Broadly speaking, it made him a symbol of art and humanity overruling political pragmatics." But he couldn't have accomplished it without a willing partner in the Kremlin.

Of course, antagonistic pronouncements toward the West continued. In November 1959, an official delegation of Soviet composers arrived in the United States, following a visit to the Soviet Union by American musicians, including Roy Harris, Ulysses Kay, Peter Mennin, and Roger Sessions. Several members of the Russian group wrote reflections of their trip. Dmitri Kabalevsky attacked émigré Igor Stravinsky's flirtations with the avant-garde—"What an ignominious end for a creative career so promisingly begun!"—disparaged "Broadway music" and Louis Armstrong's "strident tones . . . Hysteria, exaggerated crescendos, the tearing to shreds of any substance." Jazz seemed to him a disease, in which "the hypnotized jazzmaniacs began to twitch, stamp, snap their fingers, and even howl."

Soviet musicologist Boris Yarustovsky had his own host of criticisms, from the job insecurity faced by his Western colleagues to the "cult of violent combat" found on American television: "It is difficult to imagine a more dreadful, a more pathological spectacle." The young, he wrote, are too devoted to sensation and fashion, leading to the idolization of such terrible composers as Bartók, Schoenberg, and Messiaen. Yet, he concluded, "the wider and more systematic our contacts become, the greater the gain for the peace and people of the world."

Attitudes were undeniably shifting, and in 1959 Ian Fleming felt compelled to replace the villainous Soviet-backed SMERSH organization in his James Bond novels with a noncommunist criminal syndicate, SPECTRE. In another sign of cultural blending, the Soviets embraced their own version of Bond—a character named Avakum Zakhov—in a spy series by Bulgarian writer Andrei Gulyashki. Beginning with *The Zakhov Mission*, his books became best-sellers in the Eastern bloc.

The channeling of Soviet "students" into America—however high-minded the justification—turned out to be an enterprise rife with real spies. Oleg Kalugin was one of them. Nevertheless, his presence in the United States was naively met with fanfare, including a *New York Times* profile headlined "A Popular Russian." The article "went on to say that I was the son of a Leningrad city clerk and was chosen for the Fulbright student exchange by my professors at Leningrad University and by 'Soviet educational authorities.' I had to chuckle, of course," he later wrote. "It was all a lie. The Soviet educational establishment had not sent me to America for a year. The KGB had."

Anticommunist political conservatives who seemed to be standing in the way of progress were indeed right to be wary. Livingston Merchant, assistant secretary of state, said he had an "instinctive revulsion" against accepting Soviets into "one of our great universities . . . when we know that they would be carefully selected . . . to represent a philosophy which is dedicated to our destruction." He had a point.

Yet, the journey to America had unexpected consequences for agents like Kalugin. Even as he first traveled to an airport in the West, he experienced "the shock of leaving the gray, monochrome world of the Soviet Union and landing in a place virtually exploding with colors and sights." After a taste of American freedom, many of his colleagues similarly became instruments of a growing pro-Western democratic movement within the Soviet bureaucracy.

Kalugin, one of four members of the exchange assigned to Columbia University, explored the length and breadth of the American landscape—to the detriment of his minders. "We were treated to an intimate view of the American heartland," he wrote of his group, "which was then riding the boom years of the late 1950s. It was a land of Cadillacs and Chevrolets, of Zenith and Motorola TV consoles, of the latest refrigerators and dishwashers and toasters, of drive-ins and jukeboxes and countless miles of gorgeous roads. The supermarkets were packed with a dizzying description of goods, and everywhere the people seemed friendly and guileless . . . That trip—and all my time in America—gave me a brief twinge of doubt about our Communist system." The freedom he experienced to poke around the country and engage people in discussions contrasted sharply with the mood in his own country. "As the years went by and I would return to the USSR from operations abroad, I increasingly experienced the sense that I was slipping behind some gloomy Communist curtain."

Between 1958 and 1988, fifty thousand Soviet citizens visited the United States through cultural-exchange initiatives. Kalugin called the returning participants a "Trojan horse" within the Soviet Union. They "played a tremendous role in the erosion of the Soviet system. They kept infecting more and more people over the years."

One of the most startling examples was that of Alexander Yakovlev, a member of Kalugin's Columbia University group who had been sent by the Central Committee of the Communist Party. Yakovlev grew close to Mikhail Gorbachev, and ultimately became one of the architects of perestroika—the restructuring (and ultimate dissolution) of the Soviet empire. "In 1958," wrote Kalugin of Yakovlev, "no one would have dared predict that he would later team up with Gorbachev and Eduard Shevardnadze to begin the revolution that would ultimately topple Soviet Communism."

Though there was no straight line connecting the fall of the Soviet Union to the effect Van had in Moscow—obviously, many factors came into play—the pianist clearly contributed to the alchemy of that moment. It would be difficult to find a Muscovite who didn't think so.

Van's fame in his own country remained undiminished, and three years after the Tchaikovsky win, his appearance at New York's Lewisohn Stadium could still trigger a "melee." It "looked like the running of the bulls at Pamplona," reported *Time* in August 1961. "With elbow, knee and hip, the lovers of the arts and the avid curious jostled and shoved in a wild struggle to get inside. Those who failed craned their necks over the fences or peered from apartment house windows more than a block away. Inside, early arrivals snatched all available folding chairs, forcing many a reserved-seat ticket holder to hunker on the ground. The scene was an impressive if chaotic tribute to the continuing musical phenomenon known as Van Cliburn."

Critical response was another story. The *Los Angeles Times* had written in 1958 that he "fully merits all the adulation," citing "the formidable control of massive sonorities, the perfect control of tonal subtleties, and a sweeping disdain of manual difficulties . . . Even more remarkable in so young an artist," it continued, "was what might best be described as heart."

Two years later, Mozart was said by one critic to be "in his fingers but not in his emotional grasp." *The New York Times*'s Harold C. Schonberg complained that the pianist was "determined to underplay," and found Van's performance to be "over-careful" and lacking in tension, direction, or variety. None of this affected ticket sales in the least. Like a blockbuster movie railed against by weekend newspaper reviewers, Van was bigger than his critics.

He continued to oblige audience demands for the Tchaikovsky and Rachmaninoff concertos, while starting to voice other ambitions, including aspirations to make his mark as a conductor. "Conductors were each like kings in their own kingdoms," he said. "There was Fritz Reiner and the Chicago Symphony, Eugene Ormandy and Philadelphia, Erich Leinsdorf in Boston, Kirill Kondrashin in Moscow."

The idea began in 1961, when he was invited to play and conduct Prokofiev's Piano Concerto no. 3 with the Los Angeles Philharmonic in Carnegie Hall at a memorial concert for Dimitri Mitropoulos. Van paid $1,800 of his own money for three hours of rehearsal time with the orchestra, at which Bruno Walter stood by his side, coaching him at every step. He was also booked to give a recital the afternoon of the Carnegie date at Constitution Hall in Washington, DC—for which he arrived a mere twenty-two minutes late. He performed, flew quickly back to New York, and when he appeared onstage it was with the piano that Steinway had built in 1953 for Mitropoulos, who had played and conducted that same Prokofiev concerto. The instrument featured a plastic, see-through lid for ease in making visual contact with the orchestra.

The concert went well enough that an invitation to lead the Philadelphia Orchestra at its pension-fund concert came next. The offers rolled in. "I did twenty-seven concerts as a conductor," Cliburn later reported with pride. At Lewisohn Stadium, he not only played and conducted the Prokofiev concerto but also conducted Kabalevsky's overture to *Colas Breugnon* and Rachmaninoff's last work, the Symphonic Dances. Whether he had the stuff of a great conductor was questionable. The critical reaction was lackluster. According to Raymond Ericson in the *Times*, "Mr. Cliburn came close to getting the results he wanted from his players"—hardly a ringing endorsement. "In playing the piano he has a musicality that flows superbly through his fingers directly to the keys," Ericson pointed out. "He is not yet able to communicate with the same immediacy through an orchestra, so that the music often lost tension and grew slack."

Jumping in to the role of conductor without years of preparation was not going to be an easy transition. The reaction was disappointing even in the Soviet Union, when he conducted the Moscow Philharmonic in the same program in 1965. RCA secured the master tape of that concert for a recording but deemed the result not up to snuff, and the company decided not to release it. Instead, it issued a record of Van conducting the Interlochen Youth Orchestra in a performance of Ralph Vaughan Williams's *Serenade to Music*.

Wisely, Van soon focused on recording his first solo album, *My Favorite Chopin*. RCA booked Manhattan's Webster Hall, a former ballroom, for the sessions, and Van was to arrive at ten o'clock on a Monday night. He didn't show. RCA's executives were unfazed, knowing Van was never one to punch a clock. Everyone simply reassembled the next night.

He finally arrived on Tuesday at around 11:30 p.m., with "a tall, ghostly woman, ageless, with straight dark hair down to her waist," as producer Jack Somer recounted in an article for *Stereo Review*. She mounted the stairs followed by the taller pianist. "I greet Cliburn," Somer recalled, "and he introduces me to his companion, his *astrologer*. She immediately asks for details of my birth: date, time and place.

"My answers prompt a brief dialogue aside," he wrote. "Happily, it ends in my being granted full astrological sanction. The sessions may now begin." Things still didn't go easily. This romantic repertoire should have been a breeze, but gremlins of self-doubt invaded the recording studio and assaulted Van with a vengeance. The situation was more fraught than a live performance. He couldn't shake loose the image of Juilliard students sitting around a stereo player, scrutinizing his performances and pointing out all their faults.

As he played, there were dropped notes, bad takes, moments of mounting frustration. By four in the morning, Van had tentatively approved just one brief segment. "Suddenly, after a particularly rough passage," writes Somer, "he rises, angrily slams the cover down on the keyboard, *kicks* the piano, and turns his back on it. The noise, like two rifle shots, reverberates through the gaudy, mirrored hall as the engineers, the tuner, and I swiftly converge to assuage Cliburn's anxiety. But it is pointless." That blowup ended the session.

Days later, Van was still at it, plugging along step by agonizing step. Toward the end of the week, during a long break, the piano had unexpectedly stirred to life. Hearing the sounds, the technicians rushed back to their equipment, hoping to capture something useful. "But wait," thinks Somer. It's not Chopin. "It's 'You and the Night and the Music,' and Cliburn is *singing*, in a husky, torchy voice, accompanying himself in a wonderfully warm and easy style . . . Cliburn sings six or seven songs." Then, almost without pause, "he begins playing the [Chopin] etude. He plays with the introspection that has eluded him all week. He plays with the several levels of Chopin's deceptively simple piece exquisitely balanced. He constructs Chopin's arch. At four o'clock Friday morning, after several completely sublime takes, the E Major Etude is completed, and, with it, the album." *My Favorite Chopin* would become an instant best-seller.

At this point, none of what was transpiring was easy for Van. He told *Guideposts* magazine in 1960, "I should have been ecstatic, for the fragrance of fame is sweet. But I wasn't. All I saw ahead then was the desperate need to pray for the strength to continue whatever was meant for me."

As professional pressures bore down, the pianist used what tools he could to cope, including visits to astrologers and metaphysical seers. It didn't always bode well for projects in which he was involved. Radio broadcaster Robert Sherman recalls the time when Van was supposed to narrate a script for a program on New York radio station WQXR. "He cancelled the first session," Sherman recalls, "because the stars weren't in proper alignment that day."

Van's friend Ruth Covelli spent many evenings on the phone with him discussing the implications of those heavenly constellations. "Van and I could talk about predictions and what the aspects were for his travel, or for his next concert," she explained. "This would be after a late dinner, when we would each get home at one or two in the morning, and it could go until eight in the morning."

She directed him to a psychic named Irwyn Greif, who specialized in past-life readings. Greif claimed to have been an eyewitness to the destruction of Atlantis, and boasted among his clients numerous celebrities, including actor William Shatner and singer Judy Collins. His books included *The Soul Is a Traveler in Time,* and *The Many Faces of Reality.* Van drove out to Brooklyn to consult with Greif and was told that one of his past lives was in Russia. "Van was in uniform as a high-ranking member of the army," said Covelli, "and Greif said that Van and I had a short relationship there." Given those details, she says, it was no wonder that he was so well received in Moscow. "Van's chart is very unique," she said. "He was a Cancerian. He had a huge group of planets at the top of his charts, indicating public attention. He also had Libra rising, and Libra is charming. Jupiter was in his first house, which is why he was so tall. His chart really did describe his life."

They had dinner together often in New York, and Van was usually with his mother, she says. "Van was the first to introduce me to champagne," Covelli said, "and not just any champagne, but Dom Pérignon." She was aware, however, of times when Van's deep insecurity, and his search for heavenly certitude, could have paralyzing effects. "He could be waiting in the wings of a concert and call me to ask if it would be okay to go on," she remembered.

His friends were not the only ones keeping tabs on those emotional ups and downs. "Van Cliburn is very discouraged . . . [and] feels that he was not in good favor in certain places," said a report by the Federal Bureau of Investigation in 1962. Over the next several years, as his reliance on seers and advisors intensified, the bureau tracked it all. At one point, aware that the FBI was scrutinizing him, Van enlisted the help of a family friend, Texas congressman Sam Rayburn, speaker of the House, who vouched for the pianist's patriotism. A few years later the agency was still so concerned about his connections to the Soviet Union that it listened in on his conversations with a woman they described as a medium or spiritualist. "It appears," said their report, "that [Cliburn] is completely dependent on [her] for guidance and encouragement and obeys all her orders."

Excerpts from their interactions included the following:

"You seem disturbed," she says. "I am," he replies. She received a psychic message, she reports, that all the great musicians were standing around him, helping him.

"Could I have a shot tonight?" he asks her. "Could you do it yourself?" "Yes, I feel I need it every day," he responds. Her advice: twice-daily shots will keep him going. (The contents of the shots are not discussed.)

"Should I have some beer tonight?" he asks. "Yes, it will relax you."

"Will they like my conducting?" "Yes. I had a vision," she says. Nevertheless, he feels he needs help: "I hope you will project to my mind so I will not make any slip." Don't worry, she tells him. "The forces will be with you."

She also offers more mundane advice. "The embassy is short of tuna fish," she reports. "Send tuna fish to the embassy. It will make a good impression."

While Van was grappling with these issues, outwardly he remained the same bighearted boy from Kilgore. When Jimmy Mathis received a second-place finish in the 1961 National Federation of Music Clubs contest, the entire Cliburn clan sprang into action on his behalf. Rildia Bee announced that he should have won first prize, and organized a group to raise funds for him. "They gave me a pot of money—I think it was $4,500," remembers Mathis. Then Van stepped in to offer additional help.

He gave $1,000 to the National Federation of Music Clubs for another award in memory of Theodore Steinway, with a recital at New York's Town Hall as the prize, and Mathis was the winner. "Van and I were in a taxi talking about setting the date for Town Hall," says Mathis, "and Van asked me, 'Jimmy, wouldn't it be more exciting if you were to play at Carnegie Hall? I'm going to make that possible for you.' In the end, he gave me a check so I'd have enough money for all the advertising I'd need. I was so touched when he made Carnegie Hall viable."

Of course, Van's glowing persona remained as outsized as ever. "When I gave the concert [on January 17, 1962]," explains Mathis, "he felt he had to make a speech in the middle about 'the House of Steinway.' I said, 'Now Van, I know how you get carried away, and I don't want you to mess up the intermission. I'll be late for the second half and get nervous and it will affect my playing.' He talked for only ten minutes. You just had to tell him."

Van, Continued

GENEROSITY WAS A RECURRING MOTIF in Van's life; another was a powerful attachment to his childhood roots. It was no accident that he named his early original piano composition "Nostalgia." He often seemed, in fact, to live as much in the past as in the present, recalling conversations and meetings from decades earlier with remarkable specificity—recounting, with dramatic import, exactly when so-and-so said thus-and-such. His mother, even in her dotage, would occasionally pipe in with a correction, as if the keeping of such details were a moral imperative. Both appeared to be driven by a curatorial ambition to assemble and preserve the story of his life. When he moved from his tiny apartment at the Osborne to lodgings just a little farther east on Fifty-seventh Street at the Salisbury Hotel, the new, larger digs became a storehouse of memories, with entire rooms set aside for items he had accumulated.

He had also purchased a house in Tucson in 1961. "Someone in Arizona left him a lot of money," speculates Ivan Davis. His advisors plowed some of his earnings into real estate, with a focus on the western portion of the country. "All of those Dallas bankers invested wisely for him," recalls Jimmy Mathis, "including low-income housing projects in California." It secured him financially.

Meanwhile, the home crowd beckoned. Texas music teachers Grace Ward Lankford and Dr. Irl Allison had long admired Van's talent. Lankford was head of the Fort Worth Piano Teachers Forum. Allison was founder of the larger National Piano Guild. Both were on hand at a dinner at Fort Worth's four-year-old Ridglea Country Club on November 30, 1958, with Van—who had performed that day with the Dallas Symphony—and his parents as guests of honor. Van suffered nausea and fever after that Dallas performance, likely a result of his usual nervous agitation, always worst when the hall was filled with neighbors and friends. By the time of the dinner, though, he felt well enough to show up.

Lankford had intended to share the news that her group was expanding, and would offer a first prize of $1,000 to a winning pianist. But midway through the meal, she was handed a note from Allison. "Hold on," it said. "I'm going to make a startling announcement." He made good on the claim, proposing an international competition named after "Rildia Bee's little boy," and pledging $10,000 every four years to make it possible. Van, as surprised as the other five hundred guests, later added substantially to the pot by giving a benefit concert. At that dinner, Lankford and Allison agreed to join forces. They enlisted the help of the local business community and 450 volunteers. Texas Christian University placed its facilities at the group's disposal.

The United States Information Agency offered to distribute brochures to every American embassy in the world. The event's maiden voyage was scheduled for the fall of 1962. And just like that, the Van Cliburn International Piano Competition was born.

Van served as an inspiration rather than a hands-on participant, recalled Alann Bedford Sampson, who served as the competition's chair for sixteen years before becoming president and CEO of the Cliburn Foundation. "Yet he cared about two things. He felt the prize should be more than just a photo opportunity, a check, and a medal. It was to incorporate opportunities to perform, with four years of management—a first in the competition world. The goal was to launch a career. Sol Hurok helped get engagements for the winners. And he felt strongly that one of the best measures of artistic ability was in making music with others. So a quartet was brought in for chamber music. That was also a first."

Given Van's lack of interest in the Marlboro experience, the emphasis on chamber music at the Fort Worth competition is surprising, but musically sound. "The most striking thing for me," explained Sampson, "was the love Van had for the young people who came to compete. Looking back, that is one thing that maybe we took for granted."

Amid all the excitement over the new venture, Juilliard would again assume the role of spoiler. Correspondence between the school and Fort Worth officials reads like a series of diplomatic cables issued during a Cold War impasse. Grace Ward Lankford's letter to Juilliard offering William Schuman a place on the new competition's advisory board was met with disdain. Schuman's assistant, Mary H. Smith, explained that the institution could not be seen as a "sponsor" of any competition, especially since

Schuman and Mark Schubart had not been given an opportunity to approve the requirements, the judges, and the organization's method of operation.

Considering Van's strong feelings about his Texas brethren, his reaction to the snub could easily have been predicted. Nevertheless, it set off shock waves. On December 13, 1961, Juilliard's new dean, Gideon Waldrop, had a telephone call from Van, "the gist of which," he reported, "is that he cannot now play for the benefit concert to which he had originally agreed." Schubart, now vice-president of Juilliard, responded the very next day, explaining that he invariably declines such requests, since contestants from Juilliard are usually involved. He reminded Van of his own misgivings about the Fort Worth contest. "If I am not mistaken, at one point you were seriously considering the possibility of withdrawing from it altogether," he wrote, adding that, "in any event, I do hope, Van, that you will not allow this matter, clearly a misunderstanding all around, to interfere with your warm relationship with Juilliard." It did.

It took until July 1963 to find a resolution to the impasse, when word came from a new president of Juilliard, composer Peter Mennin, that Van's benefit concert for the school was back on, now set for October 4 in Lincoln Center's new Philharmonic Hall. It had originally been scheduled for Carnegie Hall, but, as Mennin explained in a note to Schuman—who was now president of the newly created Lincoln Center cultural complex, where Juilliard was to be relocated—the venue was changed so that the event would be held in a constituent of the budding arts center. Van offered money to keep Carnegie Hall as the location for the concert, but Mennin was insistent—even though, since the Juilliard Alumni Association had already booked Carnegie Hall, the school was still obligated to pay Carnegie's rental charges. Van played the benefit recital and the following year, Mennin officially agreed to join the advisory board of the Van Cliburn Competition. The rift was over.

The Fort Worth competition had an impressive start even without Juilliard's endorsement. Mikhail Voskresensky was one of four Russian entrants in the initial Cliburn Competition—a sign of continued international cooperation (and a reflection of the enduring strength of Van's reputation in Russia). Voskresensky, a student of Lev Oborin and a multiple prizewinner in European competitions, is still a professor at the Moscow Conservatory. At the first Cliburn Competition, he received third prize. But his most enduring memory of the visit, during which he fell ill, is of Van nursing him back to health with chicken soup.

The winner of that outing was American Ralph Votapek, who, like Van years before, faced the career-stalling prospect of being drafted into the armed forces. He informed his hosts about it only after he won. "I remember Grace Ward Lankford's remark in her broad Texas accent," he says: "'Well, we'll see about that, honey.' Lankford called Texas governor [John] Connally, and he contacted my local draft board, and I got a deferment. Otherwise the prize would have gone to the Russians."

The biggest aspect of the award was a contract with Sol Hurok. "It spoiled me," Votapek admits. Yet the first Van Cliburn Competition prizewinner never achieved anything like household name recognition. The new competition's promoters quickly learned that the stunning impact of Van's experience was simply unrepeatable.

In 1958, Van had told *The Dallas Morning News*, "An artist cannot be a machine, although some people seem to expect him to be one." He would never have said so, but his mother was one of them. As the gears of a life in music slowly began to grind him up, Rildia Bee was there to push him along. "She was in effect the root, the taproot, that kept him going," said record producer John Pfeiffer.

As Cliburn's road manager, she maintained order in his life, but it came at a cost. Over the months and years, he found the treadmill of a concert career less and less bearable. Before long, as Tchaikovsky said of his own music, Van's seams were showing. Even his beloved Soviets began to complain of an artistic decline. Georgian pianist Eliso Virsaladze, a respected teacher at the Moscow Conservatory, found the change troubling. "For me, his performance in Moscow in 1958 was the brightest, the most unforgettable musical event of my life," she told author Mark Zilberquit in 1983. "I remember from beginning to end each of his appearances on the stage in all the three rounds, every phrase he played. I emphasize I mean the competition, not his later visits." His playing on his returns to Russia, she said, "was not simply a disappointment. It is like you loved someone passionately, with all your heart, and then were disappointed in him. It is like the death of your idol." Her explanation for the change was unforgiving: "I believe the main reason is insufficient love for music," she declared.

She has now amended that view, attributing the initial harsh pronouncement to her own immaturity. "When you are younger you can make such simple judgments," she said recently. But the sense of loss for her was real—and, as for so many Muscovites, personal. She recalled his early playing as a harmony of wonderful qualities: virtuosity, a sense of improvisation—most of all, freshness. Van's performances on subsequent visits were often less consistent. A Chopin étude would be noble, at one recital,

with "subdued waves of sound in the left hand and a beautifully passionate, singing right hand," wrote a critic in 1972; at
the next recital, the same piece could sound false and mannered.
Everyone had expected Van's earlier, youthful qualities to mature
and deepen over time, but he never seemed to grow into the old
master they had hoped for. Instead, interpretive idiosyncrasies
began to pop up with increasing frequency. The eloquent balance
between rhythmic drive and soaring lyricism that once character-
ized his playing seemed to have been lost.

At some point, said Mathis, Van began to equate slow with
profound. "I bumped into the Cliburns in Paris, where he was
doing the Tchaikovsky with Georg Solti," he remembered, "and
I had played with Solti earlier. So I went backstage and said,
'Maestro, this is the old Van. It's brisk and wonderful,' and he
said, 'Jimmy, it wasn't easy.'" The pianist's new ideas tended to
undermine the beauty of his earlier approach. "At some point he
decided to get away from rhythm into the purity of sound," said
Mathis. "He developed this concept of *lingering* on the tones.
That can be very dangerous. [Conductor and pianist] Christoph
Eschenbach told me that Van had done the same thing with
some Mozart. You can linger so long on a phrase in the second
movement of a Mozart concerto that you lose all semblance of
where it's heading." The music will simply go limp.

At home, critics increasingly accused Van of staleness, and
concluded he was chasing after momentary success with too little
interest in artistic growth. But his perfectionism in the recording
studio argued against the view that this pianist was looking simply to cash in on instant fame. He yearned for something more.
It just somehow seemed just out of reach. He was not unaware
of the dilemma. Van had said himself, after returning from Moscow, that he was not yet a success—merely "a sensation." Indeed,

when pianist Jerome Rose ran into him in Vienna in 1961, Van told him, "It isn't how you live, it's how you die that determines your position as a pianist." Legacy was very much on his mind.

By the 1970s he just wanted to stop. Associates like John Pfeiffer sensed it; the pianist told his Shreveport friend Raymond Boswell that he was simply "worn out." Though he experienced occasional high points, like a 1973 White House performance for Golda Meir, the prime minister of Israel, difficulties were mounting, and the decade was fraught. In 1974 he was hard hit with two personal tragedies: first, the loss of his father; then Hurok passed away.

At that point, his world was collapsing. "I said to myself some time ago—starting in 1975," he later explained, putting the best possible face on the situation, "that I want to take a sabbatical and enjoy myself before it's too late. So, every time someone called me to play a concert I just kept saying that I was busy on that date. I didn't tell anyone that those were *my* dates, that I was busy having a good time. My manager told me to make an announcement but I said, 'Why make an announcement? What if in two months the canned goods run out?' I'm grateful I was able to do it without my mother starving to death."

Some saw the circumstances as more serious. He had asked André Previn for help in obtaining European performance dates, saying there was no interest in him there. He didn't help his cause with the 1976 television debut of *Live from Lincoln Center*, featuring Van's performance of the Grieg Piano Concerto under Previn's baton. Pianistically, it was a terrible mess. "I think he was nervous," Previn now says.

Van seemed ill prepared. The playing was indecisive and sloppy. Between movements, the camera caught him sitting uneasily at the piano, protectively folding his arms around his torso, as if trying to comfort himself. "In the cadenza," remembered Jeaneane Dowis, "he put so much pressure on his wrists that he was visibly shaking."

He was, in fact, reaching bottom. "Nineteen seventy-six was a low-energy time for me," Cliburn later admitted. "I actually tried to get the date of the Grieg Concerto moved to April. It was performed in January. I remember the weather as being so very cold. And I was desperately trying to gain weight—I was below 160 pounds. I even tried drinking malteds, but nothing worked. I was tired. I had been playing a lot of concerts: some for good reasons, and some [just] because someone asked me to play . . . So Jeaneane was right; I was not feeling physically at ease." Two years later, in Toledo on September 29, he gave his very last performance for nearly a decade.

The sprawling suite at the Salisbury Hotel where Van and his mother had settled expanded over the years until it occupied fourteen rooms on two floors. When Van first moved there from his tiny apartment up the street at the Osborne, he handled the task of relocating on his own, in little stages. "I would bump into Van carrying a chair or a small table," Gary Graffman told *The New York Times*. "That's how he moved."

The space was extravagant, especially for just a mother and son, though in 1977, the family unit expanded to include Tom Zaremba, a mortuary-science teacher with whom Van had developed an intimate relationship beginning in the summer of 1966. The pianist's pattern of finding someone to serve as a general manager of his life took on a new urgency as his mother entered her eighties, and Zaremba's duties soon included shopping, paying bills, dealing with various other aspects of the household, and looking after Rildia Bee.

For a while, New York was an appealing playground. Van's

calendar filled with evenings at the opera (sometimes he'd attend both the afternoon and evening performances on the same day), concerts, and stylish dinners, capped by late-night gatherings, always with Rildia Bee at his side. By the 1980s, though, the old homestead began to exert its pull. For one thing, his mother had had enough of their living conditions. "Well, I'm certainly glad my mother isn't still alive to see how I'm ending my days sitting around in a hotel room," she complained. So in 1985, Cliburn searched for and found his "dream house"—a huge estate once owned by Kay Kimbell, who had endowed Fort Worth's art museum.

One of the moving men engaged for the job, John McGinnis, recalls what he and his colleagues found in the various apartments that the Cliburns had occupied. "We were there for a couple of weeks, because everything had to be appraised before we packed it up," he remembered. "Mrs. Cliburn sat down and played piano for us. She said she wanted to be back in Texas."

Over the years Van's method had been to fill up a room completely, and then leave it and move on to the next one. "We packed a whole room full of nothing but empty shopping bags—from places like Macy's or Lord & Taylor," recalled McGinnis. "We would enter a room and find old flowers and vases—you wouldn't know that there were also valuable items hidden there. Everything was stacked up, including ashtrays with piles of ashes still in them, but underneath that would be a Ming vase, or stuff from the shah, or ornately carved Louis XIV chairs. There was trash everywhere. He said the valuables would be safer that way—someone would think it was all junk." One room was devoted to the empty suitcases he had used over the years, going back to his childhood. "If a decision had to be made about whether to keep something or not, he'd keep it," said McGinnis. "He seemed to know what everything was and where it came from, even though these items hadn't seen the light of day for years."

Peter Goodrich, who was an artist liaison for Steinway & Sons, remembered the dimly lit hallways of the Salisbury filled with new mattresses, which the management had attempted to deliver. The pianist wouldn't allow anyone to enter his rooms. Pianist Sara Davis Buechner was a frequent visitor and recalled seeing "papers and tchotchkes and boxes and Fabergé eggs and paraphernalia all over the floor, which had not been vacuumed in a very long time. In the corner of the living room was a fully decorated Christmas tree, a touch startling to see in late October; obviously it had lingered there since the previous December." The contents of the clutter, says Ivan Davis, were actually a key to understanding the pianist. "There would be a Schweitzer humanitarian award that he received," he says, "and next to it, a roll of toilet paper made out of phony dollar bills. That is Van."

"Every piano in his house was in horrific condition," remembered Goodrich. "I would say, 'Van, let me send someone to put your pianos in shape.' He never let me do it." Cliburn told a writer for *Texas Monthly* that he had actually never been wild about pianos; that even as a youngster living in his first apartment in New York, he would spend "his lunch money" on flowers. "The odd thing about me is that I enjoy flowers as much when they get old and dried out as when they were fresh," he said. "I don't know—I just look at those flowers, and in my mind, I still see the beauty they once had. I never threw any of them away."

On the way to Fort Worth, said McGinnis, the movers had to stop at the Philippine embassy to pick up "a huge portrait of First Lady Imelda Marcos dressed in a gown, next to her husband in military regalia. It had a heavy gilt frame." Marcos had played a substantial role in Van's life, beginning in 1973, when a Cliburn "minicult" in Manila was supported by government-controlled radio stations broadcasting his recordings nonstop. Filipino clothing designers turned out a Cliburn line, described as "an array of gowns to make anyone beam with pride . . . while imbibing Cliburn's music." Manila-born pianist Emilio del Rosario was forbidden from performing any pieces in Van's active repertoire. The Texan came to enjoy special status at Malacañang Palace, and at the Waldorf Towers in New York, where Marcos loved to entertain guests in the posh thirty-seventh-floor suite once occupied by General Douglas MacArthur.

Marcos surrounded herself with a coterie of celebrities, like actor George Hamilton and Dame Margot Fonteyn, who ended up establishing a ballet company in Manila. Dame Margot received a pension from Marcos. So did Van, after the dictator established the Rildia Bee O'Bryan Cliburn Foundation, of which the pianist was a founding director. Cliburn's monthly stipend for life was part of the Philippines' first International Artist Award conferred on him in 1973, with the announcement that "he has charmed the savage breast of discord with the unifying power of his universal art."

One of Goodrich's tasks for Steinway was periodically to walk over to the Salisbury Hotel to pick up cash from Van to purchase pianos for Imelda. Van did other small favors for the first lady of the Philippines. When he took her to the Metropolitan Opera, she was star-struck. "The Met—it was fabulous—those chandeliers, those paintings, the audience," she recalled. "My God, the Rockefellers, the Du Ponts, the Fords, the Magnins, the Lindsays, the painter Marc Chagall." She asked Van to help her bring some of that glamour to Manila.

"Around 1975," remembered Schuyler Chapin, "I was general manager of the Metropolitan Opera, and Van came to my office

and closed the door. He wanted me to come to his box at intermission to meet a very important guest." It was Marcos. Chapin
had no desire to meet her. At the time, the company was about
to make a tour of Japan, and Van asked if they would make a
detour and include the Philippines. "I said, 'No, you couldn't
possibly afford it,'" remembered Chapin. "The Japanese trip was
costing us $2.5 million. She offered to put up a million and a
half for us to come to an auditorium that was not adequate, and
with a capacity that couldn't possibly make the money back. It
was viewed as an insult that I wouldn't bend over backwards for
her. These were absurdly bad judgments [on Van's part]." When
things went downhill for the Marcoses and they became political
outcasts, the Van-Imelda relationship soured.

Soon after the Tchaikovsky win, Van had talked of building a
home one day. "I don't think my house will be pretentious or
small either. It will be comfortable, old-fashioned maybe—in
keeping with my family background . . . Sometimes rather prissy,
but always warm and sincere." The one thing that could not be
said of the Kimbell estate was that it was small. "We had looked
at so many houses," said Rildia Bee, "ranch-style houses on one
level so that I could get around. We couldn't have considered this
house except it had an elevator, but since it did, it was just perfect
for us." The place was large enough to accommodate the relent-
lessly expanding mass of collectibles. "Van and Rildia Bee sometimes can't bear to take down their Christmas decorations until
April," reported *The Dallas Morning News* in 1988, "and there are
still signs of Rildia Bee's 90th birthday party, which took place
more than two years ago." In a 1993 article, the cake was cited as
still standing in an upstairs hall.

Visitors noted the continuing eccentricities, including the Tennessee Williams–tinged dialogue that had become the palaver of a mother and son who addressed each other as "Little Precious" and "Little Darling." But a sense of playfulness had begun to replace the dark shadows. Mary Russell Rogers, in the *Fort Worth Star-Telegram*, wrote about her two a.m. meeting with Van: "He says he enjoys intelligent wit, but doesn't care for comedy. He is devoted to opera and adores old movies. He owns hundreds of films; *Random Harvest* with Ronald Colman and Greer Garson is one of his favorites. He likes *Jeopardy* and sometimes watches soap operas . . . He was, he says, old when he was young." A guest stopping by the house early in the day might find Zaremba in a bathrobe sitting around the kitchen table with Rildia Bee, while Van happily ran to the flower shop for new arrangements. The odd but charming trio lived by their own unique set of personal rules.

Perhaps it was the tempering effect of years of endless peaks and valleys, or the advancing state of his mother's age, or even the alignment of the stars in the sky. Whatever the reason, though he now seemed content, Van was at this point primed for something new to enter his life; he found it at a political fundraising party at socialite Martha Hyder's house in the late 1980s.

"You two should meet," Hyder told the late-arriving Van as she introduced him to Tommy Smith, a tall, handsome man with a gentle nature who was twenty-nine years the pianist's junior. Smith, a music student at Texas Christian University at the time, was naturally a bit awestruck. "It was hot, it must have been August or September, but he was in a dark suit and tie— his uniform," Smith remembers. "He asked me some questions about my family, and I told him I had three brothers and a twin sister. 'Are you identical?' he asked. I paused, glanced down at

myself, and said, 'I don't think so.'" The exchange was funny and
charming, though Van later admitted that he was embarrassed at
having asked the question. It lasted all of five minutes, but a seed
had been planted.

A few months afterward, Smith received an invitation to
attend a birthday celebration for Rildia Bee at the Fort Worth
Club. "It was a major party," he recalls; "it seemed to last three
days." Before long, a dinner invitation to the Cliburn residence
was extended.

Smith hadn't been a guest at any of the late-night parties Van
regularly gave, attended mostly by friends and people affiliated
with the Cliburn Foundation. So as the hours stretched on at
Van's home, he was taken by surprise. "It must have been nine
p.m. when Rildia Bee came down in her wheelchair with her
nurses and her dog," he recalls. "We didn't sit down to dinner
until around midnight. I had never been exposed to that kind
of insanity before!" Smith remembers. "We had dinner, and suddenly it was two a.m. I was tired . . . I tried to say good night,
and Van said, 'No. I want you to listen to something.'" They
moved to the library, and Van put on a recording of Strauss's *Der
Rosenkavalier*—the final trio and duet. "Something happened
to me then, and I started crying," says Smith. "It was the most
beautiful thing I had ever heard in my life. By now it was at least
three a.m., and I decided it was time to go. The day Van died,
I thought of that trio and duo. I almost had it played at the
funeral. I wanted to, but didn't.

"After that evening," he says, "our friendship developed." A
deep connection was just beginning to take root.

CHAPTER 13

The End of the Road

"THE LAST TIME I SAW VAN," recalled Schuyler Chapin, "was when Emil Gilels 'snuck' into Carnegie Hall on a Saturday afternoon." It was during April 1983, and the Soviet pianist had not been scheduled to appear in the United States. Then Carnegie Hall announced on short notice that he would be giving a recital, touting "the spirit of cooperation that has made possible the return of this great artist." In *The New York Times*, chief music critic Donal Henahan found that announcement strangely cryptic, and drily asked whether the CIA had struck a deal with the KGB.

Chapin had been invited to the Gilels recital by Seymour Rosen, then manager and artistic director of Carnegie Hall, and decided to give a supper party afterward, hosting ten or fifteen people, including Van. At the dinner Gilels turned to Van and asked, "Van, why no more play? It's wrong." It was an awkward moment, remembers Chapin, and Gilels, sensing the pianist's reaction, backed off. Afterward, he put his hand on Van's shoulder and they left to talk privately.

That meeting figured in Van's claim, four years later, that Gilels had unusual prescience, an assertion redolent of the magical thinking by which the pianist managed to elevate ordinary moments into cosmic, star-shaped events. At the time of his comment, Soviet premier Mikhail Gorbachev and his wife were about to make an official visit to the White House and had requested that Van play for them. "Emil Gilels was gifted with second sight," Van reported. "He told me that he felt that when I did play again, it would have something to do with Russia and America." In some versions of the story, Van gave the prediction even greater weight by claiming that Gilels had seen it all in a dream. Whether their interaction was accurately reported or a product of Cliburn's imagination, the Gilels encounter seemed to have helped spur him to return to the stage. It had been nine years since he gave a public performance, and he was clearly growing restless.

Russian devotion to Van had never flagged. But he was no longer certain about his own pianistic abilities. "You may be sure that before I agreed to go to the White House, I went to play for my mother," he said. "And she said to go ahead."

Richard Probst, who was at the time director of concerts and artists for Steinway & Sons, sat near Rildia Bee at the White House event, and recalled that she was "the piano teacher to the end, gesturing the tempo, and following every phrase." The impressive celebrity audience included philanthropist and diplomat Walter Annenberg and his wife, conductor Zubin Mehta and his wife, cabinet members, and other notable figures. The decorations were festive, Probst remembered. "There was a wonderful Christmas tree made of azaleas." Before the concert, Van, Rildia Bee, and Probst met at one o'clock in the morning to try out a variety of pianos. Van disliked most of them, and settled instead on the instrument owned by the Cliburn Foundation in Fort Worth, a piano known as the "Silver."

He began his recital with the Soviet national anthem. "It took the Soviets two lines of music before they realized what was happening," recalled Probst. Then he played "The Star-Spangled Banner," followed by his old standbys, including "Widmung." "When he finished, Van stood up, the president and Nancy Reagan stood up, and the Gorbachevs followed suit," said Probst. "Then Mrs. Gorbachev whispered to Van that she regretted not being able to hear him perform the Tchaikovsky First Piano Concerto. He asked, 'Would you like to hear something else?'"

Up until then, the atmosphere had been stiff, recalled Probst. "The Americans and Soviets didn't know how to interact, and it had been a long day. But Van started to play and sing 'Moscow Nights,' and the Russians began to sing. Then everyone joined in. At the end, the emotional tone of the room had changed—like going from a temperature of thirty-five degrees to seventy-two degrees. Thereafter, people were smiling at each other."

The pianist's career was instantly rebooted. Van had always feared that once gone, he would be forgotten by the musical world. It was time to put that thought to the test. Following his White House appearance, the offers again began to arrive, and he remained selective. Organizations like Steinway hoped to lure him back to the stage for their own purposes. For the piano maker's 1988 Carnegie Hall celebration of its 500,000th piano, the firm tried to maneuver him into the performer's spotlight by bestowing an award on Rildia Bee. It was a surefire way to compel his attendance at an event. Van and his mother showed up at the Steinway bash to acknowledge the honor, but he didn't take the bait. By the end of 1989, though, he had given performances at the Mann Center in Philadelphia and in Moscow and Leningrad, where the crowds again were fervent.

He agreed to anoint Dallas's new, magnificent Morton H. Meyerson Symphony Center, performing the Tchaikovsky concerto with the Dallas Symphony, under Mexican conductor Eduardo Mata. The hall, designed by architect I. M. Pei and acoustician Russell Johnson, was gorgeous, and the sound impeccable. In *The New York Times,* Donal Henahan found the performance "rhythmically slack . . . The visceral excitement, the purely sonic 'rush' that the Tchaikovsky concerto affords the listener, simply did not develop." Rildia Bee, however, thought it was "wonderful!"

The next year, Van played shakily at Kilgore College at a recital to raise money for the Harvey Lavan and Rildia Bee Cliburn Scholarship in his old hometown. The performance rituals (including a very late start) unfolded as usual, but as the recital began his hands started to tremble so badly that after barely making it through the first piece he left the stage. "It's always hardest to play before those who know you only too well," he said later. The sight brought to mind Mark Twain's painful description of Tom Sawyer in the grip of a bout of stage fright: "His legs quaked under him and he was like to choked. True, he had the manifest sympathy of the house but he had the house's silence, too, which was even worse than its sympathy . . . Tom struggled awhile and then retired, utterly defeated."

Van stayed backstage long enough that audience members began to mutter to each other. Is he coming back? After perhaps twenty or thirty minutes, he reappeared and continued, suddenly cool and calm. The change in his demeanor was surprising and mysterious, yet, after the false start at the beginning, the concert went according to plan.

After the ordeal, a weight seemed lifted from Cliburn's shoulders. The evening still being young, Van convinced the organist of Kilgore's First Presbyterian Church, James Lynn Culp, to open up the church and give a late-night organ recital for invited guests. How could he refuse? About a dozen people attended what turned into a beautiful, strange, and utterly Van-like evening. That night encapsulated the agony and the triumph of his career.

Despite the difficulties, he was determined to carry on. The size of his fee helped to control the flow of offers—$125,000 for a recital was more than most presenters could afford. Nevertheless he received an inquiry from the new Irving S. Gilmore International Keyboard Festival in Kalamazoo, Michigan. The Gilmore Festival was founded both to celebrate the piano and to discover hidden talent deserving of wider recognition. As a fledgling endeavor, it needed a big splash for its 1991 launch. Bringing in the elusive Van Cliburn added an element of glamour.

The Gilmore's artistic director, David Pocock, paid an emotional price for his gamble. Van and his entourage arrived by private plane at six in the morning on the day of the performance. "People from the festival had been waiting up for hours to greet him," remembered Pocock. "We had gotten several phone calls during the night that he was on his way." The plane had left very late, of course, and encountered turbulence along the way; as the jet bucked and trembled, those onboard could hear Rildia Bee shouting, "You tell that pilot to cut it out!" All seemed fine after the group landed, however. Van handed out generous hundred-dollar tips, and retired to his hotel suite until about four in the afternoon, when it was time to choose a piano.

He placed people at different locations in the hall to help him pick the instrument with the best sound. "Then he decided that he didn't like any of the pianos," said Pocock, whose inner alarm bells were starting to go off. Van turned to pianist José Feghali, a Cliburn Competition winner, and said, "José, I don't really want to play tonight. Why don't you do the concert?"

"It was scary," Pocock said. "I'm sure he meant it." Several days before, in New York, Van had instructed Susan Tilley, chairman of the Cliburn Foundation, to cancel the Kalamazoo appearance, but she ignored that decision. Now, like an athlete before a really big match, he was choking. As the selection process continued, "he ultimately picked the worst piano," said Pocock, "but it was the brightest one."

About thirty minutes past the official start time of the concert, the Gilmore's director of marketing and public relations, Julie Cook, had a look of horror on her face. Robert Silverman, editor and publisher of *The Piano Quarterly*, had told her that Van probably wouldn't show up. She was in a panic. Those who knew him predicted that he would eventually show, and he did—an hour late. According to Pocock, Van wouldn't begin until he was handed the fee. Then, business resolved, he walked out onstage and began to talk to the audience.

"He gave a touching speech," said Pocock, "but it was too long." The playing, however, had moments of great beauty. "Even 'The Star-Spangled Banner' was extraordinary. He played the hell out of it. But after, he was disappointed. He wanted more from the audience. I think he would have gotten more if he had shown up on time. What bothered people the most was that he was an hour late, but never apologized for it."

Some time during the recital, Rildia Bee lost a contact lens, and when the music ended and the audience left, she could be seen sitting helplessly in the hall, tears flowing down her cheeks and causing her voluminous makeup to streak. When Van set eyes on her, he became panicky. "Find an eye doctor," he barked at Tom Zaremba, his face flushed with growing agitation.

Astonishingly, an ophthalmologist was found at that late hour. When Van finally calmed down, he confessed with a sheepish look, "I can't bear the thought of her suffering." The episode settled matters—they would head home that night. "If I knew this would happen, I never would have come," he told Pocock. "And what was it all about?" asked the festival's director. "She just lost a contact lens," he shrugged.

The career relaunch had been a sporadic affair. By 1994, Van was planning a more serious foray into American concert life with a national tour featuring the Moscow Philharmonic, led by Vassily Sinaisky. The program featured the Tchaikovsky First Concerto and the Rachmaninoff Third, plus an orchestral performance of Copland's patriotic *Lincoln Portrait* with Van as the narrator. Rildia Bee, ninety-seven, was in no condition to make the trip.

Journalist Donna Perlmutter's visit to the Fort Worth residence found Van readying himself for those upcoming appearances. "Steinway grands abound, nine downstairs and another three upstairs," wrote Perlmutter. "And framed photographs are everywhere. Rildia Bee and Van. Van and Rildia Bee. A heady, glorious couple, beaming at each other, at the camera. Other photos include Van and Maria Callas. Van and Sol Hurok. Van and Nikita Khrushchev. Van and the Ronald Reagans." Nothing else was as comforting as those reminders of glorious times.

At a Hollywood Bowl performance on July 11, less welcome ghosts of the past re-emerged, demonstrating once again that recapturing the miracle of Moscow was a futile pursuit. "Meet the new Van, same as the old Van," wrote Michael Walsh in *Time*. "At the intermission of the tour's first concert . . . the nearly neurasthenic Cliburn experienced what he called 'light-headedness,' and the program was delayed while a doctor took his blood pressure. Eventually he returned to the stage, sheepishly informing the audience of 14,000 that he felt unable to play the Rachmaninoff concerto, and so substituted a series of solo encores."

It seemed to Walsh that Van was less interested in the life of a traveling virtuoso than ever before. Nevertheless, noted the reviewer, there were still moments of greatness. Van dropped the Rachmaninoff concerto permanently from the program and kept in the solo pieces to fill out the concerts. As the tour edged along the continent from California, through the Midwest, on toward New York's Metropolitan Opera House, Rildia Bee suffered a severe stroke. Van returned to Fort Worth on Thursday, July 28, long enough to realize the seriousness of the situation, then returned for his planned concert in New York on August 2. "I have a feeling she would want me to do it," he said. Likely, without her hovering presence, he wouldn't have embarked on the tour at all.

The *New York Times* arts writers greeted his arrival with an internal notice appearing on the paper's computer screens: "The Cliburn circus comes to town." That evening, with his mother on her deathbed, he stood at attention as the orchestra played the Russian national anthem, walked quickly to the piano for his own rousing version of "The Star-Spangled Banner," and then joined in a performance of the Copland work. From the stage of the opera house, he recited a poem he had written for his mother when he was just fourteen. It sounded, wrote critic Tim Page in *Newsday,* "like a not terribly well-organized outtake from Tennyson's 'In Memoriam,' and I might have dismissed it as mawkish had I not realized, when it was over, that my eyes were wet." Without pausing for applause, Cliburn played musical selections by Szymanowski, Debussy, and Chopin.

After intermission, the time for the Tchaikovsky concerto had arrived. Allan Kozinn of the *Times* found the performance "both heartening and puzzling . . . The pity is that there is a spark in Mr. Cliburn's playing that begs to be fanned into flame." Sadly, fanning the flames of passion is simply too great a challenge when your entire world is going up in smoke. Page found the playing to be "solid, impassioned, idiomatic, and sometimes less than perfectly coordinated." But the evening had left its impact on sensitive listeners. "One had the extraordinary (if not entirely comfortable) sense that 4,000 people were eavesdropping on an intensely private moment," Page concluded, "as Cliburn, oblivious to the world, child and man, conquering hero and bereft son, sat alone on the stage, playing his heart out, triumphant and inconsolable."

The swirl of emotions must have been dizzying. Yet after the Tchaikovsky, Cliburn offered an encore, his old nostalgic companion—Liszt's arrangement of Schumann's tender "Widmung." Van's thoughts must have been drawn in that moment to the song's lyric: "You the world in which I live; you my heaven, in which I float . . . My good spirit, my better self!" The love of his life was dying.

"I had an excruciating pain in my head during the concert," he said later. "There was terrible trouble in my right arm. I knew she was going." The next day, she expired. A charter flight had brought him back in time to see her in her last moments. "I was holding her," he said. "She went oh so peacefully. Oh so beautifully." He stayed with her for several hours, and later reported having a mystical experience at the moment of her passing.

The funeral was unusual, at least for anyone not familiar with the ways of the Cliburns. Every attendee was given his or her own limousine, remembered Steinway's Peter Goodrich. "The funeral home was decorated to look like Rildia Bee's bedroom. She was settled in the bed. Her dog, Baby Chops, was with her. It all seemed so weird."

"Van's mother was fully dressed," recounts Tommy Smith, who had joined the household as Cliburn's life partner around 1994, remaining a fixture during the pianist's last two decades, "and when you went into the parlor it looked like she was sleeping. Van sat on one edge of the bed, and I sat on the other, and Baby Chops was also on the bed, walking around. The janitors came in and almost fell over, seeing the dog walking all over Rildia Bee, just as if she were alive. But Van couldn't stand the thought of putting his mother in a casket—or his father, either, though I wasn't around back then."

Friends had long speculated about what would happen when Rildia Bee passed away: would Van breathe a sigh of relief, they wondered, or might he completely collapse? In the end, the transition was smooth. The greatest impact on his life at this point was the deep love he had found through his partnership with Tommy.

Smith is the Van Cliburn story's happy ending. Many years before, Schuyler Chapin had described Van's life as "a tragedy in the grand sense. This is a man of basically terrific instincts," he said, "caring about people, a belief in spiritual values, a God-given talent to communicate, not a bone in his body of nastiness. He was an innocent—a kind of artistic Billy Budd. What happened? The rigors and difficulties and angst of the real world, coupled with a curious and disturbing relationship with his mother—an on/

off, love/hate affair . . . The great outside world is harsher than I imagine he dared think. He was a high romantic. He thought he could embrace Khrushchev and say, 'Come on, Nikita, we don't want to do that . . .' In the end, he couldn't cope. It shouldn't be this way, but the world is not going to change."

Yet it did. With Tommy Smith, Van at last found a fulfilling, loving union. Zaremba was gone, though the dissolution was acrimonious. His parting gift to Van was a frivolous, vindictive palimony suit, which was promptly thrown out of court. The intent was no doubt to embarrass Van, though none of his neighbors and friends cared in the slightest. At this point Van was finally shedding the old shell of a life in which he had been trapped, though he could look back with some satisfaction on a record of remarkable achievements. He had, after all, helped change the world, inspiring love and admiration in generations of Russians, and propelling efforts at diplomatic exchanges between the rival superpowers. Political crises continued to spring up, of course, marked by terrifying headlines: the U-2 spy plane disaster in 1960, the creation of the Berlin Wall in 1961, the 1962 Cuban Missile Crisis, proxy wars in the Middle East and Asia. Still, Van had served as a constant reminder that even between hostile nations the real possibility of "soft power" and effective diplomacy remained.

He also created a lasting legacy of musical beauty—issuing recordings of Rachmaninoff, Prokofiev, Tchaikovsky, Chopin, Brahms, Liszt, Beethoven, Schumann, Mozart, and more—and spurred the creation of an international competition and festival that continues to this day to touch the lives of many young musicians. According to Mary Lou Falcone, his charitable giving amounted to more than anyone will ever know: "More young pianists have been helped by him than you can count, often anonymously." He performed for heads of state around the world, including every president from Harry Truman to Barack Obama.

Of course, it was never easy, and one wonders if Rildia Bee—the wind that filled his sails—was also the albatross that sank him. "I thought about that," says Smith. "But without the force of Rildia Bee, what would have happened? Van might not have done with his life what he did. And what an extraordinary life it was."

That part of his journey was now coming to an end. His sporadic efforts to reclaim the concert stage had proved fruitless. "The last memory I have of Van was the terrible occasion [in May 1998] when they opened Bass Hall in Fort Worth for him to play the Rachmaninoff Second Concerto, and he fainted, supposedly," remembered Ivan Davis. "I was there with [critic] John Ardoin. It was a terrible performance, memory slips even in the first movement. At the most difficult part of the third movement, just before he got there, he swooned."

The sixty-three-year-old Cliburn was taken to the hospital. "Doctors examined him and sent him home for some rest," reported the Tribune News Service. "They said he had fainted from heat exhaustion, stress, and the effects of smoke and haze that have blanketed much of Texas because of fires in Mexico and Central America." It was time to put the piano to rest.

There were compensations, though. At home and in his travels, Tommy Smith was by his side, and it made all the difference. "He did not miss the piano," says Smith. And there were rewards in a companionable life off the stage. "The last ten or fifteen years, we could go to concerts or fundraisers," recalls Smith, "but 90 percent of the time we ran home afterward."

For most of his life, the pianist had hidden his sexuality from the public. But when Van received an award at the Kennedy Center Honors in Washington, DC, in 2001, Smith could be seen on camera sitting behind him. When he was given Russia's highest honor, the Order of Friendship—presented to him by Vladimir Putin in 2004, for his contributions in the promotion of Russian-American friendship and cultural cooperation— Smith was again with him. Things seemed good. He was no longer haunted by the past.

In 2012, his health faltering, Van offered a group of items for auction at Christie's in New York—a collection of English furniture, Russian works of art, and silver and jewelry he had accumulated over a lifetime. He knew every piece intimately. There were 166 items in all, and each one had a story—from a pair of George II gilt mirrors attributed to Matthias Lock, to a Russian silver soup tureen that had belonged to Grand Duchess Olga Nikolaevna. ("I was playing a concert on the twenty-third of June, 1963, and I passed a shop and saw it," he said. "It had been in possession of a daughter of Nicholas I. My mother used it for chicken soup.")

Every object brought back memories. "The first week I had come back from Moscow I played the concert at Carnegie Hall on May 19," he recalled, "and that week I was with Princess Wolkonsky, Rachmaninoff's daughter . . . I bought these cufflinks and that bowl." Cliburn's hundred-year-old piano, the one he had practiced on as a child—Steinway no. 157754—was also offered up for sale. The receipts were to be divided between the Moscow Conservatory and the Juilliard School of Music. The total assemblage fetched nearly $4.4 million.

The auction set off warning alarms in those who knew him. He was selectively divesting. In a preauction presentation held at the New York Public Library, Van seemed off balance. He wept after hearing young Korean-American pianist Joyce Yang (who had netted a silver medal at the Cliburn Competition) performing Rachmaninoff ("I miss Rachmaninoff so much!" he exclaimed through tears), and reiterated several well-worn anecdotes, including an ever-evolving story about the day he and his mother purchased expensive antiques for each other as gifts.

The lament about missing Rachmaninoff was telling. The two had never met, of course; yet their artistic trajectories followed similar paths: Rachmaninoff was beleaguered by self-doubt, and sought relief through untraditional remedies, like hypnotherapy. (He dedicated his Second Piano Concerto to Dr. Nikolai Dahl, whose "autosuggestion" techniques had freed him to write the piece.) The Russian master never overcame his psychological burdens; he continued to believe throughout his life, as he told Vladimir Horowitz, that he had "tried to succeed in three things—composition, piano playing, and conducting—and had succeeded in none." Perhaps Van's affinity for Rachmaninoff's music reflected that shared emotional undercurrent. His remark about missing Rachmaninoff was revealing in another way: this repertoire continued to be available any time he cared to play it. Clearly, it wasn't the music itself but the act of sharing it with an audience that had brought him fulfillment.

When the artless interviewer at the library asked him to describe himself in just seven words, he rattled off: "Hallelujah. Great music. Wonderful parents. Marvelous friends." The response was upbeat, as usual, but the pianist was gaunt and pale. Something was wrong. Then came an announcement: bone cancer. Smith cared for him throughout his decline. Among the friends who made a special journey to see him on learning he was ill was Liu Shikun, his Chinese rival at the Tchaikovsky Competition; his tender feelings for his musical comrade never faded.

Somehow, though frail and hoarse—months after the date at which doctors had predicted he would be gone—Cliburn gathered the strength to appear onstage at the Cliburn Foundation's fiftieth-anniversary gala at Fort Worth's Bass Hall on September 5, 2012. "I'm so thrilled to be here tonight," he told the stunned, welcoming crowd in a hoarse whisper, ending his remarks with, "Never forget: I love you all from the bottom of my heart—forever."

"He was so ill," recalls Smith. "He was brought backstage in a wheelchair. But he was the absolute pro. It exhausted him—just those twenty steps knocked him out. He went straight home. What people don't realize is that he was able to separate the job [of being a celebrity] from the rest of his life. Fame never affected him. He had no idea even that people knew him. But when he was in public something switched on—an almost tactile 'spotlight.' He had an amazing life. But did it knock him down sometimes? You bet."

Smith wistfully recalls the pianist's last moments. "There was a Russian woman named Irene who had been in the audience when Van won in 1958, and she wrote to him devotedly for fifty years. She died about a month before Van did—hit by a car while crossing the street. The night Van died [on February 27, 2013], he suddenly said, 'Irene, isn't this the most beautiful room?'

"At the end, he was so weak. I peered into his face, trying to make contact, and said, 'Hello!' He could barely open his eyes. But he answered, 'Hello . . . I *love* you!' An hour later he died, absolutely at peace. He was certain that he was going to meet some old friends. As sad as it was, it was beautiful. That's the sweet, loving person I miss."

The remnants of a remarkable life remained. "The suitcases from his childhood—I still have all of those," says Smith. "I would say, 'For God's sake, why can't we throw some of this away?' He would answer, 'Because I remember what they were when I got them.' In his mind, the [wilted] flowers were still fresh. And there was his coat: he always had it on: I don't care if it was 120 degrees. It was his security. God knows what was in the pockets. I didn't even look. I folded it up and put it in the casket with him." The coat—like those ritual objects placed in the tombs of Egyptian pharaohs to accompany them on their journey to the afterlife—was laid to rest with its owner.

Cliburn was mourned the world over, especially in Russia, where he is still lovingly remembered. At the funeral, a statement by Russian president Vladimir Putin avowed that "during the most difficult historical times, the art of Van Cliburn brought together people from different countries, different continents, and united them." Former president George W. Bush, who had honored Cliburn with the prestigious Presidential Medal of Freedom in 2003, told mourners that the pianist had surprised the Soviets by rising above the stereotype of the Texas cowboy. He was a gracious, humble young man, said the president, "beloved, even by the enemy."

In Van Cliburn's world, of course, there were no enemies. Only musicians, and the audiences they served.

The Other Competitors

For the West, the Tchaikovsky trials had yielded a single winner, Van Cliburn, the golden-toned hero who single-handedly vanquished the mighty Soviets. That narrative was a delight to American concert managers and record producers. However, many formidable players participated, each with commendable attributes. As Lev Vlassenko said, "some really good, serious musicians went almost unnoticed. I'll name just two: the French Roger Boutry and the American Jerome Lowenthal . . . From today's point of view we may call them the 'intellectuals' of the 1958 competition." Indeed, Boutry, Lowenthal, and several others—especially the finalists—continued to make important contributions. The doors had opened especially wide for Van, but they had by no means slammed shut on his fellow competitors.

Boutry, for example, quickly established himself in France as an important pianist, composer, teacher, and conductor. At the time of the competition his main interest was in furthering his career as a composer; he had already received the prestigious Prix de Rome in composition. The Moscow visit was for him mostly "a tourist occasion," he said, as well as an opportunity to perform a piano work he had written expressly for the event, entitled Scherzo Fantaisie. In the end, the competition had indeed helped him to promote that work—several other pianists eventually played it. Kabalevsky, for one, sent him a note praising his skill. Boutry's compositional orientation had informed his pianism; his reviews before the Moscow adventure noted the "luminescent structure" of his interpretations, along with a "transcendent technique." But, wrote French composer and musicologist Pierrette Mari, he was "too intelligent a musician to limit himself to the role of brilliant interpreter." After Moscow, Boutry went on to become harmony professor at the Paris Conservatory and music director of the Garde républicaine. To date, over sixty of his compositions have been published.

Nadia Gedda-Nova also returned to Paris, where she continued a professional track already under way before her trip to Moscow, helping to prepare singers at the Opéra. She also served in that capacity for Herbert von Karajan at the Salzburg Festival and Claudio Abbado at La Scala in Milan.

Many of the French players gravitated to the United States, where they established important teaching legacies: Annie Marchand (d. 2015) at Immaculate Heart College in Los Angeles and then at Northern Illinois University and at the Chicago Musical College at Roosevelt University; Evelyne Crochet at Brandeis University and the New England Conservatory in Boston. She also became Rudolf Serkin's teaching substitute during his sabbatical year at the Curtis Institute of Music in Philadelphia.

Annie Petit took on positions at the University of Wisconsin, Muhlenberg College in Pennsylvania, and the Curtis Institute.

Jerome Lowenthal is on the faculty of the Juilliard School in addition to teaching summers at the Music Academy of the West in California. His extensive performing career has included concertos under the batons of Leonard Bernstein, Daniel Barenboim, Seiji Ozawa, Eugene Ormandy, Pierre Monteux, and Leopold Stokowski.

Daniel Pollack concertized extensively throughout the Soviet Union, where he was the first American to record for the Melodiya label. He subsequently embarked on a piano career spanning five continents, performing often with the world's major orchestras. He is a professor at the University of Southern California.

Norman Shetler went on to teach at the Mozarteum in Salzburg, as well as to work with several important artists, including baritone Dietrich Fischer-Dieskau, tenor Peter Schreier, and violinist Nathan Milstein. He demonstrated unique gifts as a musical collaborator.

Lev Vlassenko (d. 1996) continued to perform and record, and was a fixture on the faculty at the Moscow Conservatory for thirty-nine years, also teaching at schools in the United States and Australia. In 1991 he was honored as a People's Artist of the Soviet Union.

Not all of the contestants were afforded similar opportunities. For some, the brief, shining moment in Moscow led only to years of disappointment and struggle. This was particularly the case for two pianists, Liu Shikun and Milena Mollova, who were praised by Emil Gilels in a postcompetition article for *Pravda* in which he described them as representatives of "fledgling" but important national schools. "Incidentally," he noted, "the talented pianist Milena Mollova [of Bulgaria], who was among the prizewinners was, at only eighteen years old, the youngest participant in the competition."

Anointed by one of the world's great pianists, Mollova went on to an artistic dead end. When the contest was over, she returned to Russia at Gilels's invitation for a year, to study with him at the Moscow Conservatory. Sadly, as a result of the policies of the Bulgarian regime, she had no future. "The situation at the time made it impossible to have a career—with or without the recognition I gained at the Tchaikovsky Competition," she says. "Nothing could help that. The country was closed." Bulgaria did not open up to the world until the 1990s.

Liu Shikun, who had the bad luck of becoming a professional musician during Communist China's reign of terror, fared far worse. Like Mollova, he continued studying in Moscow for a while.

"When I returned home to China after the Tchaikovsky Competition," he reported, "the culture had changed." Common labor was valued above art, and he was forced to engage in physical work for two months to serve as an example to others. Meanwhile, Mao Zedong was promoting the idea that music and art must be based on folk traditions. If Liu wanted to compose, he had to adhere to those principles. "I thought this wasn't a bad idea," he recalls. "So in 1959 I wrote a piano concerto—it was called Youth Concerto—and for the first time China had a piece that utilized both Western and Chinese instruments."

He went back to Moscow in 1960 for two years of further study, but when he returned home, the political climate had worsened further. As a professor at the Beijing Conservatory, he performed for both Mao and Zhou Enlai. Both criticized his playing as not suited to Chinese audiences. "Mao chatted with me," he recalls. "They both gave me suggestions, like playing the melody louder. Since Chinese audiences didn't know classical music, they thought that people would understand the music better if I emphasized the melody." He tried to accommodate them.

In 1966, the Cultural Revolution under way, things deteriorated quickly. Officially, he was under suspicion both because he played Western classical music and because he had studied in the Soviet Union; China and the Soviets were no longer on good terms. "Richter and Kabalevsky loved me and had invited me to their houses," he explains, "so I was accused of being a Soviet spy. But the real reason for my trouble was that Mao's wife, Jiang Qing, was trying to force me to give false testimony against my father-in-law, who was a man of some political standing."

Things moved downhill swiftly. He was placed under a form of house arrest at the Beijing Conservatory. When he left one day to visit his three-year-old son at home, he was confined in a police booth in front of the school, where people were encouraged to throw things at him. Then he was moved into the notorious Qincheng Prison, an environment populated by serious criminals. He cleaned toilets. Guards repeatedly struck his right arm with a military belt—fracturing the bone. He was tortured. "In summer and winter I had only one shirt. There were no showers. For food they gave me some moldy bread and rotten leaves with insects, loaded with lots of salt. I had to spend hours bowing to a portrait of Mao. They kicked me. My hair became white from lack of sun."

"They never got what they wanted," Liu said with pride. They told him that his father-in-law was already destroyed, and that he should give up hope. "But I realized that on some days the newspaper they allowed me to read didn't arrive, even though my neighbors received a copy." It was a hint that there was information being withheld from him. "One day the guard forgot and gave me the newspaper when it contained an article describing how inspirational Mao was to the people who met him," says Liu, "and it included my father-in-law's name as one of the people the Chairman received. So I knew he was still in good standing."

The challenge became to find a way to get word out about his predicament. He found a broom, sharpened the handle's end to a point, then used it to cut out characters from the newspapers he was allowed to receive. His moldy bread became a glue to paste them together to form a letter, which he addressed to Mao. "It was about how they tried to push me to tell a lie, and that I wasn't a spy," he said. Seven years had passed. Finally, his first wife was allowed to visit, and she smuggled out the letter and managed eventually to get it to the Chinese leader. "I didn't give in. If I had, I probably would have died there."

When at last he gained release in 1973—a month and a half after his letter was brought to Mao—he spent months in the hospital before resuming his career as a pianist and as a soloist with the Central Philharmonic Orchestra of China, performing such officially sanctioned works as the *Yellow River* Concerto (which he learned by listening to the piece as it was broadcast over the loudspeakers outside his prison cell). "I hadn't touched a piano in seven years and the orchestra members wanted to see if I could still play," he remembered. He could. After the ordeal and the disgrace, when Eugene Ormandy visited with the Philadelphia Orchestra, Mao asked him to perform, and he did.

His fortunes underwent a complete reversal. In 1978 he became the first Chinese national to visit America and perform at the White House. "President Jimmy Carter told me, 'We knew you very early on, because you won a prize at the same time as Van Cliburn,'" Liu recalls. "'Van is the pride of America and the world, and you are the pride of China and the world.'" The following year Deng Xiaoping invited Seiji Ozawa and the Boston Symphony to China, and Liu recorded the Liszt First Piano Concerto with the ensemble. It became a bestseller.

In 1985, with his oldest son living in Los Angeles, the pianist flirted briefly with the idea of asking for asylum in America. Supporters had contacted members of Congress, got their support, and found an immigration lawyer for him. The FBI was already on board. "I would have become more famous," he reflected. "I thought about it very much. But China was starting to change, and my relatives were still there. My friends in America had tears in their eyes when I left. They were afraid I would get the same treatment again."

Those fears were unfounded. In 1990, the pianist settled in Hong Kong, where he began teaching piano ten hours a day. After two years, he had gathered enough money to create his first music school. The pianist has now founded more than a hundred such schools in over thirty cities, serving a total of almost seventy thousand Chinese students. He is flourishing. And, once again, so is Western classical music in China, with virtuoso celebrities like Lang Lang, Yuja Wang, and Yundi joining the formidable Liu on the front lines.

Appendix

I. JURORS AND PIANISTS

Jury:

  Emil Gilels (USSR) [Chairman]
  Sir Arthur Bliss (Great Britain)
  José Carlos Sequeira Costa (Portugal)
  George Georgescu (Romania)
  Armand de Gontaut-Biron (France)
  Camargo Guarnieri (Brazil)
  Lajos Hernádi (Hungary)
  Dmitri Kabalevsky (USSR)
  Boris Lyatoshynsky (USSR)
  František Maxián (Czechoslovakia)
  Heinrich Neuhaus (USSR)
  Lev Oborin (USSR)
  Fernand Quinet (Belgium)
  Sviatoslav Richter (USSR)
  Pavel Serebryakov (USSR)
  Henryk Sztompka (Poland)
  Pancho Vladigerov (Bulgaria)

Finalists:
  1. Van Cliburn (USA)
  2. Liu Shikun (China), tied with
     Lev Vlassenko (USSR)
  3. Naum Shtarkman (USSR)
  4. Eduard Miansarov (USSR)
  5. Milena Mollova (Bulgaria)
  6. Nadia Gedda-Nova (France)
  7. Toyoaki Matsuura (Japan)
  8. Daniel Pollack (USA)

Special Diplomas:
Roger Boutry (France)
Evelyne Crochet (France)
Anton Dikov (Bulgaria)
Julian Gutman (USSR)
Alexander Igharev (USSR)
Jerome Lowenthal (USA)
Inna Malinina (USSR)
Annie Petit (France)
Alexey Skavronsky (USSR)
Sérgio Varella-Cid (Portugal)
Natalia Yuzbasheva (USSR)

First Stage Only:
José Eduardo Agirre Alvarado (Ecuador)
Melita Edith Bán (Hungary)
Klára Bella (Hungary)
Alex Biel (Czechoslovakia)
Dmitry Blagoj (USSR)
Blandine Crosti (France)
Sylvie Decret (France)
Danuta Rogulska Dworakowska (Poland)
Dhen-li Hu (China)
Annie Marchand (France)
Norman Shetler (USA)
Hans Siesert (Federal Republic of Germany)
Josef Sitek (Czechoslovakia)
Imre Szendrei (Hungary)
Hans Thürwächter (Federal Republic of Germany)
Thorunn Johannsdottir (Iceland)

II. TOTAL SECOND-ROUND SCORES WITH AND WITHOUT RICHTER'S VOTE

	AVERAGE	RANK		AVERAGE	RANK
Dikov	13.88		without Richter	14.56	
Gutman	14.56		without Richter	15.33	
Gedda-Nova	17.35	8	without Richter	17.5	
Mollova	19.30	6	without Richter	19.56	7
Liu	23.75	2	without Richter	23.81	2
Cliburn	23.12	3 tie	without Richter	23	4
Miansarov	17.69	7	without Richter	18.67	8
Yuzbasheva	17.31		without Richter	18.27	
Lowenthal	14.59		without Richter	15.31	
Boutry	16.71		without Richter	17.56	
Varella-Cid	16.76		without Richter	17.5	
Shtarkman	23.12	3 tie	without Richter	23.63	3
Igharev	13.94		without Richter	14.63	
Petit	12.71		without Richter	13.31	
Vlassenko	24.18	1	without Richter	24.19	1
Malinina	13.53		without Richter	14.19	
Matsuura	19.65	5	without Richter	20.69	5
Pollack	20.29	4	without Richter	20.62	6
Crochet	15.75		without Richter	16.56	
Skavronsky	15.82		without Richter	16.63	

III. SECOND-ROUND SCORECARD IN ENGLISH

	A. Dikov	D. Gutman	N. Gedda-Nova	M. Mollova	L. Shikun	V. Cliburn	V. Miansarov	N. Yuzbasheva	J. Lowenthal
A. Bliss	19	22	19	24	25	25	20	20	22
P. Vladigerov	16	13	15	25	24	25	21	22	13
E. Gilels	16	14	18	20	24	25	16	17	17
C. Guarnieri	12	13	16	16	23	17	19	18	15
G. Georgescu	20	19	20	23	25	25	22	21	19
D. Kabalevsky	15	15	17	21	24	25	17	19	15
F. Quinet	10	13	14	15	23	23	16	16	12
B. Lyatoshynsky	15	12	20	20	23	25	17	16	15
F. Maxián	13	16	15	17	23	22	21	17	14
H. Neuhaus	10		21	21	25	25	10	10	10
L. Oborin	14	15	17	20	24	23			14
S. Richter	3	3	15	15	23	25	3	3	3
P. Serebryakov	15	13	16	21	24	24	20	20	15
S. Costa	14	13	15	17	20	15	18	17	13
L. Hernádi	12	18	19	19	24	19	22	18	17
H. Sztompka	16	16	19	17	25	25	21	22	18
A. De Gontaut-Biron	16	18	19	17	25	25	20	21	16
AVERAGE OF POINTS FOR ROUND II	13.88	14.56	17.35	19.30	23.75	23.12	17.69	17.31	14.59

R. Boutry	S. Varella-Cid	N. Shtarkman	A. Ikharev	A. Petit	L. Vlassenko	I. Malinina	T. Matsuura	D. Pollack	E. Crochet	A. Skavronsky
24	20	23	19	20	25	20	23	24	25	20
12	14	24	10	8	25	14	20	21	15	14
19	17	23	15	15	25	15	21	20	16	17
15	18	25	15	12	21	13	23	19	14	20
20	20	24	21	14	25	19	20	23	18	21
19	19	24	15	15	25	15	23	22	20	15
15	12	23	14	10	25	10	17	15	13	16
13	20	24	15	15	25	15	25	23	15	15
16	20	23	16	12	24	10	20	20	16	11
10	10	23	1	10	24	10	20	22	15	10
19	14	24	15	12	25	12	16	20	14	15
3	3	15	3	3	24	3	3	15	3	3
20	17	23	15	13	25	15	22	20	17	17
17	18	25	14	10	18	13	20	15	12	18
18	21	22	17	15	25	15	21	22	18	18
22	20	24	16	16	25	15	20	22	19	20
22	20	24	16	16	25	16	20	22	18	19
16.71	16.76	23.12	13.94	12.71	24.18	13.53	19.65	20.29	15.75	15.82

Acknowledgments

I have many people to thank for making this book possible. First on the list must be my intrepid editor Jonathan Segal, along with his assistant, Julia Ringo.

I began work on this project while in residence at the National Humanities Center in North Carolina as a Meymandi Fellow, an honor made possible by the generosity of the outstanding scholar, humanist, and healer Dr. Assad Meymandi. Among my colleagues there, the Russia expert Dr. Ernest (Erik) Zitser of Duke University was an incredibly charitable mentor.

I am indebted to many institutions for the access they granted me to archival materials—in particular, to Julia Kruger of the American College of Musicians; Rachel Chatalbash of the Archivists Round Table of Metropolitan New York; the Arthur Bliss Trust; Valoise Armstrong of the Dwight D. Eisenhower Presidential Library and Museum; the Federal Bureau of Investigation; the Glinka National Museum Consortium of Musical Culture in Moscow; Jane Gottlieb of the Juilliard School; the Kilgore School and Library; the La Guardia and Wagner Archives; the National Archives in College Park, Maryland; George Keck of the National Federation of Music Clubs; the New York City Municipal Archives; Gabe Smith of the New York Philharmonic Archives; the New York Public Library; the Paley Center for Media; Laura Ruede, Van Cliburn Archivist of the Mary Couts Burnett Library at Texas Christian University; Maggie Estes of the Van Cliburn Foundation; and the Yale University Oral History of American Music project.

Special thanks are due my Russian consultants and translators, including Artem Bizimov, Lev Gankine, Sarah Glacel, Hannah Khromov, Nina Lelchuk, Maya Pritsker, and Alexandra Solomina; French translators Sonia Gluckman Buxbaum, Adrian McDonnell (assistant to Roger Boutry), and Debra Popkin; and Chinese translator Yu-Ching Hsu, who was an invaluable help in my exchanges with Liu Shikun.

Others who contributed mightily to my efforts include Sergei N. Khrushchev, Senior Fellow, Watson Institute for International Studies at Brown University; Dmitri Alexeev; Sara Davis Buechner; the ever-helpful David Dubal; Sara Fishko; Leon Fleisher; Edith Friedheim; Eric Gibson; Gary and Naomi

Graffman; author A. E. Hotchner; Iya Itin; Dr. Dennis Klein; Mary Ellen Koenig of the United States embassy in Moscow; Seymour Lipkin; Galina Atemieva-Lifschitz; Konstantin Lifschitz; Albert Markov; Roman Markowicz; Benita Meshulam; Evans Mirageas; Simon Morrison; Polina Nazaykinskaya; pianist Paul Ostrovsky; Richard Probst; Yale Richmond; Richard Rodzinski; Jerome Rose; David and Vivian Rubin; David Schoenbaum; Craig Sheppard; Alexander Shtarkman; Joseph Smith; James Stream; William R. Trotter; Hans Tuch; Solomon Volkov; Stanley Waldoff; André Watts, James Graham Wilson, Office of the Historian, U.S. Department of State; and Sergei Zelenev. Radio documentarian Sara Fishko kindly shared her interviews of Schuyler Chapin and Jerome Lowenthal.

On the Russian side of the globe, I am most grateful to the Vlassenko family—Ella, Irina, and Natasha—for their generosity; Aschen Mikoyan has been invaluable with her friendship, stories, and photographs; faculty members of the Russian music conservatories are included elsewhere in the text, but in Moscow, Victor Bunin deserves special attention; Sergei Kurzhkovskiy helped me obtain the photo of the three winners; and in St. Petersburg I was well treated by Elena Vitenberg, Lidya Volchek, and piano department head Ekaterina Murina, faculty member Sergei Urivaev, and Dean Leonid Zaichick.

Finally, to my wife, Adrienne, I owe everything.

Notes

Two previous biographies of Van Cliburn were helpful, though both are highly flawed. *The Van Cliburn Legend* by Abram Chasins with Villa Stiles was rushed to press barely a year after the pianist's Tchaikovsky Competition win, and Chasins, though close to the subject, was a notoriously untrustworthy storyteller; he admitted to me that he made up some of the material in order to make the book more interesting. Howard Reich's *Van Cliburn*, done with the pianist's full cooperation, is often a full-throated defense against any criticisms the pianist received over the course of his career. As a result, the text crosses the line into hagiography.

In addition to the books, articles, and media resources cited here, I conducted numerous interviews with Cliburn and his friends, associates, and colleagues, both here and in Russia—including his early Kilgore neighbors, Juilliard colleagues, fellow Tchaikovsky contestants, and many music professionals with whom he worked. I am thankful for their cooperation.

Interviews for this book were conducted with the following people, in both the United States and Russia:

Dmitri Alexeev, Jessie Armstrong, Vladimir Ashkenazy, Dodi Ashkenazy, Lou Ballard, Dmitri Bashkirov, Angeline Battista, Joseph Bloch, Roger Boutry, Victor Bunin, Lucille Butts, Martin Canin, Schuyler Chapin, Van Cliburn, Ruth Covelli, Evelyne Crochet, Bella Davidovich, Ivan Davis, Andea de Forest, Misha Dichter, Velma Dickson, Jeaneane Dowis, David Dubal, Mary Lou Falcone, José Feghali, Vladimir Feltsman, Sara Fishko, Max Frankel, Edith Friedheim, Olegna Fuschi, Peter Goodrich, Vera Gornostaeva, Gary and Naomi Graffman, Lottie Lou Lipscomb Guttry, Ann Frasher Hudson, Sarah Keene, Sergei Khrushchev, Nina Lelchuk, Seymour Lipkin, Liu Shikun, Jerome Lowenthal, Glenn Mack, Lucy Mann, Albert Markov, James Mathis, John McGinnis, Evans Mirageas, Milena Mollova, Annette Morgan, Ekaterina Murina, Paul Ostrovsky, Dmitry Paperno, Annie Petit, David Pocock, Daniel Pollack, André Previn, Richard Probst, Isabella Rafaelovna, Richard Rodzinski, David and Vivian Rubin, Lubov Davidovna Schukina, Neil Sedaka, Craig Sheppard, Annie Marchand Sherter,

Norman Shetler, Alexander Shtarkman, Tom Smith, Henry Steinway, Jenny and Sherry Thompson, William R. Trotter, Sergei Urivaev, Eliso Virsaladze, Lev Vlassenko, Natasha Vlassenko, Solomon Volkov, Mikhail Voskrensky, André Watts, Nanette Wickham, Harriet Wingreen, Leonid Zaichick, Vladimir Zakharov.

Many other important sources used for the book are cited in the Acknowledgments.

On the valuation of the ruble: the correct exchange rate for 1958 is difficult to pin down, especially because there was an official rate and a black-market rate. I based my calculations on information from the usually reliable Russian economic newspaper *Kommersant* (http://kommersant.ru/doc/2649852).

NOTES ON INDIVIDUAL CHAPTERS

Chapter 1
Edith Friedheim, Arthur Friedheim's daughter-in-law, pointed me to a passage in Friedheim's *Life and Liszt* by the volume's editor, Theodore Bullock, that asserts a strong connection between Van's piano sound and that of his mother's teacher, Friedheim:

> "When I went to hear Van Cliburn play in Brussels in 1958, I knew nothing about him," wrote Bullock. "The fact that he was performing the Tchaikovsky Concerto for which Friedheim had no love, and which I loathed, gave me no clue to what was coming. I was puzzled for a moment and then I sat up with a start. Surely I had heard this man before. What incarnation was this? Could memory be playing tricks on me? Then I recalled the words of Louis Carpath, written long ago in Vienna: 'When I listen to Arthur Friedheim, I close my eyes and I seem to hear the master, Franz Liszt.' Here, incredibly, impossibly, was Arthur Friedheim in 1958 playing in Brussels. Here was the poise I had known so well, the same great, rich sweep. The same uncanny use of the pedals. The same incredible mastery of subtle detail. I listened to Cliburn with my eyes open and I knew that Arthur Friedheim was playing again as Liszt played before him. Friedheim . . . was Liszt's most receptive pupil. Certainly Friedheim had no more receptive pupil than Rildia Bee Cliburn. Her son she shaped in her image and his."

Quotes from Van Cliburn about his early music lessons are from interviews conducted by me. The story about being trained to serve at the dinner table was revealed by him during his onstage interview at the New York Public Library at the time of the auction at Christie's; his revelations about the idea of serving audience members came during an interview with me for *Piano Today*.

Information from Van's childhood neighbors—Lottie Lou Lipscomb Guttry, Bill Morton, Lucille Butts, Nanette Wickham, Velma Dickson, Annette Morgan, Lou Ballard, and Jessie Armstrong—was captured in Kilgore in 1990 when I visited to attend Van's piano recital there. The interviews with Jimmy Mathis and Jeaneane Dowis took place in New York in 1990 and 1991; Ivan Davis's interviews occurred in New York in the early 1990s and in Florida in 2013. Information about Olga Samaroff's relationship to the Cliburns came from Samaroff's assistant Angeline Battista.

The late Joseph Bloch, a dear friend, supplied years of stories and insights, along with an interview conducted in 1990. Martin Canin recounted Van's audition at Juilliard in an interview in 2010. The correspondence from Rildia Bee to Rosina Lhévinne can be found in the Juilliard archives.

Chapter 2
The interview with Glenn Mack took place in New York in the early 1990s. Several former Juilliard students confirmed the stories of Van's social life and drinking habits. Gary Graffman's recollection of Van's appearance at Carnegie Hall (and of his own nightclub adventures) appears in his hilarious autobiography, *I Really Should Be Practicing: Reflections on the Pleasures and Perils of Playing the Piano in Public*. Van's confession about his reliance on cigarettes was made to an acquaintance from his Juilliard days, Andea de Forest. Van's remark about being a Christian, as opposed to a Baptist, was made to me.

Matisse's description of his difficulties in capturing the spontaneous beauty of a bouquet appears in his limited-edition book *Jazz*.

Van's theory teacher at Juilliard was composer Robert Ward, and the anecdote about the theory exam and the pianist's spotty memory was conveyed by him to pianist Joseph Smith, who related it to me. The note from Van to Lhévinne about the Michaels Award is in the Juilliard archives.

Van's folksy remarks to Mrs. Leventritt are reported by Gary Graffman in his book.

Robert Freeman reported his Marlboro experiences during a 2015 interview. Van's remarks about late Beethoven will appear in a forthcoming book by pianist Sara Davis Buechner about her own life story.

Chapter 3
I conducted several interviews with Jerome Lowenthal, beginning in 1991. Mary Lou Falcone shared her observations with me in 2013. Naomi Graffman's remembrance of being Van's "alarm clock" appeared in "Old Acquaintances Remember Cliburn" by James Barron, in *The New York Times*, February 27, 2013. My interview with Schuyler Chapin took place at Steinway Hall in New York in 1990.

Naomi Graffman cited Van's chronic nosebleeds as the reason he was rejected from the army, in a conversation with me.

Van's encounter with the clairvoyant was related to me by two of his friends, Sarah Keene and Andea de Forest. "He was lying on the bed with his feet dangling off the edge," says Keene, when he suddenly announced, "I'm going to Russia, girls." At that point he filled them in on the details of the prediction.

Lazar Berman's book is not available in English translation; I received help in deciphering the text from two friends: Artem Bizimov, a former graduate student of mine, and Lev Gankine, who translated two of my books for my Russian publisher. I communicated directly with Vladimir Ashkenazy and Dmitri Bashkirov about Berman's assertions regarding their participation in the precompetition meeting with Soviet officials.

Chapter 4

The movie poster for the Russian version of *The Silent Man* appears in the photo section of this book. Recent revelations about Russia's training of its Olympic athletes highlight the recurrent pattern of cheating disclosed by Maya Plisetskaya in her book.

Chapter 5

Lev Vlassenko's comments were derived in part from his writings and recollections gathered by his family, and in part from an interview I conducted with him in 1990.

The story of Flier's dog howling at the opening strains of the Tchaikovsky concerto was confirmed to me by pianist Vladimir Feltsman, another Flier student. "It's absolutely true," he said. "The dog developed an allergy to the opening of the concerto, and no other music affected him that way. If Flier was in a good mood and wanted to entertain guests, he would play those opening notes just to set the dog off. I witnessed it many times."

Chapter 6

The Gogol quote is from his *Nevsky Prospekt*. The story of the French judge standing on a chair and railing at the chandelier was told to me by jury member Sequeira Costa during an afternoon-long interview I conducted at his home.

Shostakovich remains a controversial figure; Solomon Volkov's book purporting to be the composer's memoirs (*Testimony*) has been depicted in some quarters as fiction. However, the text seems to me generally believable, and it certainly has the flavor of the era, even if some details are difficult to confirm. Other sources used here include *Story of a Friendship: The Letters of Dmitry Shostakovich to Isaak Glikman, 1941–1975; Dmitri Shostakovich, Pianist* by Sofia Moshevich; and *Galina: A Russian Story* by Galina Vishnevskaya.

Chapter 7

The sad story of Ecuador's Alvarado was reported to me by Annie Marchand Sherter. Aspects of "Russian piano style," and Rosina's penchant for moderation, were conveyed to me by the brilliant piano expert David Dubal.

An English translation of the chart of scores in the second round may be found in the Appendix, along with a comparison of competition rankings as they would appear with and without Richter's votes.

Chapter 8

The Cliburn-Shetler relationship left a deep impression on many of the competition participants, though none wanted to be quoted. I am grateful to Norman Shetler for his willingness to speak openly about it.

The exchanges between Neuhaus and Goldenweiser are reported in Dmitry Paperno's *Notes of a Moscow Pianist.*

The discussion among Khrushchev's advisors about whether to award first prize to Van is recorded in the Russian edition of *Memoirs of Nikita Khrushchev,* ed. Sergei Khrushchev, volume 2: *Reformer, 1945–1964* (but not in the English-language version). Nina Lelchuk first made me aware of this, and the translation here is by Sarah Glacel.

The Max Frankel quotes are from an interview I conducted with him.

Chapter 9

US State Department documents quoted here reside in the National Archive in College Park, Maryland. Some of the correspondence involving Juilliard officials can be found in the collection of the Juilliard library. The exchanges between Mark Schubart and Rosina Lhévinne are also available in the archives of the New York Public Library at Lincoln Center. Internal Soviet memos from the Central Committee concerning the event were made available to me by the Glinka National Museum Consortium of Musical Culture.

The reference to Dr. Sikirsky comes from Nina Lelchuk.

My interview with Vera Gornostaeva in her Moscow apartment was facilitated by Alexandra Solomina. Sadly, the venerable teacher passed away not long after our meeting.

Chapter 10

A video of the incident in which Van reads a fan's note before beginning the Rachmaninoff concerto is available on *Van Cliburn in Moscow,* volume 3.

The exchanges in regard to the ticker-tape parade, including the telegram from Michael Caracappa of *The New York Times* to Mayor Wagner, are in New York's Municipal Archives.

Chapter 11

Khrushchev's home movies were made available to me by his son, Sergei.

Chapter 12

The FBI reports on Van are often unreliable, sometimes offering little more than rumor mongering. However, the telephone taps seem too specific to be discounted.

Juilliard's insistence on keeping its distance from any hint of affiliation with Van's activities seems ridiculous in retrospect. Whether it was a stance aimed at institutional purity or at Van Cliburn in particular is hard to discern.

Chapter 13
I am deeply grateful to Tommy Smith for his willingness to meet with me.

Epilogue
Liu Shikun shared the story of his imprisonment with me when we were both in Fort Worth in 2013. He was on the jury of that year's Van Cliburn Competition.

Selected Bibliography

BOOKS

Apparat TsK KPSS i Kul'tura (Staff of the Central Committee of the Communist Party of the Soviet Union and Culture), *1958–1964*: Dokumenty / Sost. E. S. Afanas'eva, V. Iu. Afiani (otv. red.), Z.K. Vodop'ianova (otv. sost.), T. A. Dzhalilov, T. I. Dzhailolova, M.Iu. Prozumenshchikov, Published by Russian Political Encyclopedia Press (ROSSPEN)—1958–1964: Documents.

Benjamin, James. *The Most Musical Nation: Jews and Culture in the Late Russian Empire.* New Haven: Yale University Press, 2010.

Berman, Lazar. *The Years of Peregrination: Reveries of a Pianist.* Moscow: Klassika XXI, 2006.

Bliss, Sir Arthur. *As I Remember.* London: Faber & Faber, 1970.

Brzezinski, Matthew. *Red Moon Rising: Sputnik and the Hidden Rivalries That Ignited the Space Age.* New York: Times Books, 2007.

Bulgakov, Mikhail. *The Master and Margarita,* trans. Diana Burgin and Katherine Tiernan. New York: Vintage, 1996.

Castro, Christi-Anne. *Musical Renderings of the Philippine Nation.* New York: Oxford University Press, 2011.

Chasins, Abram, with Villa Stiles. *The Van Cliburn Legend.* Garden City, NY: Doubleday & Company, 1959.

Capote, Truman. *The Muses Are Heard: An Account.* New York: Random House, 1956.

Caute, David. *The Dancer Defects: The Struggle for Cultural Supremacy During the Cold War.* New York: Oxford University Press, 2003.

Dudintsev, Vladimir. *Not by Bread Alone,* trans. Dr. Edith Bone. New York: E. P. Dutton & Co., Inc., 1957.

Ehrenburg, Ilya. *Post-War Years: 1945–54,* trans. Tatiana Shebunina in collaboration with Yvonne Kapp. Cleveland: World Publishing Company, 1967.

———. *The Thaw,* trans. Manya Harari. Chicago: Henry Regnery Company, 1955. Russian text first published Moscow: Sovietsky Pissatel, 1954.

Finn, Peter, and Petra Couvée. *The Zhivago Affair.* New York: Pantheon Books, 2014.

Friedheim, Arthur. *Life and Liszt,* in *Remembering Franz Liszt,* ed. Mark N. Grant. New York: Limelight Editions, 1986.

Gaddis, John Lewis. *We Now Know: Rethinking Cold War History.* New York: Oxford University Press, 1997.

Geldern, James von, and Richard Stites (eds.). *Mass Culture in Soviet Russia: Tales, Poems, Songs, Movies, Plays and Folklore 1917–1953.* Bloomington: Indiana University Press, 1995.

Gerschenkron, Alexander. *Reflections on Soviet Novels.* Cambridge: Cambridge University Press, 1960.

Gogol, Nikolai. *The Collected Tales of Nikolai Gogol,* translated and annotated by Richard Pevear and Larissa Volokhonsky. New York: Pantheon, 1998.

Gorokhova, Elena. *A Mountain of Crumbs.* New York: Simon & Schuster, 2011.

Gorsuch, Anne E. *Youth in Revolutionary Russia: Enthusiasts, Bohemians, Delinquents.* Bloomington: Indiana University Press, 2000.

——, and Diane P. Koenker (eds.). *Turizm.* Ithaca, NY: Cornell University Press, 2006.

Griffin, Nicholas. *Ping-Pong Diplomacy: The Secret History Behind the Game That Changed the World.* New York: Scribner, 2014.

Graffman, Gary. *I Really Should Be Practicing: Reflections on the Pleasures and Perils of Playing the Piano in Public.* Garden City, NY: Doubleday & Company, Inc., 1981.

Grum-Grzhimailo, Tamara. *Tchaikovsky Competition. History, Faces, Events.* Moscow: Grant (ГРАНТЪ), 1998.

Hasty, Olga Peters, and Susanne Fusso. *America Through Russian Eyes, 1874–1926.* New Haven: Yale University Press, 1988.

Hixson, Walter L. *Parting the Curtain: Propaganda, Culture and the Cold War, 1945–1961.* New York: Palgrave Macmillan, 1998.

Hoberman, J. *Army of Phantoms: American Movies and the Making of the Cold War.* New York: New Press, 2011.

Hotchner, A. E. *Choice People: The Great, Near-Great, and Ingrates I Have Known.* New York: William Morrow, 1984.

Hurok, Sol, with Ruth Goode. *Impresario: A Memoir.* Westport, CT: Greenwood Press, 1946.

Iossel, Mikhail, and Jeff Parker (eds.). *Amerika: Russian Writers View the United States.* Champaign, IL: Dalkey Archive Press, 2004.

Janis, Byron, with Maria Cooper Janis. *Chopin and Beyond: My Extraordinary Life in Music and the Paranormal.* Hoboken, NJ: John Wiley & Sons, 2010.

Kalugin, Oleg, with Fen Montaigne. *The First Directorate: My 32 Years in Intelligence and Espionage Against the West.* New York: St. Martin's Press, 1994.

Kenneson, Claude. *Musical Prodigies: Perilous Journeys, Remarkable Lives.* Portland: Amadeus Press, 2003.

Koch, Scott A. *Selected Estimates on the Soviet Union, 1950–1959.* Washington, DC: United States Central Intelligence Agency, 1993.

Koestler, Arthur. *Darkness at Noon.* New York: Macmillan, 1941.

Kraus, Richard Curt. *Piano and Politics in China.* New York: Oxford University Press, 1989.

Khrushchev, Nikita. *Khrushchev Remembers,* ed., and trans. Strobe Talbott, with introduction, commentary, and notes by Edward Crankshaw. Boston: Little, Brown and Company, 1970.

————. *Memoirs of Nikita Khrushchev, vol. 2: Reformer,* ed. Sergei Khrushchev. Moscow: Vremy, 2010.

Lapin, Slava. *From the Inside.* Osaka: Luniver Press, 2009.

Lerner, Alan Jay. *The Street Where I Live.* New York: W. W. Norton, 1978.

Lertzman, Richard A., and William J. Birnes. *Dr. Feelgood: The Shocking Story of the Doctor Who May Have Changed History by Treating and Drugging JFK, Marilyn, Elvis, and Other Prominent Figures.* New York: Skyhorse Publishing, 2013.

Liao Yiwu, *For a Song and a Hundred Songs: A Poet's Journey Through a Chinese Prison,* trans. Wenguang Huang. Boston: New Harvest/Houghton Mifflin Harcourt, 2013.

Maksimenkov, Leonid. *Muzyka vmesto sumbura: kompozitory i muzykanty v Strane Sovetov* (Music Instead of Muddle: Composers and Musicians in the Land of the Soviets), *1917–1991.* Moscow: Mezhdunarodnyi fond "Demokratiia," 2013.

Mazour, Anatole G. *Russia: Tsarist and Communist.* Princeton, NJ: D. Van Nostrand Co., 1962.

McCauley, Martin. *Who's Who in Russia Since 1900.* New York: Routledge, 1997.

McReynolds, Louise, Joan Neuberger, Richard Stites, and Julie Buckler. *Imitations of Life: Two Centuries of Melodrama in Russia.* Durham, NC: Duke University Press, 2002.

Medvedev, Roy Aleksandrovich. *Khrushchev: The Years in Power.* New York: W. W. Norton & Company, 1978.

Mitter, Rana, and Patrick Major (eds.). *Across the Blocs: Cold War Cultural and Social History.* Portland, OR: Frank Cass, 2004.

Monsaingeon, Bruno. *Sviatoslav Richter: Notebooks and Conversations,* trans. Stewart Spencer. Princeton, NJ: Princeton University Press, 2001.

Moshevich, Sofia. *Dmitri Shostakovich, Pianist.* Montreal and Kingston, ON: McGill–Queen's University Press, 2004.

Mulroy, Kevin (ed.). *Western Amerykanski: Polish Poster Art and the Western.* Seattle: University of Washington Press, 1999.

Nabokov, Nicolas. *Old Friends and New Music.* London: Hamish Hamilton, 1951.

Neuhaus, Heinrich. *The Art of Piano Playing,* trans. K. A. Leibovitch. New York: Praeger, 1973.

Norris, Jeremy. *The Russian Piano Concerto, vol. 1: The Nineteenth Century.* Bloomington: Indiana University Press, 1994.

Nye, Joseph. *Soft Power.* New York: Public Affairs, 2005.

Paperno, Dmitry. *Notes of a Moscow Pianist.* Portland, OR: Amadeus Press, 1998.

Paulicelli, Eugenia. *The Fabric of Cultures: Fashion, Identity, and Globalization*, ed. Hazel Clark. New York: Routledge, 2008.

Parrott, Jasper, with Vladimir Ashkenazy. *Ashkenazy: Beyond Frontiers*. New York: Atheneum, 1985.

Pedrosa, Carmen Navarro. *Imelda Marcos*. New York: St. Martin's Press, 1987.

Plisetskaya, Maya. *I, Maya Plisetskaya*, trans. Antonina W. Bouis. New Haven: Yale University Press, 2001.

Rabinovich, D. A. *Performer and Style*. All-Union Publishing House "Soviet Composer," 1981.

Raleigh, Donald J. *Soviet Baby Boomers: An Oral History of Russia's Cold War Generation*. New York: Oxford University Press, 2013.

———— (ed.). *Russia's Sputnik Generation: Soviet Baby Boomers Talk About Their Lives*. Bloomington: Indiana University Press, 2006.

Rauch, Georg von. *A History of Soviet Russia*, trans. Peter and Annette Jacobsohn. New York: Frederick A. Praeger, 1967.

Rasmussen, Karl Aage. *Sviatoslav Richter: Pianist*. Boston: Northeastern University Press, 2010.

Reich, Howard. *Van Cliburn*. Nashville: Thomas Nelson Publishers, 1993.

Richmond, Yale. *Cultural Exchange and the Cold War: Raising the Iron Curtain*. University Park: Penn State University Press, 2004.

Roper, Robert. *Nabokov in America*. New York: Bloomsbury USA, 2015.

Rosenberg, Victor. *Soviet-American Relations, 1953–1960: Diplomacy and Cultural Exchange During the Eisenhower Presidency*. Jefferson, NC: McFarland & Company, 2005.

Salisbury, Harrison E. (ed.). *The Soviet Union: The Fifty Years*. New York: Harcourt Brace, 1967.

Saxe, Serge. *Universal Pursuit: The Creative World of Serge Saxe*. "About Serge Saxe" by Van Cliburn, Austin: Texas Quarterly Studies, 1965.

Saunders, Frances Stonor. *The Cultural Cold War: The CIA and the World of Arts and Letters*. New York: New Press, 2000.

Sazonova, E. (Evgeniia), and M. (Mark) Serebrovskii. *Moskva—Konkurs imeni P. I. Chaikovskogo: 1958–1978, piat' konkursov: istoriia, razmyshleniia*. Moscow: Sovetskii kompozitor, 1978.

Schwarz, Boris. *Music and Musical Life in Soviet Russia, 1957–1981*. Bloomington: Indiana University Press, 1983.

Shapiro, Doris. *We Danced All Night: My Life Behind the Scenes with Alan Jay Lerner*. New York: William Morrow, 1990.

Shostakovich, Dmitri. *Story of a Friendship: The Letters of Dmitry Shostakovich to Isaak Glikman, 1941–1975*, trans. Anthony Phillips. Ithaca, NY: Cornell University Press, 1993.

Siloti, Alexander. *My Memories of Liszt*, in *Remembering Franz Liszt*, ed. Mark Grant. New York: Limelight Editions, 1986.

Stites, Richard. *Russian Popular Culture: Entertainment and Society Since 1900.* Cambridge: Cambridge Russian Paperbacks, 1992.

Swayne, Steve. *Orpheus in Manhattan: William Schuman and the Shaping of America's Musical Life.* New York: Oxford University Press, 2011.

Starr, S. Frederick. *Red and Hot: The Fate of Jazz in the Soviet Union.* Pompton Plains, NJ: Limelight Editions, 2004.

Tassie, Gregor. *Kirill Kondrashin: His Life in Music.* Lanham, MD: Scarecrow Press, 2009.

Taubman, William. *Khrushchev: The Man and His Era.* New York: W. W. Norton, 2004.

Thayer, Charles, *Bears in the Caviar.* Montpelier, VT: Russian Information Services, 2015.

Tornoff, Kiril. *Virtuosi Abroad: Soviet Music and Imperial Competition During the Early Cold War, 1945–1958.* Ithaca, NY: Cornell University Press, 2015.

Trotter, William R. *Priest of Music: The Life of Dimitri Mitropoulos.* Portland, OR: Amadeus Press, 1995.

Tuch, Hans N. *Arias, Cabalettas, and Foreign Affairs: A Public Diplomat's Quasi-Musical Memoir.* Washington, DC: New Academia Publishing, 2008.

———. *Communicating with the World: U.S. Public Diplomacy Overseas.* New York: St. Martin's Press, 1990.

Vishnevskaya, Galina. *Galina: A Russian Story.* New York: Harcourt Brace Jovanovich, 1984.

Vlassenko, Ella (ed.). *Lev Vlassenko: Articles, Reminiscences, Interviews,* trans. Maria Kravhencko. Brisbane: Allstate Printing & Graphics, 2009.

Volkov, Solomon. *Testimony: The Memoirs of Dmitri Shostakovich.* Pompton Plains, NJ: Limelight Editions, 2004.

Wellens, Ian. *Music on the Frontline: Nicolas Nabokov's Struggle Against Communism and Middlebrow Culture.* Burlington, VT: Ashgate Publishing Company, 2002.

Wild, Earl. *A Walk on the Wild Side.* Palm Springs: Ivory Classics Foundation, 2011.

Zilberquit, Dr. Mark. *Russia's Great Modern Pianists.* Neptune, NJ: TFH Publications, 1983.

Zubok, Vladislav Martinovich. *Zhivago's Children: The Last Russian Intelligentsia.* Cambridge, MA: Harvard University Press, 2009.

ARTICLES AND REPORTS

Ahles, Andrea. "Cliburn juror has special connection to competition's namesake." Fort Worth *Star-Telegram*, June 5, 2013.

Annals of the American Academy of Political and Social Science 200 (November 1938).

Arbatsky, Yury. "The Soviet Attitude Towards Music: An Analysis Based in Part on Secret Archives." *Musical Quarterly* 43, no. 3 (July 1957).

Bachus, Nancy. "Inside Competitions with Daniel Pollack." *Clavier Companion*, January/February 2010.

Barron, James. "Old Acquaintances Remember Cliburn." *New York Times*, February 27, 2013.

Bellow, Saul. "Literary Notes on Khrushchev." *Esquire*, March 1961.

Biryukova, Ekaterina. "Fame or money for you? Ekaterina Biryukova on Russian musical awards." *Critical Mass*, 2006, no. 2.

Black, Jessica Catherine. "The New York Philharmonic Behind the Iron Curtain: Goodwill Tour or Cold War Propaganda?" *Thesis*, University of Melbourne Conservatorium of Music, 2012.

Borge, Anders V. "Discordant Diplomacy: Goodwill and the Cultural Battleground of the 1958 Tchaikovsky Competition." *Hopkins Review* 6, no. 1 (winter 2013) (New Series).

Bracker, Milton. "Jubilant Cliburn Arrives Here After Piano Triumph in Soviet." *New York Times*, May 17, 1958.

Brook, Tim. "The Revival of China's Musical Culture." *China Quarterly*, no. 77 (March 1979).

Bryk, William. "Dr. Feelgood." *New York Sun*, September 20, 2005.

Central Committee CPSU Reports. Moscow: USSR Ministry of Culture, n.d.

Ciboski, Kenneth N. "A Woman in Soviet Leadership: The Political Career of Madame Furtseva." *Canadian Slavonic Papers/Revue Canadienne des Slavistes* 14, no. 1, (spring 1972).

Dallin, Alexander. "America Through Soviet Eyes." *Public Opinion Quarterly* 11, no. 1 (spring 1947).

Davidson, John. "Van Cliburn: His Very Private Life." *Texas Monthly*, May 1987.

Dunne, Dominick. "Imelda in Exile." *Vanity Fair*, August 1986.

Frankel, Max. "Russians Cheer U.S. Pianist, 23." *New York Times*, April 11, 1958.

———. "U.S. Pianist, 23, Wins Soviet Contest." *New York Times*, April 14, 1958.

Fulford, Robert. "Glenn Gould's 1957 Russian Tour." *Globe and Mail*, March 11, 1998.

Gerovitch, Slava. "Mathematical Machines of the Cold War: Soviet Computing, American Cybernetics and Ideological Disputes in the Early 1950s." *Social Studies of Science* 31, no. 2.

Gilels, Emil. "Art Brings People Closer." *Pravda*, April 15, 1958.

Hallinan, Victoria. "The 1958 Tour of the Moiseyev Dance Company: A Window into American Perception." *Journal of History and Cultures* (1) 2012: 51–64.

Harris, Joyce Saenz. "Cliburn: Myth and Reality on a Legendary Scale." *Dallas News*, May 23, 1993.

Hsu, Madeleine. "The Naked Face of Talent: Rosina Lhévinne." *American Music Teacher,* November/December 1981.

Hudson, G. F. "Mao, Marx and Moscow." *Foreign Affairs* 37, no. 4 (July 1959).

Isacoff, Stuart. "The Rise and Fall and Rise of Van Cliburn." *Ovation,* September 1989.

———. "Van Cliburn Then and Now." *Piano Today,* Summer 2001.

Kabalevsky, Dmitri. "A Russian Traveler's View of American Music," trans. Joseph Suhadolc and Virginia Moseley. *Music Educators Journal* 49, no. 2 (November–December 1962). First published in *Literaturnaya Gazeta,* February 11, 1960.

Korovkin, Michael A. "An Account of Social Usages of Americanized Argot in Modern Russia." *Language in Society* 16, no. 4 (December 1987).

Lipman, Jeaneane Dowis. "Rosina." *American Scholar* 65 (summer 1996).

Madigan, Tim. "Van Cliburn: Mementos of the Musician." *Fort Worth Star-Telegram,* May 13, 2012.

Mason, Colin. "Paris, May 1952." *Tempo,* no. 100 (1972), Cambridge University Press.

Mosely, Philip E. "Freedom of Artistic Expression and Scientific Inquiry in Russia."

Pollack, Noemi Levinsons. "We Went to Europe." *Juilliard Review* 6, no. 1 (winter 1958–59).

Rabinovich, David. "Van Cliburn." *Musical Life,* 1972.

Richmond, Yale. "Cultural Exchange and the Cold War: How the West Won." Speech delivered at the Aleksanteri Institute's 9th Annual Conference, University of Helsinki, Finland, October 2009.

Rogin, Michael. "Kiss Me Deadly: Communism, Motherhood, and Cold War Movies." *Representations,* no. 6 (spring 1984), University of California Press.

Sargeant, Winthrop. "Cliburn Plain." *New Yorker,* February 28, 1959.

———. "Musical Events." *New Yorker,* May 31, 1958.

———. "Musical Events." *New Yorker,* October 25, 1958.

———. "The Wages of Fame." *New Yorker,* March 17, 1962.

Schubart, Mark. "Moscow Rolls Out Red Carpet." *New York Times,* April 20, 1958.

Schulman, Michael. "Bling Ring." *New Yorker,* May 13, 2013.

Scott-Smith, Giles. "The Congress for Cultural Freedom, the End of Ideology and the 1955 Milan Conference: Defining the Parameters of Discourse." *Journal of Contemporary History* 37, no. 3 (July 2002).

Siegelbaum, Lewis. "Sputnik Goes to Brussels: The Exhibition of a Soviet Technological Wonder." *Journal of Contemporary History* 47, no. 1 (January 2012).

Somer, Jack. "Van Cliburn, Crooner." *Stereo Review,* December 1973.

Stein, Gladys. "Rosina Lhévinne: Personality Enigma." *Piano Quarterly,* winter 1984–85.

Stein, Howard F. "Psychological Complementarity in Soviet-American Relations." *Political Psychology* 6, no. 2.

Teroganyan, Minkall. Interview with Lev Vlassenko. *Sovetskaya Musyka,* November 1981.

Time:

    April 21, 1958, p. 65.

    April 28, 1958, p. 59.

    May 19, 1958, p. 13.

    October 6, 1958, p. 52.

    January 1, 1959, p. 38.

    June 22, 1959, p. 38.

    July 18, 1960, p. 22.

    September 5, 1960, p. 36.

    August 11, 1961, p. 54.

    January 5, 1962, p. 40.

    January 12, 1962, p. 61.

    May 18, 1962, p. 79.

    October 26, 1962, p. 63.

    October 27, 1967, p. 56.

    November 22, 1968, p. 77.

    September 19, 1977, p. 106.

    July 3, 1989, p. 72.

    July 25, 1994, p. 71.

    May 13, 1996, p. 39.

Tuch, Hans. "American Culture in the Soviet Union." US State Department
dispatch, Moscow embassy, July 18, 1960.

Vartanyan, Ruben. "After the Contest." *Soviet Culture,* May 28, 1958.

Vlasov, Vladimir. "Van Cliburn Plays." *Current Digest of the Russian Press* 12,
no. 23 (July 6, 1960).

Weiner, Jack. "The Destalinization of Dmitri Shostakovich's 'Song of the Forests,'
op. 81." *Rocky Mountain Review of Language and Literature* 38, no. 4 (1984).

Williams, Don. "Cliburn Gives Time, Money, Name to Piano Competition."
Piano Guild Notes, September–October 1962.

Yale Oral History files on Mrs. Schuyler Chapin and Schuyler Chapin (August
1, 1979), and Van Cliburn (October 2, 1980).

Yarustovsky, Boris. "Journey to America," trans. Richard F. French. *Journal of
Research in Music Education* 10, no. 2 (autumn 1962).

VIDEOS

Arkatov, Salome. *The Legacy of Rosina Lhévinne.* Arkatov Productions, 2003.

———. *Memories of John Browning.* Arkatov Productions, 2006.

Feyginberg, Yosif. *Glenn Gould: The Russian Journey*. Atlantic 4 Productions Inc., 2002.

Nikita Khrushchev home movies, courtesy of Sergei Khrushchev.

Paley Center for Media, "Nikita Khrushchev," *Face the Nation,* CBS, June 2, 1957.

Paley Center for Media, "Leonard Bernstein and the New York Philharmonic in Moscow," CBS, October 25, 1959.

Van Cliburn in Moscow, vols. 1–5. Video Artists International, 2008.

Index

Index

Index

Index

First Insert

Van Cliburn at age nine: *Courtesy of the New York Philharmonic Archives*
Cliburn at age twelve: *Courtesy of the New York Philharmonic Archives*

At Juilliard: *Courtesy of the New York Philharmonic Archives*
At the Marlboro Festival: © *Clemens Kalischer, used by permission*

Russians demonstrating at the U.S. Embassy, Moscow: *UPI Radio Telephoto*
Movie poster: *Used by permission of the Autry National Center of the American
   West*
The Boston Symphony in the Soviet Union: *Courtesy of the Glinka National
   Museum Consortium of Musical Culture*

St. Basil's Cathedral: *Adrienne Isacoff*
The Hotel Peking: *Stuart Isacoff*
Cliburn and Lev Vlassenko: *Courtesy of Irina Vlassenko*

Dimitri Shostakovich: (public domain)
Sviatoslav Richter: (public domain)
Emil Gilels: (public domain)

Cliburn in rehearsal with Kirill Kondrashin: *Courtesy of the Glinka National
   Museum Consortium of Musical Culture*
Cliburn discussing a point with Kirill Kondrashin: *Courtesy of the Glinka
   National Museum Consortium of Musical Culture*
At the Tchaikovsky Competition: *Courtesy of the Glinka National Museum
   Consortium of Musical Culture*

Cliburn in performance: *Courtesy of the Van Cliburn Foundation*
The official first-round scorecard: *Courtesy of the Glinka National Museum
   Consortium of Musical Culture*

The official second-round scorecard: *Courtesy of the Glinka National Museum Consortium of Musical Culture*
Handwritten jury notes: *Courtesy of the Glinka National Museum Consortium of Musical Culture*

Second Insert
Encore performance in Moscow: *Courtesy of the Van Cliburn Foundation*
The competition's three top winners: *Courtesy of the Foundation of the Nikolai G. Rubinstein Museum*

Cliburn with Nikita Khrushchev: *Courtesy of the Van Cliburn Foundation*
Fans on the Moscow airport rooftop: *Courtesy of Aschen Mikoyan*

New York City ticker-tape parade: *Courtesy of the Van Cliburn Foundation*
Cliburn and Robert Wagner: *Courtesy of the La Guardia and Wagner Archives*

Cliburn meeting President Eisenhower: *Courtesy of the National Park Service and the Dwight D. Eisenhower Presidential Library and Museum*
Cliburn with Ivan Davis: *Courtesy of Ivan Davis*

Cliburn in airplane, Moscow: *Courtesy of Aschen Mikoyan*
Cliburn singing at Mikoyan home: *Courtesy of Aschen Mikoyan*
Cliburn playing "Moscow Nights": *Carl Mydans for* Life *magazine, used by permission of Getty Images*

Cliburn's parents with Schuyler Chapin: *Kal Weyner, courtesy of the La Guardia and Wagner Archives*
Cliburn with Sol Hurok: *Kal Weyner, courtesy of the La Guardia and Wagner Archives*
Misha Dichter: *Courtesy of Aschen Mikoyan*

Cliburn with competition finalists in Fort Worth: *Ken Howard, used by permission of the photographer*
At Lev Vlassenko's grave: *Courtesy of Irina Vlassenko*

Vera Gornostaeva: *Adrienne Isacoff*
Liu Shikun: *Courtesy of Liu Shikun*
Cliburn with Tommy Smith, Moscow: *Courtesy of Aschen Mikoyan*

Stuart Isacoff is a writer, pianist, composer, and lecturer. He has appeared on many stages, including New York's Metropolitan Museum of Art and Lincoln Center, the Verbier Festival in Switzerland, and Settembre Musica in Italy. He is a regular contributor on music and art to *The Wall Street Journal* and a winner of the ASCAP Deems Taylor Award for excellence in writing about music, as well as founding editor of the magazine *Piano Today*, a position he held for nearly three decades.

Mr. Isacoff performs piano recitals that combine classical repertoire with jazz improvisation. He is also the author of *A Natural History of the Piano: The Instrument, the Music, the Musicians—from Mozart to Modern Jazz and Everything in Between* and *Temperament: How Music Became a Battleground for the Great Minds of Western Civilization*. He lives in New Jersey.

A NOTE ON THE TYPE

This book was set in Adobe Garamond. Designed for the Adobe Corporation by Robert Slimbach, the fonts are based on types first cut by Claude Garamond (c. 1480–1561). Garamond was a pupil of Geoffroy Tory and is believed to have followed the Venetian models, although he introduced a number of important differences, and it is to him that we owe the letter we now know as "old style." He gave to his letters a certain elegance and feeling of movement that won their creator an immediate reputation and the patronage of Francis I of France.

Composed by
North Market Street Graphics, Lancaster, Pennsylvania

Printed and bound by
Berryville Graphics, Berryville, Virginia

Designed by
Maggie Hinders

WILLIAM FAULKNER
of Yoknapatawpha County

TWENTIETH-CENTURY AMERICAN WRITERS

WILLIAM FAULKNER of Yoknapatawpha County
  by Lewis Leary

ERNEST HEMINGWAY and the Pursuit of Heroism
  by Leo Gurko

RING LARDNER and the Portrait of Folly
  by Maxwell Geismar

THORNTON WILDER: The Bright and the Dark
  by M. C. Kuner

TWENTIETH-CENTURY AMERICAN WRITERS

WILLIAM FAULKNER

of
Yoknapatawpha
County

By LEWIS LEARY

Thomas Y. Crowell Company   New York

Manufactured in the United States of America

1   2   3   4   5   6   7   8   9   10

Library of Congress Cataloging in Publication Data
Leary, Lewis Gaston, date

    William Faulkner of Yoknapatawpha County.
    (Twentieth-century American writers)

    Bibliography:
    1. Faulkner, William, 1897–1962. I. Title.
PS3511.A86Z875   813'.5'2 [B]   72–7551
ISBN 0–690–89173–3

For two daughters, one niece, and many students who have allowed me to talk about Faulkner, and for Joe Blotner, who has saved me from much error.

Contents

The County
and the Man

I

In his early thirties William Faulkner created a new world. Ever since he could remember, he had been hearing stories told or telling them himself. Most often they were accounts of people whom he or his family or friends had known or heard about in Mississippi. They seemed to him, these friends and relatives and the people of whom they spoke, much like other people. They were driven by the same impulses. They responded to the same human needs. So he put them all together into an imaginary county which he called Yoknapatawpha, and he wrote about it and its people for more than thirty years. Its population, like that of almost any other place, contained many well-intentioned sinners, some rascals, and a few saints. It became an accurately reduced image of a larger world.

Soon the larger world caught up with and welcomed

Faulkner's private world. Even before he had finished telling all about it, his stories of Yoknapatawpha County found readers in many languages. His voice was a reminder to all people that people everywhere are much the same as they are. He became recognized then as one of the great storytellers of his or any generation, an artist to be placed confidently beside the best which any country had to offer, and in his own country a successor worthy of standing shoulder to shoulder with Nathaniel Hawthorne, Herman Melville, or Henry James.

Faulkner's own life was unpunctuated by great events. He was born in New Albany, Mississippi, on September 25, 1897. He moved to Oxford in that state at the age of five, and resided there and worked there for most of his life. As a young man he lived briefly in New York and New Orleans, and he traveled for several months in Europe. Later, to supplement the small income which writing brought, he worked for varying periods in Hollywood as a writer of motion-picture scenarios. After being awarded the Nobel Prize for literature in 1950, he occasionally journeyed abroad as a cultural ambassador, to South America, Europe, and Japan. He lectured from time to time at universities in this country and spent some of his last years as a writer-in-residence at the University of Virginia. He died in Oxford on July 6, 1962, in his sixty-fifth year.

But no man's life can be so briefly told. Nor is the simple setting forth of what he did the whole true story of his life. A man is the product, Faulkner would have said, not only of what happens to him while he lives, but also of events and attitudes which happened or were held long before. Much of what he is is determined by memories or traditions of a past from which his outlook and activities derive. For Faulkner there were four kinds of past, and each weaves itself, one entangled with the other, inextricably to the pattern of what any man can be.

First, there is a mythical past, handed down by scripture or folk memory—a time when the world was young and primitive and wild and good, before man spoiled it through disobedience. This was an Edenic time, both cradle and haven. There is also the real past, of historical events, when towns were established or railroads built, when men battled and conquered or were defeated. Close to that is the legendary past of events handed down in memory from father to son—deeds which happened or are so strongly believed to have happened that they become tradition. Finally, there is the remembered past, which every man knows because he has lived through it, his own experience certifying what he has done or seen or suffered.

The mythical past is bolstered by the conviction that once, long ago, a good land existed, with deep woods to hunt in, streams to fish in, and fields to furnish all that was necessary for the nourishment of man. Nature was respected then as powerful and complacent, a friend and a sustainer, benevolent but also ruthless, destructive in storm or flood or when misused by man. Nature was good, even human nature, but it became a prey to corruption when men in greed despoiled the good land, cheated the red man, enslaved the black, or took from neighbors and friends more than their share of the common inheritance.

Recorded past can be read about in books. Remembered past is available to every man, each according to his experience. Either can be distorted by deeply rooted certainties of a mythic good time long past or of that other time when tradition tells of men who behaved nobly and well. To Faulkner, that time of tradition was the period of the great civil war from 1861 to 1865, when his great-grandfather had commanded a Confederate regiment in battle against enemy invaders. It had been a time of drama, of dauntless courage, of illimitable endurance. A people had been defeated and a way of life submerged, but legends remained of gallantry and goodness. Something had been lost of graciousness and strength. But had these really been lost? Was this tradition of a braver time of grace and gallantry, of kindly master and contented slave, really true? Faulkner would think about that, and write about it also, sometimes to the discomfort of his Southern neighbors.

He had been named in part for his great-grandfather: he was William Cuthbert, his great-grandfather was William Clark. The last name was spelled Falkner (and still is so spelled by many of the family) until William Faulkner changed it. William Clark Falkner was born in Tennessee in 1825 but crossed to Mississippi, probably at the age of fourteen. Largely self-educated, he became a lawyer and a planter, and was so active in the rough-and-tumble affairs of frontier Mississippi that he was involved in at least three duels, in two of which he killed his opponent. He seems to have been a man who could turn his hand successfully to almost anything. After being wounded in the Mexican War, he wrote a long poem about that war called *The Siege of Monterey* and a novel called *The Spanish Heroine*. He married twice, had one child by his first wife, eight by his second.

When the Civil War began, William Clark Falkner organized a company of riflemen and became the Colonel of the Second Mississippi Infantry Regiment, which fought with conspicuous distinction at the first Battle of Bull Run. After the war he helped organize and became principal owner of the Gulf and Ship Island Railroad, entered profitably into the lumber business, continued in the practice of law, and wrote more books, the most successful of which was a romantic novel, *The White Rose of Memphis*, published in 1880. Nine years later he was shot and killed by a onetime business associate.

The tradition which grew out of Colonel Falkner's bravery and daring, and the noble hardships which he and others of his generation had suffered during the war, was to become one of the themes prominent in the writings of his great-grandson. John Wesley Thompson Falkner, the Colonel's oldest son, carried on his father's enterprises, expanding the railroad, developing farm and forest lands, being active as a lawyer, a banker, and in politics, and as a trustee of the University of Mississippi. He was an imposing figure, convivial but respected. His white suit and silver-headed cane bespoke elegant distinction. A leader certainly in Oxford, he was also one of the most prominent men in all of northern Mississippi.

John Falkner's older son, Murry Cuthbert Falkner, did not do as well. After two years at the University he became a railroad man: first a fireman, then an engineer, a conductor, a passenger agent, and finally an officer of the railroad which his grandfather had built and of which his father was then President. He eloped with the daughter of a onetime local sheriff, and he and his wife had four sons, of whom William Faulkner was the eldest. When the railroad was sold to a larger competitor, Murry Falkner established in Oxford a cottonseed mill and an ice plant, and later a livery stable and then a hardware store. After World War I he became Secretary and Business Manager of the University of Mississippi on the outskirts of the town.

Like his father, Murry Falkner was a convivial companion, fond of hunting and horses and the company of men, and his sons were early taught to ride and hunt. Even when very young, they tinkered with engines and dreamed of becoming aviators. Schooling seemed less important than hunting possum or squirrel, or listening to tales told around a campfire or by the drivers and grooms in their father's livery stable. William Faulkner was eight before he first went to school, and he remained there through the grammar grades and then went two years to high school, though in fact he attended mainly during the fall term when he could play football. Though small, he was wiry and quick, a daring and imaginative quarterback. But the forced feeding of the schoolroom did not appeal. He preferred the more serviceable lessons which were to be learned in the fields and forests and low-lying delta lands of the Mississippi countryside. He preferred his own adventures in reading and observing.

When the Falkner family discovered that William was not really attending high school, he was placed in his grandfather's bank as a bookkeeper, a position which he did not enjoy. He preferred to read or draw, and he drew so well that some of his sketches were sought by student publications at the University of Mississippi. An older friend, Phil Stone, who had gone to Yale and now studied law at the University, introduced him to Keats and Swinburne, to Shakespeare and Conrad, whom his mother also encouraged him to read, and to Melville's *Moby Dick*. Most of the neighbors considered him aloof and withdrawn, a person who chose to be alone, and who was somewhat wild. Estelle Oldham, the daughter of a prominent Oxford lawyer, wore his ring, but her parents thought that he was certainly not the man their daughter should marry.

When the United States entered World War I in 1917, the tempo of his life suddenly accelerated. Faulkner stuffed himself with bananas to become heavy enough to qualify for pilot training in the Aviation Section of the Army's Signal Corps, but to no avail: he was turned down as too short. In April of 1918 Estelle Oldham, urged by her parents, married another, presumably more promising man. But by that time Faulkner had departed for Connecticut for a visit with Phil Stone, who had transferred his law studies to Yale. For a time Faulkner worked as a clerk at the Winchester Arms Company in New Haven, unhappy and restless. Then, in June, he was accepted as a cadet in the Royal Canadian Air Force and reported for training at the School of Military Aeronautics in Toronto. Meanwhile, his brother Murry, who was nearly two years younger than he, had joined the Marines, and had fought and been wounded in France. When the war ended in November, William Faulkner was disappointed not to have completed his training as an aviator.

He returned to Oxford a month later, jaunty in a British uniform, with a swagger stick, an overseas cap, a tightly belted trench coat, and a limp which he is said to have encouraged friends to believe resulted from a crackup in which his plane had crashed into—but what it had crashed into, or when, or why, or even if it had ever crashed at all, was not always clear, for William Faulkner seems to have changed his story several times over the next several years, adjusting it to the requirements of the situation in which it was told or the credibility of the person to whom he told it. He had always been capable of putting together a good story.

That is one reason why telling the story of William Faulkner's life is difficult. He could usually be counted on to invent incidents or to make something which had happened seem greatly more dramatic than it really had been. Furthermore, he thought that what he did or had done was his own business. He resented people who pried into his private life. Unlike Ernest Hemingway, whose personal activities became a legend and who seemed to enjoy being in public places and in the public eye, Faulkner preferred to be left alone. What he wanted told about what he did, he would tell. People were free to talk all they wanted to about what he wrote: that was public. But he discouraged people who intruded to discover how he lived or how he wrote or what he thought about most public matters. One method of discouraging them was by answering questions with statements which were palpably untrue. Some people believed him; others reported what he had said in irony or exasperation, so that, in spite of his reticence, legends have grown up around him, several of them of his own making.

Some details, however, can be known. After his return to Oxford at the end of the war, he did little for several months except wander and read and write, mostly in poetry. He visited friends in Memphis and New Orleans, and people in Oxford thought that some of the friends he visited were not especially respectable. One was a notorious gambler who presided over an illegal establishment at nearby Clarksdale. There Faulkner would sit quietly, glass in hand, listening, observing, storing up materials about how people acted and how they spoke or thought. Estelle visited her parents in Oxford with her new baby daughter, and he saw something of her also. That summer he sold his first poem, to the *New Republic* in New York, for fifteen dollars.

Urged by his family, in the fall of 1919 he enrolled at the University of Mississippi as a special student, taking courses in English, French, and Spanish. He contributed drawings and verse to the student publications, and at the Commencement exercises in June 1920 received a prize of ten dollars for the best poem written during the academic year. Short and dapper, with a small flaring mustache, he was quiet and still somewhat aloof—more English in his mannerisms than American, some of the townsmen thought. Much of his time was spent alone or with select collegiate drinking companions. He seemed to be drifting, without any visible aim. People who did not like him called him "Count No 'Count."

In the fall of 1920 he enrolled again at the University, but by then he had dropped the course in English, apparently because he considered it badly taught. Literature could be spoiled by too much talking about it. But he continued to write, and when Estelle again visited Oxford that spring, he made her a gift of a hand-crafted, hand-written volume of poems composed especially for her. For the dramatic society at the University, he wrote and illustrated a fanciful one-act play, *Marionettes*, about Marietta, who is loved and then left by Pierrot, and he laboriously prepared, drawings and all, handmade copies for half a dozen friends. All that summer he was employed as a handyman at the University, principally as a painter who is still remembered for his careful work.

Then, with one hundred dollars which he had saved, he

went to New York and got a job in a bookstore at eleven dollars a week. He lived, as an aspiring young writer should, in Greenwich Village, which at that time was a center of bohemian literary activity. Elizabeth Prall, who managed the bookstore, remembered him as an effective salesman, helpful to customers, quietly knowledgeable about what books were best and disdainful of books which were not. But he was not good at keeping records of sales he had made—that did not seem important.

By December 1921 he was back in Oxford as postmaster of the University post office, a position which he held for more than two years. Meanwhile, he read and he wrote, and he visited New Orleans to meet Sherwood Anderson, who had married Elizabeth Prall and who was just then at the height of his reputation as a short-story writer and novelist. Though no longer a student, Faulkner continued to contribute verse and drawings to publications at the University of Mississippi, and, encouraged by Phil Stone, he put together a collection of his verses, which was submitted to a publishing company in Boston.

But mainly he seemed to be doing nothing. He played golf often, he visited his disreputable gambler friends, and he was scoutmaster of a local boy scout troop, a favorite among the boys because of the stories he told. But he was not successful as a postmaster. He is reported to have said that he resented being at the beck and call of every fool who wanted to buy a stamp. Mail which seemed to him unimportant or magazines he considered trashy were often set aside, sometimes deposited in the refuse can outside the back door. His records were a shambles. His accounts never seemed to come out right. Soon people began to complain, and a postal inspector arrived to put the place in order. By midsummer of 1924 Faulkner, now almost twenty-seven, was out of work again.

Some satisfaction may have been derived from the appearance of his volume of poems that fall. Phil Stone had helped him pay for its publication, and it was called *The Marble Faun*. It spoke in one poem after another of the disappointment of a faun carved in stone that he could not follow the mythical Greek goat-god Pan as he danced reckless over meadows and hills. Imprisoned in marble, the unfortunate faun was condemned to watch, rather than participate in, the life around him. Faulkner must have felt that he, too, was a captive among people who failed to understand his desire for freedom. The girl he had wanted to marry had married someone else. The glories of war such as his great-grandfather had known had eluded him. He did not fit in Oxford, where people considered him strange, a drifting ne'er-do-well, without ambition. He later remembered himself as having been at this period "a harmless, passionless vagabond." He was restless and he wanted to get away.

These yearnings were passionately a part of his poems. But the words and images which he used to express them came from books, not from experience. Faulkner's favorite reading had been in English writers, in Algernon Swinburne especially, and in A. E. Housman, whose *The Shropshire Lad* was then widely admired. As a result, the landscape of his poetry was a literary landscape, utterly unlike anything which he actually knew or daily saw in Mississippi. It was filled with copses and glades and brakes and wolds, with downs where heather grew, with thatched-roofed cottages about which flew rooks and nightingales and sweet-voiced blackbirds. The captive marble faun who was Faulkner yearned for a beauty which was past and unreal, and he looked with despair on what people had done to spoil possibilities for beauty in his own time. The feelings were genuine—that something had gone out of the world which should be there and which might, just might, come again, if only in dream—but the voice in which Faulkner now spoke was not his own voice. It echoed with phrases borrowed from other men, and it did not ring true.

What he needed, he thought, was experience, and opportunity to see more of the world, to travel and absorb, and to be with other people who struggled to express themselves. Much of that winter was spent in New Orleans among literary people there. Faulkner submitted poems and essays to a newly founded little magazine, *The Double Dealer,* and he wrote sketches of New Orleans life for the *Times-Picayune.* He became friendly with Roark Bradford—a young newspaperman whose later book, *Ol' Man Adam an' His Chillun,* would form the basis for the long-running play *The Green Pastures*—and with Lyle Saxon, whose stories of Louisiana life would later bring him brief fame. With these young men he led a bohemian hand-to-mouth existence. They wrote earnestly and they talked of other writers, not much older than they, who were writing successfully and well.

They responded to the ironic despair of T. S. Eliot's *The Waste Land.* His febrile Prufrock, the timid man who dreamed but seldom dared, seemed a portrait indeed of many of their contemporaries. They admired the fragile lines of Conrad Aiken, the witty and weary sophistication of Aldous Huxley, the daring imaginative flights of James Branch Cabell's *Jurgen,* which was so insinuatingly free-spoken that it was banned. People were beginning to talk of James Joyce, whose magnificently bold *Ulysses* could sometimes be smuggled in from Europe. These were exciting times for young writers. Despair was in the air, but opportunities also seemed present for new freedoms in expression. Faulkner hoped that he could earn enough by writing for newspapers to allow him to go abroad, as other young Americans had, to live and write in Paris, where things happened and writers dared be bold.

He returned briefly to Oxford, where Estelle was again visiting, now with two children. But Europe called, and so did New Orleans, for Sherwood Anderson was there again, and Anderson seemed harbinger of much that could be fresh and truthful in modern writing. His *Winesburg, Ohio* had appeared a few years before, in 1919, and his *Poor White* a year later. No one since Mark Twain had written of simple people with more sympathetic honesty. Anderson admired the spare style of Gertrude Stein and her sensitive feeling for characters who had the dignity of great simplicity. His own style was direct and earthy. He wrote, not yet repetitiously, of what he knew and deeply felt. Anderson was a bluff, friendly, outgoing man, interested in and helpful to young writers like Ernest Hemingway, whom he had known in France. He was attracted now to the slight and quiet young man from Mississippi, and he wrote him into a short story called "A Meeting South" as a war veteran, wounded and disillusioned.

And Faulkner admired Anderson. He envied the older man's daily program of writing in the morning and recreation in the afternoon: that, he thought, was how a man should live, should write. It may have been now that he began to turn from poetry, and the kind of newspaper sketches he had been writing, to thoughts of more serious work in fictional prose. He moved to a room in Pirates' Alley and sent off stories to national magazines—to *Collier's* and the *Saturday Evening Post*, each of which rejected them. He wrote again for the *Times-Picayune*, and that spring of 1920 did an essay on Anderson for the *Dallas Morning News*; and he and Anderson collaborated, each writing in turn, on a series of outlandish tall tales about a mythical Al Jackson, a descendant of Old Hickory, who was half-man, half-sheep, half-shark, and who lived and had absurd adventures in the Louisiana swamplands.

This was the kind of thing which Faulkner was to do increasingly well. There was something of history in it, though distorted, and a great amount of humor—which Anderson urged him to be serious about. The older man seems early to have recognized Faulkner's flair for the comic, his sense of the sham and pretense behind many human motivations, and his perception of the extraordinary but human weaknesses which lead to their discouragement or downfall. "You are just a country boy," Anderson is said to have told Faulkner, "and you must write about those country things that you know."

But Faulkner had not yet discovered what he really knew. He worked now on a novel about a soldier who returned from war horribly wounded, and about the troubles which people had in adjusting to him. During the course of the novel, the wounded soldier's fiancée goes off with another man. In some sense this was what Faulkner knew. He had been hurt in a wartime accident, or let people believe that he had. People in Oxford had not adjusted well to him, nor he to them. The girl to whom he had given his ring had married, though not after his return from war, another man. It was experience, but experience distorted by personal hurt.

Life in New Orleans, however, was pleasant, and there a young man might both remember and forget. There were boating trips on Lake Pontchartrain. There were rumors of madcap adventures in bootlegging and rum-running. There were poets and playwrights and painters, many of his age, who were actively creating or talking about creating. None seems to have worked harder or played harder than William Faulkner. He continued his newspaper contributions and by the spring of 1925 had completed his novel. Tradition, which Faulkner did little to discourage, says that when he showed the finished manuscript to Sherwood Anderson, the older man promised that he would recommend it to his New York publisher if Faulkner did not insist that he read it first. Whether this is true or not, Anderson did recommend it, and Faulkner shipped it off.

Much of the early summer of 1925 was spent in Oxford, where Estelle was visiting again, or with some of the Stone family at their vacation place at Pascagoula on the Gulf of Mexico. In July Faulkner boarded a freighter from New Orleans which would take him to Europe. There he spent the next six months, traveling as inexpensively as he could through Italy and Switzerland to France. He found a room in Paris, in the Latin Quarter near the Luxembourg Gardens, and there he settled in to live quietly and write. He worked over a novel about a feckless young man named Elmer Hedge who had ludicrous adventures at home and abroad, but it did not go right, and he later discarded it. He sent occasional stories to the *Times-Picayune*. Most of the time he was alone, not seeking out those other American writers who in the 1920's lived or visited long in Europe —not Ezra Pound in Italy, nor Ernest Hemingway or John Dos Passos in Paris. He took a walking tour through northern France, and in October spent nine days rambling through England. By the end of the year he was back in Oxford, his money gone, travel-worn, and with a beard. The first thing his mother is said to have said to him when he stepped off the train was, "For heaven's sake, Billy, take a bath."

When *Soldier's Pay* appeared a few months later, in February 1926, it was reasonably well received, largely perhaps because it was so like many other novels of postwar malaise which were then appearing. It begins with a rollicking comic scene of returning soldiers drunkenly roistering on a train. It then jumps to another train, on which two of the soldiers, still somewhat the worse for wear, quite inadvertently find themselves. There they come upon another soldier, a young officer of the British Royal Air Force, who is being returned to his home in Georgia, almost blind, his face horribly scarred, and with no memory at all. The comic mood then becomes one of sympathetic though irresponsible camaraderie as the two soldiers share their bottle and their whiskey-inspired goodwill with the derelict Donald Mahon. One of them is a young aviation cadet who, as Faulkner had been, is disappointed because the war ended before he could get into it. The other is a hard-bitten enlisted man named Joe Gilligan, who saw action in France and who has a large capacity for loyalty and for rot-gut whiskey. They are befriended by Margaret Powers, a young war widow, who joins them in drinking and in taking care of the wounded aviator. Margaret and Joe determine to see Lieutenant Mahon safely home. The young cadet falls in love with Margaret but must return to his mother in California, from where he promises to—and quite too often does—write her letters, which are young and callow.

In Georgia, Donald Mahon had been reported dead. As he returns, his clergyman father is depicted puttering in his garden, joined there by a plump, sardonic young man named Januarius Jones, a dilettante superb in repartee and practiced in the seduction of women. They talk aimlessly and cynically in airy suppositions about matters which are far removed from the reality of Donald's wound. The clergyman wonders whether it is not jealousy which makes older people criticize young people for doing what, when younger, they themselves had not the courage to do—which, now that they are old, they have not the power to do. Januarius speaks in tendentious, Thoreau-like borrowed phrases about men being slaves to their possessions and required either to labor or to steal in order to maintain them. These things of which the two men talk are true enough, but they are platitudes, and Faulkner's use of them is effectively ironic, suggesting the heady emptiness of words which are unconnected with reality. Like most people, these two ambling males in the garden talk too much.

The two moods of comedy and irony dominate most of *Soldier's Pay*. When Donald is brought home, his father refuses to accept the fact that his son is dying. Donald's pretty fiancée faints when she first sees his disfigured face. Only a servant girl, with whom Donald had once made love, really cares for him. The young war widow, Margaret Powers, is a faithful attendant, but mostly because she has feelings of guilt for having married a young man much like Donald with whom she had not really been in love and who had been killed before she could tell him so. Joe Gilligan is faithful because of his dogged devotion to Margaret. Of all the characters, only the plump and lecherous satyr, Januarius Jones, comes vividly to life, though his aliveness is parasitic since he preys on almost all the others. The morbid curiosities of small-town life, its petty gossip and febrile amours, its legacy of shallowness and failure in human understanding—this is the soldier's pay.

Faulkner's attitude of disillusionment was partly an inheritance from Sherwood Anderson, whose *Winesburg, Ohio* had pictured just such a town as he wrote of in *Soldier's Pay*. It represented a view prevalent at that time, shared by T. S. Eliot, who wrote of hollow men and wasted lands. In Donald Mahon's Georgia town—which might have been almost any town anywhere—each person remains tight within himself, bound by memories or lack of them. When Donald's fiancée marries someone else, Margaret in pity marries Donald. Then Donald dies, and Margaret refuses the hand of loyal Joe Gilligan. The characters separate, each to go his own way, having shared an experience but not having communicated—except on superficial levels, by talking in evasive disguises. The reader supposes that life will go on for each of them in just that manner, the past blotted over or forgotten, as poor Donald's wound had made him forget, or bottled up inside, uncommunicable and unsharable, like Margaret's feeling of guilt. And all the while, plump and plausible predators like Januarius, for whom there is no past, only a present filled with opportunistic adventuring, prey on people who are weak or selfish or willful or wounded.

Soldier's Pay contains much to admire, in characterization and in dialogue. It moves and it is moving. It anticipates themes which Faulkner would later develop, but it fails, finally, to cohere. Faulkner had spread his net too wide. He still heard and imitated voices which were not his own. His second novel, which appeared in 1927, is even less successful. It was called *Mosquitoes*, and is a rambling narrative of a yachting excursion which is organized by a wealthy and talkative middle-aged woman who collects celebrities. Among the group which she brings together are a sculptor, who may have been an ironic self-portrait, an effete young poet who was an equally ironic portrait of one of Faulkner's New Orleans friends, and a middle-aged writer who tells tall tales about Al Jackson and who seems to have been modeled on Sherwood Anderson. In fact, it may be that almost every character in *Mosquitoes* is a portrait or partial portrait of someone Faulkner had known in Louisiana. Principal among them is an eccentric young man who spends most of his time carving a pipe and who, to provide a stem for it, borrows a piece of tubing from the steering mechanism of the vessel. As a result, the yachting party finds itself aground. But their insistent, sophisticated conversation continues unabated, punctuated by the sound of their slapping at the mosquitoes. Faulkner seems to have intended their talk to seem as bothersome as the little insects that nip at their arms and ankles.

But it does not quite come through. There is almost nothing of plot in *Mosquitoes*, only talk. There are young people aboard the yacht, most of them morosely self-centered, and there is some tentative, inconsequential love play among them. The older people drink or play bridge and talk incessantly. Almost everybody has too much to say, and with sophisticated disregard of matters which are meaningful. How petty and irrelevant people can be, how unresponsive to other people, how wrapped in self and self-regard. Faulkner did not say this directly in *Mosquitoes*. He did not have to, for now he was beginning to master a style which would be unmistakably his own.

It became then, and would remain, a poet's style, suggesting more than it ever divulges. Faulkner was not satisfied with the simple declarative manner of Sherwood Anderson or the laconic and uninvolved prose which Ernest Hemingway at just this time was beginning to make seem representative of the stoic disillusionment of the 1920's. Faulkner preferred a language which dared to use metaphors that could distract a reader from the simple story he was telling to show him vistas revealing something vague but significant beyond. The homespun storytelling of Sherwood Anderson was parodied in *Mosquitoes*, and was parodied again in an introduction which Faulkner wrote to a volume of caricatures drawn by one of his New Orleans friends called *Sherwood Anderson & Other Famous Creoles*. Anderson was hurt, and perhaps rightly. But it seems to have been clear to Faulkner now that Anderson's advice had been correct: he must write of what he knew, and in his own manner. He was indeed a country boy from Oxford, Mississippi, and that discovery opened for him a rich vein of local lore and history, and of experience remembered, which from this time on he mined with great success.

For in his next novel, *Sartoris*, published in 1929, Faulkner found all at once his own authentic voice, the characters he could most effectively present, and a place to put them. The place was Yoknapatawpha County, a gullied red-clay area of swamp, timberland, and fertile fields some seventy miles south of Memphis in northern Mississippi. It is bounded on the north by the Tallahatchie River, and on the south by the Yoknapatawpha River. Between is a land of dusty roads beside which lie cotton fields, lush bottom-lands, and deep forests of pine. In 1936 it contained 15,611 people—6,298 of them white, 9,313 black. Through its middle, running north and south, is the railroad which Colonel Sartoris built after his return from commanding a regiment during the Civil War. Its principal town is Jefferson, where the Colonel's son Bayard is President of a local bank.

Yoknapatawpha is a replica of a real county in a real Southern state. It is much like Lafayette County, in which Oxford is located, and people there have sometimes thought that they recognized themselves, their ancestors, or their friends in the characters which Faulkner created in novels and short stories during the next thirty years. But it is an imaginary county also, William Faulkner's "mythical kingdom," of which he claimed to be sole owner and proprietor. As he reveals it in story after story, Yoknapatawpha exhibits a geography, a history, and genealogies of its own. Jefferson, its county seat, resembles Oxford. Men in overalls or shirt-sleeves lounge before its courthouse, which is traditionally columned and porticoed, and which looks out over the town square and its memorial monument to the Confederate dead.

The countryside around it contains well-kept barns and ill-kept houses, sharecroppers' shacks, Negro hovels, and dilapidated mansions. It is strung with country roads over which mules draw heavy loads of farm produce, timber, or cotton. Rising clouds of dust reveal the presence of men on horseback or in surreys, later in automobiles. It contains crossroad stores where country men swap yarns on shaded porches. It has rickety country hotels, blacksmith shops, cotton gins, and backstreet restaurants where simple food is sold and complicated bits of gossip are exchanged.

It is inhabited by small farmers, lawyers, bootleggers, itinerant salesmen, horsetraders, politicians, preachers, and poor whites, and by landed aristocrats or their descendants, often submerged in memories of better times long past. Men in Yoknapatawpha do battle against nature and against the trickery of men. Often the battle is with themselves. Some are ridden by greed or lust or fear, burdened with guilt or madness, but inspired often by desperate obsessions fed by memory of or desire for some ideal good. Their women are generally of three kinds: the lush, fertile, earthy, and amoral; the old, reminiscent, and wise; or the dried, pretentious but unproductive, patterned by tradition to prudishness. Yoknapatawpha is a county in Mississippi, but it is also a microcosm of the modern world. Men who once have been powerful, but who fail to maintain an ethical center, proceed inevitably to ruin. Lesser men, of little morality, mean and grasping and with no qualms of conscience, scheme their way to success. Those of simple heart courageously prevail.

Long ago, the land of Yoknapatawpha was inhabited by Chickasaw Indians. Its virgin forests were alive with game: wild turkey, deer, bear. But early in the 1800's the white man came, and bought or bartered land from the Indians. Among them were the McCaslins and the Compsons, each of whom acquired large tracts in the early 1830's. Not long afterward Thomas Sutpen arrived and purchased from the Indian chief Ikkemotubbe one hundred square miles of rich bottomland near the Tallahatchie. A few years after that, John Sartoris came from Carolina and built a fine mansion four miles north of Jefferson. Soon others came: Lucius Priest, the Beauchamps, the Coldfields, the Benbows, the Stevenses—solid men all, who built tradition. But as the century progressed, a new breed of people rose toward power. They were a numerous band, all named Snopes, who came from nowhere and had no breeding, but who swarmed over the land like locusts, taking over stores and banks and public office. All of these people, their ancestors and descendants, appear in one or another of Faulkner's tales of Yoknapatawpha. Most of them appear more than once, so that a reader begins to feel that he knows them almost as well as Faulkner did, and knows their backgrounds and what can be expected of them, and why.

For Faulkner did know these people. He had grown up listening to stories about country people and town people much like them. He had hunted and fished with people of their kind. He knew the way they talked and acted, and he liked them, even those he could not admire. Some were weak, some were dishonest, almost all were prejudiced to one degree or another. They were sometimes brave, sometimes pathetic or preposterous, but always human. And because they were human, not even the simplest of them could be simply explained. Each had been shaped to what he was by numberless influences. Myth, legend, history, and adventures in disappointment or success had joined to form them all. No one of them could explain himself, even to himself, though several of them incessantly tried. To other people, each was likely to present a facade which concealed as much as it revealed.

Faulkner's recognition of this complicated nature of even the simplest person is reflected in his style. To a reader accustomed to the spare, staccato prose of a writer like Ernest

Hemingway, Faulkner's writing can seem unnecessarily roundabout and obscure. He often withholds information which it is necessary for a reader to have in order to understand a person or a situation. He moves backward and forward in time so that a reader has difficulty in determining exactly where he is. Rather than telling a story simply and directly, from its beginning to its end, he often proceeds in circles. For life is fluid, and what man does often moves in circles. Nothing stands still. Each simplest action is conditioned by influences which impinge on it from the past or which distort it by anticipations of the future. To present an impression of life as it is, folding back on itself and incessantly moving, Faulkner often employs sentences which are long and involved, gliding sinuously through observation, action, conscious ·and unconscious thought, musing, and memory.

He is often, therefore, thought to be a difficult writer who places large demands on readers. His style has been described as "a calculated system of screens and obtrusions, of confusions and ambiguous interpolations and delays." His controlling purpose has been said "to keep the form—and the idea—fluid and unfinished, still in motion, as it were, and unknown until the dropping into place of the last syllable." In life, he seems to say, no story is ever finished. Lovers die, but not love. The secrets of no person are ever completely revealed. Life is motion. To arrest motion is to make it inert and static, like the carved or painted figures on a Grecian urn of young men who forever chase but never catch young girls. Faulkner preferred to hint at motives for the chase, to explain its excitement and suggest its consequences.

Thus he denies himself the luxury of direct statement.

Almost everything that he writes is qualified by modifiers or by parentheses which extend or obscure simple meanings. For a statement is final and static, arresting motion. It is incapable of capturing the constantly moving experience of living. Nouns which name need modifying. No man is simply a man. He is a kind of man, and to describe his kind requires subtle nuances. Any attempt to snare in words what he is or what he does is finally unsuccessful, unless the words arrange themselves as elusively and unexpectedly as do the forces, past and present, of shame, despair, or jubilation which twine and twist together to make him what he is.

Poets have always known this. Henry David Thoreau at Walden Pond compared truth to a wild animal which is frightened away when approached directly. It must be taken by surprise, cautiously and craftily approached from one side or another. Faulkner suggests much the same thing, and more besides, in his story "The Bear," in which the boy Ike McCaslin can come near to the great beast only when he puts aside his compass and watch and gun, instruments which provide precise direction in time or place, or which accomplish cessation of life—like assertive sentences which are exact but deadening. Faulkner must be read as a poet is read. His sentences flow massively toward meaning beyond what they say.

Sartoris is another story of young men returning from war, but set forth with richness of texture and depth of background not found in Faulkner's earlier writing. Bayard Sartoris, an aviator, returns to Jefferson haunted by the memory of his brother John, who was killed in air combat and for whose death he feels himself to have been somehow vaguely and indirectly responsible. Caspey, a Negro servant in the Sartoris household, returns also, bringing with him new attitudes learned in Europe about his rights as a person. Horace Benbow, a young lawyer, brings back from his experience as a Y.M.C.A. worker abroad some small skill learned in Italy for making delicate small objects out of blown glass. Buddy McCallum returns with a medal won for bravery but he must keep it hidden from his father, who, with memories of the Civil War still with him, cannot forgive his son for having fought in a Yankee army.

Memories play a large role in *Sartoris*. Many of them are centered about the brave activities of Colonel John Sartoris long before, during the Civil War, and about the even more reckless gallantry of his brother Bayard, which had become legendary in the Sartoris family. Whatever happens to any one of the characters in the novel is measured against these treasured golden deeds. The stories are told and retold by Colonel Sartoris' octogenarian sister, Miss Jenny Du Pre, and they become more expansive with each retelling. The repetition of names in the Sartoris family heightens the sense of tradition, but also adds confusion. Some attention is required to discover which Bayard or which John, from which generation, is being talked about.

The Bayard who returns from war in 1918 has much bottled inside him that he can only express through violent action. He drives his automobile recklessly at breakneck speed through the country roads of Yoknapatawpha. His grandfather, also Bayard, and President of a bank in Jefferson, clings to older ways. As a banker, he will not even lend money to a person who owns an automobile. For years he has been accustomed to being driven every workday morning in his carriage over the four miles which separate the old Sartoris mansion from his office in Jefferson, and every afternoon to being called for by the same Negro retainer who drove him in. Arriving home, old Bayard will call for his saddle horse and ride over the Sartoris land, which was once a great plantation but which is now broken into small plots worked by sharecroppers. Nothing is as it used to be, but he does his best to preserve old decencies and old amenities.

With a kind of stoic fatalism he does ride with his grandson in the automobile. One afternoon, when it swerves into a ditch, old Bayard succumbs to a heart attack. He dies, explains Miss Jenny, from the inside out, not in the devil-may-care manner of a true oldtime Sartoris. Young Bayard, his grandson, flees Jefferson, raging with guilt at having been responsible for another Sartoris death. He wanders about the country, and word of his headstrong adventures trickles back to Jefferson. Finally he is killed when a plane which he flies as a test pilot comes to pieces in the air. In a sense his death is suicidal, for he knows the plane to be untrustworthy. In another sense he impetuously gambles with death, and loses. That is in the gallant, foolhardy Sartoris tradition.

But what is outlined above presents only the bare bones of the novel *Sartoris*. So simply sketched, it may seem stark and grim, as if its mood were tragic. Faulkner has sometimes been supposed to be a tragic writer who broods over man's inevitable doom, and there is indeed a brooding quality about almost all of his work. In his stories many people die, actually and often violently. Others die spiritually, eaten from within by guilt or greed or simple lassitude. But death to Faulkner is not necessarily tragic. It is required of every creature. Faulkner's emphasis is on life, its pathos and its comedy. He writes with compassion and abounding humor about the foolish things and the lovable things that people do. Life goes on, sadly, drolly, bravely.

In *Sartoris* some characters are plainly ridiculous, like Horace Benbow, who blows glass baubles and talks a kind of baby talk to his sister. He courts the wife of another man with pompous gallantry, and when he marries her becomes puppylike as her slave. His sister is named Narcissa, and she is often in the Sartoris house as a companion to Miss Jenny, alternately bullied and petted as she listens to the old lady's tales of her own gallant and devoted brothers and to her complaints about what the Sartoris family has come to now. Narcissa is a quiet and pliant girl who had been greatly attracted to the young John Sartoris who was killed in World War I. She is worried but secretly excited by anonymous love letters, mostly obscene, written to her by Byron Snopes, a bookkeeper in old Bayard's bank and a Peeping Tom who spies on her through her bedroom window. Young Bayard Sartoris frightens her. His sprees and madcap adventures and his arrogance repel her. But when he is injured in an automobile accident, Narcissa helps nurse him back to health and then marries him, and she gives birth to his son on the same day that young Bayard is killed. Death comes but life continues. Perhaps this new Sartoris will freshen and strengthen traditions which have been weakened or soiled.

All of these characters will appear again in later stories. And many of the minor characters in *Sartoris* will be more fully developed, often in larger roles. Old Doc Peabody (Lucius Quintus Peabody, M.D.) will be many times seen, all three hundred pounds of him. The Snopeses become ubiquitous; neither Faulkner nor, as he might say, the world would ever be rid of them: Byron Snopes, who, foiled in his pursuit of Narcissa, absconds with money from old Bayard's bank; Montgomery Ward Snopes, who evades the draft by holding a plug of tobacco under his armpit to increase his heartbeat and later joins Horace Benbow abroad as a Y.M.C.A. worker; and, chief of them all, Flem Snopes, who comes to Jefferson as proprietor of a small side-street restaurant and then works his insidious way to the vice-presidency of old Bayard's bank. Most sympathetically treated are the McCallums, the father and six sons whose farm lies some miles northeast of Jefferson. They stand tall in pride and self-respect, an independent, strong-willed people, the best product of the land. They cultivate its acres, hunt in its forests, and make the finest whiskey in Yoknapatawpha County. Young Bayard finds momentary comfort when he visits them after his grandfather's death.

The relations among all these people, the contrasts among them, the words they speak and the attitudes which are unspoken, are woven into a rich tapestry which Faulkner spent most of the rest of his career enlarging and embellishing. In *The Sound and the Fury*, also published in 1929, he related the decline of the Compson family, who, like the Sartorises, had once been rich landowners. A year later, in *As I Lay Dying*, he treated the pilgrimage of a poor white family from their farm below Frenchman's Bend: Addie Bundren's husband and six children surmount extraordinary difficulties in transporting her body in a homemade coffin on a farm wagon to Jefferson, where her husband has promised she will be buried. Each is an involved and involuted book which puzzles many readers. Neither is like any book ever written before, in insight or subtlety of execution. Critics praised them cautiously, and Faulkner in his early thirties became known as a writer of power and promise. But few people bought any of his books. Increasing fame did not bring increasing fortune. Only the appearance in 1931 of *Sanctuary*, a novel so shocking that people flocked to bookstores to buy it, did he begin to make any appreciable profit from his writings. Most of the stories which he submitted to magazines were rejected as too difficult for popular taste.

Meanwhile Faulkner assumed new responsibilities. Estelle, divorced from the husband her parents had chosen for her, had returned to Oxford. She and Faulkner were married in June 1929 and, accompanied by Estelle's two children, spent a quiet honeymoon at Pascagoula. Soon afterward they moved to a dilapidated old house which Faulkner had purchased on the outskirts of Oxford, and he set to work with his own hands to restore it. For money to live on, he worked as night supervisor in the local power plant. There, when his townsmen were asleep and the need for power was diminished, he did a great deal of writing, using the back of an upturned wheelbarrow as a desk.

The short story "A Rose for Emily" appeared in the *Forum* in April; "Red Leaves," the first of several tales of Indians of northern Mississippi, appeared in the *Saturday Evening Post* in October. Like Hemingway and F. Scott Fitzgerald, Faulkner learned that short stories were likely to be more profitable than novels. He might expect as much as five hundred dollars for a single story. No novel before *Sanctuary* had brought him that much. But from thirty-seven submissions of short stories during the first nine months of 1930, he received only six acceptances.

With a family to maintain and a house to keep up, he was glad then to accept a short-term contract with Metro-Goldwyn-Mayer in Hollywood at five hundred dollars a week. It would be like selling a short story every seven days.

Faulkner was not happy in Hollywood, but when he learned its methods, he did good work there, now and in several later brief visits. He adapted his short story "Turn About" into the motion picture *Today We Live*, which when released in 1933 starred Joan Crawford, Gary Cooper, and Robert Young. On a second visit in 1935 he became what he called "a motion-picture doctor" for *The Road to Glory* with Frederic March and Lionel Barrymore in leading roles. He later collaborated on the screenplay of Ernest Hemingway's *To Have and Have Not* and of Raymond Chandler's *The Big Sleep*, in both of which Humphrey Bogart and Lauren Bacall appeared. In 1954 he accompanied producer Howard Hawks to Egypt for the filming of *Land of the Pharaohs*. Altogether, during occasional visits over a period of more than twenty years, Faulkner received screen credits for six major productions and worked without credit on at least nine more. In 1933 Miriam Hopkins played the title role in *The Story of Temple Drake*, adapted from Faulkner's *Sanctuary*. Four more of his novels were to be made into pictures, and others were purchased for that purpose by Hollywood but have not yet been produced.

Faulkner was seldom at his ease in California. People seemed rootless there. He liked many of the actors, who were hardworking people, and he was drawn especially to Howard Hawks, who directed each of the pictures for which he received screen credits. But Hollywood was principally a source of quick money which would allow him to spend time quietly in Oxford, where he could be with his family and write. A collection of short stories about his townspeople appeared in 1931 as *These Thirteen*. His reputation was growing, as well as his capacity for work. Publishers began to vie for his books. Random House in New York issued a special, limited edition of his story *Idyll in the Desert*; the Book Club of Texas, an edition of *Miss Zilphia Grant*; and the Casanova Press reprinted three of his essays and five of his poems in *Salmagundi*. Each of these small volumes has become a collector's item.

Light in August, his seventh novel and by some readers thought to be his best, was published in 1932, again drawing on people and events in Yoknapatawpha County. During the next year he brought out a second volume of poems, *A Green Bough*, and collected more of his short fiction into *Dr. Martino and Other Stories*. With money earned by the success of *Sanctuary* and his work in Hollywood, he bought an airplane, a cabin Waco, and took up flying again, and in 1935 turned some of his experience and observation of other fliers into a novel about barnstorming aviators called *Pylon*. A year later his powerful novel *Absalom, Absalom!* appeared, and appended to it was a map of Yoknapatawpha County and a genealogy of the principal characters who acted out the drama and history recorded in that book.

The seven years between 1929 and 1936 reveal Faulkner at the height of his achievement, with *Pylon* the only novel of that period not laid in Yoknapatawpha County and peopled by its inhabitants. Introduced in *Sartoris*, this land and these people, brought to popular attention by the lurid *Sanctuary*, were magnificently detailed in *The Sound and the Fury, As I Lay Dying, Light in August,* and *Absalom,*

Absalom! In these four books Faulkner penetrated with insight and great subtlety the aspirations and deviations of the human spirit. He was reportorially realistic, but his sentences wound devious intimations of forces beyond those of everyday experience. None of the four novels is easy to read or can be casually understood. Each requires concentrated attention from the reader, sympathy and tolerant compassion for the backslidings, shortcomings, sins, and feckless ambitions of the often quite ordinary, aspiring people whom Faulkner presents—their moments of triumph and the depths of their despair. The reader who can find any of these qualities within himself will find each of these books rewarding. Faulkner would write other stories of Yoknapatawpha and its people which would be easier to read, but none so profoundly revealing.

During these busy years the most important occurrence in Faulkner's personal life was the birth of his daughter Jill in 1933. Another child had been born two years earlier, but had lived only a few days. Its death had been overpowering. Faulkner's grief was partly responsible for his embarking that fall on a notorious spree of which more gossip remains than record. One tale which can be substantiated is that of his curing a severe case of hiccups by flying upside down in a private plane. Another, details of which are handed down by people who were shocked or confused, tells of an uproarious long evening of convivial revel with Dashiell Hammett, already famous for his thriller *The Maltese Falcon*, and soon to be better known for *The Thin Man* and *The Adventures of Sam Spade*.

But work called more consistently than play. *The Unvanquished*, published in 1938, is made up of stories of a boy's adventures during the Civil War, exciting yarns well told, and bustling with action intermixed with humor. In *The Wild Palms* a year later, two stories are told concurrently, chapters of the first alternating with chapters of the second. One recounts the hardships of an honest convict adrift in a Mississippi flood and of his attempts to return to his fellow prisoners; the other is a tale of runaway adulterous love. The first story was later published separately as *The Old Man,* and has seemed to some readers to suggest profundities of meaning not unlike those found in *Adventures of Huckleberry Finn.* But Faulkner meant the stories to be read together in a kind of antithetical balance. In one story, someone has said, a man sacrifices everything for freedom and love; in the other, the convict sacrifices everything to escape from freedom and love in order to return to the regularized security of the prison camp. But the impact of either story, read separately or together, can probably not be so simply explained. They shimmer with suggestions greatly more profound.

In 1940 Faulkner released a book about the Snopeses called *The Hamlet,* on which he had been working for more than ten years. Friends who had seen portions of it thought they contained the funniest writing they had ever read. No one, not even Mark Twain, had done better. The saga of the rise of Flem Snopes to power, and the adventures and misadventures of other Snopeses who followed him, was to be continued in 1957 in *The Town,* in which Flem has moved from the hamlet of Frenchman's Bend to become an important man in Jefferson. It would be concluded two years later in *The Mansion,* in which Flem meets his end, childless and unmourned. Faulkner seems to have had great fun with these stories, so deceptively humorous. They ramble and are repetitious, and the modern

world of Yoknapatawpha is darkened by deeds at which
tradition-ridden people wince and wonder.

Go Down Moses, published in 1942, is another collection
of short stories, bound together by the frequent appearances
of Ike McCaslin, his father Theophilus (Uncle Buck), and
his uncle Amodeus (Uncle Buddy), the latter two being
eccentric twins who had appeared, one or the other or both
together, in earlier tales of Yoknapatawpha County. The
McCaslins, the Compsons, the Beauchamps, and the
Snopeses are families that appear so often in the novels and
short stories that Faulkner or his admirers have provided
them with genealogical charts. Most highly thought of
among the stories in Go Down Moses is "The Bear," an
account of a boy's initiation to important truths. Its elusive
suggestiveness and insights have inevitably invited comparison with those in Herman Melville's Moby Dick. But, like
Melville's masterwork, "The Bear" is also a good yarn of
men hunting, this time in the deep woods, and of their
respect for wild creatures.

In spite of the excellence of these stories, Faulkner's
reputation went into a decline during the early 1940's. Most
of his better novels of the late 1920's and early 1930's were
out of print, and restrictions on printing during World War
II made their republication difficult. Though Faulkner
wrote as steadily as ever before, he did not seem effectively
to reach even his previous public, limited as it had been.
Some seem to have been turned away because of what they
thought to be a loss of power in Faulkner, or a failure in
integrity. Much of his work now seemed to attempt to
meet rather than mold public taste. Though he was beginning to receive serious critical attention abroad, especially in France, he was neglected at home. Between 1942

and 1945 he was often in Hollywood, meeting expenses with hack work.

The turmoil in which the world found itself during these years distracted him. He spoke out against the regime of General Franco in Spain. The outbreak of World War II troubled him (he served as an air raid warden in Oxford), and before its end he had begun a long book about war and what might be done about it. He began also to express opinions on the race question which were not popular with his Mississippi neighbors. Not until 1946, when samples of much of the best that he had written were brought together by Malcolm Cowley in *The Portable Faulkner*, did he receive consistent critical and popular attention in this country.

Faulkner's long lover's quarrel with the South can in retrospect be discovered even in his earliest writings. He loved the South but he hated what was being done to despoil its land and what had been done to its people, even by themselves, as intolerance allowed the color of a man's skin to determine where he must eat or ride or worship. *Intruder in the Dust* in 1948 spoke to just that problem. A white man kills another white man and shifts the blame to a Negro, against whom the town of Jefferson rises in anger, demanding retribution. The Negro is finally freed, largely through the activities of fourteen-year-old Charles Mallison and his uncle, Gavin Stevens, a lawyer who had studied at Harvard and Heidelberg and who thought of himself as a kind of guardian of the conscience of Yoknapatawpha. *Intruder in the Dust* was made two years later into a popular motion picture, filmed in Oxford. By that time Faulkner was becoming more widely recognized.

In 1949 he brought together six short stories, most of

which had previously appeared in magazines, as *Knight's Gambit*. They were detective stories in which Gavin Stevens and his nephew solved crimes and mysteries which had baffled the rest of Yoknapatawpha. During the next year the *Collected Stories of William Faulkner* won the National Book Award for fiction. Faulkner was also awarded the coveted Howells Medal by the American Academy of Arts and Letters, to which he had been elected two years earlier.

In December 1950 he received the Nobel Prize for literature "for his powerful and independent artistic contribution to America's new fictional literature." His daughter, Jill, accompanied him to Stockholm, where, on receiving the award, he delivered an address which made clear the depth of his compassion toward people who struggled and wrangled, destroying each other and themselves, but whose indomitable spirit would not only endure but would finally prevail. A few months later he was decorated in New Orleans as an officer of the French Legion of Honor. In the spring of 1952 he addressed fellow Mississippians on the inalienable right for all men to equality in the pursuit of liberty.

Faulkner now had become a public figure, honored and respected. *Requiem for a Nun*, part drama and part subtly revealing intricate prose, appeared in 1951 as a sequel to *Sanctuary* and as a kind of moral expiation, or explanation, of what had been considered sordid in that book. *A Fable*, his novel about war, appeared in 1954 and won both the National Book Award and the Pulitzer Prize for fiction. An intricately structured parable about a common soldier who with twelve disciples brought World War II temporarily to a close, *A Fable* is among the most overtly meaningful of Faulkner's works, with a Christian message clearly apparent, but it has not been considered among his most successful. He tried his hand at television now, collaborating in an adaptation of his short stories "The Brooch" and "Shall Not Perish," and he wrote an original script called "The Graduation Dress." Between 1954 and 1960 nine more video presentations based on Faulkner's writings appeared, including versions of the short stories "Smoke" and "Barn Burning" in 1954, of *The Sound and the Fury* by NBC in 1955, and a redaction of *As I Lay Dying* by CBS in 1956.

In 1951 he delivered the commencement address when Jill was graduated from the University High School in Oxford. Two years later, he spoke at her graduation from Pine Manor Junior College in Wellesley, Massachusetts. He urged the young people in Mississippi to raise their voices fearlessly against injustice, and he spoke to the students of Pine Manor about avoiding shibboleths of race or color or creed. He became increasingly outspoken and increasingly unpopular among some elements in the South. Even in Oxford he received obscene telephone calls and vague anonymous threats.

During the mid-1950's he traveled abroad several times on cultural missions as a representative of the Department of State, one trip taking him around the world: to Japan and other countries of the Far East, to Rome, Munich, Paris, and other cities of Europe. He was impressed by the extent to which people in other lands looked to the United States for moral leadership, and he was disappointed that that leadership was not more active. He considered writing a book of essays on *The American Dream: What Has Become of It?* But his approach was nonmilitant. His tone was more of sadness than of anger, and by some black leaders was considered equivocal. He advised patience and nonviolence to leaders of the NAACP. "A Letter to the North" in *Life* magazine asked for tolerance and understanding of his southland. He protested when three white men were merely given prison terms for the murder of three black children. He protested again when the young Negro Emmett Till was killed in Mississippi. Must we murder children in order to survive, he asked?

With the poet Robert Frost, Faulkner in 1954 attended an International Writers' Conference in Brazil, but hurried home before it was over in order to take a father's part in Jill's wedding. Soon afterward she and her husband moved to Charlottesville, and in 1956 Faulkner and his wife joined them there, as he accepted an appointment as writer-in-residence at the University of Virginia. He liked the people of that state, he said, because they were true snobs and therefore did not bother him. He also liked the riding and fox hunting that Charlottesville provided. Not at all to his surprise, he liked the students also, for he had always responded to young people. They and their point of view and their promise had figured importantly in his fiction.

He left Charlottesville briefly for another goodwill journey, this time to Greece, where he received a medal from the Athens Academy. In this country he talked to students from Princeton, Vassar, and the United States Military Academy, and addressed a conference of the United States Commission for UNESCO at Denver. But he retained his reticence, preferring most often to be alone with his family, even declining an invitation to the White House because, he told friends more than half seriously, that was too far to go just to eat with strangers. He was more comfortable at home, where there were now grandchildren nearby for him to admire.

Meanwhile he wrote of Mississippi and his boyhood there for *Holiday* magazine, and he did pieces on ice hockey and horse racing for *Sports Illustrated*. A group of hunting stories, including a revised version of "The Bear," was gathered for publication in 1955 as *Big Woods*. During the late 1950's, while he completed the Snopes saga with *The Town* and *The Mansion*, Yoknapatawpha County and its people were vividly with him. He turned then to another reminiscent account, told this time by a grandfather to a grandson, of humorous and very human adventures which once had taken place there. A month after this his last novel, *The Reivers*, appeared, William Faulkner was dead. He had gone for a routine check at the hospital at Oxford, and on the night of July 6, 1962, succumbed to a heart attack. But the new world which he had created, of Yoknapatawpha and its people, lives on.

The Sound and the Fury

2

Tomorrow, and tomorrow, and tomorrow
Creeps in this petty pace from day to day
To the last syllable of recorded time;
And all our yesterdays have lighted fools
The way to dusty death. Out, out brief candle!
Life's but a walking shadow, a poor player
That struts and frets his hour upon the stage
And then is heard no more. It is a tale
Told by an idiot, full of sound and fury,
Signifying nothing.

—MACBETH, V, v.

Much that Faulkner would write about is suggested in that passage from Shakespeare. His concern was with yesterdays and with the pettiness of contemporary life. In *The Sound and the Fury* he wrote of three brothers, one

of whom is an idiot and who is first to tell the tale. The
second is a walking shadow, doomed to suicide. And the
third is a poor player who struts and frets and worries. But
the novel is not so much about them as about their
sister.

Faulkner once explained that *The Sound and the
Fury* had its beginning when he saw, perhaps in imagination, a little girl the seat of whose drawers was dirty as she
climbed a tree to look through a window into a room
where her grandmother's funeral was taking place, and to
report what she saw to her small brothers on the ground
below. Why she was brave enough to climb that tree, he
said, is what the novel is about. In a sense, it was a forbidden tree, and climbling it led to knowing something
from which adults protected children. She climbed toward
knowledge, while her brothers remained on the ground
in the innocent paradise of childhood. Faulkner never says
that directly. He suggests it obliquely, allowing each reader
to make what he can of this most complicated and difficult
book.

For the sister never appears in the story, except in the
memory of her brothers. Caddy (her true name is Candace)
Compson is seven when she climbs the tree. Her older
brother, Quentin, is nine. It is he who earlier had pushed
her so that she fell into the mud and got her underpants
dirty. Her younger brothers are Jason, who is six, and
Benjy (then named Maury), who is four. Jason is already
a poor player, a tattletale and something of a miser. Symbolically, he keeps his hands in his pockets, and he cries
when he is not allowed to be a leader. Benjy is loved and
protected by Caddy. He needs protection, for he is not
normal. He never learns to feed himself. He never learns

to talk, only to bellow. Yet, quite incredibly, the tale which is told is first told by him.

What actually happens takes place almost thirty years after Caddy climbs the tree. Events move through three days, April 6 to April 8, 1929, from Good Friday to Easter Sunday. But this present time is roiled and confused and determined by things which happened many years before. The narrative moves backward and forward through time in the consciousness of each of the brothers, as each in his turn reveals what he knows or feels or remembers. Central to each is his reaction to Caddy's marriage in 1910, and the love that was lost on that day. For *The Sound and the Fury* is about love. It is about misdirected love and true love, and about what happens when love is absent or distorted. The novel is divided into four parts. After each brother has given his version, filled with sound or fury or despair, the story is concluded with some serenity in a section dominated by Dilsey, a faithful Negro servant in the Compson household. She had known and watched over and loved the children for many years.

Much has been written about the three Compson brothers and what they can be thought to represent. In Freudian terms, Benjy has been said to be a personification of the id, Quentin of the ego, and Jason of the superego. Attention has been called to Benjy's apprehension of reality through his sense of smell: he likes the natural smell of trees, the sweetness of honeysuckle disturbs him, and he bellows when Caddy wears perfume. Quentin is dependent on sound—the remembered sound of his father's voice, the sound of a watch ticking, of bells ringing. Jason's world is revealed by sight, by the keeping up of appearances, by seeing what seems to be rather than what really is.

Time does not exist for Benjy. To him past and present merge into one. Quentin is obsessed by time, by what—for one thing—it has done to the Compson family, which was once powerful and rich and which now struggles for existence. To Jason time is something to be overcome: time is money. Dilsey, the Negro servant, with eternity and eternal verities as her guides, moves placidly beyond time and is a corrective of time. Only she can tell what time it really is by looking at the clock in the Compson kitchen which is old and broken and always wrong.

Some years after *The Sound and the Fury* appeared, Faulkner explained to a group of students that he had originally thought of it as a short story. He had wanted to present a child's report of adult activities. His story would present the commentary of innocence upon experience. In order to achieve the most complete and unsoiled innocence, he decided to have the tale told by an idiot who was artless and more dependent than even a child would be. But as the narrative progressed, other characters began to emerge. The brothers and the sister of the idiot intruded, his mother and father, the Negro servants in his family, and other people from the outside also.

Because an idiot does not tell a very coherent story, Faulkner determined to allow his older brother to tell it also. But Quentin was not coherent either, and he died before the story was completely told. Faulkner therefore let it be told again by Jason, who, though as self-centered as either of the others, was more logical, but like them also confused. Finally the story was told again by the author himself, but with focus on Dilsey. "I wrote the same story four times," he explained.

Exactly what that story is, and what it signifies, is left

for the reader to discover. He learns of it in the same way he discovers the truth about anyone or anything in real life: he observes and he listens to the testimony of other people. He may never completely know the truth about what happened, only what he can put together of bits and pieces of evidence or invention. That is the way a reader of *The Sound and the Fury* discovers the truth about Caddy. And that is why different readers see her differently. If it can be said that there are as many Hamlets as there are readers of Shakespeare's play, it may also be said that there are as many Candace Compsons as there are people who talked about her in Yoknapatawpha County or who read about her now.

Benjy is not often to be believed, insofar as facts are concerned. He had depended too much on Caddy, who has been gone for almost nineteen years, and the memory of her is confusing to him. He is first seen peering through a fence which faces on a golf course. He is thirty-three years old and he is watched over by a Negro boy who is not much more than a third his age. When one of the golfers whom Benjy is watching calls to his caddie, Benjy, on hearing that word, is reminded of his sister and begins a bellowing, lonesome moan, which continues as he follows along the fence while the players proceed toward the putting green. Past and present to Benjy are the same. What happens on April 7, 1928, which is the day on which his version of the story is told, merges with memories of other days. His impressions and sensations are a montage of what was and what is. When on April 7, 1928, he snags his clothing on a nail and he crawls through the fence, he is reminded of another day many years before when one Christmas Eve he climbed through a fence with Caddy.

Some readers have found symbolic suggestions in April 7, 1928, being the Saturday of Holy Week and also Benjy's thirty-third birthday, as well as in Christmas Eve being the date of his climbing through the fence with Caddy. For these readers Benjy signifies man uncorrupted or a Christ figure. And it is possible so to interpret Benjy, for Faulkner will be found throughout to be deeply concerned with truths of Christian doctrine and with such eternal verities as are set forth in the Sermon on the Mount. Blessed for him are the simple, the artless and uncorrupted people.

On that Christmas Eve Benjy remembers his hands having been cold, and that memory causes his mind to jump to another cold afternoon long ago when he had been bundled up and allowed to stand by the front gate to meet Caddy as she returned from school. When she arrived, he had babbled at her happily but wordlessly. "What are you trying to tell Caddy?" she had asked. But, unable to speak in words, Benjy could never tell her. All that he could realize was that Caddy was, always had been, and always would be kind to him. She had known that he liked bright things like flame and flowers and mirrors which reflect the confusing world he cannot comprehend, only experience. She had allowed him to play with her jewel box, which had seemed to him full of stars. Caddy was, and is, and always would be fresh and loving and kind. She smelled like trees.

Later, when she had affairs with boys or used perfume, she no longer smelled like trees, and then Benjy bellowed until she washed herself and smelled like trees again. Everything in Benjy's world revolves about himself, his comfort in dependence on Caddy, and his misery when she is gone. With no sense of the passage of time, his sensations of well-being and grief are virtually simultaneous, one folding back over another, to color or confuse. He is a Compson, and he is the Compson closest to a natural state. Every other member of the family is also egocentric, even Caddy. Each is more demanding of other people than of himself. Each also is taken advantage of by others, as Benjy is taken advantage of by the Negro boys who are assigned to take care of him.

Faulkner offers some help toward understanding Benjy's tangled and fragmented introduction to the Compson family by indicating jumps in time, backward or forward, by changes in type face from roman to *italic*. Changes in the succession of boy servants who watch over Benjy also point to changes in time. When Versh is his companion, events recalled take place before 1905 when Benjy was less than ten years old. When T. P. takes care of him, the time is from 1905 to 1912. Each of these two is Dilsey's son. Luster, who is Benjy's attendant in 1928, is her grandson. But even with these hints, the sequence of events as set forth by Benjy's sensations is difficult to follow. But this first baffling section finally reveals many things about the Compson family which are made clearer in the following three sections.

What is learned is that the Compsons are not what they used to be. Their once fine, large house needs painting. Their carriage house and barn are in disrepair. Mr. Compson is a kindly man, but he has given up and he drinks quite too much. Mrs. Compson is a querulous hypochondriac who meets every crisis by taking to her bed. She thinks the Compsons feel that she, a Bascomb, has married above her station, for Compsons of former generations were important people: one was a General, another a Governor.

Her older sons are named after Compson forebears, but she names her youngest son after her brother Maury, a wastrel who takes advantage of Compson hospitality by using the children as go-betweens in an affair he is having with a neighbor's wife. By the time this youngest son is five years old, it becomes plain that he is an idiot, and Mrs. Compson insists then that his name be changed to Benjy so that he will not bring discredit to the Bascomb family.

Among the Compson children Caddy is clearly the leader, though Quentin, two years older than she, thinks that he should be. As the oldest Compson of his generation, he feels it is his duty to protect his sister and to see to it that her reputation remains unsoiled. That is what chivalric Southern tradition requires of older brothers. But Quentin does not do well as a protector, even as a child. On the day of their grandmother's funeral Caddy falls into a stream as she is romping with her brothers. When she then takes off her wet dress, Quentin in reprimand pushes her so that she falls backward in the mud and dirties her drawers. He knows that, as the oldest, he will be held responsible for Caddy's actions, so that this childhood scene becomes symbolic of later relationships between this brother and his sister, when other attempts at protection are also not effective and when Quentin blames himself for what happens to Caddy.

Jason, two years younger than Caddy, is never close to his sister. He tries to get the other children to do what he wants to do by threatening to tell on them if they do not. He is an ominous presence, even in Benjy's murky recollections. Sometime later Faulkner wrote of these children again in a short story, "That Evening Sun," in which each character is more clearly set forth than in the novel. To some readers this story is thought to be good preparation for understanding Benjy's inarticulate memories of the Compson family and their impression on him as revealed in *The Sound and the Fury*.

As Caddy grows older, boys are attracted to her, and she to them. It is as if she seeks among them the affection which she does not find in her family, each member of which seems increasingly concerned with himself. When she succumbs to a young man named Dalton Ames, Quentin threatens to kill him unless he leaves town. Then, when Ames remarks that all girls are bitches, Quentin attacks him but is humiliatingly overpowered. But Ames does leave, and Caddy takes up with other young men and becomes pregnant. She is taken by her mother to fashionable French Lick Springs, where she meets an older man who marries her.

At her wedding in 1910 fifteen-year-old Benjy stands on a box outside a window to watch her; she has flowers in her hair and wears a long veil which seems to him like shining wind. His Negro companion finds a bottle of champagne which Jason had stolen for himself and hidden for his own later use, and Benjy and the Negro boy get drunk. When Benjy falls down and bellows, Caddy and Quentin rush from the house to help him. Benjy, though stupefied and uncomprehending, is pleased, for he has taken Caddy away, at least momentarily, from the man who would take her away from him. But it is too late: she is already married and will leave home. Quentin, who has failed to avenge his sister's seduction by Dalton Ames, angrily manhandles the Negro boy who is responsible for disturbing the wedding which will make her at seventeen a respectable woman.

Meanwhile, the pasture in which the children had played is to be made into a golf course. Mr. Compson sells it to pay the expenses of Caddy's wedding and to send Quentin to Harvard. Not long after his sister's marriage, Quentin commits suicide. Then Caddy has a baby girl, whom she names Quentin after her dead brother. The child is sent to the Compsons' after Caddy's husband divorces her when he learns that he is not its father. Shortly thereafter Mr. Compson dies, and Jason becomes the head of the family. When Benjy one day slips through the gate at which he had long ago waited for Caddy as she returned from school, he rushes affectionately forward and frightens other schoolgirls whom he mistakes for his sister. Jason then has him castrated so that he will not do harm to little girls.

The arrival of the girl Quentin is disconcerting to Benjy. He confuses her with his dead brother, after whom she has been named. When later he senses, hears, or smells that she has been with boys on the vine-shaded porch of the Compson house, he confuses her with Caddy, who years before was on that same porch with other boys. He and his Negro companion Luster are the only members of the Compson household who have seen the girl Quentin climb down the tree that grows by her window for secret meetings with young men. It is possible for a reader to suppose that it is the same tree, grown taller, which her mother climbed almost thirty years earlier in order to report to her brothers on their grandmother's funeral.

Benjy, who cannot talk, is not able to tell other people what his niece has been doing, and Luster, as a Negro, dare not. All through that Saturday in April 1928, during which Benjy bellows and remembers, his small Negro companion looks for and cannot find a quarter which he has lost. Luster needs that quarter so that he can go to the carnival which is to open in Jefferson that evening.

All these events are made clear in the sections of the novel which follow the long first section, in which they are first fleetingly revealed through Benjy's consciousness. By the time a reader has finished *The Sound and the Fury*, he will discover the story all to have been there in the rush and overlapping of Benjy's kaleidoscopic sensations in which past and present are one. Events flash through his consciousness dramatically. Action is simply action. He receives sensations as a camera might, and he has no mind to search for reasons why something has happened. A time-less view of the Compson family has been presented, all at once, the whole span of it since Benjy was four years old. What he recalls is what he has seen or heard. Though of the surface only, his sensations reveal facts which eventually are proved to be correct.

In the second section, his brother Quentin confuses fact with imagining. He is greatly concerned with reasons why something has happened. Benjy views events on the level of sensation, Quentin views them on the level of emotion or passion. Whereas Benjy makes no connections between what was and what is, Quentin makes too many connections. He cherishes romantic notions of pride and of family tradition. His inherited code of conduct requires a man to be responsible for and to protect his sister, and in this he has failed. He wishes that time could be turned back, so that things might be done better. Quentin's long interior monologue, which makes up the second section of *The Sound and the Fury*, reaches retrospectively into the past and it also reveals his activities during a single day at Harvard and in the countryside near the university. The day is June 2, 1910. Before it is over Quentin will have committed suicide.

For Quentin requires that all experience be made to conform to an impossible pattern made up of notions of family honor and of the sanctity of womanhood. Instead of being satisfied to allow Caddy to develop naturally, he has insisted that she become what he thought she should be. As a child, he pushed her into the mud or slapped her when she acted as he thought she should not have acted. When, at fifteen, Caddy kissed a boy, Quentin scoured her face in the grass. At the same time, he was hurt that she was not upset when she discovered him pawing a neighbor girl in the Compson barn. He took Caddy's affair with Dalton Ames much more seriously than she did. When he assumed an avenging brother's role by ordering her seducer out of town, he ignominiously failed.

It is a father's role, also, that young Quentin has assumed. For Mr. Compson also seems undisturbed by his daughter's affairs, so that the burden of upholding family honor falls, thinks Quentin, on himself. Mrs. Compson, however, is dramatic in response to her daughter's downfall. From the day that she discovers that Caddy kisses boys, Mrs. Compson begins to wear the black of mourning. Mr. Compson asks Quentin whether he, Quentin, has told his mother about Caddy's conduct. Quentin assures his father that he has not. The talks between father and son during the months before Quentin leaves Jefferson for Harvard are remembered in voluminous detail. Mr. Compson's world-weary cynicism is that of a disillusioned idealist. "No battle is ever won," he has told his son. "They are not even fought." Victory is an illusion. Virginity is only a word. Time is a trickster, and each tomorrow does creep in petty pace guiding man closer toward oblivion. But time can also provide a balm. It will only be a matter of time, he has said, before the anguish which Quentin feels about Caddy's downfall will be assuaged.

So time and honor become confused in Quentin's mind. One of the first things he does on that June morning in 1910 is to smash the face of his watch and tear off its hands. But time will not be so easily set aside. Quentin can still hear the time-recording chiming of the college bells. But honor, he thinks, might be overcome. What if it had been he, and not Dalton Ames, who seduced Caddy? He had asked his father just this question a few months earlier. Incest, Quentin had explained, was a crime so abysmally base that he and Caddy could have gone to hell together for having committed it. To his disordered and romantic mind that seems the better thing, sounding the depth and the death of Compson tradition. His little sister, he tells himself, is death, and his sister is dead morally. In shared despair, some months earlier, Quentin and Caddy had considered suicide together, but he had been unable to go through with it. Now that she is married to a man she does not love, and lives as if in living death, he must kill himself in retribution.

As Quentin wanders aimlessly on that final day, he reconstructs and lives through memories of past time. The thought of Caddy's wedding reminds him that a collegemate has jokingly referred to his roommate, Shreve, as Quentin's "husband." He fights, again with disastrous failure, with a young man who, like Dalton Ames, calls women bitches. A little girl follows him, and he calls her Sister. Incest and honor are both suggested when the little girl's brother attacks Quentin, suspecting him of immoral designs on his sister, who in Quentin's subconscious associations is his sister also. This brother is a workingman, not an aristocrat, yet he is a more efficient protector of a sister than Quentin has been. Disillusioned and distraught, Quentin nevertheless continues to the end to observe traditional proprieties. He carefully cleans his vest with gasoline and brushes his teeth before he leaves his Harvard room to drown himself.

In the third section of *The Sound and the Fury*, Jason on April 6, 1928, retells the story of the Compson family. It is Good Friday, but nothing good happens. Jason is now thirty-five, a monstrous man, mean and conniving, one of the most unpleasant characters in modern fiction. He resents Compson land having been sold to send Quentin uselessly to college, where he did not even last a year. He resents Caddy also, for her husband had promised him a job, and the divorce had spoiled that. In recompense Mrs. Compson gave him a thousand dollars to invest in a part-ownership of a hardware store in Jefferson. Instead he spent the money for an automobile and talked the owner of the hardware store into deceiving Mrs. Compson by taking him on as a clerk anyway.

Jason is ruthlessly logical; he demands his rights, not only in taking every minute of the time his employer allows him for lunch, but also in demanding full family attendance, Benjy excepted, at meals over which he sullenly presides as head of the Compson household. He has inherited his neurotic mother's tendency to have blinding headaches under stress. Though he cherishes his automobile, the smell of gasoline makes him ill. He had been named Jason after his father, but Mrs. Compson thinks him really more like members of her Bascomb family. He is her comfort and support. As head of the family, he controls its affairs.

That is, he thinks he does. Benjy is fed in the kitchen and watched over as he rambles moaning through the yard by Luster, who mourns the loss of the quarter which would have admitted him the next day to the carnival. The girl Quentin is a problem to Jason, for he cannot control her, but she also has helped to support him. She is insolent and headstrong. She stays away from school in order to meet boys and do all manner of unmannerly things with them —like mother, like daughter, Jason says, and his first words as he begins his account of the Compsons are "Once a bitch, always a bitch." But for years he has been stealing the money which Caddy sends regularly for Quentin's support, and he even manages to intercept her mail and steal money which Caddy sends directly to her daughter for the purchase of special little things.

Jason is elaborately cunning. If all women to him are bitches, all men to him are scoundrels, ready to relieve a sucker of his money or reputation. But not Jason: he will beat them all at their own game. He knows his way around, and no one takes him in. But, for all of his cunning and his logical pragmatism, Jason always loses. He makes small investments in the stock market, which he is convinced is manipulated by men who are intent on defrauding him. He keeps the money which he has stolen from his niece in a strongbox behind a board in his closet, for he has no trust in banks.

His character is revealed in small meannesses. It was he, not Quentin, who spied on Caddy when she sat with boys on the Compson porch. It was his tale-bearing which brought Mrs. Compson to the wearing of mourning for her errant daughter. It was he who told Caddy's husband that her child had been fathered by another man, so that he, Jason, was responsible for Caddy's divorce. But he outsmarted himself, for Caddy's husband did not find the promised job for Jason, and he hated Caddy for that. To his disordered mind she seems the one person singly responsible for his troubles, his lack of success, his being stuck in Jefferson as a hardware clerk.

Once, when the girl Quentin was a baby, her mother had slipped into town and offered Jason one hundred dollars if he would allow her to see her child. He had taken the money, wrapped the baby in a blanket, and in a carriage rushed by the corner where Caddy waited, allowing her only a fleeting and tantalizing glimpse of her daughter. A later example of his meanness occurs on the day of the carnival, when he receives two free tickets of admission. As the Negro boy Luster watches, brokenhearted, Jason sadistically drops them one by one into the kitchen fire. No wonder Faulkner later described Jason as the most vicious character he had ever created, though at another time he suggested that he was the only sane Compson of his generation.

In the fourth section of the novel attention turns to Dilsey, the Negro cook. Mrs. Compson has never really been a mother to any of her children. She is querulous and self-pitying. Her failure to love has contributed to the decline of the Compsons, for when women fail or love fails, families decline. The Negro Dilsey has taken her place as mother to the children, loving them, scolding them, protecting them. She places her frail black body between the girl Quentin and Jason, when the uncle in rage threatens to take a strap to his niece. On Easter Sunday morning in 1928 Quentin does not appear for breakfast, and Dilsey mounts the stairs to waken her. But Quentin's room is empty. Mrs. Compson suspects that her granddaughter has committed suicide, like the uncle for whom she was named. Then Jason, who is always suspicious, suspects something. He rushes to his room, where his strongbox is hidden. Opening the box, he finds his hoard of money gone. Quentin has climbed down the tree by her window and run away with a young man from the carnival. Enraged, Jason calls the police.

But the police refuse to join in pursuit of the fugitives. There is too little evidence against them, and besides the police guess something about whose money it really is that Quentin is said to have stolen. For all his practical cleverness and concern for appearances, Jason is found out. He chases frantically over the countryside in his automobile in hectic, unsuccessful pursuit of the runaways. His head aches unbearably. The fumes from the gasoline make him desperately ill. Nothing comes of his search. Nothing good comes to, or of, or from Jason.

Meanwhile Dilsey has taken Benjy to the Easter service at her Negro church. Though people stare at her as she walks through the town with the mumbling idiot beside her, she is unperturbed. Appearances mean nothing to her. She has labored placidly for years amid the chaos of the Compsons, and she has always found time for kindness. Now, as the narrative focuses on her, the Compson family is for the first time seen, not just talked about. Benjy is revealed as a massive man who slobbers; his eyes are a pale, clear blue, like cornflowers. Jason is a heavy man whose hair is slicked down on each side of his forehead like that of an old-fashioned bartender. Mrs. Compson does indeed dress in black. Her gestures, like her voice, are querulous and mannered. Quentin is a slender girl of seventeen, wistful and petulant, who wears too much makeup and whose dresses, Jason thinks, are too short. Dilsey covers her own serviceable blue gingham dress with an old army overcoat and puts on a man's felt hat when she takes Benjy to church. What a person wears is to her no index of what a person is. Not only has Dilsey been a mother to all of the children, but a surrogate father also, the true head of the Compson household.

Dilsey is selfless, without the innocent egocentricity of Benjy, the inward-looking nightmarish egotism of Quentin, or the ugly self-seeking of Jason. Sensation, emotion, logical reasoning, each of which have been seen to dominate singly each of the Compson brothers, in her operate all together, so that she feels and loves and is sensible all at the same time. Service and compassion are Dilsey's guides. She is simple, but she is whole. She endures, and of such, a reader can almost hear Faulkner say, is the kingdom of heaven.

Dilsey accepts things and people for what they are, without requiring that they become what she would like them to be. In the last scene of the book Luster is driving Benjy to the cemetery to visit his father's and his brother's graves. Instead of going to the right of the statue which stands in front of the Jefferson courthouse as Benjy had always been accustomed to going, the mischievous small Negro boy directs the carriage to the left. Benjy howls because, though mindless, he likes things to remain the way he is used to their being, each in its ordered place. Hearing the howls, Jason dashes from his store, grabs the horse's bridle, and turns him in the right direction. He is angry because people can see Benjy, a Compson, making a spectacle of himself.

In *The Sound and the Fury* the only true order is supplied by Dilsey. Her unselfish love suggests that this tale —first told by an idiot; then retold by Quentin, the walking shadow; and then told again by Jason, who struts and frets—does signify something. It speaks of possibilities for weaknesses and for strength within the human spirit. It suggests that when love is not found where it should be, it will be sought for somewhere else, as Caddy sought it, and her daughter also. Love cannot be coerced by tradition, as Quentin would have it, nor by pride, such as Mrs. Compson's. The girl Quentin tells Jason that she is bad because he made her that way, but it is she who makes that statement. Faulkner does not supply reasons or meanings. He allows each reader an opportunity to know what has taken place, but he also allows each reader to discover the significance of these actions for himself or herself.

So tightly ordered is *The Sound and the Fury* that readers have discovered depths of meaning too various for simple explanation. Any description of it leaves something out. Incidents recur, and gestures recur. A reader begins to remember cushions and soiled slippers, mirrors and firelight. Fences climbed and fences which restrict begin to assume symbolic importance. Children become muddy and, in a sense, adults do also. Honeysuckle means different things to different characters. Old friends will be recognized, like Doc Peabody, who is so heavy that the children who ride with him in his buggy have to hold on tight not to slide off the tilted seat. A member of the Snopes family appears briefly, as does the legend of Colonel Sartoris's bravery. Anyone who enjoys reading as an exciting game will find *The Sound and the Fury* a well-stocked playground. Those who require meaning must provide their own.

It has sometimes seemed useful to count off the oppositions which can be discovered in *The Sound and the Fury*. Antitheses there certainly are: between self-love and selfless love, between erotic love and spiritual love, between chaos and order, time and eternity, self-control and lack of self-control. But focusing on any one, or on all of these places word-made limits on a novel which refuses to submit to limitation. Faulkner is telling a story of what happens to a brave little girl and to her family. His concern is with what he later became fond of describing as truths of the human heart, and of the human heart most often in conflict with itself.

Many years after the novel was published, Faulkner supplied it with an appendix. He explained then some matters of chronology which readers had found unclear. He described the origins of the Compson family in Yoknapatawpha, how one Compson named Quentin had been a Governor and another named Jason had been a General, both men of proved integrity. He told then of how the family had fallen—its fine house, spacious lawns and promenades, and fertile acres all finally sold or fallen to ruin. He also explained what happened to the Compsons who were left when the novel ended. He revealed that as soon as Mrs. Compson died, Jason had Benjy committed to the state asylum and sold the Compson mansion to a man who made it into a boardinghouse (but years later, in his novel *The Mansion*, Faulkner further amended the history of what happened to the two surviving Compson brothers). The girl Quentin disappeared, but her mother, Caddy, lived on. She was married again in Hollywood, was divorced in Mexico, and was last seen in a newspaper photograph during World War II, in which she was recognized seated in a sports car beside a Nazi General on the Riviera. The appendix is valuable as further history of Yoknapatawpha County and its people. It is an extension rather than a part of *The Sound and the Fury*. Most readers find that novel quite capable of standing alone.

It finally reveals itself as a warmly compassionate examination of what can be done to love to destroy it, and what might be done to keep it whole. Beneath its tone of disillusionment rings a note of hope. What is crippling because it is lost is not the inherited aristocratic code which Quentin Compson and his father mourn or the pride in family into which Mrs. Compson withdraws. These are well lost, for searching through the past for weapons with which to subdue the present is not only futile but an invitation to defeat. What is lost—and need not be lost—is innocence and uncorrupted simplicity. To view life as a child might view it, or as a poet might, is suggested as a worthy and not impossible end. Caddy could not do it because she became caught in the barren trap set by her family's failure in disinterested love. Nor could her brothers, who were trapped by excessive concern with themselves. The brave little girl who climbed the tree becomes a saddened woman. Caddy's story is central to *The Sound and the Fury*. She gropes unguided toward sexual maturity, and finds disaster. What could have been a life-creating experience becomes furtive, leading to a kind of living death both for her and her daughter.

Benjy sensed this, and if his love for Caddy could have been spoken, he might have saved his sister. Dilsey knew it also, but she was black, and no Compson except Benjy really heard her voice. When love fails or love is distorted, then its story is filled with sound and fury, its significance diminished. But not to nothingness. Dilsey with her simple faith survives. Even Jason will be heard of again in Jefferson. However maimed by what experience has contributed to his character, he clings to something of the stubbornly persisting, indomitable human spirit. Like Dilsey, he endures. Perhaps that is why Faulkner called him the sanest of the Compson family. Jason's kind continues to exist, and Dilsey's kind continues to exist also, each indestructible. Faulkner would examine the friction created by the inevitable survival of each of these kinds in much of his subsequent fiction.

As
I Lay Dying
3

The story of Candace Compson in *The Sound and the
Fury* is recalled through the consciousness of four witnesses,
three of whom, her brothers, communicate directly to the
reader, while the fourth, Dilsey, reveals her attitudes as she
is objectively presented by the author. The story of Addie
Bundren in *As I Lay Dying* is told by fourteen witnesses,
each of whom speaks in one or another of the fifty-nine
unnumbered sections into which the book is divided. Six
of them are members of her family: her four sons, her
daughter, and her husband. The others are neighbors,
friends, or chance bystanders who comment on what happens as a kind of chorus. Addie herself speaks only once, in
a monologue of hardly more than twelve hundred words.
The story is about what her dying does to the rest of her
family.

As I Lay Dying is among the most engaging and, at first glance, the most formless of Faulkner's novels. Few novels by any author contain as many characters so vividly portrayed, so alive, so human, and so comic. Its narrative outline, however, is very simple. Addie had been a schoolteacher in Jefferson when she married Anse Bundren, who lived on a small, never very successful cotton farm some miles below Frenchman's Bend. She had become the mother of five children, four of whom are young adults when the narrative begins.

Addie had extracted a promise from her husband that when she died, he would see to it that she would be buried in Jefferson among her own people. As the story begins, Addie lies dying. When she does die, her body is laid in a coffin placed on a mule-drawn wagon, which her husband and her sons and her daughter will accompany on its journey to her grave. But it has been raining, so that rivers which must be crossed are flooded and bridges have been made unsafe or have been washed away. As a result Addie's family is forced to take a long and tedious roundabout route. After overcoming strange and tremendous obstacles, the Bundren family reaches its destination, and Addie is laid to rest. Her husband's promise to her has been kept. The mission undertaken by her family has been completed.

But an outline of the plot of *As I Lay Dying* does scant justice to a story which is boisterously humorous at the same time that it is perhaps the most profound of Faulkner's novels. It is also his shortest novel, compact with insight. In it he presents unsophisticated country people whose pride and ambition and capacity for failure are not greatly unlike those of the once aristocratic Sartorises or Compsons, but whose indomitable, dogged determination allows them finally to succeed. They are human and they make many mistakes, some of which are absurd, but it is people such as these, Faulkner may seem to be saying, who shall ultimately inherit the earth.

Like the Compsons, Addie takes pride in her forebears. Tradition dictates that she be buried among them. And the tradition is reinforced by her desire to be removed, if only by death, from the trap into which her acceptance of inherited ideas had led her. Love had been an inherited idea. When the country man whom she would marry had spoken of his love for her, she had believed him, partly because she had not wanted to spend all of her life as an old-maid schoolteacher. But love as he had spoken of it had proved to be an empty word, attractive but meaningless. It had tricked her into being a mother more often than she had wanted to be. Life had not been kind to Addie, but she was a strong force. She held her family together.

As she lies dying, she can hear her oldest son, Cash, who is a carpenter, as he works carefully at the making of her coffin. Her daughter, named Dewey Dell, stands by the bedside fanning her. Darl and Jewel, Addie's second and third sons, are returning to the house from work in the cotton fields. Vardaman, her youngest son, has gone fishing. Her husband, Anse Bundren, talks disconsolately to a neighbor named Vernon Tull, whose wife has brought Addie a cake which was baked to sell; but the prospective buyer decided not to take it, and Cora Tull will now present it to the dying woman.

None of this is told directly. First, the reader is presented with a brief monologue, not five hundred words long, spoken by Darl as he and his brother come in from the fields, silent, in single file. Jewel walks behind Darl.

He wears patched overalls and a frayed straw hat. He is tall, straight-striding, and impetuous. The path which they follow approaches, then circles around, a log cotton-house, then on the other side of the house it continues straight again. Darl follows the path around the house, but Jewel proceeds straight ahead. Without breaking his stride, he steps through a paneless window on one side of the log house and out through a window on the other side, thus catching up with and passing his older brother who walks behind him.

Jewel is not described as a tall man. He does not have to be. His height is suggested by Darl's statement that anyone watching them as they approach the cotton-house could see that even though Jewel walks fifteen feet behind, his hat towers a full head above Darl's hat. Their father, Anse Bundren, will be similarly undescribed. Darl presents no portrait of Anse. Instead he notices his thumb and finger joined to place snuff behind his upturned lip. When Darl later describes the faded shirt which stretches over the hump in his father's back, he is more concerned with how the cloth looks than with Anse's physical deformity. But Anse is nonetheless recognized as a country man bowed by labor who finds pleasure in snuff. Other members of the Bundren family are presented in the same casual manner, most of them by people who have known them so long that what they look like is taken for granted.

As Darl approaches the house where his mother lies dying, he sees his brother Cash at work on the coffin, and it gives him comfort to think what comfort it must give his mother to know that her coffin is being so painstakingly made. Then the story is taken up by Cora Tull. Her thoughts and conversation are revealed as those of an opinionated woman whose observations are always just a little off the mark. Like almost everyone else, she sees or thinks what she wants to see or think. Neither she nor any of the other reporters achieve an objectivity which allows them to recognize the sometimes very stupid valor, the often dubious loyalty, but the nonetheless dogged persistence of the Bundrens, and their absurdity also.

For on its surface, As I Lay Dying is a hilariously, though often gruesomely, funny story. Addie's oldest son, Cash, is revealed as a careful carpenter, but he has already carelessly fallen off a roof and broken his leg, and he will break his leg again and it will be carelessly, though lovingly, set by a veterinarian and then encased by his brothers in an improvised cast made of concrete inside of which his leg swells and gangrene sets in. Cash is meticulous. The coffin over which Cash works is meticulously made. Each plank is neatly beveled to make it watertight. It is a good coffin, flaring wide toward the head and narrowing toward the feet. But Addie had wanted to be buried in her wedding dress, which had a wide flaring skirt. When she is placed in the coffin, her head, therefore, is put where her feet should have been so that the flared-out skirt can fit neatly into the wide and flared-out part of the coffin. Then Addie's youngest son, Vardaman, worrying that his mother cannot breathe in such a tightly built coffin, borrows his oldest brother's auger and bores holes in the top of the coffin to let air into it. But Vardaman is very young, and he is not a careful borer, so that he bores holes into his mother also. But the Bundrens are resourceful. They improvise a mosquito-net veil which will cover the holes in Addie's face when the coffin is opened for viewing during the funeral service.

Almost everything that happens becomes a comedy of absurd human errors. The Bundrens are delayed in setting out for Jefferson with Addie in her coffin because Darl and Jewel have gone off with the wagon to deliver a load of wood, to earn three dollars which will help meet expenses during the journey. They would have returned with the wagon sooner, except that it becomes mired in the mud, turns over, loses a wheel, and has to be repaired.

While these two sons are away, old Doc Peabody arrives at the Bundren home, which sits on a high bank above the road. Too heavy to climb the bank without assistance, the corpulent physician is hauled up to the house with a plow rope. When Addie dies, the boy Vardaman blames her death on the doctor, whom he thinks might have saved her. He rushes down to the road, unties Peabody's horses, and beats on them until they run away, with Peabody's carriage careening perilously behind them.

On the next day the neighbors gather for Addie's funeral. The service is spoken by the Rev. Mr. Whitfield, an itinerant preacher who is also, though the fact is unknown to any of the Bundren family except Darl, the father of Addie's favorite son, the impetuous and swift-striding Jewel. When alive, Addie had shown special affection for Jewel by beating him and caressing him more often than she did her other children. He was her jewel, though conceived without love, whose father was a man of God. And Jewel has a horse which he beats and caresses because it means more to him than almost anything else. He earned the horse, which is as spirited as he, by hard labor. It is his prized possession, won by the sweat of his brow.

Addie's second son, Darl, possesses an uncanny, almost supernatural knack of knowing things without ever having been told them. He simply senses that Whitfield is Jewel's father. Only he knows why his sister, Dewey Dell, insists that their father carry out his promise to have Addie buried in Jefferson. Dewey Dell is pregnant and wants above everything else to get to a drugstore where she can buy something which will produce an abortion. She clings earnestly to the ten dollars which the father of her unborn child has given to her for that purpose. And curiously, though Darl at the time is miles away from the Bundren home, involved with Jewel in the attempt to deliver the load of wood, it is through his words that the reader learns of Addie's death and of how each member of the family then at home reacts to it. There is something incredible, almost of divination, about Darl's ability to know things.

Of the fifty-nine interior monologues through which the story is revealed, nineteen belong to Darl. He is not only the most knowing, but is also the most sensible of the Bundrens. At the same time, what he says or what he thinks about what is happening is often expressed in language heightened to the level of poetry, so that it suggests greatly more than it ever says. Darl's voice, however, is capable of variation. When reporting what another character has said, he uses colloquial speech patterns. When revealing his conscious thought, he employs a formal, controlled, and literary language. When expressing unconscious thought or uncontrolled rumination which more often than not is emotional, then the imagery and free association of poetry appear, so that the reader is directed toward intimation of what must be true.

Nine-year-old Vardaman, who is torn by emotion, speaks only in images. All that he knows of death is that fish die when taken out of water. His mother, therefore, has become a fish. Dewey Dell, who is self-centered and frightened, deliberates on a conscious level. A reader never is in doubt about what Dewey Dell wants or why she wants it. Her father, Anse, is a man of words who speaks in colloquial cliches which have little meaning. Jewel is a man of impetuous action who seldom speaks at all. Cash is sensible, but only within limits. Darl alone encompasses all of these attributes or attitudes. He seems to be the sanest and most complete of all the Bundrens, yet in the end he is committed to an asylum as insane.

He has to be committed for the protection of the rest of the family. For, as their coffin-laden wagon makes its trek toward Jefferson, the Bundrens become victims of one disordered incident after another. They have trouble even before they get started. By the time their wagon has been repaired and brought back to the Bundren home to be loaded with the coffin, Addie has been dead for three days. Cash conscientiously balances the coffin in the wagon bed. Beside it he packs his box of tools, so that if repairs are necessary during their trip, he can make them. Jewel rides his horse, often galloping impatiently ahead of the mule-drawn hearse. Dewey Dell is also impatient because they proceed so slowly. The journey is hardly begun before troubles entangle them all. They are prevented by flood waters from crossing one bridge and have to detour for eight miles in search of another.

When, on the fifth day after Addie's death, a fording of the swollen river is attempted, the wagon is swept away, Cash's leg is broken, and his cherished box of tools is up-tilted so that its contents are scattered helter-skelter in the rushing water. The two mules that pull the wagon are drowned, and Addie's coffin is hurtled downstream with

Darl in pellmell but unsuccessful pursuit. Jewel, the silent man of action, rescues the coffin and retrieves the tools. Muleless now, the Bundrens pull the wagon ashore and reset the coffin. A nearby farmer named Armstid provides a span of mules to draw it to his farm. Jewel dashes off to Frenchman's Bend to get Doc Peabody to set Cash's broken leg. The doctor is not there, so Jewel returns instead with Uncle Billy Varner. With a glass of whiskey as anesthetic and depending on his experience with mules and horses to make him expert, Uncle Billy sets the broken bone. Cash faints. When he recovers consciousness, the first thing that he asks for is his beloved box of tools.

The next morning Anse sets out on Jewel's horse to trade with a man named Flem Snopes for a new team of mules. Snopes proves to be a canny trader. Anse has to give him a chattel mortgage on his cultivator and seeder—as well as eight dollars he has filched from the stricken Cash's pocket, money which his son has been saving for the purchase of a talking machine. Anse even has to sacrifice money of his own which he has hoarded to buy store teeth with, for a man certainly has to eat, he explains, if he is to keep his strength. Worst of all, he promises to include Jewel's horse in the trade. If he can go without eating, his son can go without riding. Enraged, Jewel leaps on his horse and gallops off. By the next morning Armstid suspects that he must be halfway to Texas. But Jewel returns during the night and leaves his horse in Armstid's barn for Snopes' emissary to pick up when he brings the mules.

Meanwhile the smell from the coffin has become unbearable. Buzzards begin to hover over it as, with new mules, the wagon moves on. Addie has been dead for eight days when it arrives in Mottstown, a settlement not far from Jefferson. Horrified townspeople cover their noses as it passes. When Anse halts the mules briefly, the town marshal orders him to move on. Anse, however, is obdurate. He has as much right to park his wagon on a public street as any other man. There is business to attend to in Mottstown. Darl buys ten cents' worth of concrete to encase Cash's broken leg. Dewey Dell goes to the drugstore with her ten dollars, but the druggist refuses to sell her what she wants.

That night the Bundrens stop over at another farm. They promise the farmer to keep the wagon far from his house. When rain begins to fall, they move it into his barn. Young Vardaman sits up all night to keep the buzzards away from his mother. During his vigil he sees his brother Darl set fire to the barn. That seems to sensible Darl the sensible thing to do: to get rid of Addie and her odor through the cleansing power of fire. Impetuous Jewel rushes through the flames to save, first, the animals who are trapped by the flames, and then his mother in her coffin. The next day the wagon and its burden arrive in Jefferson. There Anse borrows two shovels and, his promise kept, supervises the burial of Addie in her family plot.

Meanwhile Darl is taken off to the insane asylum at Jackson. Only an insane man would have set fire to a barn with his dead mother in it. His family, which under normal circumstances would have to pay damages to the farmer whose barn had been burned, certainly could not be held accountable for what an insane man had done. Committing Darl to the state asylum seemed certainly to prove that he was insane, and that they therefore were blameless and not liable for damages.

Darl gone, Cash is taken to Doc Peabody, who dresses his gangrened leg. Country-girl Dewey Dell is seduced by a drugstore city slicker under the pretense that what he does to her will produce an abortion. Anse, discovering that his daughter has ten dollars, takes the money from her and buys himself a new set of false teeth. As the wagon, released now of its grisly burden, is prepared for the homeward journey, Anse with new teeth gleaming introduces his children to a "duck-shaped" woman who carries a Gramophone in her arms. She it is who lent him the shovels which prepared Addie's grave. Now she is the new Mrs. Bundren.

A cycle is complete. Life will go on much as it always has, but now for Anse to the accompaniment of music from his new wife's talking machine. Addie's children will not again be what they have been. Cash will limp for the rest of his life. Darl is in the madhouse. Jewel will certainly dash off somewhere, perhaps to Texas. Pregnant Dewey Dell will probably marry. Little Vardaman—what will happen to him? Without Addie to hold them together, the Bundrens as a family will fall apart. As long as they remembered her, toiling together to carry out her wish, she was a living force. She lay dying until her body was deposited in its grave.

But the Bundrens' neighbors and the country people who helped them and the townspeople who watched them would not forget them. Their misadventures would certainly become one of the legends of Yoknapatawpha County. And each reader of As I Lay Dying will piece together the hints and allusions in the testimony given by sometimes contradictory witnesses to share knowledge of that legend, which is comic to the point of being slapstick burlesque but which contains seriously probing suggestions of something more.

For the Bundrens' legend crackles with intimations. On

one level it follows a familiar folk-tale motif, as Anse, charged with a mission, accomplishes it and, like the classic hero of the folk legend, receives gifts as reward—in his case, new teeth and a new wife. Simple Anse is the simple Hans who bumbles through many a household story. But on another level Anse is more than simple: he is an innocent. He allows others to do his work when it is strenuous, because, as his children more than once testify, he dares not sweat—if he sweats, he will die. It may, therefore, be possible to suspect that Anse represents man in his simple innocence before he was tempted and corrupted by a woman and expelled from the Garden of Eden, condemned forever afterward to earn his bread by the sweat of his brow. Anse had been tempted toward marriage by Addie, who had been a schoolteacher tired of tending children. But, tempted, Anse promised Addie more than he could supply.

Anse is revealed as a man of words, of empty words like love and duty and promise. He had given Addie his word that he would bury her in Jefferson. But words, Addie says, go up in the air like smoke. Only deeds cling along the ground of reality. Silent Jewel performs deeds. He saves his mother's body when it is threatened by fire and water. Jewel's father is Whitfield, a man who speaks the word of God, and Jewel is willing to sacrifice even his beloved horse to make possible the carrying out of the word-promises made by Anse. In the beginning was the word. Actions, however, speak louder. Jewel suggests redeeming force. Darl can also be found to be a person who is sacrificed so that others may be saved.

But these circlings toward meaning provide only glimpses of what *As I Lay Dying* can reveal. On its surface it is a comic grotesque, creating a legend on a fairy-tale motif. At the same time it is an appealingly sympathetic portrayal of simple people who mean well but who, like most people, make mistakes. Freudian critics have discovered in it variations of the Oedipus complex in the relationships of each son to his mother. It is classic in structure in that people who observe the Bundrens act as a chorus which comments on the main action. In *The Sound and the Fury* Dilsey is the only spokesman who is not personally involved in what happens to the Compsons. In *As I Lay Dying* eight different characters who are not members of the family comment on the Bundrens. Each reports from his own viewpoint. To some they are pathetic, to others comic, to still others a menace to the health of the community.

What happens to the Bundrens suggests conflict, not only between saying and doing, but between alienation from the community and acceptance of assistance from other people, and also between stubborn self-reliance and social responsibilities. Religious currents sweep through it like the flood which swept through the Yoknapatawpha countryside. As a parable of death, purgatory, and salvation, of trial by water and trial by fire, of sacrifice and redemption, it communicates, not always clearly, but persuasively.

Whatever it is—a burlesque, a parable, or a religious fable—*As I Lay Dying* is among Faulkner's most sensitive and complex books, and Addie Bundren, dead or alive, is at its center. She can be thought of as the human spirit which encompasses both good and evil. She can be interpreted as the earth-mother, productive both of love and violence. Her name may suggest her to be a female, fallen Adam, the progenitor of all men. She is an Adam forced out of Eden and faced by a world in turmoil because of

the "wild blood boiling along the earth." She had eaten of
the tree of knowledge and as a schoolteacher had been
guilty of the greater sin of passing to others knowledge not
based on experience. She was corrupted by knowledge
which was patched together by words.

Experience teaches her that words mislead. They are
mouthed shapes, "profoundly without life." They seldom
succeed in saying what they are trying to say. Her first son,
Cash, was born as a result of a word called love. Addie had
been tricked by a biological impulse. By the time Darl was
born, she and Anse were so far apart that this second birth
seemed an outrage. Already spiritually cuckolded, Anse was
then cuckolded in fact when Addie sought out Whitfield
as the father of her third child. Their act was merely physical, for in order to come to her Whitfield had to forget all
the good words which he as a clergyman used. Then, in
recompense for having cheated Anse, Addie had Dewey
Dell to "negative" Jewel, symbolically wiping out the son
who had been "mothered by violence, fathered by no one,"
only by a man of the word who, when stripped of his
words, became nothing. Finally Vardaman was born to replace the son she had robbed her husband of. But her
children are hers alone, the fruit of her violence and frustration. Jewel is her cross and her salvation. In reality, she had
lain a long time dying. She remembers her father having
told her that "the reason for living was to get ready to stay
dead a long time."

She learns that much of life is illusion, made absurd by
words like duty, repentance, pride, and sin which people
use to escape from life. Though dead, she lives among her
children, each of whom is shaped by her influence. Once
she had believed that death was annihilation. As she lies

dying, she recognizes death as only another convenient word. It is neither an end nor a beginning, only a continuation, a function of the mind. Life lives on, whether in the wordless, sustaining violence of nature or in the wordy, continuing aspiration of men. *As I Lay Dying* may seem to be a book about death, which is the end of living, but it can be read also as a book about life and its requirements. Faulkner presents no easy answers to the mysteries which inevitably accompany living. Horror and humor, selfishness and courage, love and fear are intermingled, as they are in life. What is funny to their neighbors is not funny at all to the Bundrens. Reality can be suspected to be what anyone's perspective makes it. Perhaps it is not even that simple. To pretend that reality can be plainly explained is to depend on words which only congeal reality into conventional, stated meanings. Faulkner had too much respect for the rich complexity of life to do that.

Light
in August
4

The shaping power of Faulkner's imagination rises to new heights in *Light in August,* the longest of his early novels. It tells the story of two people who are strangers in Jefferson and who never meet, but whose lives are affected by the same series of events which take place during a period of eleven days in Yoknapatawpha County. One of them is Lena Grove, and of her background little is told—only that on one hot August day she travels up a dusty road toward Jefferson and sees a flame-filled pillar of smoke ahead of her, which rises from a burning house. She is pregnant and is in the midst of a long, patient search for the father of her unborn child: every child, she thinks, deserves to have a father. Of the past of the other person, a great deal is revealed, some of it true, some of it imagined. It is he, Joe Christmas, who has set the house on fire, creating a light in the August sky, and he is pursued by the people of Jefferson and is finally killed. On the day of his death, Lena's child is born. She is last seen on the road again, in quiet continuing search of its father.

Between these two stand a quiet man named Byron Bunch, who befriends them both, and the Rev. Gail Hightower, who helps to deliver Lena's baby and who is present when Joe Christmas is killed. Byron is the comic hero of the story, a simple and honest man who lives for the present, doing each day what he can according to the opportunity which each day offers. Hightower is a defrocked clergyman who dreams of days long ago when brave ancestors accomplished deeds of great daring. Byron is a man of quietly inconspicuous action, but Hightower is inertly entangled in a past which, much like that of the Sartorises and the Compsons, is in some part of his own making.

The structure of *Light in August* can be likened to that of a great circle with a straight line running through it, extending on either side beyond the circumference of the circle. The straight line is the path followed by Lena in her steadfast quest. As it enters the circle, it is buffeted by the activities of other people who are in Jefferson, but it continues its straight way to emerge from the opposite rim of the circle, as Lena, still steadfast, continues her quest. The great circle represents the roundabout wanderings of Joe Christmas as he searches to discover who he is. For though what happens in Jefferson during that hot August covers only a period of eleven days, the quest of Joe Christmas extends over a period of more than thirty years, and it is on his futile quest that the focus of the narrative remains the longest.

Light in August is the most well-balanced in structure of

Faulkner's novels. It opens as if with a prelude as in the first chapter Lena is seen trudging one Friday afternoon toward Jefferson, where she is confident that she will find and marry a man named Lucas Burch, so that, when born, her child will have a father. She is befriended and stays that night with the Armstids, country people who played a minor role as witnesses to the Bundrens' pilgrimage in *As I Lay Dying*. The next morning Armstid drives her to Varner's store in Frenchman's Bend, where she catches a ride to Jefferson with another country man. As they approach the town, she sees on its outskirts the smoke and flame of a house on fire. Chapter two introduces Byron Bunch, the foreman of a local sawmill. He is an earnest, quiet man who works on Saturday, he says, in order to keep himself out of trouble.

As Byron putters about the mill that morning, he remembers a Friday morning three years before when Joe Christmas arrived in Jefferson and signed on at the sawmill for the menial task of shoveling sawdust, a work usually done by Negroes. And Byron also remembers a man who called himself Joe Brown, who only six months before wandered into Jefferson and found work at the mill. Both men quit their jobs some six weeks ago and have been living, somewhat mysteriously, in a cabin on the Burden place just outside of town. Nearby, in the main house, lives Joanna Burden, a Yankee spinster whose abolitionist grandfather and brother were killed sixty years before by Colonel John Sartoris because they had attempted to organize local Negroes in voting.

Byron also thinks of his friend the Rev. Gail Hightower, who twenty-five years before had been a Presbyterian clergyman in Jefferson, but who lost his wife and then his church, and who now lives alone, isolated and entangled by his dreams of the past. Only Hightower knows that every Sunday Byron Bunch rides thirty miles into the country to lead the singing in a small rural church. Now, on this Saturday morning, as he works quietly at the mill, Byron notices that smoke is rising from the direction of the Burden place, but he pays little attention to it, only keeps on working.

Then Lena arrives at the sawmill, for she has heard that Lucas Burch works there, a mistake which seems to have come about because the name Burch sounded like the name Bunch. When she discovers that Byron is not the man she has been searching for, Lena accepts disappointment with quiet resignation, but Byron has suddenly and unaccountably fallen in love. From Lena's description of Lucas Burch, he recognizes that the man she seeks is the Joe Brown who had worked at the mill but who now lives in the cabin on the Burden place with Joe Christmas. He does not tell Lena this, but takes her into town, finding a place for her to stay with his landlady.

The third chapter focuses on Gail Hightower, on his past and on the effect upon his life of his continual immersion in dreams of a legendary past. Even as a young man, more than a quarter of a century before, he had somehow confused the glory of religion with the martial glory of deeds done by his Civil War ancestors. He could hear their hoofbeats as they galloped recklessly toward acts of gallantry. Years before, he had married a woman whose family had influence enough to secure for him a church in Jefferson, for it was there he had always dreamed of being because tradition told that it was there, in Jefferson and in the countryside around it, that many of those glorious deeds of

82   Light in August

his ancestors had taken place. But so wrapped was he in the past and in dreams of galloping horsemen bravely adventuring that he could keep neither his pulpit nor his wife. Now he lives alone, isolated from the community—obsessed, untidy, but talkative. Byron Bunch is also isolated, but by his quietness. He has apparently never been a person who calls attention to himself. He has learned the protective value of patient labor. When he wants to make a joyous sound unto the Lord, he leaves Jefferson to lead his country choir.

Each principal character in *Light in August* is isolated. Lena Grove is a stranger in Jefferson, but so in their own ways are Hightower and Bunch, who in chapter four sit together talking of the strange happening which disturbed the town that weekend. Byron Bunch, with responsibilities now for the care of Lena, even failed to ride out to his little church in the country. He and Hightower now talk of Joe Brown and Joe Christmas, each of whom is also isolated, a stranger in town. But these two men have been living off the community by peddling bootleg whiskey. Joe Christmas and Joanna Burden, who was isolated also as a Northerner and a champion of the Negro, had been revealed as having lived intimately together for three years. But now Joe Christmas has murdered Miss Burden and has set her house on fire, and is in flight as a fugitive. His companion, Joe Brown, is a Judas who is eager to turn him in for the reward which has been offered. He has told the townspeople that Joe Christmas is partly Negro. As the sheriff and his posse pursue the murderer, Hightower muses over what will happen when Christmas is finally caught: "Poor man," he says. "Poor mankind."

That is the order in which characters are introduced in the four opening chapters of *Light in August*: first Lena

Grove, then Byron Bunch, then Joe Christmas, and then Hightower. And after eleven intervening chapters in which the story of Joe Christmas is told, these characters appear again, exiting roughly in reverse order to the order of their appearance. Incidents of the fugitive's boyhood and young manhood—and his arrival in Jefferson, his love affair with Miss Burden, the murder, the chase, and his capture—are presented. As the book draws to a close, Hightower and Bunch are again revealed in conversation, much as they were in chapter four. Then three chapters are devoted to the birth of Lena's child, the flight from Jefferson of its father, and the killing of Joe Christmas by an avenging mob. The book ends as it began. Hightower is still musing, still alone. Byron Bunch and Lena Grove, joined now, though not in marriage, are last seen traveling together down a dusty road. Lena's child is in her arms, and Byron is faithful beside her as she continues her patient quest for the father which her child, like every child, should have.

Starting quietly, the book ends quietly, as with assurance that unpretentious, quiet perseverance will finally prevail. But between the calm beginning and the quiet ending violence and corruption reign. Self-seeking men follow thoroughfares which lead hopelessly only to the past. As much as Gail Hightower is victimized by the imagined sound of thundering hooves and by visions of bygone gallantry, so Joe Christmas is also a victim of a past which may be just as legendary. Hightower knows too much of his ancestry and its claims to glory. Joe Christmas knows too little of his, and it is precisely his lack of knowledge which pursues and isolates him.

His mother had eloped with a traveling carnival man, who was darker-skinned than she—a Mexican perhaps, or

perhaps, as her father insisted, a Negro. He, Joe's grandfather, was an unpleasant and bigoted man named Doc
Hines. He preached white supremacy in Negro churches.
He had pursued the dark-skinned seducer of his daughter
and killed him. He had refused to allow a physician to
attend his daughter when she gave birth to a son. As a
result, she died. Shortly afterward Hines left young Joe, his
grandson, at the door of an orphanage on Christmas eve—
hence his name, Christmas. And the grandfather followed
him there, finding a position at the orphanage as a janitor,
to watch over and persecute the child. He thought of himself as the instrument of an avenging God who carries out
the divine will. He told the other children that Joe was
Negro, and they mocked him in the play yard. Doc Hines
was virtually insane with eagerness that punishment for
the sin of the father should descend upon the infant son.
He equated sex with evil, "bitchery" with "abomination."

None of this, however, is revealed to the reader until
Joe's story as he remembers it himself is told. His first
recollection is of the orphanage when he was five years old.
Hungry for affection and for sweet things, he wanders one
day into the room of a young woman dietician who has
been kind to him. He explores as a child might, and when
he discovers her toothpaste, he tastes it, likes it, and eats
quite too much. When he hears the dietician coming, he
scurries behind her washstand curtain to avoid being caught
at something which he knows he should not be doing.
There he cowers, so frightened and so miserably ill because
of what he has eaten, that he does not notice at all that the
dietician and her companion, a young intern, are making
love. When his gagging betrays his presence, the dietician
is certain that he has been spying on her. She is terrified

lest the small boy tell what she supposes he has seen. She turns on him in anger, calling him the lowest and vilest name she can think of—a nigger. Later she tries to bribe him to silence with money. Joe is bewildered. He does not understand why she should alternately be angry and kind. Thus, even as a child, Joe is unable to know certainly whether he is a Negro or not. His past is blank and his future becomes a quest for self-identification. Hurried into adoption by the dietician, who fears that he might reveal her love affair, Joe spends his boyhood in the strictly regulated home of a rigid Presbyterian family named McEachern. Simon McEachern sternly demands an exacting standard of conduct. Mrs. McEachern is confusing to the boy because she is often kind. At eight Joe is beaten by his foster father because he will not learn the catechism. When barely in his teens, he has his first sexual experience, with a young Negro girl in a barn. At seventeen he begins to hoard and hide money, some of which is given secretly to him by kindly Mrs. McEachern. He slips out at night for a young man's adventuring.

Then, in a restaurant not far from the McEachern farm, he meets a young waitress named Bobby Allen. She is kind to him, and they become lovers. Like the girl in the ballad which her name suggests, she seems to a seventeen-year-old boy fresh and lovely, everything that a girl should be. In reality, she is a small, childlike woman of over thirty. Her eyes are described as like an animal's. Joe steals money from the McEacherns to entertain her. He is happy but guilty in his love. His foster father's Presbyterian teachings suggest that he is being tempted by feelings that are sinful, so Joe shoots a sheep and washes his hands in its blood in order to give himself what he calls immunity from the sin.

As he slips out at night to meet Bobby, he is so conscious of wrongdoing that he sometimes hopes he will be caught. He does not know at first that Bobby is really a prostitute who has been brought by the owner of the restaurant to attract customers. One night he confesses to her what he thinks to be his secret—that he has Negro blood. She refuses to believe him, but from that time onward he gives her money, presumably for her services.

McEachern follows them one evening to a dance hall, to which he is guided as if by divine direction as an avenging archangel. When he accuses Bobby of being a Jezebel, Joe turns on the man who once attempted to whip him toward righteousness. He viciously clubs his foster father with a chair, perhaps killing him. Neither Joe nor the reader is sure of this or is completely clear about all that follows afterward. Bobby turns against him, shrieking with anger, "Bastard! Son of a bitch! Getting me into a jam, that always treated you like you were a white man. A white man!"

Joe then enters on the long road which he will follow for fifteen years in flight from and in quest of himself. He steals money from Mrs. McEachern. He is badly beaten and robbed by Bobby's friends. Women have been responsible for much of his confusion. The dietician at the orphan home, like Bobby, was kind and then vicious. Even Mrs. McEachern, in deceiving her husband by being kind to Joe, finally seems to him tainted with duplicity. For years, Joe attempts to resolve the conflict within him created by a double burden. He assumes that he has black blood and is therefore doomed. He is increasingly disturbed by the disparity between what he does and what he knows he should do.

Rejected and unhappy, belonging nowhere, he wanders to Oklahoma, Missouri, Mexico, to Chicago and Detroit. He works in oil fields and wheat fields; at one time he is a day laborer, at another a miner, a prospector, an employee in a gambling house. He enlists in the army, but deserts after four months. Sometimes he lives with Negroes as a Negro; at other times he is a white man among whites. But either way he rages within himself, confused between a yearning for the kind of order which McEachern stood for and the violent, disruptive passion generated by the confusion within himself. Once he almost kills a prostitute because she says that she does not care whether he is black or not.

At thirty, he arrives in Jefferson, a white man who accepts a Negro's menial task at the sawmill. On his way to town he had stopped at Miss Burden's house, looking for food. She is a spinster of forty whose life has been dedicated to the support of a school for Negroes. He and she enter into an affair which lasts for three years, she abandoning herself without reserve to the demands of physical passion.

The road which Joe Christmas follows in search of himself has become a sewer, he now thinks, and a sewer that runs mostly at night. Joanna Burden is wracked by middle-aged fantasies of bearing Joe's child, but her ardor is cooled by middle-age menopause. Now she wants to do something kind for Joe. She wants to improve him by giving him a scholarship to the Negro college which she supports. She no longer thinks of him as an individual capable of love. She will reform him to the stock figure of a "respectable Negro" who is grateful for what white people do to help him. She asks him to kneel with her and pray for forgiveness for what they have done. Instead he kills her and sets fire to her house. She is another woman who is not to be trusted. Joe resents people who force him toward religion as his Presbyterian foster father had tried to force him. Women and religion both seem false, and soiled.

And so Joe Christmas begins to run again, this time in smaller circles, in flight from the vengeance of man. He is certified a Negro now by Joe Brown's accusation, and a white woman has been killed. All at once, he who has been an alien, isolated from his fellows, receives instant social identity as a fugitive. The community of Jefferson, members of which are now introduced for the first time, provides him with a traditional social role, the black seducer of a white woman. More than a week of chase follows, during which Joe enters a country church and terrifies its Negro congregation, and enters a white man's neighboring town unnoticed because he seems to be a white man. When finally caught, Joe receives a traditional social punishment. His fanatic grandfather appears again and vindictively urges the community to destroy the abomination against God and the sin against itself which the fugitive represents. Manacled but attempting to flee, Joe Christmas is caught, shot, castrated, and dies.

Because symbolically he is crucified by castration, and had come to Jefferson at the age of thirty-three, Joe Christmas can be recognized, like Benjy Compson and Darl Bundren, as another ironic Christ figure. Faulkner supplies several obvious parallels between Joe's life and the life of Jesus. Joe Christmas was born of an unwed mother. His initials, J. C., correspond to those of Jesus Christ. When as a small boy he first arrives at his foster parents' home, Mrs. McEachern ceremoniously washes his feet. When, in flight after the murder, he clears the Negro church of its fright-

ened congregation, Faulkner makes it plain that this happens on a Tuesday, the day of Holy Week on which Jesus
cleansed the temple. Two days later, on the day of the Last
Supper, Joe enters a Negro cabin where a meal mysteriously
appears before him, but he eats alone, for he has no disciples, except for the Judas whose name is either Joe Brown
or Lucas Burch, and who has already betrayed him. Other
parallels are lightly touched: Bobby Allen presents a fleeting
likeness to Mary Magdalene. Joe's refusal to deny his
identity when captured, and his boyhood cleansing of himself after sexual temptation with the blood of a new-slain
lamb both suggest biblical counterparts. Joe Christmas has
been described as a savior who cannot redeem, only suffer.

And why he is this is what *Light in August* is about, but
Faulkner never gives the answer clearly. His triumph is to
have revealed Joe Christmas less as a symbol than as a suffering human being, and to have left the reader with a sense
that, in spite of Joe's stumbling and his blind frenetic
searching, his lack of knowledge of himself and his lack
of love—in spite of these, something important of human
dignity and human decency survives. When last seen, Lena
Grove and Byron Bunch are questing still. She is a
madonna, her infant son in arms, the son who had been
born on the day that Joe Christmas died, as if in promise
that mankind might have a second chance. And Byron
Bunch is a faithful Joseph beside her. They are unpretentious people who accept life as they find it. Theirs is the
confidence and the humility and the simple resourcefulness
by which alone mankind can survive.

For pride in one's past can cripple, as it crippled Hightower, whose visions of bygone glories cut him off from his
fellows. And fanaticism is also isolating, whether it is the

eye-for-an-eye kind of ruthless retribution which made Joe's grandfather, Doc Hines, so monstrous a caricature of biblical justice, or whether it is the self-soothing and self-deceiving charities of Miss Burden. Each of these assumes that there are only two kinds of people, the black and the white, the evil who require punishment or redemption and the good who remain forever good however despicable their actions.

And words are isolating, like the ritualistic words of the catechism which McEachern would have Joe Christmas memorize. Even words like love, of the kind which an idealistic young Joe felt for Bobby Allen, can be shattered against revelations of reality. For *Light in August* is not only a study of degrees of isolation and rejection, or of varieties of shallow religious attitudes and of racism. It speaks also, like *As I Lay Dying*, of the crippling effect of abstract words and phrases, which, learned in childhood, can color and distort whole lives.

Faulkner has many unpleasant things to say about people and how they act or react, and he calls on biblical legend and romantic poetry to reinforce his sense of their essential inhumanity. Echoes of Old Testament wrath are heard in the shrill recriminations of Doc Hines. The wordy and legalistic rigor which can distort Calvinist Presbyterianism is revealed in McEachern's reliance on inherited doctrine. Hightower's religion is composed of empty phrases, interrupted by dreams of human glory. It is again like the Grecian urn of John Keats, static, serenely removed from reality, fair but forever lifeless.

Not only are most of the men in *Light in August* presented as monstrous caricatures; the women whom Joe Christmas meets also repel him. He has learned to resent and be angered by their occasional misdirected kindnesses. They become sterile, sexual objects, to be used and abused. To the disillusioned and finally cynical, unhappy young man, they too are urns, but cracked and oozing filth. He meets none who do not finally repel him.

Even the townspeople of Jefferson who are introduced late, as the chase after the fugitive Joe begins, are unpleasant or casually uncommitted figures. The Harvard and Heidelberg educated Gavin Stevens remains coolly aloof from the human drama which is taking place in his town. The vengeful, glory-seeking Percy Grimm, who leads the National Guard in search and capture and castration of Joe Christmas, is, after Jason Compson in *The Sound and the Fury*, as unsavory a character as Faulkner ever produced, and is perhaps even more disturbing because he seems so real. It is significant that he appeared briefly in *As I Lay Dying* as a nephew of Flem Snopes.

There are good people in Yoknapatawpha County, but Joe Christmas never knows any of them, except for Byron Bunch, and Byron keeps pretty much quietly to himself. Joe's and Lena Grove's paths never cross. Nor does he know Mrs. Armstid, the kindly countrywoman who gives Lena comfort and shelter as she approaches Jefferson, nor Mrs. Beard, Byron's landlady, who provides a temporary refuge for Lena in town. The long road which Joe frantically runs is illumined by no redeeming light. Even on the shorter last road down which he flees as a man already condemned by society, he puts on a black man's shoes to throw his pursuers off the trail.

But Joe's murder of Joanna Burden and his own death are redeeming, if to no one else, briefly to Gail Hightower. Joe has been described not only as a Christ figure, but also

as a Puritan saint, because the Calvinist doctrine which
McEachern, after all, succeeded in teaching him leads
toward a feeling of guilt. What Joe does as a person of
natural impulses does not square with what he has been
taught should be done. To his grandfather Hines, dark
blood certifies the presence of the Black Man, the Prince
of Evil, Satan himself. To Joanna Burden, black blood is
a reminder of the white man's guilt. It is a dark stain which
might be wiped away by kindness. Faulkner plays these
views one against the other, not so much to say that they
are characteristic of actual geographical locations, North
or South, but to suggest that they represent attitudes to be
found among any group of people. They may even be found
clustered in contradiction within one person.

Joe Christmas distrusts himself because of his consciousness of unexpiated guilt as much as he does because he does
not know who he is. Money becomes a symbol of his guilt
when he recalls the bribe which the dietician at the orphanage had offered him. Mrs. McEachern supplied him with
money which he spent on Bobby Allen. The prostitute had
accepted money from him. Sweet things like toothpaste
became associated with guilt. After the incident with the
dietician he never wanted any more sweets. Most of all,
women are sources of guilt. They do not understand
morality. When Joe had gone to bed feeling himself to be
like a Christian martyr for having withstood a beating from
his foster father, Mrs. McEachern had spoiled his martyr-
dom by secretly bringing him a tray of food. He could not
eat it. Women disrupt the order which men try to impose
on the world. Throughout the book, women, food, and
money attract but also repel.

That is not to suggest that women are evil, only that Joe

Christmas thinks they are. Lena Grove is not redeemed by
what he has done, for she needs no redemption. Her steadfast purpose is not altered at all. Hers is an implacable
human force, pagan and decently amoral. She is a creature
of the earth, beyond good or evil. Her name suggests a
sheltering grove. She asks few questions of life, and receives
few answers. She accepts things as they are because that
is the way they must be. Nor is Byron Bunch greatly affected by Joe. With greater experience of the world, he
assumes social responsibilities. He befriends Lena and
watches over her as a mother might. His last name recalls
the bunch, the group, the communal whole. But his first
name is incongruously Byron, and he romantically falls in
love with Lena at first sight.

Despite his love, Byron unselfishly searches out the man
who calls himself Joe Brown but who is actually Lucas
Burch, because he knows that Lena thinks it proper to
marry the father of her child. When he sees Joe Brown
attempting to hop a freight to escape from Jefferson, Lena,
and the baby, he tries to stop him and is badly beaten.
Byron's interest in Joe Christmas is more casual. He had
thought it strange that Joe three years before had stooped
to a menial job at the sawmill. He was not especially disturbed, only interested, to learn that he had turned bootlegger. Even after the murder or during the chase, Joe becomes for Byron mainly a person to speculate about with
Gail Hightower.

But the defrocked clergyman is redeemed. He reenters
the society from which he had withdrawn. Like Christmas,
he too has been a dropout from normal contacts with his
fellows. He too is troubled by disparities. Memories of times
when his forefathers were bold impinge on every present

thought. Simply, he was shut away in the high tower of his seclusion until the gale created by Joe Christmas shook him free.

Like Joe, he too lives with shame. His feeling of guilt for the loss of his wife and the loss of his church presses on him, only relieved by phantoms from the past of legend. Deprived of speaking God's word from the pulpit, he had for a time offered himself as a transcriber of words on hand-painted Christmas and anniversary cards. He had lived alone with a Negro woman who cleaned and cooked for him. Townspeople suspected them of immoral, unnatural acts. Masked men frightened the Negro woman into quitting her position. And a note signed by the Ku Klux Klan ordered Hightower to leave Jefferson at once. When he refused to go, he was found two days later in the woods, tied to a tree and beaten unconscious. Since then he has lived alone. Byron Bunch is his only visitor.

Byron first brings Hightower out of the shell of his isolation when he persuades him to act as midwife at the birth of Lena's baby. Helping to bring life into the world, Hightower reenters the world. Doc Hines's wife is there also, a pathetic old woman whose mind is so deranged that she confuses the newborn child with her own grandbaby, whom her husband had taken away from her to place in an orphan's home. Later in that day, when Joe Christmas is pursued into Hightower's home, the clergyman makes a heroic attempt to save him. He uses the false word of a lie to improvise an alibi for the murderer.

In a final revery which may contain much of the intellectual impact of the book, Hightower argues with himself about any man's right to destroy himself as long as he harms no one else by doing it. He thinks of all the quiet walls behind which men isolate themselves. He considers how ingeniously they fashion words which guard them from the necessity of discovering truth. He thinks of how false even the best of words are, even when they appear in the best of books. It is an error of youth, he tells himself, to create heroes. He still continues, however, to imagine that he hears the thundering of the hooves of horses on which his ancestors rode to glory. Hightower's redemption is perhaps only fleeting. A little redemption goes a long way.

Light in August contains violence—the wild, rich blood which courses from the heart of nature. It contains corruption and human error. It is about death, including the dead life of men who overlay humanity with creed. Like *As I Lay Dying*, it is also a book about life and its renewal. The light in August is an actual light which reddened the sky above Jefferson when Joe Christmas exorcised some of his guilt and frustration by setting fire to Joanna Burden's house. It is also a spiritual light. Among country people, a cow is sometimes said to be light after she has given birth to a calf. In Germany and France, Faulkner's novel was translated over its original title. In the Netherlands, like Mississippi a land where cattle are cherished, it was called *Born in August*.

Absalom, Absalom!

5

Like *The Sound and the Fury* in which Caddy Compson appears only as remembered by other people, *Absalom, Absalom!* tells of the rise and decline of Thomas Sutpen only by having someone else talk about him. There is a difference between the two novels, however. In *The Sound and the Fury* every character who speaks or thinks of Caddy has known her. In *Absalom, Absalom!* only one of the narrators has known Thomas Sutpen. The others piece together details of his story from what other people have told them or from what they themselves imagine must have been true.

Thus *Absalom, Absalom!* is, among other things, a disclosure of how history is made and legends are developed. No one knows the story of Thomas Sutpen completely, not even Miss Rosa Coldfield, who for almost half a century has nursed her outrage against him because of the way he

treated her when she was a girl. Her memory is distorted
by her grievance. In her view Thomas Sutpen had been a
demon, an ogre, a ruthless and relentless man who was
driven by ambition to which he would sacrifice anyone and
anything. The great house which he had built twelve miles
beyond Jefferson is falling into ruin. It is an ominously
mysterious house, inhabited by strange dark people who
seem to be custodians of some baleful secret. It is a house
haunted by legends which the townspeople for years have
known and repeated among themselves. It is a house of
ill omen.

Thomas Sutpen has been dead for forty years when, on a
September afternoon in 1909, Miss Rosa Coldfield calls to
her house in Jefferson young Quentin Compson—the same
Quentin Compson who appeared in *The Sound and the
Fury*. He is now twenty, and very soon he will leave for
Harvard. Perhaps he will never return to Jefferson. But he
is a smart boy who someday, Miss Rosa thinks, may become a writer who will record the story of her outrage. So
there she sits, a fiery little old lady whose tiny feet dangle
from her chair without reaching the floor. She is bitter,
frustrated, vengeful, and breathless as she tells Quentin her
version of the story of Thomas Sutpen, a man from
nowhere who with a band of half-wild Negroes had descended on the wilderness land and in violence had torn
from it a great plantation of one hundred square miles
and had erected on it a great house surrounded by splendid
gardens.

She wants Quentin to borrow his father's horse and drive
her that evening out to the great house, now in ruins. There
she will reveal to him more of its awful secret. As a result,
he will be able to make plain to all the world the kind of

demon that Sutpen had been. Meanwhile, she talks on interminably. Quentin listens politely, as a young man should.

Before Miss Rosa was born, this ogre named Sutpen had come to Yoknapatawpha and had married her sister and had fathered two children, each of whom was older than Miss Rosa. After her sister's death, Miss Rosa, an orphan and twenty years old, moved to Sutpen's great house, and she lived there for two years just at the end of the Civil War. Thomas Sutpen was away from home during that time, fighting in the Confederate Army. When he returned, a widower of fifty-eight, he offered marriage to the twenty-two-year-old sister-in-law whom he found living in his house. She accepted, or she wanted to accept, but then something dreadful happened which now, when she is sixty-five, still fills her with indignant, sputtering wrath.

Miss Rosa is not always easy to follow in what she tells Quentin. Her narrative jumps back and forth, recounting at one moment events which happened before she was born, at another detailing what she remembers of her own shocking experience. She thinks there had been something strangely demonic about her niece, Judith, who was four years older than she, and something doomed and sensitive about her nephew, Henry, two years older than his sister. Miss Rosa explains to Quentin what she had learned from her own sister about Sutpen—violent and aggressive, naked to the waist, in fearful, deadly combat, fighting in the barn for the joy of fighting with one of his savage black slaves, while his children watched, Henry terrified at ringside, Judith fascinated from a hiding place in the loft above.

Everything that Miss Rosa says is colored by her loathing for Thomas Sutpen. He was not a gentleman. He was a monster. Before he had married her sister, men from Jefferson used to gather at his place to gamble, to drink, and to watch Sutpen in combat with his wild Negroes. Even her father, a Methodist churchman and a respectable merchant, had gone there long before Miss Rosa was born. No good came of that, for he soon became involved in mysterious dealings with Sutpen. She thinks there must have been a curse on her family and on the whole South which allowed a demon of this kind to descend on them to despoil tradition. What was the crime bedded deep in her family and in the land of Yoknapatawpha which she and her sister, both innocent, were fated to expiate?

Her account is thus confused by emotion. Truth and fancy are merged by her bristling anger. What she knows and what she has been told are fused to a pattern warped by her long-festering resentment. She lives haunted by ghosts from her unhappy past. And Quentin Compson, sitting there with her on that late summer afternoon, is confused also. He listens considerately, responding only with an occasional "Yessum" or "No'me." But what she tells him makes him think of his own family and the ghosts which inhabit its past.

He thinks that if perhaps he can tell the story of Sutpen, the telling of it may lay those ghosts also, at the same time wiping out the name and memory of Miss Rosa's demon, and somehow explaining, especially to Quentin himself, why God in retribution had allowed the South to flounder in agony after losing the Civil War. For Quentin, alert to history and his family's part in it, is also haunted. Miss Rosa—wan, haggard, reminiscent, and bitter—seems to him a ghost, a remnant from the past, and he thinks of himself as a ghost also, born in the baffled ghostland of the South and fated to be destroyed as Sutpen had been destroyed. Quentin is a romantic young man, and his thoughts are not always logically consecutive.

That evening, having left Miss Rosa, he sits on the porch of the Compson house listening to his father. From him Quentin hears another, more extended version of the history of Thomas Sutpen. Much of what Mr. Compson knows of the subject has been learned from his father, General Compson, who was a friend of the strange and boisterous man. Other details of the story as Mr. Compson tells it have been gleaned from local tradition. It is bolstered also by documentary evidence in the form of a letter which Judith Sutpen gave Quentin's grandmother forty years before. There were other letters which might have thrown additional light, but they have been lost or destroyed.

From all of this testimony—the hints, allusions, reminiscences, and local gossip—Quentin gradually reconstructs his own version of the fortunes and misfortunes of the Sutpens. He has grown up knowing bits and pieces of it, but now, spurred on by Miss Rosa and concerned about his own family and his forthcoming departure from Jefferson for college, he begins to put them all together. Readers of *The Sound and the Fury* will remember how upset Quentin is presented as being during this late summer of 1909. His sister, Caddy, has been made pregnant by one man and married to another. Quentin has tried to avenge her as a brother should, and has failed miserably. The meadow where the Compson children once played has been sold to provide money for Caddy's wedding and Quentin's college expenses. Sutpen's downfall therefore seems to him a bleak portent of the downfall which threatens the Compsons also.

Then, four months later, when Quentin is at Harvard, he

receives a letter from his father telling him that Miss Rosa is dead. His roommate, Shreve McCannon, seeing that Quentin is upset by the letter, asks him about it. All through a long January evening the two young men talk, reconstructing between them the Sutpen saga. Quentin tells what he knows, and Shreve, a Canadian who has never been South and who has never heard of the Sutpens, supplies details, often in good-natured raillery.

This is the way that history is made, that legends are born—from hints of truth and hearsay evidence molded by imagination and emotion. Quentin is too closely involved with fears for his own family to interpret clearly. What Shreve contributes are traditional Northern notions of what the South is like. He is the most Northern of Northerners, from Canada where Negro slavery never existed. Yet Shreve confidently supplies narrative links which make the story of Sutpen complete.

Because the collegians at Harvard are young and romantic and casually bookish, the story which they reconstruct assumes several borrowed guises. It resembles a Greek tragedy, darkened by incest and fratricide. It takes on overtones of the Old Testament story of King David and his son Absalom, from which Faulkner derived the title of this novel. It comments ironically on Christian doctrine which speaks of love and compassion by having uncompassionate and loveless things happen during the Christmas season. Sutpen's son Charles Bon (Charles the good) is thirty-three when he is murdered. He, his father's first begotten, who might have redeemed the family, is symbolically crucified. Throughout the narrative lurks the ominous and corroding influence of time. Sutpen is finally felled by a vengeful old man with a scythe such as Father Time is popularly pictured as wielding. The narrative which the young men piece together finds its beginning and its ending in the consequences of man's inhumanity to man.

The story of Sutpen unfolds as a mystery story unfolds. What happens is not directly revealed, but bit by bit in fragments, some of which overlap, and some of which do not fit snugly with other fragments. Reading *Absalom, Absalom!* is like doing a jigsaw puzzle some parts of which are warped or missing. New pieces must be whittled out before the picture can be seen complete. It is a novel about how people arrive at what they call truth. A fragment here, another there, is discovered, not necessarily in chronological order, each with its own coloring of prejudice or pride. No one knows the story entire. Each version is colored by the predispositions of the person who tells it. Some details are not remembered at all until a chance remark by one person reminds another person of something he might not otherwise have recalled. A reader soon discovers that much of the story which Quentin and Shreve piece together may not be true at all.

When the pieces are all assembled and fitted into place, a design does come clear. Thomas Sutpen had been born of a poor mountaineer family in West Virginia. His father was a shiftless man who, when his wife died, moved down to the lowlands, where he settled as a tenant farmer on a large plantation near the James River in Virginia. Here, as a boy, Thomas Sutpen was for the first time confronted with a situation in which his assumed superiority because he was white was rudely challenged. When at fifteen he was sent by his father to deliver a message to the plantation owner, he in innocence went to the front door of the planter's mansion. A handsomely dressed Negro servant turned the ragamuffin boy away, ordering him to go around to the back door. Angered and humiliated, the boy vowed vengeance. He would become rich, and he would father children who would never be turned from any door. He would perpetuate his name in honor forever. This became Sutpen's grand design, to which all else had to be subordinated.

Four years later he became an overseer on a sugar plantation in Haiti. Displaying almost superhuman strength and boundless courage, he put down a slave rebellion there. As a consequence he was rewarded with the hand of the wealthy French plantation owner's daughter. Her name was Eulalia Bon, and a son named Charles was born to the young couple. Sutpen prospered, but when he discovered that his wife was partly Negro, he turned over all his property to her except for twenty Negro slaves and returned without her to the United States. His two-year-old octoroon son was left on the island with his mother.

At twenty-six Thomas Sutpen turned up in Jefferson, a taciturn but determined man, a mystery to the townsfolk. Exploring the countryside on horseback, he met the Indian chief Ikkemotubbe and somehow acquired from him title to one hundred square miles of undeveloped land. No sooner had he filed title to this land with the County Recorder than he disappeared from Jefferson. Two months later he returned with his twenty savage slaves and a captive French architect. Working side by side with his slaves, he erected a splendid mansion. When the architect ran away, Sutpen forcibly brought him back. Nothing was allowed to interfere with the building of the great house. Only when its walls and roof were erected and in place, and the gardens and promenades laid out, was the Frenchman allowed to leave.

Throughout, Sutpen is drawn larger than life, a man of

heroic strength and inexhaustible energy battling against nature and subduing it to his design. People in Jefferson remembered him as a massive man, red-haired, and consumed by ambition. He was as mysterious as he was powerful, and he soon became a subject of gossip. The source of his wealth was unknown and mysterious. Rumor accused him of nefarious dealings, even as an armed bandit. But Sutpen faced down all suspicion and walked boldly among the townspeople, even when threatened by mob action. In 1834 his daughter Clytemnestra was born to one of his female slaves. The great house had been erected but was still unfurnished, its windows gaping holes, its gardens unplanted. It became a place of ill repute among many good people of Jefferson. Men from town drove out to Sutpen's place for days, and especially nights, of mysterious activities which caused tongues to click with disapproval. What they did there was magnified by gossip to become legend.

Quentin's grandfather, General Compson, had been as close to Sutpen as any man in Jefferson. Sutpen had confided to him his grand design for a great house and a splendid family. Though he accepted a loan of cotton seed from the General, he refused an offer of money which would allow him to furnish and decorate his house. Instead he entered into a mysterious and presumably illegal partnership with the local merchant, Goodhue Coldfield. Leaving Yoknapatawpha again on a surreptitious and unrevealed venture, Sutpen returned with four huge, ox-drawn wagons filled with everything needed to complete and outfit his mansion.

In June 1838 he married Coldfield's daughter, Ellen, in a wedding service attended by only a handful of the one hundred people of Jefferson who had been invited. By March of the next year a son, Henry, was born to the couple. Nineteen months later a daughter, Judith, was born. Four years after that the children's aunt, Rose Coldfield, was born in Jefferson. As a child, she was frightened but fascinated during visits to her sister's family in the great house twelve miles from town. She seems to have been a timid little girl, plagued more than most by her niece and nephew and tremendously awed by their father.

Meanwhile, Thomas Sutpen had become the most prosperous cotton grower in Yoknapatawpha County. His fields and gardens were carefully tended. His mansion was splendidly imposing. He commanded respect if not affection from his neighbors. He had a son who would carry on his name, inherit his lands, and insure the continuance of Sutpens forever. The accomplishment of his grand design seemed guaranteed.

When that son at twenty entered the University, he met there an attractive young law student from New Orleans named Charles Bon. Henry Sutpen proudly brought his new friend home for a visit during the Christmas holidays. Judith Sutpen was attracted to Charles Bon, and he to her. A match between them was encouraged by Thomas Sutpen's wife. But Sutpen, after an unexplained visit to New Orleans, forbade the marriage. He had apparently learned, though he did not at the time reveal it, that Charles Bon, whom he must have recognized at once as his Haitian octoroon son, had been married in Louisiana to a woman who was also partly Negro, and had himself a son named Charles Étienne Saint Valery Bon, who, as the oldest son of Sutpen's oldest son, might be presumed to be rightfully heir to Sutpen's estate. Even if Charles Bon were never revealed as part-Negro and a half-brother to Judith, the union between them had to be stopped. Their marriage and their offspring would contravert Sutpen's magnificent plan. Though other people might never know the relationship to be incestuous and though in the public view Sutpen's grand design would seem to be successfully carried out, such success, Sutpen confided to General Compson, would be falsely grounded, without worth or meaning.

When the Civil War started, Thomas Sutpen joined John Sartoris in forming an infantry regiment. After a year he was elected its Colonel in Sartoris's place. Henry Sutpen and Charles Bon joined the University Greys and were attached to General Compson's regiment. Before the war ended, Ellen Sutpen had died and her young sister, Rosa, had moved out to the plantation. Charles Bon was wounded at Shiloh. Thomas Sutpen was cited for bravery by General Robert E. Lee. When Bon proposed to Judith Sutpen that they wait no longer to be married, he was soon thereafter shot and killed at the gate of Sutpen's Hundred by her brother, Henry. He had learned from his father something (how much is not made clear) of Bon's past history. Quentin and Shreve are very sure that Sutpen himself had covertly approved, perhaps even engineered, the killing. The deed done, Henry Sutpen disappeared. Little Miss Rosa, Judith, and the inscrutably foreboding Clytemnestra remained alone in what had become a war-despoiled and deteriorating mansion.

As a result of the war Thomas Sutpen lost all but one square mile of his great plantation. But he was determined to persevere in the creation of his grand design. He asked Miss Rosa to become his wife, but only on the condition that she first prove herself worthy by bearing him a son. In outrage she refused, and she lived in outrage and in poverty the rest of her life, in her deceased father's house in Jefferson. Sutpen apparently made the same proposition to Milly, the daughter of a poor white neighbor named Wash Jones. When Milly bore him only a daughter, Sutpen told her that it was too bad she was not a mare so that he could give her a good stall. Enraged, her father attacked and killed Sutpen with a scythe.

The half-sisters Judith and Clytemnestra had lived alone for years in the decaying Sutpen mansion, which became to the people of Jefferson more a place of mystery and menace than ever before. They were joined by Charles Bon's son, Charles Étienne, who grew up to become a reckless and roistering troublemaker, arrested for brawling at a Negro dance. He finally married a black woman, and they had an idiot son named Jim, who became known through the countryside as Jim Bond. His father occupied a cabin on Sutpen land, but Jim Bond lived in the great house with his aunts Judith and Clytemnestra, one white, one black. When Judith died and then Charles Étienne died, Jim Bond and Clytemnestra lived apparently alone in the dilapidated mansion—the last of the Sutpens, the tattered remnant of Sutpen's grand design.

On that evening in September 1909 when Quentin Compson drives Miss Rosa to the old house, they find it silent. The door is locked and there is no response to their knocking. Quentin climbs through a window to unlatch the front door for Miss Rosa. She rushes in, pushing past Clytemnestra, who stands in the doorway as if to block her entrance. She clambers up the stairs and in a second-floor bedroom discovers her nephew, the long-time fugitive murderer Henry Sutpen, now seventy years old, weak and ill. Quentin follows her and speaks briefly to the old man.

At Harvard a few months later he learns from his father's

letter that Miss Rosa, vindictive still, returned to the old Sutpen place soon afterward with a deputy sheriff and an ambulance. As they approached the house, it burst into flames and was soon destroyed, Clytemnestra and Henry Sutpen perishing with it. Only the idiot Jim Bond remained. The last of his family, he howled grotesquely as he watched the final relic of his great-grandfather's dream consumed by fire. Then he disappeared.

The driver of the ambulance and the deputy sheriff restrained Miss Rosa as she attempted to dash into the flaming house. Frustrated, overcome finally by her outrage and anger, she collapsed. She was taken back to Jefferson in the ambulance which in angry, outraged lust for vengeance she had supplied to bring her bedridden nephew to jail. She remained in a coma for almost two weeks, and then died.

Those are the bare bones of the story of the fall of the house of Sutpen as Quentin, prodded by his roommate Shreve, reconstructs it. The only facts that Quentin knows are that he heard Miss Rosa's angry story, he went with her on that September evening to the old mansion, he saw old Henry Sutpen in an upstairs bedroom, and he saw Clytemnestra as she attempted to block Miss Rosa's entrance. His father showed him a letter in which plans for the marriage of Charles Bon and Judith Sutpen were revealed. Everything else is based on what other people have told him and is patched together by conjecture. What is conjectured is colored by Quentin's worry about the decline of his own family and by Shreve's quizzical but romantic outsider's view of what it must be like to be a Southerner.

Thomas Sutpen, however, comes magnificently alive. He appears as a legendary figure, looming large in menace and in might. The boy who had descended from his mountain birthplace to find rebuff even among the servants of the rich man living on the plain becomes a resolute man of single purpose who ruthlessly sweeps aside whatever threatens his dream of wealth and reputation. His is the traditional American success story, of rise from rags to riches. His grand design reflects what any boy may be encouraged to dream. But it is a distorted reflection, made of fantasy and then nightmare. It omits humility in respect for nature, especially for human nature. Sutpen's illusion is that he can go it alone, relying only on his own strength and determination. Other people are pawns to be moved by him, overwhelmed by his turbulent will. His unfaltering, furious single-mindedness removes him from the community of men, but not from their envy, their anger or mystification, or, finally, their sympathy.

Sutpen is the frontiersman who hews a wilderness to submission. His strength is that of other familiar supermen, like Paul Bunyan, for example, whose deeds of strength and daring have also become legendary. Sutpen becomes the ogre of the fairy tale, whose castle contains ominous and evil secrets. He is the remorseless brigand of many a household story. He is a modern Agamemnon, though so unlearned in Greek drama, says Mr. Compson, that he named his first daughter Clytemnestra instead of Cassandra, who, in her dark foreboding, she seemed to him more clearly to suggest. Like the hero of classic tragedy, he is pursued by the consequences of his misdeeds and proves to be the author of his own disaster.

Sutpen achieves power through reliance on traditional virtues of courage and determination. What he lacks are the greater virtues of compassion and love. The first of these was submerged by the wave of bewilderment and anger which flooded over him when as a boy he was turned away from the rich man's door. The second was overridden by ambition. What other people call love has become for Sutpen a mere biological instrument for carrying out his grand design. That which should hold a family together tears it violently apart. Judith's love for Charles Bon is thwarted by her father, not because it is incestuous but because it threatens to spoil the symmetry of his plan. Henry Sutpen becomes a victim of his attachment to his father and his love for his sister. He defends what he supposes to be Judith's honor as Quentin had not been able to defend his sister in *The Sound and the Fury*. But his action leads to no good end. Like David in the Old Testament, Thomas Sutpen loses his son, and for many of the same reasons.

Parallels have been discovered between *Absalom, Absalom!* and the Oresteia trilogy in which Aeschylus told of the fall of the house of Atreus. Agamemnon sacrifices one of his sons, much as Thomas Sutpen sacrifices one, perhaps two, of his. Each father thinks the sacrifice to have been justified as a means toward a laudable end. In each case the sins of the father descend on his children. In each, a Clytemnestra presides over a retributory doom.

But parallels between the Old Testament story in which Faulkner found his title are more pronounced. Like Sutpen when he takes a message from his father to the rich man's house, David is also sent by his father on an errand which changes the course of his life. His slaying of the giant Goliath finds an analogue in Sutpen's suppression of the slave rebellion in Haiti. Each is promised a bride as a reward. David is deceived when Saul substitutes another daughter for the one he promised. Sutpen is deceived because his bride is not the white girl he expected her to be.

Each flees as a result of the deception. Later, when David becomes a king, he schemes to marry Bathsheba, just as Sutpen, approaching wealth, schemes to marry Ellen Coldfield. When David's son Amman has an incestuous relationship with his half-sister Tamar, he is slain by his brother Absalom, as Charles Bon is slain by Henry Sutpen when an incestuous relationship threatens. The fall of the house of David is complete when Absalom dies. The house of Sutpen is doomed when Henry disappears. There is, however, a difference in the endings of the two stories. King David, repenting what he has done, cries out in anguish, "O my son Absalom . . . would God I had died for thee O Absalom, my son, my son." Thomas Sutpen does not repent. He stubbornly perseveres, and tries again, but then time in retribution catches up with him.

As Quentin reconstructs Sutpen's story, it is a tragedy, because Quentin's brooding mind irresistibly links it to what he recalls of New Testament or Greek legends of doom. But as an idealistic young man, he resists the dark interpretations put on it by his Northern roommate; by his father, whose mind is mired in disillusioned brooding on the past; or by Miss Rosa, who quivers with righteous indignation. Whether in Miss Rosa's dingy parlor or on the front porch with his father, Quentin listens as his elders spin out the tale. What he contributes is most often troubled rumination as in his mind he constructs imagined conversations and wonders about what they can mean. Nothing in what he hears explains to him why things happened as they were said to have happened, or indeed whether they even happened at all. When Quentin speaks, it is often to ask a question. He is troubled by the absence of love in what he hears.

Some readers have supposed that when Quentin and
Miss Rosa come on Henry Sutpen hidden in the old house,
the old man must have revealed some secrets to Quentin,
or perhaps to Miss Rosa, who later passes on the information. Quentin seems to know more than his father and
Miss Rosa and his grandmother's letter reveal. But Faulkner
himself did not find it necessary to explain Quentin's access
to new information. As Quentin tells the story to his roommate, his sympathetic detailing of Henry's tortured concern
with incest and with the protection of his sister's and
family's honor parallels his own troubled concern for Caddy
and the Compson family in *The Sound and the Fury*.
Judith Sutpen, as he presents her, is a courageous and suffering girl, much like Caddy. Whatever good things are done
in the Sutpen household are done by her. Miscegenation
horrifies Quentin, but he defends Thomas Sutpen as an
innocent man misguided. Without experience of his own
to aid him, Quentin can only explain Sutpen in borrowed
terms. But he does not hate the South, he insists to his
roommate: *"I don't. I don't! I don't hate it! I don't
hate it!"*

So magnificently self-sustained is *Absalom, Absalom!*
that it is not necessary however to read it with memory in
mind of what had happened in *The Sound and the Fury*.
It is complete in itself. Nor is it necessary to read it as an
indictment of the South and of the South's guilt because
of the white man's treatment of the black man. It plumbs
deeply to reveal sources of evil in any man. Sutpen's innocence—if that is indeed the word for his single-minded
refusal to heed ancient admonitions about love and compassion—though it may remind a reader of an older time
when men were stout-hearted conquerors, provides a mirror

also in which modern man may find his own image. The story is double-pronged and open-ended. It reveals as much about Quentin as about the man whose history so troubles him. Perhaps it tells as much about each reader and what he puts into it or takes from it.

Absalom, Absalom! is the last of Faulkner's four great novels which appeared between 1929 and 1936. In it and *The Sound and the Fury, As I Lay Dying,* and *Light in August,* he presented what he later liked to describe as the human heart in conflict with itself. Characters struggle to overcome forces which are inexorably present in nature or in human nature. Some accept their humanity and its requirement of sacrifice. Others are observers who are able to forget their own shortcomings when they comment on the faults of others. What is presented is life, which can be corrupt or troubled or serene. During these seven years and afterward, Faulkner published other stories, some of which were more immediately popular. Most of them are more explicit, with meaning more clearly underscored. All of them contain characters who are often comic, always human, and inevitably erring. None, however, has the depth and density of these four. Each reader finds his favorite among them. Mine is *Light in August.*

The
County and Beyond
6

William Faulkner once said that he had deliberately written *Sanctuary* as a shocker, and it was certainly received by the reading public of 1931 as a shocking book. Chronologically it falls between *As I Lay Dying*, which had appeared the year before, and *Light in August*, which appeared a year later. But in structure and theme it seems to belong to an earlier period. It is uneven in tone, sensational, and lacks thematic unity. Grotesque or burlesque comic scenes distract attention from the mood of disillusionment or despair which makes *Sanctuary*, however imperfect otherwise, one of the most powerful expressions of the attitudes of the post-World War I generation of young Americans known as the "lost generation." The world which it presents is soiled by sordidness and sin, and by the hopeless despondency of people who would, if they could, do something about it, but who are too weak or too willful to try.

As in *Light in August*, two stories are told, one of a man, the other of a woman, except that in *Sanctuary* the two stories meet and merge. The central character of the first story is Horace Benbow, who in *Sartoris* was introduced as an effete idealist who had returned to Jefferson after the war, having served as a Y.M.C.A. secretary in Europe. He brought with him glass-blowing equipment with which he dreamed of creating delicate objects of transcendent beauty. Now, ten years later, the henpecked husband of the former wife of another man, he is, at forty-three, a dreamer still, devotedly dedicated to ideals of purity and saintliness in woman. To him, a woman is the repository, the temple, the sanctuary of all things which are good. Like Quentin Compson in *The Sound and the Fury*, he thinks of woman as a creature to be cherished and protected at any cost. What Horace Benbow finally discovers, but never really allows himself quite to believe, is that the sanctuary which is woman can be soiled. Woman is not an ideal. A woman is a person, just like any other person, and is as vulnerable as any other person to the very human capacity for making mistakes.

The second story is that of Temple Drake, a headstrong girl whose father is a judge. Though thematically her story is subordinate to that of Horace Benbow, actually her sensational and shocking adventures overshadow his bumbling and sorrowful ineptness. It was what Temple did and what was done to Temple which made *Sanctuary* shocking and the first of Faulkner's books to reach a wide audience. When some years later the story was made into a motion picture, it was called *The Story of Temple Drake*. And perhaps that was as it should be.

What is not always noticed about the voices of despair and disillusionment which appear in Faulkner's fiction is that they almost always belong to weak and temporizing men—like Quentin Compson, for example, or his father. Horace Benbow is of that kind, but without the solemn, misguided dignity of the Compsons which makes them appear as almost tragic figures. That they are not tragic, only pathetic, may be suggested by Faulkner's present portrait of the well-meaning but completely undignified and almost wholly comic Horace Benbow. He is an educated but unmasculine man, tired now of the routine of marriage and its responsibilities. He is tired of the shrimp he must buy each week for his wife, and the way the juice from the carton in which they are carried drips down over his trouser leg. Horace has been described as a twentieth-century Don Quixote. He is so innocent and fumbling that he can neither drive a car nor handle the simplest of tools. As the story opens he is in flight from his wife and his home in Kinston, on his way to nearby Jefferson, where his widowed sister (she who in *Sartoris* had married young Bayard) lives and where, unknown to his wife, he has maintained ownership of the house in which he spent his boyhood.

He is resting from his journey beside a spring near Frenchman's Bend. There he is accosted by a gangster from Memphis named Popeye, a sinister little man who looks as if he had been cut out of tin. His distance from the true nature of things is certified by his spitting into the spring by which they sit and by his fear of bird noises, which he hears in the woods as day darkens toward twilight. Popeye is alien to the natural world, and he will be discovered to be isolated also from the world of men. His pistol is his only virility. His hand twitches impulsively toward it at the first sign of danger.

Benbow accompanies Popeye through the woods to the Old Frenchman Place, a onetime fine mansion now falling to ruin, where a bootlegger named Lee Goodwin plies his trade. There Benbow talks and talks about his wife and her daughter, about his disillusionment with marriage and his fear that his eighteen-year-old stepdaughter, Little Belle, on whom he now centers his battered ideals of female purity and spiritual beauty, will be corrupted by the boys she is beginning to date. He talks on and on through the evening, though no one listens to him. He continues then on his way toward Jefferson.

Four days later, on a Saturday afternoon, Temple Drake, who is just about the age of Little Belle, is brought to the Old Frenchman Place by her date, Gowan Stevens, a student at the University of Virginia, who is drunk but out of whiskey. When he wrecks his car and becomes drunker still on Lee Goodwin's bootleg booze, in shame he leaves Temple there, to be protected by Lee Goodwin's common-law wife Ruby La Marr, who continuously insists that Temple leave the Old Frenchman Place before darkness falls. No longer protected by the chivalric code which reveres womanhood as sacred, she might be attacked by Popeye or even Lee, or one of the other men who hang around the bootlegger's establishment.

This prospect both terrifies and fascinates Temple. She runs and runs, and hides, imagining that men pursue, half knowing but not admitting that her running is of itself an incitement and an invitation. Finally, guarded by Ruby, she spends the night. On Sunday morning she hides in a corncrib, watched over by a feeble-minded, loyal man

named Tommy, who promises to keep the other men away.
Popeye enters the crib, shoots Tommy, and rapes Temple
with a corncob. Later that day he takes her to Memphis
and finds her a room in a house of ill fame run by a pleasant, middle-aged, and motherly woman known as Miss
Reba. There she is protected as Popeye's girl. Though
Popeye is impotent, unable to make love to Temple, he
supplies her with a lover, named Red, and he watches
greedily as Red makes love to her. When she responds to
Red and conspires to see him privately, without Popeye
present, Popeye shoots Red through the forehead and
kills him.

At first in her experiences with men, Temple is frightened
but unresisting, even in the corncrib, but as time goes on
she becomes utterly bereft of shame, glorying in sen-
suality. It is not so much that she deteriorates morally as
that she recognizes and responds to something which already existed within her. But Temple does not accept the
moral consequences of what she does. When Lee Goodwin
is arrested for the murder of feeble-minded Tommy in the
corncrib and is brought to Jefferson for trial with Horace
Benbow as the lawyer defending him, she perjures herself
by testifying that it was Lee, not Popeye, who had killed
Tommy and raped her.

After Goodwin is convicted and condemned, but then
taken at night from the jail and burned by a mob intent on
avenging female virtue despoiled, Temple is taken by her
father to Europe, where she can rest and forget. Benbow,
defeated and more disillusioned than ever, returns to his
wife in Kinston. Popeye is later arrested, charged, convicted,
and executed for the murder of a man in Alabama whom
he could not possibly have killed, because that killing took

place on the same evening that Popeye was in Memphis putting a bullet through Temple's lover's forehead.

That shooting makes possible an ironic and grotesque scene of no special importance except that it is gruesomely funny. During the wake which Red's friends hold for him, his dead body reposes in horrid dignity on a table, until the loving celebration of his mourners becomes so raucous, and they so drunk and careless, that Red is knocked from the table and the wax peg which filled the gunshot wound in the center of his forehead is dislodged and rolls along the floor. Only a few days after that incident the missing Temple Drake is discovered to be at Miss Reba's by means of another comic diversion. Faulkner appropriated the familiar folk tale of country bumpkins who, in the city for the first time, mistake a bawdy house for a boardinghouse and engage rooms there. Young Virgil Snopes and a companion named Fonzo stumble on Miss Reba's place. They admire her pretty daughters. They hope she will not discover that they visit girls in bad houses and then make them leave because they are not fit to live in her house. It is Virgil's older and more corrupt kinsman, Senator Clarence Snopes, who, as a veteran visitor of houses of ill fame, discovers Temple's presence at Miss Reba's and sells that information to Horace Benbow so that Temple can be returned to Jefferson to testify—for Lee Goodwin, Horace thinks. Faulkner seems to be suggesting that in a world roiled by corruption even death may seem comic and prostitution a source of slapstick humor.

Miss Reba is a warm and kindly person, honestly amoral. She takes great professional pride in the orderly management of her house of prostitution, and is shocked by Temple's disorderly and, it seems to her, immoral attitude toward sex. And Ruby La Marr had been a prostitute once also, and for honest reasons. Lee Goodwin had been in prison, and she had needed to support herself and the child which she bore him out of wedlock. Now she is willing to prostitute herself again, if it will enable her to raise money for his defense against the murder charge. As a matter of fact, that is exactly what such a good and righteous woman as Horace's sister, Narcissa, suspects that Ruby is doing. She is shocked that Horace allows Ruby to live in the old Benbow home. She is sure that the two are living, as she might say, in sin. Making conventional statements about God and morality, she and other righteous women of Jefferson insist that Ruby leave the house, even the town. Who is more corrupt, the former prostitute or the exemplary and outraged women who persecute her?

Three moral environments may be discovered in *Sanctuary*. The first is the little world which centers about the Old Frenchman Place. There Ruby and Lee and their baby live in a kind of idyllic peace, he distilling nature's good corn into honest whiskey. But then another world intervenes as Popeye comes to buy the whiskey, which he smuggles into Memphis, and Temple comes to destroy the natural good relationship between Lee and Ruby. It is an amoral world at the Old Frenchman Place, better than the second world, the underworld of Memphis, where relief for honest human appetites is sold. But is Jefferson, the third world, superior to either of these? Words rule there —words like honor and reputation, which go up in the air like smoke. It is a false world, built on illusion. Covering up that which within itself is evil, or hounding from its sight that which it considers evil in other people, it fails in honest apprehension of reality. It refuses to admit that doing wrong just comes naturally, and that in recognition of the commonality of error lies the true brotherhood of man.

Horace Benbow in *Sanctuary* almost comes to such knowledge. He finally recognizes that his ideals are illusions. The actions of his wife, his sister, Temple Drake, and even Ruby La Marr convince him that women are more than sanctuaries: they are people, and subject to error. But Horace is not a strong man. He retreats into himself, and is not heard of again in Yoknapatawpha County. But the story of Temple Drake was to be continued twenty years later in another book, which Faulkner called *Requiem for a Nun*.

Sanctuary had seemed to say that people are corrupt because the world in which they find themselves is corrupt. Human evil is made to seem a manifestation of a universal or cosmic evil. The novel's mood is of disillusionment complete. *Requiem for a Nun* sets forth a different mood. It is written as a three-act drama, with long passages of exposition preceding each act. The play itself picks up the story of Temple Drake eight years after the events recorded in *Sanctuary*. Temple is married to Gowan Stevens and has had two children. But the younger child, an infant daughter, has been smothered in her crib by a Negro servant named Nancy Mannigoe. Nancy is a former prostitute whom Temple later admits she hired in order to have someone to talk to. For though Temple was out wardly made respectable by becoming Mrs. Gowan Stevens, she knew herself, though at first only subconsciously or privately, as a person who had enjoyed living in a house of ill fame. Nancy, she thought, was the only person in

Jefferson who spoke her language or who understood what she had done and why. Nancy had been a corrupt person, and Temple had been corrupt, and Temple wanted to believe that all people were corrupt.

Gowan Stevens married Temple as if in atonement for having deserted her in *Sanctuary* at the Old Frenchman Place. But he suspects that her older child is not his, though he is somehow convinced that in any case it is his in a moral sense, for it was his drunken cowardice or thoughtlessness or carelessness, whatever it could be called, that was responsible for making Temple into the kind of person who would have a child by someone else. Gowan is a decent man of conscience. He is able to face up to and accept the consequences of what he had done. His marriage to Temple seems to be tolerably happy, but that is all. Both he and his wife are tortured human beings, bound to misery by their past.

Temple in the past has been less able to admit responsibility for what she does. Now, faced with a new crisis, she runs away again. After Nancy is sentenced to be hanged, Temple flees to California. Nancy's lawyer is Gavin Stevens, an uncle of Temple's husband, Gowan. He is a well-educated man, a Phi Beta Kappa with degrees from Harvard and Heidelberg, who after *Sanctuary* replaces the less competent Horace Benbow in Faulkner's fiction of Yoknapatawpha County as a kind of representative of the conscience and explainer of the motives of its people. He asks Temple to return so that she can join him in petitioning the Governor to pardon Nancy. Temple insists that Gavin Stevens may be able most simply to save Nancy by proving her to have been insane when she smothered the baby. But the lawyer seems to suspect something which the reader does not yet know, and insists that Temple go with him to the Governor.

Temple finally does accompany Gavin Stevens to the statehouse at Jackson, and there in anguished confession reveals that she was being blackmailed by the brother of Red, who had been her lover in *Sanctuary*. She explains to the Governor that Nancy knew that she, Temple, planned to run away with the blackmailer rather than submit to the social disgrace which revelation of her affair with Red might bring, and to take her younger child with her, leaving the older with Gowan. Nancy believed that by killing the younger child she would somehow keep the family together. When through confession Temple admits her share of responsibility for what has happened, she realizes that Nancy has offered herself as a sacrifice. Her sin of murder will expiate Temple's perhaps greater sin of failure to accept herself honestly for what she is—a human being prone to error. Nancy will die for Temple's sin, so that Temple may find redemption.

This story, on its surface so sensational and even improbable, takes on multiple suggestions of meaning. Although a play, it contains more talk than action, though as adapted for the stage in France by Albert Camus it was performed to some critical acclaim. When presented on the stage in New York, it was described as a long and dark dialogue flowing endlessly from some hidden reservoir of the world's evil. But even simplified, it does not seem simple. Numerous suggestions of meaning have been discovered in it, most of them religious. Gowan and Temple have been described as an Adam and Eve who have fallen and been expelled from the garden of innocence. Their child suffers for the sins of her parents. The Negro Nancy is a nun who attempts to save Temple's soul—if indeed, says Temple, I have a soul. Nancy's is a primitive faith. She is a servant of (the) Temple, she offers herself as a human sacrifice, she suffers, and she believes. Much of what Faulkner seems to have been trying to say in *Requiem for a Nun* may be suggested in a question which he poses but does not answer. Does the salvation of the world depend, he asks, on the patient suffering of men?

But *Requiem for a Nun* inevitably speaks also of the past, and of how the past affects and becomes part of the present—of how *Was*, Faulkner would become fond of saying, becomes *Is*. Temple's salvation can be thought of as her recognition of this, and her final admission of responsibility for the consequences of what she had done. The long prose passages which precede each act reinforce such suggestions of meaning. The first act, "The Courthouse," tells of the early days of Jefferson and of how that town got its name and its courthouse and a sense of community among its inhabitants—all in an attempt to cover up and hide forever an illegal piece of comic rascality involving the theft from a government mail sack of a lock for the town jail.

The prelude to the second act, "The Golden Dome," moves back to geologic time, advances to the coming of the red man, and then moves on to the coming of the white man, who attempted to establish man-made law and order over a great, lush, and natural territory out of which was carved the state of Mississippi with its capital at Jackson, where the golden dome of its statehouse continues to symbolize the ambition and presumption of men. The third act is introduced by "The Jail," and here the history of Jefferson is told, from its first settlement to the present, the presence of the past symbolized by a girl's name which was scratched on the window of the jail in 1861 and which still survives.

Some of Faulkner's most magnificent and tantalizingly evocative prose is found in these preludes. Single sentences, as if by magic, are made to speak, all at once and at the same time, of the mythic, historical, and remembered past, each merging with the other, and all merging, singly or together, with the present, so that they become sentences which are both timeless and encompassing all time, as what has been past is made to explain or to influence the direction of anything which happens or is thought to happen, or even which is thought. The prose moves in massive but intricately contrived cadences toward suggestions of meanings beyond any which words can supply. Each sentence becomes a gigantic net into which Faulkner seems to have attempted to entrap all meaning. He speaks as a poet speaks, through insight toward intimations of truth.

To some readers his reach has seemed greater than his grasp. Sometimes he may appear to try too hard, and to fail. It was Faulkner's attempt to make words accomplish what seemed an impossible task for words to master which made Ernest Hemingway once say that he wished he could manage Faulkner, as a prizefighter's manager manages a prizefighter, keeping him from attempting more than his ability allows. But Faulkner once said that among his American contemporaries he most admired Thomas Wolfe, who dared risk failure by attempting to use words and rhythms which reached toward meanings never revealed before. When they failed, theirs was a brave failure. They had taken risks by experimenting.

As an incorrigible and audacious experimenter himself, Faulkner may have failed in *Pylon*, which appeared in

1935. It is at one and the same time a comic tale of a barn-storming flying team, a poem in sometimes fractured prose about the glory and the insanity of man in his contest against the sky, and a plaint of disillusionment with man in all of his undertakings in the moral and mechanical wasteland in which he finds himself floundering. And it has been found to be one of the most original but also one of the most derivative of Faulkner's novels. Its language does often mount toward poetry, but in doing so uses many of the same symbols and allusions that T. S. Eliot had used in his poems of disillusionment. Faulkner experiments with using words as James Joyce had done, jambing them together to speak of "gasolinespanned" or "sunstipulated distances." His words, like his fliers, soar in adventurous flight. But the disparate elements of theme or structure in *Pylon* never quite fuse. The action is often melodramatic. Symbols such as the pylon itself, which stands both for sex and for speed, are not subtle. Religious undertones may be discovered, hints at searchings for salvation, but what Faulkner means to suggest does not come clearly through.

The flying team of which he writes is made up of an aviator, a parachute jumper, a woman who is or has been the property of each, and a journeyman mechanic named Jiggs who drinks too much and is careless but kindly. They are befriended by a reporter whose name is said to be so ridiculously incredible that it is never mentioned in the novel, though there is some suggestion, because of the title of one chapter, "Lovesong of J. A. Prufrock," that he may be, or at least have the name of, T. S. Eliot's bumbling hero, who timidly wonders whether he dare eat a peach and who wears the bottom of his trousers rolled. Whatever his name, he is a wonderer and a bumbler also. He wonders at the bravery of airmen, but he wonders also whether they are not insane. He kindly takes the flying team in when they are homeless, but then allows them to drink so much that the plane which the flier races the next day is not properly checked out. The flier crashes and is killed, the rest of the team moves on, and the reporter is left alone, still wondering.

Homeless and rootless, the airmen have an existence above and beyond society. As barnstormers, they are here today and gone tomorow. Where they come from few men know, and they move on to who knows where. They are ephemeral as butterflies, Faulkner once explained to a student group at the University of Virginia: "they are outside the range . . . not only of respectability and love, but of God too," for they have "escaped the compulsion of accepting a past and a future." Yet they are sustained by the fruits of man's most advanced ingenuity. Their planes are mechanical marvels, but they are also a threat and a menace to man when they are not managed and kept with care. For flying, like any other human activity, can be tainted by corruption. The airfields from which the airmen fly are donated by or named after men who through questionable practices have become wealthy in business or politics.

Pylon has not been a favorite among many of Faulkner's readers. It seems hurried and inchoate. It is the first novel since the earlier and even less successful *Mosquitoes* to be laid completely outside of Yoknapatawpha County. Part of the action in *Sanctuary* had been in Memphis, and part of the action of *Requiem for a Nun* would take place at the state capital at Jackson, but in each of these books the focus is on people from Jefferson or the Old Frenchman Place.

Though Faulkner knew fliers and had even done some barnstorming himself, his attitude toward them seems to have been ambivalent. They control machines which can be vicious, but which can also be tamed, literally to rise to heights which show in new perspective. Though potentially masters of man's finest achievement, fliers are careless or rash, as if attempting at the same time to destroy it. They are equally rash in morals. Young Bayard who flies to his death in *Sartoris* is made plausible because of his involvement with the people and the past of Yoknapatawpha. Though Faulkner may have intended to reveal the airmen in *Pylon* as rootless men who lacked precisely that commitment to background, he does not succeed in providing them with substance and credibility as characters. They are, perhaps purposely, presented as creatures who are half human and half metallic, like Popeye in *Sanctuary* exiled from the secrets and the sorrows of the human heart.

The Wild Palms, published in 1939, can be called a laminated novel. Two stories are told, neither having any apparent relation to the other. First a chapter of the first story is presented, then a chapter of the second, and chapters continue to alternate in a kind of counterpoint until each story is completed. As we have seen, each story was later printed separately, one over the original title, the other as *The Old Man*. But they should be read as Faulkner intended them to be read, for there are, after all, relationships between them.

The first is a love story about a man who runs away with another man's wife. It is not a pleasant romance, for the love between the young physician Harry Wilbourne and Charlotte Rittemeyer seems even at its beginning unnatural, and becomes increasingly sordid. Throughout, the woman is the aggressor, a predator who consumes her mate. She believes that marriage is an empty form which destroys love, because love should be free, unrestricted by codes of conduct devised by man. For two years the couple leads a skulking life, cut off from society, in Chicago, in a mining camp in Utah, and finally in a resort colony on the Gulf of Mexico. When Charlotte becomes pregnant, Harry performs an abortion. When she dies of toxemia as a result, he goes to prison.

The second story begins with a man in prison. The Mississippi River is in flood, and convicts are being called upon to help rescue people from the rising waters. Two of them, one tall, the other fat, are sent off in a skiff with instructions to pick up a woman who is stranded in a tree and a man who clings to a cotton-house roof. The skiff is caught by the force of the flood and is overturned. The fat convict gets to shore, where he reports his comrade drowned. But, actually, the tall convict recovers the boat and for weeks struggles desperately to return it and himself to the prison camp where they belong. He rescues a pregnant woman from the branches of a flood-menaced cypress tree. With almost superhuman effort he battles the raging currents of the rampant Mississippi, the Old Man of Waters, which surges on indomitably.

When he attempts to surrender the skiff to men on shore, he is shot at as if he were a fugitive instead of a man who is attempting to return what does not belong to him. He wants to get rid of his woman companion and finally does, but not until he has helped her give birth to a child in a snake-infested Indian mound which rose above the waters. When he gets her ashore and does return the skiff, his mission accomplished (though he laconically admits, "I never did find that bastard on the cotton house"), his sentence is extended for ten years because he is said to have attempted to escape.

Certain parallels or oppositions between the two stories are immediately apparent. The tall convict, at the beginning of the account of his adventures, is already a prisoner, and he remains a prisoner at the end; Harry, at the beginning of his unhappy story, is symbolically prisoner to his love for Charlotte and her influence on him, and at the end he is a prisoner in fact. Harry is a victim of a woman who will not let him go, and the tall convict has custody of a woman whom, though he must meet tremendous challenges to do it, he wants to get rid of. Harry, trained as a physician, is responsible for the death of a woman after he performs an operation which prevents her giving birth. The tall convict, with only the edge of a tin can to cut the umbilical cord and a shoelace to tie it with, successfully helps to bring new life into the world.

But the stories can also be read as ironic commentaries on the misleading and corrupting view of life which can be presented by literature that falsifies relationships between men and women as they really are and life as it really is. The tall convict is in prison in the first place because as a younger man he had been a victim of a literary fraud. He had believed what he read in pulp fiction magazines about sure-fire methods for robbing a train. What the men in the fiction had successfully carried off, he was ignobly captured in attempting. He thought of suing the writers and the publishers of such misleading trash for using the mails to defraud.

The story of the love between Harry and Charlotte satirizes distortions of romantic love as presented in literature. Harry is a ridiculously inept lover. Rather than being the manly and chivalric conqueror of a girl who is innocent and pure, he is the victim of an aggressive woman. Faulkner may even have had a particular book in mind on which this story of unconventional but blighted love is commentary. Harry can be thought of as a caricature of Frederick Henry in Ernest Hemingway's A *Farewell to Arms*, and Charlotte, perhaps, provides ironic commentary on Catherine Barkley, who in that novel also dies in giving birth to a child who does not live. The settings which Faulkner chose resemble such familiar Hemingway settings as a camp in the deep woods or a cottage beside a body of water. Love that is romanticized in literature so that it seems sacred and separate from reality leads finally, in life, to disaster.

Harry and Charlotte are people of sophistication who attempt to rearrange things. They want to live the kind of life which they want to live, not the kind which they can or should live. Each is something of an artist, a creator: Harry, when he loses his place as a medical intern, turns to the writing of fiction; Charlotte is adept at arranging displays in store windows. The tall convict, however, is simple, clumsy, and ignorant, but he is strong in determination to carry out the task which has been given him. Nameless, he is everyman or any man. He does not attempt to alter anything; he accepts what he cannot understand. He is elemental man struggling against great forces of nature, even against the rampaging Old Man, the river rampant in flood. And the nameless woman to whom he provides protection is the elemental mother, the child-bearer whose guarantee is that life will continue. Without pretense and without any attempt to change anything from what it naturally must be, they survive and, however confined, are free.

The
Short Stories
7

Several of Faulkner's short stories may ultimately be remembered as among his finest achievements. The first to appear in a magazine of national circulation was "A Rose for Emily" in the *Forum* of April 1930. It was followed by "Red Leaves" in the *Saturday Evening Post* on October 25, 1930, and by "Ad Astra" in the annual anthology called *American Caravan* in 1931. These early stories define the areas which Faulkner would most often explore in his short fiction. First, most often, and most importantly, he wrote of the people of Yoknapatawpha County; second, of the Indians of northern Mississippi from whom the white man acquired his land; and third, of men at war who were reckless and brave. Many of the best of his stories are pieces of the gigantic jigsaw puzzle which, as Faulkner finally put it together, became not only a history of the imaginary Yoknapatawpha County, but also a paradigm of the history and condition of modern man. "Ad Astra," for example, though about soldiers in France, discloses something more of the impetuousness of the aviator Bayard who had appeared in *Sartoris*. "Red Leaves" tells of the competition among early Indians for the white man's favor, a story which would be retold in larger detail in *Go Down, Moses*.

Each short story thus seems part of the greater narrative. Sometimes an incident is related which will later find its way into a novel. The short story "Wash," for example, which appeared in *Harper's Magazine* in 1934, anticipates the ending of the story of Thomas Sutpen in *Absalom, Absalom!* two years later. "Afternoon of a Cow," written in the 1930's, contains the germ of an episode in *The Hamlet*, and "Barn Burning" in 1939 first recounts the story of Ab Snopes's vengeful habit of destroying other people's property, which would also be retold in that book. At other times the short stories are extensions or explanations of incidents which have been narrated before. "That Evening Sun" in 1931 makes clear certain references to a former Negro servant which had appeared in *The Sound and the Fury* two years earlier. "There was a Queen" in 1933 adds dimensions to the character of Horace Benbow's sister, Narcissa, who had appeared in *Sartoris* and *Sanctuary* and who would appear again in *The Town*.

For Faulkner seemed to think of each story as part of a total pattern. When he collected them into volumes, he arranged them in an order which could suggest their relationships one to another. *These Thirteen* in 1931 contained in its first section four war stories, in its second section six stories of Yoknapatawpha County and its people, and in its third section three stories of Americans abroad. Each section is linked in meaning to the other by its final sentence, which suggests a mood that is brooding and somber. The first section ends with a description of a wounded soldier who makes babbling sounds that are "meaningless and unemphatic and sustained"; the second section closes with a glimpse of a "dark world . . . stricken beneath the cold moon and lifeless stars"; and the collection is concluded with the story "Carcassonne," which has been described as Faulkner's attempt to capture in words the ecstasy and agony of a writer's creative experience. As an artist who is a man of man-made limitation, what he can reveal is small indeed beside "the immensity of darkness and silence within which . . . muses the dark and tragic figure of the Earth, his mother."

Dr. Martino and Other Stories in 1934 seems to have been less carefully arranged, but the *Collected Stories* of 1950 reveals a form as painstakingly devised as that of any of Faulkner's novels. It begins with a section entitled "The Country" which contains stories of poor-white sharecroppers like the Snopeses and of sturdy farmers like the McCallums, with whom, in *Sartoris*, young Bayard took refuge after his father's death. The next section, "The Village," presents tales of people in the town of Jefferson, and the next, "The Wilderness," is about the Indians from whom their land derives. Then, in "The Wasteland," appear five stories of men of war, and in "The Middle Ground," eleven stories of men uprooted and disillusioned, lost and defeated. Finally, in a section called "Beyond," a note of hopeful anticipation is struck with six stories which suggest glimpses of truths beyond those certified by experience. Again "Carcassonne" is the final story, whimsical and poetic and ironically autobiographical, a parable of a little man whose Pegasus is a buckskin pony on which he thunders up the long blue hill of Heaven, hoping that he may *"perform something bold and tragical and austere."*

"A Rose for Emily," which opens the second section, is a bold story—shocking perhaps, but not really tragic or austere. Emily Grierson, who for forty years has slept beside the physical remains of her dead lover, is pathetically a victim to a father who for years dominated her and drove suitors away. She is victimized also by a lover who would leave her, and by a passion which would murder rather than let him go. When love is gone and the lover is killed, Miss Emily clings to the illusion of love. However macabre, her keeping of her lover's body forever beside her represents a kind of furtive strength. Isolated, she becomes a minor legend during her lifetime; after her death, when her ghastly secret is revealed, hers becomes a story so appalling that no one can forget it. But it is a story which speaks symbolically of every person who allows love to die or who murders love, yet clings to the sham, the unreal semblance, the dead body of love.

A favorite theme throughout many of these stories is the bravery or honesty or loyalty of boys. Sometimes such stories are sentimental, as is "Two Soldiers," in which an eight-year-old attempts to go off to war with his nineteen-year-old brother, who enlists after the Japanese attack on Pearl Harbor. In "Barn Burning" a poor white boy is so shocked by the lack of morality in his family that he runs away. Such a conflict between divided loyalties appears again in "Mountain Victory," in which a Tennessee boy attempts to protect a Confederate officer who at the end of the Civil War is with his Negro servant on his way home to Mississippi. The boy's family plans to ambush and kill the officer, but the boy admires the soldier's bravery and bearing, and warns him. Nevertheless the officer is killed, as are the boy and the Negro servant—for bravery and compassion are menaced in a world roiled by hatred or avarice.

The wartime adventures of boys are told in greater detail in *The Unvanquished,* a series of stories about a white boy and a black boy from Yoknapatawpha County during and after the Civil War. The white boy is the same Bayard who in *Sartoris* is a grandfather and a banker. His father, the fabled Colonel John Sartoris, is busy fighting the Yankees. The Colonel's mother-in-law, Rosa Millard, remains at the Sartoris mansion just north of Jefferson. She harasses the Yankees also, in her own way, aided by her grandson Bayard and by his Negro companion Ringo. The boys are of the same age and have played together all of their lives. Rosa is aided also by Ab Snopes, a little, unscrupulous man, willing to enter into any scheme which will bring him profit.

The Unvanquished is often recommended as the book with which people who have not read Faulkner before may most profitably begin. It introduces characters who will appear again in other stories of Yoknapatawpha County, like Virginia Sartoris Du Pre, Colonel John's young widowed sister, who in *Sartoris* is Miss Jenny, the talkative matriarch of her nephew's household, and who is briefly seen in *Sanctuary* and in other stories. Judge Benbow, an ancestor of the lawyer Horace, also appears, as do General and Mrs. Compson, grandparents of the children who grow up in *The Sound and the Fury.* The Burdens, who come to Jefferson from the North and who incur the wrath of Colonel John Sartoris, will be recognized as the grandfather and the brother of Joanna Burden of *Light in August*. The story of Thomas Sutpen, pieced together in *Absalom, Absalom!*, is briefly told again. Also making their appearance are Theophilus McCaslin, known as Uncle Buck (he had had a minor role in *Absalom, Absalom!*) and his twin, Amodeus, known as Uncle Buddy, who is introduced for the first time. Each of these eccentric but stouthearted brothers would play later parts in accounts of Yoknapatawpha. Their belief that the land does not belong to the people, but that the people belong to the land, becomes an important reflection of one of Faulkner's own most consistent convictions.

But *The Unvanquished* is also a good introduction to Faulkner's world because the seven stories of which it is composed are told more simply than many of his others. They were written for a popular audience, the first five appearing in the *Saturday Evening Post*, the sixth in *Scribner's Magazine*; only the last was written for this volume, to provide the boy's adventures with a climax in which Bayard moves toward maturity. Though of a narrative structure less involved than that of many of Faulkner's other stories, *The Unvanquished* does present some difficulties. Almost everything which happens takes place in the 1860's but is recalled by Bayard Sartoris many years later. Yet what he recalls is so vivid that successive episodes are presented as if through the mind of a twelve-, then a thirteen-, a fourteen-, and a fifteen-year-old boy, and finally through the mind and conscience of a young man of twenty-four. The past seems really present as he reconstructs it.

To a twelve-year-old the Civil War was a grand display of heroism and bravery. His father, though a small man, seemed to him gigantic and wondrously brave. Bayard and Ringo scratch a battlefield into the dirt of the Sartoris yard, and they play at mock battles in which Yankees are always losers. But the year is 1863, and General Grant has just defeated the Confederate army at Vicksburg. Not far north of the Sartoris plantation, Corinth falls and troops of bluecoats swarm through Mississippi. Colonel Sartoris seems to the boys unusually distracted when he returns briefly home to hide the family silver where it cannot be found by marauding invaders. The boys are disappointed that he has no stories to tell of great battles bravely fought.

After he is gone and a troop of Yankees approach the Sartoris plantation, Bayard and Ringo lug an ancient gun from the wall and shoot at the enemy, killing a horse. When an irate Sergeant pursues them into the house, they crouch in terror under Bayard's grandmother's skirts, shocked but very glad that she tells lies about there being no boys anywhere in the vicinity. The horse which they shot had been a fast horse, and the company of soldiers had expected to win great sums by betting on him when he was raced against horses belonging to other Yankee units. The Sergeant, therefore, wants vengeance against the boys. But a kindly Yankee Colonel, who has sons of his own, intervenes by calling off the search for the culprits. Though Granny, the boys think, has done something very bad by lying, they nevertheless accept as just her washing out of their mouths with soap because they had spoken of the Yankees as "bastuds."

In the second story the boys are a year older. Colonel John Sartoris has been waging guerilla war against the invaders, and Granny, afraid that the plantation will be taken over in retribution, sets out for Memphis with Bayard and Ringo and the family silver. On the way they are met by Yankees, who commandeer their mules. Instead of staying with Granny, to protect her as Southern gentlemen should, the boys set out to recapture the stolen animals. In their search they come on Bayard's father, who scolds them soundly but enlists their aid in tricking the Yankees into returning the mules. Bayard's father, who seems to his son everything that a gallant soldier should be, later fools the enemy again by making an exciting escape when they attempt to capture him at the Sartoris mansion. So glorious is the memory of his father's brave duplicity that Bayard almost forgets to mention that the house was burned in retaliation.

For war is still glamorous to young Bayard, and his father continues to seem to him everything that a dashing hero should be. But in the third story, when he is fourteen, Bayard becomes aware of the realities of war. On a trip with Granny to visit her sister in Alabama, he sees one ruined plantation after another, with tall chimneys towering starkly over masses of rubble. Whites are sharing Negro cabins with former slaves. Swarms of blacks crowd the roads, hysterically rushing toward a promised land of freedom. The wagon in which Granny and the boys ride is swept by the tide of Negroes into a river, and their horses are lost. Demanding compensation for them and for the chest of family silver which has been tumbled into the current, Granny is brought before the same Yankee Colonel who commanded the troop at which the boys had shot two years before. The Colonel has captured so many mules and so many great boxes of family treasure, and so many Negroes have come to him for protection, that he does not know what to do with them all. He turns over to Granny many times what she asks, so that she has more mules and boxes of silver and Negroes than she yet knows what to do with.

But then, in the fourth story, Granny enters into the profitable business of selling horses and mules to other Yankee units, then stealing them back again to sell for a second, or a third, or even a fourth time. It is a grim and complicated comic business, in which she is assisted by sly Ab Snopes, and by stolen requisition forms on which Ringo becomes adept in forging Yankee signatures. But then Granny is killed by a bushwhacker, and in the fifth story Bayard and Ringo, joined briefly by Uncle Buck McCaslin, set out to avenge her. After a long search they come on her murderer, shoot him, and nail his carcass to an old cotton-house door—all but his offending right hand, which they bring home to fasten to the headboard of Granny's grave. War now is grisly reality. Bayard himself experiences its terrible cycle of death and vengeance.

In the sixth story the war is over. Colonel John Sartoris has returned to his plantation, to rebuild his house and help put back together the shattered social structure of Yokna-patawpha. With him he brings Granny's niece Drusilla, a girl from Alabama who, during the last years of the war, joined his force of irregulars and in men's clothes fought with them as a man, or as an avenging Valkyrie. Because he has compromised Drusilla by living in the same house with her, Colonel Sartoris yields to pressure brought by Drusilla's mother and the respectable women of Jefferson: he marries her, making her, though not much older than Bayard, the boy's stepmother. Colonel Sartoris organizes nightriders to maintain order through the disrupted countryside. He shoots and kills the carpetbagger Burdens who would organize the Negroes. Ten years later, in the last story, he is shot and killed, much as Faulkner's grandfather had been, by a man who had formerly been his associate in developing a railroad and is now his political opponent. Bayard, a law student at the University of Mississippi, is called on to avenge him. But Bayard refuses. At twenty-four he realizes that his land cannot be saved by further bloodshed.

These stories, which can be so simply outlined, are subtly told. The picture they present of Southern aristocracy brave in defeat may be romantic and unreal, like the dreams of vanished glory which obsessed the Compsons in *The Sound and the Fury* and Gail Hightower in *Light in August*. The little old lady who bamboozles an enemy is a familiar stock character in fiction, but Granny emerges finally as a complex and lovable, conscience-stricken but indomitable person. Some of her nefarious adventures in skulduggery become slapstick comedy, others verge on pathos, but an aura of gallantry surrounds her. Many of the Negroes are stock characters also, whether loyally devoted to their old masters, sullenly betraying them, or marching in masses northward in search of a River Jordan to cross toward freedom. Ringo, the most fully developed of the black characters, is alternately a pertly quipping but naive minstrel-show character and a boy whom Bayard remembers as smarter than he. Colonel Sartoris is the *beau ideal* of a dashing, arrogant, and fearless fighter in a cause which is lost.

Bayard finally recognizes that attitudes like those of his father may be remembered with admiration and affection, but that they must ultimately be put aside. As he grows older, he perceives the past for what it was, in glory and in failure. It was a good time to remember, especially when that which was most good in it, the courage and the companionship, could become elements used to build a better future. His father, who in *Sartoris* is remembered as representative of nobility and courage, is in *The Unvanquished* gradually revealed as a brave man who is domineering and intolerant, combining within himself fine qualities and destructive weaknesses. The last story suggests Greek tragedy as Drusilla, like an avenging goddess, and former members of Colonel Sartoris' courageous troop, chanting as a chorus, urge Bayard toward a bloodshedding revenge which he knows now to be morally wrong.

What is right and what is wrong was even more directly disclosed in another collection of short stories which Faulkner published four years later, in 1942. Of the seven stories in *Go Down, Moses*, five had previously appeared in magazines. All tell of the fortunes or misfortunes of the Mc-Caslin family, descendants of Lucius Quintus Carothers McCaslin, who in Yoknapatawpha early in the nineteenth century had fathered two families, one white and one black. Taken all together, the stories comment on the injustice of man to man, on the curse which descends on men who enslave their fellow men, and on the way in which suffering for the sins of one generation is passed on to generations which follow. But their culminating focus is upon McCaslin's white grandson Isaac.

All of the other stories in *Go Down, Moses* seem subsidiary to, or in some manner a commentary on, the long story called "The Bear," which is the sixth among them.

Almost in length a novelette, this account of the initiation of young Isaac McCaslin is usually considered to be among Faulkner's most extraordinary achievements, a parable revealing meaning that had only been suggested in his four great novels. This, he seems now to be saying, as if to critics who had formerly not understood him—this is what *The Sound and the Fury, As I Lay Dying, Light in August,* and *Absalom, Absalom!* are all about. This is what I have been trying to say from the beginning. Now, stated more explicitly, perhaps you will understand it.

Isaac, who is called Ike, is the only child of Theophilus, or Uncle Buck, who is one of the twin, and only white, sons of Lucius Quintus Carothers McCaslin. After their father's death Theophilus and his twin brother Amodeus, Uncle Buddy, turns the plantation house which they inherit into a residence for their inherited Negro slaves (who are all, presumably, their half-brothers). Buck and Buddy are confirmed bachelors, sturdy drinkers and great poker players, and are custodians of a sum of money which their father left for his surviving Negro kin. They have firm ideas, strongly held. They do not believe in slavery, but they are convinced that each Negro must earn his freedom by working on their plantation until his estimated but nonexistent wages equal the amount originally paid for him.

In *The Unvanquished* a hand of stud poker decides that Buck will remain home to watch over the land and the Negroes, and that Buddy will join Colonel Sartoris' regiment as a Sergeant. Now, in *Go Down, Moses,* poker fails Buck again. In his sixties, he lingers too long at the neighboring Beauchamp plantation, where he has gone with young Cass Edmonds, the grandson of his late sister, to bring back a Negro half-brother who ran away to visit a sweetheart there. During his stay Sophonsiba Beauchamp, a spinster with her eye on matrimony at any cost, tricks Buck into a situation so compromising that he is threatened with having to marry her. Buck challenges her brother to a game of poker which, if Buck wins, will allow him to remain free. But Buck loses, and thereby wins a wife.

Born in 1867, Ike is the only child of Sophonsiba and Theophilus McCaslin. His mother dies at his birth, his father and his Uncle Buddy die when he is twelve, and he is brought up by his cousin Cass Edmonds, who is a generation younger but sixteen years older than he. But Ike's principal tutor is Sam Fathers, a former slave who is half Indian and part Negro, the son of a quadroon woman and of the Chief Ikkemotubbe whose lands had once included all of Yoknapatawpha. Under Sam Fathers' tutelage Ike learns to hunt and to know his way about in the woods. He learns to respect the great wilderness land and the creatures in it, and to know that face to face with nature all men are equal. He grows to be a man who puts aside his inheritance of land, which he feels should belong to all men, and of money which he has not honestly earned.

"The Bear" may be read as a realistic story of apprenticeship and initiation. It can be read as a tale of hunting and camping and manly adventure in the deep woods. It is a masculine story of men away from home and home cooking, relieved of the care or comfort or control of women, and released from workaday responsibilities for earning money or maintaining an inherited social structure. Like the tall tale of the American frontier, it contains characters who may seem larger than life. The mood and manner of the folktale is discovered in it, or of the familiar local legend which is passed down by word of mouth, told around some campfire or before a household hearth. It will be recognized as a nostalgic reminiscence of days which were good but are gone. Or it may be read—like Herman Melville's *Moby Dick* or, on another level, Ernest Hemingway's *The Old Man and the Sea*—as a nature myth which speaks of man's struggle against elements more powerful and consistent than he.

But no one of these readings explains "The Bear" completely. Its scope encompasses all of them, and more. It can be thought of as a capsular paradigm of Faulkner's own life experiences, or those of any person whose past impinges on and influences what he has become. It is Faulkner's most explicit, but at the same time most penetrating revelation of man in his relation to nature: what man has done to despoil the good land and abuse its creatures, and what man may do to discover a right relation to nature. "The Bear" contains overtones which are profoundly religious, so that it becomes also a parable of the fate and the possibilities of man.

Taught by Sam Fathers to shoot and to track wild game, to know the secrets of the wilderness, its menaces and its delights, Ike McCaslin kills his first buck at the age of ten and his first bear at the age of twelve. But even to see Old Ben, the gigantic bear whose cunning and courage have become legendary among the hunters of Yoknapatawpha County, Ike must put aside the accouterments of civilization: his gun, which is a man-made instrument of destruction, and his compass and watch, which are artificial guides to direction or time. He must confront the great bear simply as one creature to another.

Five years later, when Ike is seventeen, the bear is finally cornered and killed. It brushes off the attack of dogs who are recklessly and doggedly courageous—like, one may think, the dashing Confederate cavalrymen who rode gallantly toward destruction, or like any brave creature who dares more than he can do. Finally the bear is killed when Boon Hogganbeck, part Indian and a creature who among men may be thought most closely to approximate the strength and tenacity of Old Ben, jumps onto his back and stabs him. Even the most powerful of creatures must die, though in their magnificence they seem to symbolize something awesome and eternal. When Old Ben dies, Sam Fathers dies also. Young Ike McCaslin's initiation is over. He has been witness to a moment of great truth, and his tutor's task is finished.

Ike recalls these things many years later. Much of the forest land in which he formerly hunted is gone, sacrificed to the need or avarice of man. Major de Spain's hunting lodge, near to which Sam Fathers lived, is gone, and the Major is gone, as are Cass Edmonds and General Compson and the others among whom Ike as a boy learned to know the woods and its creatures. Bears are gone from the forests, and men hunt lesser game in woodlands fringed with farms or crossroad settlements. Relinquishing his title to the McCaslin plantation, Ike refuses to own land of his own. He begins now to learn more about his forebears. Laboriously piecing together bits of information found in an old family ledger, he comes to realize—and to abhor the realization—that people were held as slaves in whose veins flowed the same blood that flows in his. He lives simply as a carpenter, then as a shopkeeper in Jefferson, and he tries for years to find his grandfather's black descendants so that he can hand over the legacy of money which as heir to his father and his Uncle Buddy he now holds in trust.

Ike has no descendants. The woman he marries, disappointed at not being allowed to live in the old McCaslin plantation house, refuses him children. But he lives the life for which Sam Fathers prepared him. He respects the bounty, the beauty, and the awesome power of nature. And he respects all of its creatures, especially men or women who are respectworthy, whatever their color. Through the veins of Sam Fathers flowed the blood of human beings who were red, black, and white. Spiritually, Ike is a descendant of each of these. Though childless, he has produced heirs, who are those whose understanding of man and nature approaches his, if only because they have read what is revealed about him and his inheritance, and also what is revealed about themselves and their inheritance.

Another compilation of stories which are held together through the actions of characters appearing in each is *Knight's Gambit*, published in 1949. Again, as in *The Unvanquished*, each story had been published before, except the last. They are detective stories in which Gavin Stevens and his nephew, Charles Mallison, solve crimes which have mystified other inhabitants of the county. Each is a good story, though Stevens is often so deviously loquacious that some may seem quite too laboriously told. But admirers of stories of ratiocination have been drawn to them. One in 1946 received a prize in the Annual Detective Short Story contest conducted by *Ellery Queen's Mystery Magazine*. Admirers of the lawyer who would have so conspicuous a part in *Requiem for a Nun, The Town,* and *The Mansion* have enjoyed pitting their wits against Gavin Stevens. People who have enjoyed meeting inhabitants of Yoknapatawpha County will recognize several old friends among the characters in *Knight's Gambit,* and they will make new acquaintances, also, among people who are human and err but who are found out when justice and intelligence prevail.

Faulkner's compassionate understanding of why people behave as they do, so effectively set forth in his greater novels, is revealed also in his short fiction. Certainly to be remembered as close to the top of any list of memorable American stories are "A Rose for Emily," "That Evening Sun," "Barn Burning," and "Red Leaves," along with "The Bear" and "Was," which is the first story in *Go Down, Moses,* and "The Odor of Verbena," the last story in *The Unvanquished.* Faulkner's skill in recounting an incident or an anecdote is sometimes thought to be his most distinguishing feature. His novels are often remembered as much for separate scenes as for total impact. Some of them were begun as short stories and were then extended. Many of his stories became parts of his novels. Almost all of them are portions of a single story which is the legend of the erring people and the good land of Yoknapatawpha.

The Snopes Saga

8

For several years, probably since the mid-1920's, Faulkner had been putting together fragments of a comic history of Yoknapatawpha County. By the 1930's stories of sly trickery, like "Spotted Horses" and "Barn Burning," began to appear in magazines. In 1940 these and other stories were put together—rewritten when necessary and provided with connective material—to become *The Hamlet*, the first of three novels which recount the history of the rise and fall of Flem Snopes and the amazing history of other members of his amazing tribe. Perhaps no funnier or sadder or more tenderly compassionate books have been written by an American author than *The Hamlet; The Town*, which followed it in 1957; and *The Mansion*, which completed the trilogy two years later. They contain tall tales of a kind which Mark Twain had perfected years before, and their humor is edged with pathos, as if Faulkner were saying, "What wrongheaded and ridiculous but lovable fools all of us mortals are."

Several members of the Snopes family had been introduced in earlier novels. Flem Snopes had appeared in *Sartoris*, the first chronicle of Yoknapatawpha County, as a man who came as if from nowhere to become proprietor of a dingy, side-street restaurant and then, by mysterious means, the Vice-President of the Sartoris bank. And in that novel he brought other members of the Snopes clan with him. Byron Snopes, the bookkeeper who wrote obscene letters to Narcissa Benbow, finally fled from Jefferson with money pilfered from the bank. Montgomery Ward Snopes is remembered for having evaded the draft in World War I by keeping a plug of tobacco under his left armpit until his heart got to beating so fast that he was rejected as unfit. Flem Snopes had also been mentioned in *As I Lay Dying* as the man who brought unmanageable horses to Frenchman's Bend, and with whom Anse Bundren bargained for a team of mules. His father, Ab Snopes, had been prominent in *The Unvanquished* as the unscrupulous confederate of Miss Rosa Millard. A cousin, I. O. Snopes, was seen briefly as a cotton speculator in *The Sound and the Fury*. Senator Clarence Snopes and his young kinsman Virgil had a small but hilarious part in *Sanctuary*.

Now their stories are retold and expanded. The scene of *The Hamlet* is Frenchman's Bend, that crossroad settlement twenty miles southeast of Jefferson. There Uncle Billy Varner rules as a shirtsleeved autocrat: a farmer, moneylender, mill operator, and veterinarian. He owns the country store, the cotton gin, the gristmill, the blacksmith shop, and the outlying Old Frenchman Place for which the hamlet was named. He owns or holds mortgages on much of the best land in that area of the country. He has fathered a family of sixteen legitimate children and is said to have fathered an untold additional number throughout the county. At sixty he is still a mighty man, shrewd and courageous, but willing now to take his ease. He rules his rural empire humanely and well, without the expenditure now of too much energy. Details of his businesses and management of the store and cotton gin are left in the hands of his thirty-year-old bachelor son Jody, the ninth of his legitimate children and the only male among them to remain at Frenchman's Bend.

When Ab Snopes comes one day in 1902 to the settlement in search for a place where his family can settle, Jody allows him to rent one of the Varner farms. But then he learns from V. K. Ratliff, an itinerant sewing-machine salesman whose travels bring him information about almost everybody and everything in the county, that Ab Snopes has been known as a notorious barn-burner who, if crossed, might in angry retaliation burn barns again. As insurance against this happening to him, Jody takes on Ab's son Flem as a clerk in the Varner store. Flem is a sallow, broad-faced, hawk-nosed little man, insidiously quiet and efficiently industrious.

Soon Flem brings other Snopeses to the hamlet of Frenchman's Bend. Eck Snopes becomes the village blacksmith and marries into a local family. He fathers a son named Admiral Dewey Snopes, and then surprises his wife with an additional son, born of a previous marriage, whose name is Wallstreet Panic Snopes. Another relative, I. O. Snopes, becomes briefly the village schoolmaster. He is later found to be a bigamist, with sons by one marriage named Montgomery Ward Snopes and St. Elmo Snopes, and by another marriage a burly son named Clarence, who becomes a slippery petty politician, and twin sons named Bilbo and Vardaman after actual politicians in Mississippi. Other kin are Mink Snopes, who becomes a murderer, and Ike Snopes, an idiot, who is in some respects the most likable of them all.

Flem Snopes craftily advances. Within two years he has taken over the keeping of the Varner accounts and has wrested from Jody the management of the store. Within five years he has become the owner of cattle and property, and is known throughout the countryside as a moneylender and an unscrupulous wheeler-dealer in various increasingly prosperous enterprises. When Uncle Billy's daughter Eula becomes pregnant and the father of her expected child flees the county, Flem marries her in exchange for a deed to the Old Frenchman Place. He and his bride honeymoon in Texas for more than a year, and there Eula's child, Linda, is born. While Flem is away, his cousin Mink murders a neighbor and is sentenced to prison vowing vengeance on Flem, who, he thinks, might have and should have returned from Texas to defend him. When Flem and his bride and her daughter do return to Frenchman's Bend, there arrives at the same time a tall and taciturn Texan with a string of wild spotted horses which he attempts to sell to the Mississippi countrymen. Everyone is sure but no one can prove that Flem is really the owner of the horses.

That is the story-line of much of *The Hamlet*. As it is carried forward in *The Town* and then in *The Mansion*, it continues to follow the fortunes of Flem. But within and around this simple though ironic three-part tale of a poor boy's rise to wealth and respectability are woven other tales and other attitudes which provide the narrative with a complex texture. As in earlier novels, what happens is revealed through the words or the consciousness of several witnesses. Some incidents are recounted more than once and are differently interpreted by different people. Much that is told seems to have little direct reference to Flem Snopes, who is throughout a withdrawn and usually silent figure, ominously a presence but more often talked about than talking. The social structure through which he rises is examined, its irrevocable attitudes and comic ineptness. The truth of what happens is casually set forth through the testimony of observers who are not always well informed.

Much of what Flem and his relatives do is told by Ratliff, whose travels through Yoknapatawpha have made him an itinerant repository of news and gossip. As he goes from place to place, he manages almost always to be where the action is, or was, and he carries word of it to the next farm or hamlet which he visits. Ratliff is not, however, merely a traveling gossip. He is a creator and observer of local legend, an affable man who likes an audience and who does not hesitate to make a good story better. His imagination and his fondness for reasoning both tend to distort his tales. He is concerned not only with what happened, but with what might happen or what might have happened. He is sure, for example, that Flem Snopes makes love to Negro girls, because that is the kind of thing which country storekeepers naturally do. In reality, Flem is no more capable than Popeye in *Sanctuary* of making love to any girl.

When the lawyer Gavin Stevens later recounts what happens to Flem and his wife and her daughter, he too is often confused. He becomes personally involved because he himself is attracted to Flem's wife. As an intellectual, he is often more concerned about why something happens than with the happening itself. As he would do in *Requiem for a Nun*, he sometimes clouds issues through too much talking about them. Like Faulkner himself, of whom Stevens is sometimes thought to be an ironic self-portrait, he is fond of finding universal meanings in everyday activities. When Stevens' young nephew, Charles Mallison, reports on what happens, then things seem clearer, except that Charles, because he is a boy, is protected by older people from knowing sordid truths. He has to ferret them out for himself, little by little, as each reader must also.

The Hamlet is the simplest and most humorous of the Snopes trilogy. With *Sartoris* and *Sanctuary*, it merits a place just below Faulkner's greatest novels. It provides another version of themes which he had presented before, but reduced to homely terms, as they had been reduced in *As I Lay Dying*. Frenchman's Bend does not contain an aristocratic society, but it has its own traditional, familiar way of doing things. Its past impinges on its present. Though gallant ancestors are not remembered among its people as they are among the Sartorises and the Compsons and poor Gail Hightower, what their anonymous forebears had done does in a smaller degree control what the country men around Frenchman's Bend think it proper to do. There is conflict among them between what custom or religion teaches to be right and what their own human needs and human failings require. Because they are simple people, their passions and their fears are simply expressed. Without the veneer of sophistication as protection, what they do or think or feel seems often comically grotesque. The rise of Flem Snopes among them is amusing, but it is also disturbing to them. He upsets their values. He brings strange, new, and bewildering attitudes to the hamlet.

The first of the four sections into which *The Hamlet* is divided is rightly entitled "Flem." It tells of his coming to Frenchman's Bend, and what he saw there, and how he conquered. But Flem's tale is punctuated also with tales of other people. One is about a slick deal in horse trading in which Ab Snopes is victimized. Another allows Ab to prove that, though poor and put-upon, he is as good as any man: he tracks manure onto a rich man's carpet. When forced by the rich man to clean the carpet, Ab's womenfolk so ruin it that Ab is brought before the magistrate and ordered to give over to the rich man a share of his crops in payment. Angered, Ab burns the rich man's barn, for how else might a poor man defend himself? An eye for an eye, says his Bible. The rich man is Major de Spain, who hunted with Ike Mc-Caslin in *Go Down, Moses*. His son, Manfred, will later help even the score by taking Flem Snopes's wife as his mistress. But Flem will do him in also. He almost always lands the last blow.

There is probably no more disagreeable name in all literature than Flem Snopes. "Phlegm," however spelled, has repulsive connotations of snuffling and hawking and spitting. "Snopes" suggests all manner of unpleasant things, of which every reader can make his own listing: snoop, snout, snot, sneak, 's no hope. They are a primitive tribe, these Snopeses, often described as looking like animals. One has a rodent face, another resembles a weasel, still another has the amoral eyes of a squirrel. Mink Snopes reminds Ratliff of a hungry wildcat. Most of them are predatory packrats, hiding ridiculous small treasures. Flem is sometimes described as resembling a spider or a dog, more often a frog. He is hawk-nosed and weak-chinned. But his principal offense among the people of Frenchman's Bend or Jefferson is that he is an outsider. He is not what they are used to. He is an alien who changes things. He brings order to the Varner store. People must pay cash for what they buy. He brings efficiency to the gristmill and epigrammatic learning to the schoolhouse. What he does in moneylending or land-grabbing is no worse than what Uncle Bill did for years. The difference is that Flem is an intruder who upsets comfortable, familiar ways.

The second section of *The Hamlet* is called "Eula," and it reveals the wonderful attraction that Uncle Billy Varner's youngest daughter has for all men. She is not only luscious, but serenely indolent, sensuously exuding promise of passion. She is pictured as a goddess of old Dionysian times, a misplaced Helen of Troy whose beauty leads men to visions of ardent conquest. When she has hardly reached her teens, her schoolmaster destroys his career and thinks of destroying himself for love of her. Alone with her one afternoon in the schoolroom, he puts his arms around her, babbling of his desire. She knocks him down. "Stop pawing me," she is reported to have said. "You old headless horseman Ichabod Crane." As she grows older, she responds to boys, but she responds once too often and to a boy whose arm has been broken by other boys fighting him to possess her. The rural Venus gently supports his injured arm while he, a crippled Vulcan, gains a privilege for which most of the men of Frenchman's Bend yearn. Three months later Eula is discovered to be pregnant. Flem swaps himself as a reputation-saving husband for a deed from her father for the rundown mansion where years later Temple Drake in *Sanctuary* will meet Popeye, a man more evil than even a Snopes would ever be.

Flem is away from Frenchman's Bend during the third section of the novel, called "The Long Summer." He is with his bride in Texas, where her baby can be born without the women of Yoknapatawpha counting backward on their fingers to discover that it was born too soon. With Flem away, things get somewhat out of hand. His place in the Varner store is taken by his kinsman Launcelot Snopes, who, in spite of his name is in no way a chivalric man. He is commonly called Lump. Another kinsman, a small rodentlike creature called Mink, has only one cow but no proper pasture for her to winter on and not enough money to buy feed. He allows his animal to range on a neighbor's land with no expense to himself. When he is brought to court and made to pay the neighbor for her keep, Mink's pride is hurt. He vows revenge.

The neighbor is Jack Houston, a decent, quiet man, members of whose family played small parts in *Sartoris* and *As I Lay Dying*. At sixteen he ran away from home to escape from a country girl who plagued him with attention. After beating around through the Southeast, he settled as a railroad worker in Texas, living there for twelve years with a companionable woman he had found in a brothel. When his father died, Houston divided his savings with the woman and returned to Yoknapatawpha County to marry the girl from whom he had fled many years before. Six months after the wedding his wife was killed by a ferocious stallion. Since then, Houston has kept to himself, morose and resentful, abjuring women. The only female creature on his small farm is his cow.

Flem's cousin, Ike Snopes, is in love with Houston's cow. He follows her about through the pastureland by day and beds down with her at night in her stable. His is a pure love, and innocent, for Ike is an idiot. When he climbs the stairs in the house of the kindly countrywoman who has befriended him, he sits bellowing at the upper landing, terrified and desperate because he senses that his cow is in danger and because he, Ike, who can go up, has never learned how to go down stairs. He is happiest when pursuing his love across the meadows. When she comes to a stream and crosses it, Ike faithfully follows. But he never remembers from one time to the next that water is not solid and cannot be walked on. Consequently, each time he follows her across the stream, Ike misjudges his step and falls sprawling into the water. When Lump Snopes discovers his cousin's love affair, he leads other men from the hamlet to the cowshed for a prurient peek at the tenderly passionate wooing.

Ike as a lover is among the most admirable of the Snopeses. He is faithful to his love, not a bigamist like I. O. Snopes or twice married like Eck. Nor is he a bought-and-paid-for consort like Flem. To him love is natural and pure, and all-consuming. But other members of the Snopes clan in Frenchman's Bend think it unnatural for a young man to love a cow. Their family name is likely to be disgraced. After consultation among themselves and advice from the preacher Whitfield, they decide that the cow must be killed and their cousin forced to eat a piece of his loved one. Having thus partaken of her body whose blood has been shed for his salvation, Ike, it is reasoned, will thereafter "want to chase nothing but human women." But distraught and brokenhearted, Ike mourns the death of his sweetheart until his most kindly cousin, Eck, buys him a toy cow which the idiot-widower fondles happily, content with the replica as a reminder of love.

Meanwhile Mink Snopes avenges himself on Houston by killing him. He stuffs the body into a hollow tree, not bothering to empty the dead man's pockets of money which

Houston is said to carry with him. Mink will not stoop to robbery. But his cousin Lump, who snoops into almost everything, tries to blackmail Mink into telling him where the body is hidden so that he can rifle its pockets. Mink refuses to reveal its hiding place, but fearing that its increasing odor will lead someone to it, he drags the decaying body to a river where it can be washed away. At the riverbank he discovers that one arm is missing from the corpse, so he returns to the hollow tree to find it. There he is met by the sheriff, is arrested, and subsequently is brought to trial. In jail he refuses aid from family or neighbors, confident that his cousin Flem will return from Texas to help him. When after eight months Flem does not return and Mink is sentenced to the state prison, he again vows revenge.

In the fourth section of *The Hamlet,* "The Peasant," Flem comes back to Frenchman's Bend with his wife and her baby, which knowing country folk think quite too large for its age. Not long afterward the tall, taciturn Texan arrives with his string of wild horses. The mood of the novel now changes. It has been one of comedy edged with pathos, and with undertones of classic or religious myth. Now it becomes uproarious burlesque, but tinged with pathos still. The horses are as unmanageable and unpredictable as is the desire among the country people of Frenchman's Bend to own and tame them. Henry Armstid has come to the hamlet from his outlying farm to buy supplies with five dollars that his wife has earned by weaving. Instead, he is hornswoggled in a complicated deal for a horse which he breaks his leg trying to catch. Through slick perjury by Lump Snopes, Armstid's wife's five dollars ends up in Flem's pocket. Vernon Tull, who in *As I Lay Dying* befriended the Bundren family, is injured when run down by a horse which Eck

Snopes has purchased. Mrs. Tull brings suit for damages, which Eck is willing to pay, but the court rules that because Eck neglected to get a bill of sale for the horse, it cannot legally be proved to be his.

The wild horses quite disrupt the community of Frenchman's Bend. Breaking out of the barbed wire enclosure in which they are penned, they rampage through the back door, down the hallway, and out the front door of a neighbor countrywoman's house, creating havoc. They are to become a legend in Yoknapatawpha County. The half-tamed horse belonging to Jewel Bundren that was described in *As I Lay Dying* is one of them. Everyone is convinced that Flem is responsible for bringing the wild horses from Texas. He is a man of outrageous intrigue. He flimflams Odum Bookright, Henry Armstid, and V. K. Ratliff into buying the Old Frenchman Place by secreting a few easily discoverable coins on the premises and letting it be noised about that they are part of an immense buried treasure. Lump Snopes aids in this deception, as does a nephew, Eustace Grimm, whose last name again suggests that the unpleasant Percy Grimm who castrated Joe Christmas in *Light in August* was also one of the Snopes family. Poor Henry Armstid mortgages his farm to pay for his share of the purchase. Ratliff cannily swaps half-ownership of a small restaurant in Jefferson for his. So Flem loads his wife and her child, his trunks and boxes, onto the same mule-drawn wagon which brought them back from Texas and leaves Frenchman's Bend. The hamlet is, perhaps not better, but certainly different because of his having been there. Its store of legend is measurably increased, for Flem is not to be soon forgotten.

In *The Town* he continues to prosper. Manfred de Spain, Jefferson's Mayor, is lured by the lush and inviting body of

Flem's wife. He takes her as his mistress, winning out over Gavin Stevens, who as a less lustful and more temperate man admires her from safer distance. In another swap, in exchange for knowing nothing of his wife's affair with the Mayor, Flem is appointed superintendent of the town power plant. In that position his acquisitive compulsion gets him for the first time into trouble. In connivance with two Negro workmen whom he pits one against the other, he steals all the brass fittings from the power plant and hides them in the town water tower. When suit is brought against him, his wife visits Gavin Stevens and offers to give herself to him if he as city attorney will call off the proceedings. As a gentleman, Stevens refuses, but Flem extricates himself anyway, though the stolen brass fittings remain in the water tower where he cannot get at them.

When Colonel Sartoris dies and Manfred de Spain succeeds him as President of the bank, Flem becomes his Vice-President. Meanwhile a swarm of almost every variety of Snopeses has followed him to Jefferson. Byron, who will become an absconder, works in the bank. Eck takes over Flem's restaurant but is so honest that he is discharged. He becomes a night watchman at an oil tank, which through his well-intentioned carelessness blows up, and he with it. I. O. Snopes succeeds Eck in the restaurant but has to leave town when discovered to be defrauding the railroad by placing mules in the paths of locomotives and then suing for their death. Montgomery Ward Snopes is arrested for running a pornographic peep show. Wall Street Panic Snopes, aided by a good wife who does not like his family, prospers as a grocer by not having anything to do with his kinfolks. Irascible Ab Snopes lives retired a mile outside of town, plagued by boys who invade his watermelon patch.

Conniving again, this time with his wife's daughter as a

pawn, Flem forces Manfred de Spain out of the bank and himself assumes the presidency. The daughter, Linda, has become a not unpleasing, affectionate girl, with much of her mother's charm but without her fatal attraction to all men. For several years she is befriended by Gavin Stevens, who in the role of a kindly uncle guides her education. Flem attempts to win her confidence, mainly because he is eager to gain control of the bank shares she will inherit from her grandfather Varner. He refuses to let her go away to college lest he lose what hold he does have on her. Eula asks Gavin Stevens to marry her daughter in order to take her out from under Flem's influence. But Stevens, so much older than the girl, in decency cannot do that. Flem continues to prosper. Eula commits suicide. Manfred de Spain leaves Jefferson in disgrace. And Linda, having signed over her inheritance to Flem, leaves also.

The Town is crowded with familiar characters, either present or remembered—Sartorises, Compsons, and Mc-Callums. Old Doc Peabody appears, Ike McCaslin owns a hardware store in Jefferson, and one of Ike's black Beauchamp cousins gets into trouble by joining Flem in the theft of brass from the power plant. Most of the narrative is taken over by the peripatetic Ratliff, by the forthright though often bewildered young Charles Mallison, or by his devious but well-intentioned Uncle Gavin, who as the chronicle draws toward a close attempts to untangle its complexities. As in *The Hamlet*, short stories previously published were incorporated into the novel. Flem's pilfering from the power house had appeared as "Centaur in Brass" in the *American Mercury* in 1932, fifteen years before. I. O. Snopes's plot against the railroad had been told in "Mule in the Yard" in *Scribner's* in 1934.

As the last novel of the trilogy, *The Mansion* circles back

to begin where the first novel, *The Hamlet*, had ended—
with the trial in 1908 of Mink Snopes for the murder of
Jack Houston. The vengeful little man's defiant crime was
briefly remembered in *The Town*. Now it and its motives
are reviewed in greater detail as Mink shares with Flem the
narrative spotlight. A fatalist with a stubborn sense of justice, Mink has been perfectly willing to work out the sum
which Houston levied for the pasturage of his cow. He has
patiently paid it by working for his neighbor at fifty cents
a day for thirty-seven and a half days. Only when Houston
threatens to make him pay one dollar more as a pound
fee does Mink take what he thinks to be justifiable revenge
by killing his persecutor.

Fifteen years later, when Mink's sentence to the penitentiary at Parchman is to be reduced for good behavior, Flem
Snopes in self-protection arranges to have his vengeful kinsman kept longer in prison. He threatens Montgomery Ward
Snopes with guilefully devised evidence of having sent por-
nography through the United States mail. If the culprit will
confess to the less horrendous crime of bootlegging, he will
be sent, and for a shorter term, to the state penitentiary
where Mink is, instead of to the Federal prison in Atlanta.
As return for this kindness, Montgomery Ward is instructed
by Flem to involve Mink in a plan for escape and then to
inform the guards of the plan so that Mink will be caught
and his sentence extended. Everything works out as Flem
plans. Mink must remain at Parchman for another twenty
years. But Flem has outreached himself. Prison had mel-
lowed Mink to the point that he had almost forgotten his
vow of vengeance against his cousin. Now his rage smoul-
ders again, nursed by resentment to unyielding resolution.
After an imprisonment of thirty-eight years, Mink is finally

released. He has served one year, and a little more, for each day he worked to pay off the charge for pasturage imposed by Houston. Almost penniless but single-minded, he sets out for Jefferson.

Meanwhile, in the second section of *The Mansion*, Linda Snopes returns to her father. She had been married in New York to an idealistic Jewish sculptor named Barton Kohl. She had accompanied her husband to Europe, where he served as a flier and she as an ambulance driver in the Spanish Civil War. Kohl was killed when his plane was shot down, and she was deafened when her ambulance was blown up. Isolated by her deafness, world-wearied, and discouraged, she looks now to kindly Gavin Stevens for what comfort he can provide. Jefferson looks on her with suspicion. She had married a stranger who was a Jew and an artist— perhaps even a poet, thinks young Charles Mallison. Her husband might have been a Communist as well, and the name Kohl hardly seems to be an American name at all, much less a name to be found anywhere in Yoknapatawpha. Unlike her mother, Linda had been happily married, and she encourages Charles Mallison's uncle to marry also, so that he too may know the bond which can exist between a man and a woman. Gavin Stevens succumbs, though not without resistance, and marries, as Faulkner had, a woman with two children who had been his childhood sweetheart.

Flem Snopes resides now in magnificent splendor in the mansion which for generations had belonged to the de Spain family, and in which Manfred de Spain had lived when he was the lover of Flem's wife. There he holds forth in a spartan and troubled existence. He neither smokes nor drinks. He does not even chew tobacco, though his jaws move with an incessant nervous motion. The mansion has been remodeled as a replica of George Washington's pillared plantation house at Mount Vernon. Flem is alone and lonely. His only companion is his wife's daughter, who cannot hear him when he speaks. Though still menacing and conniving, he has become a pathetic man, among the most powerful but not most respected people in Jefferson. It is suggested now that Eula Varner would not really have had to marry him to preserve her good name because the boy who had seduced her (or whom she had seduced) had in fact been willing, perhaps even eager, to marry into her prosperous family. But Flem had seen his chance and taken it, and had parlayed his wife's lusciousness to winnings which continue even after her death to increase.

The second section of *The Mansion* is narrated in the first two chapters by V. K. Ratliff, who is shamed when unmasked as a foreigner—as a Russian, in fact, whose familiar initials stand for Vladimir Krilyvitch. The next two chapters and the last are told by Charles Mallison, who attempts to piece adult mysteries together. Gavin Stevens makes known his complicated role as a kind of surrogate father to Linda in the climactic next-to-last chapter. Each gives his own account of what happens or what has happened in the past or what he supposes to have happened. No one of them can be guaranteed completely reliable.

In the third and final section, Faulkner, as he did in the first section, tells the story, though often through the words or consciousness of one or another of the witnesses. He seems to relish the spinning of new yarns involving the people about whom he has been writing now for thirty years. Linda's ardent but futile attempts to improve the conditions of Negroes in Jefferson allow him to comment on new attitudes toward racial relations, which by 1959, when *The*

Mansion appeared, were increasingly in the public mind. He returns again to the story of the Compson family, adding details to what had been told in *The Sound and the Fury*. Now it is revealed that after Benjy was committed to the asylum by Jason Compson, his mother whined and wept until Jason brought his idiot brother home again—and two years afterward Benjy burned himself up, and the old Compson house also. Jason now lives meanly alone in an efficient, neat bungalow near the center of town. He is as devious as ever, but he has prospered as the owner of Ike McCaslin's former hardware store. When the golf course which had been the meadow where the Compson children once played is offered for sale because the golf club wants to move farther from Jefferson, Jason buys it back because he thinks he has secret information that the government wants the land for an airfield. His information, however, proves to be unfounded, so he cannily unloads the property on old Flem Snopes. Learning that the banker plans to make a lot of money by breaking it up into small lots for inexpensive housing, he tries desperately then to buy it back. But Jason Compson is no match for Flem.

Faulkner now tells more of the history of the adventures or misadventures of other members of the Snopes family. Four wild, half-Indian children of the absconding Byron Snopes descend on Jefferson and almost succeed in burning at the stake the bestial younger brother of Senator Clarence Snopes who played practical jokes on them. The career of the Senator himself is reviewed in more detail than it had been in *Sanctuary*, or in *The Town*, where it had been he, not his brother, who escaped being burned at the stake—indicating a lapse of memory on Faulkner's part which was corrected in the paperback edition of that novel so that the same man, the brother, was almost burned in both accounts.

Clarence Snopes was a burly rural ruffian from French-man's Bend until Uncle Billy Varner used his influence to have him made a constable. But he was such an embarrass-ing bully as an officer of the law that Uncle Billy had him elected to the State Senate, where he could do less harm. Now, as C. Eggleston Snopes, he aspires to higher office. As candidate for Congress he is opposed by a liberal, one-legged veteran of World War II, and goes down to blustering but humiliating defeat, the laughingstock of the county. Ratliff thinks that it may have been Uncle Billy Varner, or perhaps even the liberal opposing candidate, who encouraged two boys to rub against the Senator's trouser legs damp switches cut from a thicket where dogs were accustomed to relieve themselves. As he stood before a country crowd campaign-ing, dog after dog was attracted to him by the familiar odor and its reminder of what dogs in response to it must do. Who would vote for a man that dogs "can't tell from a fence post"?

And a new Snopes is introduced, named Orestes. A dealer in hogs who lives in the old carriage house which once be-longed to the Compson family, he feuds with a neighbor who peppers his hogs with buckshot when they wander onto his property. The neighbor is an obdurate man who will not join in selling their adjoining lands to an oil company. A strip of thirteen feet lying between them belongs legally to Flem Snopes but morally, the neighbor thinks, to him. Ores-tes slyly arranges an elaborate booby trap, so constructed that a person opening a certain window will receive a charge of buckshot. He also encourages his hogs to trespass on the neighboring property, hoping that the neighbor will shoot at them with real bullets and be liable for arrest. Orestes also involves in his plotting the suitor of the neighbor's pretty daughter, half hoping that the neighbor will shoot the young man and be jailed. Only the intervention of Gavin Stevens prevents the fiasco from getting completely out of hand. But the lawyer's solution, though more legal, is quite as complicated as Orestes' had been.

Of all the Snopeses, Mink is the most consistent and persistent. Gavin Stevens, again trying to ward off trouble, leaves money at the prison which is to be given to Mink on his release if Mink will promise to leave the state and never return. But Mink refuses to be bribed out of his rightful revenge. He catches a ride on a truck to Memphis, where in a pawnshop he spends what little money he has for an old pistol and two bullets. On the sixth day after his release from Parchman, he arrives in Jefferson. Entering the mansion, he confronts his cousin. Flem's jaws stop their chewing as if in midmotion as Mink's pistol misfires once. But on the second shot, Flem crashes to the floor.

Sympathy among the townspeople is with the murderer, who ends the reign in Jefferson of the most successful Snopes of all. Ratliff and Gavin Stevens find Mink, not hiding, only stoically waiting, among the ruins of the old cabin in which he had lived when he killed Jack Houston. They bring money to him from Linda, and they offer to send him more if he will let them know how to reach him. His vengeance satisfied, Mink is a new man. They can find him, he says, by looking somewhere across the Mississippi for M. C. Snopes. He will no longer be called Mink.

The Snopes trilogy is an anthology of country yarns and local legends, told as a country man would tell them, in good blunt country language. They are private stories not easily understood by strangers. But neither Faulkner nor his readers were by this time strangers in Yoknapatawpha County. Both he and they found pleasure in being reminded of the often foolish but always human escapades of old friends.

The three novels are held together by the astonishing career of Flem Snopes and by the stubborn persistence of his nemesis, Mink. Only another Snopes can finally do Flem in. People of the older county families have no weapons to overcome the invader whose tooth-and-nail methods are so much like those which their ancestors used to conquer and settle Yoknapatawpha. Their past is crusted with other legends, of gallantry or pride or crippling self-esteem. Flem has no past of which to be proud. Perhaps he is the man of the future. Though, like Ike McCaslin, Flem leaves no descendants, his tribe also may be thought to increase.

The
Last Novels
9

Intruder in the Dust, published in 1948 (before either *The Town* or *The Mansion*), combines several of Faulkner's familiar devices. It is a detective story in which sixteen-year-old Chick (Charles) Mallison and his longtime Negro playmate are helped by a perky old lady of nearly eighty in discovering the truth about a murder. Much of the action is heightened by macabre melodrama. Graveyards are visited at night, a body is discovered in a quicksand bog, and a vengeful mob intent on lynching the wrong man gathers menacingly in front of the Jefferson jail. The relationship to society of a black man who is partly white is again examined. The eccentric self-sufficiency of the country people of Yoknapatawpha is again revealed. Chick's talkative uncle, Gavin Stevens, again suggests a temperate and imperfect solution to a complicated problem. And once more a white boy is guided toward maturity by a tutor who is not completely white.

Because Faulkner now seemed clearly to speak of a social problem, *Intruder in the Dust* found a larger audience than many of his previous novels. Questions concerning the place and rights of Negroes were increasingly touching the conscience of the American people. The segregation and exploitation of blacks seemed to many a shameful stain on the national honor. Faulkner's was a voice from the South, where Negroes were thought to have been more discriminated against but, according to Southern tradition, better understood than in most areas of the country. That he should present himself now as their champion seemed a good sign indeed. When a year later the novel was made into a motion picture, much of the action was filmed in Mississippi, and many of Faulkner's neighbors were employed as background characters. Members of the Oxford black community provided housing for Negro actors imported from the North.

But *Intruder in the Dust* is finally more effective as propaganda than as art. The most regional of Faulkner's novels, it examines attitudes which are universal as if they were uniquely Southern. Faulkner seems to plead too hard for an understanding of the complex inherited views of the intelligent white Southerner without reminding the reader, or even seeming to remember himself, that such views are also part of the psychological and social inheritance of almost all people, anywhere. The story which he now tells is slight, the characters are more effective as representatives of ideas than as portraits subtly revealed in depth, but the message is clear. Faulkner seems increasingly concerned with being understood.

When he is twelve years old, Chick Mallison goes hunting in the woods with his Negro companion, whose name, Aleck Sander, is quaint but racially condescending, and only a little funny. When the boys fall into an ice-covered stream, they are befriended by Lucas Beauchamp, a Negro man, who takes them to his cabin, where they dry their clothes. Lucas is the grandson of Lucius Quintus Carothers McCaslin. He had appeared in *Go Down, Moses* as proudly independent, a maker of illegal whiskey, and a compulsive seeker after buried treasure. Now, in *Intruder in the Dust*, he is a proud man still. He walks with head held high through the streets of Jefferson, and he confuses and angers white citizens of Yoknapatawpha by refusing to act subserviently, as a Negro should. His attitude also confuses young Chick Mallison. The boy's inherited notions about black and white relationships are disturbed because Lucas treats him, not as if Lucas were a Negro, servile and obsequious, but just as any kindly but stern older person might.

The boy's upbringing has taught him that Negroes who do nice things for white people should be rewarded, so he offers Lucas what small money he has in his pocket. When Lucas coldly refuses it, Chick throws the money on the floor. Then he is more confused, and a little shamed, when Lucas commands Aleck Sander to pick up the coins and return them to Chick. Lucas is not acting as Chick had been taught to expect a Negro to act. He has violated the established code of relationships between the black race and the white. Even as a boy of twelve, Chick recognizes that Lucas acts generously, as any person of any color should act toward any other person. But he is only twelve, and he resents being put under obligation to a Negro.

Dried and fed, he leaves Lucas' cabin, and as a gesture of

his whiteness and his confusion, throws the money into a stream. Sometime later he attempts to repay Lucas by sending him a Christmas gift of snuff and cigars, and after that by a present to the Negro's wife. But Lucas responds by sending Chick a jug of molasses, so that the boy is still in his debt, and that worries him. When one day in Jefferson Chick sees Lucas on the street, the Negro passes him without a sign of recognition. Chick becomes obsessed with his confusion between what he instinctively knows to be one person's proper relation to another and what he has been taught that a black man's place should be in his relation with white men, even white boys.

Four years later Lucas is accused of having murdered a white man, and the people of Jefferson react as tradition has always required that white men react in such a situation. The black culprit must be taken from the jail and lynched. The family of the white victim will lose face if the crime is not avenged. That is part of an inherited ritual.

Chick, now sixteen, and confused still between his recognition of Lucas as a man and Lucas as a Negro, thinks of fleeing his responsibility toward resolution of the conflict by leaving town and staying away while the mob or the dead man's family does its work in the manner which the code demands. But when Gavin Stevens, though convinced of the Negro's guilt, agrees to defend Lucas, Chick accompanies his uncle to the jail and, responding to what he thinks to be a mute but urgent request in the prisoner's eye, returns later with a package of tobacco for him. Lucas then explains to him that an examination of the dead man's body will prove that it was not Lucas' pistol which killed him. Chick relays the information to his uncle, but the lawyer's mind is so closed to anything but certainty of his client's guilt that he will not listen. The boy, partly because he is young and has a more open mind and partly to clear himself of a nagging obligation to a black man, decides to do something about it.

He and Aleck Sander and a spunky spinster named Miss Eunice Habersham ride off at night to the country grave-yard where the murdered man is buried. On digging up his grave, they find, not the murdered man's, but another man's, body. The mystery deepens, but the boys are resolute. Aided by the sheriff, some reasonable deductions, and the further exhuming of dead bodies, they discover the murderer, who proves to be none other than the dead man's brother. Further deduction, plus some confession from the guilty man, reveals how Lucas has been purposely framed, and why. Lucas had learned that the murderer was stealing lumber from a mill which he operated with his brother. Realizing that Lucas knew of his double-dealing and suspecting that his brother knew also, he shot his brother and left behind evidence incriminating to the Negro. The evidence was not very substantial, but was enough, he seems to have thought, to keep Lucas in jail long enough for a lynch mob to do its work.

As a result of the detective work of Miss Eunice and her boy assistants, Lucas is freed. The murderer is jailed, his crime of fratricide so horrendous that the townspeople ostracize him. He seems to them not even worth lynching, and he shoots himself in his cell. Lucas returns to what he has always been, a proudly dignified Negro who refuses to grovel or accept favors from any man. Chick, his bothersome debt paid, knows that the guilt which had made that debt seem a burden cannot be assuaged. Though he looks with horror on the mob which clings blindly to an inherited code,

Chick recognizes that he inevitably shares with his townspeople the prejudice which sees the Negro, not as a man,
but as a kind of black Sambo, filled with obsequious good
humor, who must be subservient and know his place. Gavin
Stevens explains to him that all men are thus slaves to history, that prejudices of the past are not easily erased, but
that with the emergence of young people like Chick, who
are openminded and troubled with guilt, compassion and
justice may finally prevail.

But the story of the detection of evil through night-
shrouded escapades which makes up the parable of *Intruder
in the Dust* is too slight to bear the weight of rhetoric with
which Faulkner burdens it. Gavin Stevens backs and fills in
wordy circumlocutions as he attempts to explain to himself, to Chick, and to the reader the troubled, tangled prob-
ings of an older man who confronts a confused world not
of his own making but in which he must live as usefully and
as successfully as he can. While his uncle temporizes, Chick
pushes ahead, suggesting in his action and in his opposition
to inherited attitudes the biblical promise that a child shall
lead. *Intruder in the Dust* may seem to say that society will
be better when the young white and the young black work
together as Chick and his Negro companion do, especially
when they are aided by the benevolent and resolute strength
and wisdom of women like Miss Eunice. But however true
that may be, it is too simple a solution, now too simply un-
derlined. Chick finally knows that he is part of his community and shares with everyone in it a burden of inherited
guilt and shame. What angers him is his own failure, which
is the failure of his race.

What Faulkner seems to want to say about sacrifice and
compassion and justice is summed up in *A Fable*, which in

1954 again speaks of the conflict between man's wish for doing what is right and his inevitable, lovable, and often comic capacity for doing what is wrong. Patiently philosophical and crammed with Christian symbolism (even to the crosses embossed upon its cover), A *Fable* tells of an upsurge of the human spirit which momentarily ends man's greatest absurdity—war.

On a Monday morning in the spring of 1918 a lowly Corporal aided by twelve disciples persuades a regiment of French soldiers to lay down their arms. Enlisted men in the enemy trenches opposite them respond in kind, and the war is brought temporarily to a close. Only a high-level conference between German and Allied commanders gets it started again. On Friday evening of that week the Corporal is executed, flanked by two thieves. As he falls, a crown of thorns, which is barbed wire, circles his head. He is buried by women members of his family. His disciples are dispersed. Three days later his grave is struck by an enemy mortar. When the rubble is removed, his shattered coffin is found, but his body has disappeared. Sometime later it finds its way to the coffin of the Unknown Soldier which is placed beneath the Arc de Triomphe in Paris, guarded by a continuously burning flame.

These and other biblical echoes crowd A *Fable*. Faulkner ingeniously puts together a complex allegory of the possibilities and the fate of the human spirit when released from bondage. But the Corporal is not presented as a divine redeemer. He is a human and a fallible man. What he does is not made to seem miraculous, but as within the power of all men. At the same time, however, his spirit is immortal, for this is part of the heritage of mankind. What he achieves through compassion and the acknowledgment of all men as his brothers might be universally achieved, if it were not that man is also predatory and rapacious and convinced that he and people like him are somehow set apart and favored by a god who smiles upon their conquests.

These two forces meet—of what man might do and of what man, being man, must do if he is to survive amidst the jungle of past and present, dream and desire, in which he finds himself. A *Fable* points to no easy road to salvation. Reconciliation remains only a promise. If Faulkner weights the scale slightly toward hope that the measure of love will finally prove itself greater, he does not allow the reader to forget that opposing manifestations of the human spirit are also great. One thing he did know, he said in Stockholm when he received the Nobel Prize for literature, during the period that he was writing A *Fable*—and that was that man's spirit will endure. Not only deathless good but deathless folly will prevail. Man is trapped in his own humanity. As one of the Corporal's followers declares in the final scene of the novel, "I'm not going to die. Never."

A *Fable* may be a greater novel than it has sometimes seemed to be. Though difficult, it repays serious attention. Even more clearly than *The Sound and the Fury*, it is an allegory of the Passion Week of Christ which finds parallels in what Faulkner had called the Passion Week of the human heart. Like Herman Melville's *Billy Budd*, Franz Kafka's *The Castle*, and Ernest Hemingway's *The Old Man and the Sea*, its symbolism becomes obvious. But A *Fable* is greatly more complicated in structure than any of these, with multiple levels of meaning. Almost every character has its opposite. Many characters will seem to suggest more than one symbolic representation. The Marshal of the Allied forces, for example, at one time may be thought to suggest simple authority, at another time Satan tempting Christ on the mountaintop, at another the Old Testament Jehovah powerless before the New Testament doctrine of love, and at still another symbolically, if not actually, the father of the condemned Corporal, much as Captain Vere is sometimes thought symbolically, if not actually, to be the father of Billy Budd.

Faulkner's narrative method may at first confuse. Much which is spoken of early in the novel seems mysterious. The action begins *in medias res*, on Wednesday, the third day following the mutiny. It is the middle of the week, and the middle of the action. Much has taken place of which the reader is not yet informed. The scene is opened dramatically in the French town of Chaulnesmont, at some distance from the front line. The atmosphere is of pomp and pageantry. Bugles blare and sabers clash. Cavalrymen are splendid, trained to efficiency. They are reminiscent of Napoleon's brave troops. An excited assemblage of people crowds the street, waiting for something.

So alive with bustling expectation is the scene that the reader is swept along in mystified anticipation. He soon discovers that he is witness not to an exhibition of gallant soldiery, but to a police action. The cavalrymen are forcefully clearing the road so that a caravan of trucks may pass. The first truck contains standing men, packed like cattle, and battle-stained, unshaven, defiant, who are being rushed from the battle line. The last truck contains only thirteen men, battle-stained also, but chained together. One of them is a Corporal, evidently their leader. As he and his companions pass, the voice of the crowd swells, and hands are clenched. The manacled Corporal gazes calmly at the people, and his eyes lock for an inscrutable moment with those of the commanding General who stands amid the security of his military aides.

Only later, when the action turns back to Monday, is the

reason for this pageantry and confusion revealed. At noon on that day the French General, Charles Gragnon, orders a regiment of his division to attack. The officers and a few noncommissioned officers obey his command, but most of the soldiers do not. The General, disgraced, asks his superiors to have the whole regiment, including himself, placed under arrest and executed. But, after conferences among themselves during the ensuing days, these superiors decide that such a mass execution would only serve to call attention to the mutiny. A few men, more discretely shot, would be sufficient. As the narrative progresses, it moves backward and forward in time, revealing more of the activities of the leaders of the mutiny and more of the confused determination of the highest officers to get the war started again. Other people are introduced, who are also influenced or affected by the succession of events which the Corporal's mutinous armistice sets in motion.

Among them is David Levine, an eighteen-year-old British pilot, who on his first combat mission is called back because of the temporary cease-fire on the French front. Like Faulkner himself, who had not had an opportunity to fly in combat before the war ended, and like the young aviation cadet in Faulkner's first novel, *Soldier's Pay*, he is disappointed. Two days later he is sent on a patrol over enemy lines and discovers that the bullets which he shoots at German planes and the shells which the German artillery directs toward him are blanks, substituted for live ammunition to insure the safety of members of the Allied and German high commands who are flying to emergency meetings to decide what they can do to get their men back to fighting each other. Disillusioned, the young pilot commits suicide.

Another character is a former British officer who had resigned his commission in order to become a common soldier. As a runner charged with delivering messages from one military group to another, he acts as a catalyst who binds strands of the story together. Apparently an educated man, he is among the more intelligent of the Corporal's followers. Though others are killed, he survives, to become a kind of St. Paul who will carry on the message of love and brotherhood. He would turn the temporary cease-fire into a permanent peace. It is he who on the last page of the novel, though cruelly wounded, promises: "I'm not going to die. Never."

Associated with the Runner is the Sentry, who is a cockney groom called Mr. Harry or Mistairy. Much of A *Fable* revolves about his adventures, some parts of which had been published in 1950 as, Faulkner then said, "a dangling participle to a work in progress," in a small volume of limited distribution called *Notes on a Horsethief*. Mr. Harry's story begins in 1912 when he is a handler, first in Argentina and then in the United States, of a racehorse so spirited that only he can control him. When Mr. Harry is moving the horse by van from New Orleans to Kentucky, a flood-washed bridge in Mississippi gives way, and van, horse, Harry, and a Negro hostler are all plunged into the water. The horse is lamed, but rather than return him to his owner, who would put him out to stud, Mr. Harry steals the horse and races him profitably through the South. Even running on three legs, he beats the best who are pitted against him. When the police finally catch up with Harry, he shoots the horse rather than lose him. Deserting his Negro companion, he escapes, returns to England, and on the outbreak of war in 1914 joins the British army.

As a soldier, Mr. Harry is coarse and profane. He is despised at first by the former officer who is now the Runner.

As Flem Snopes had done among the countrymen of Frenchman's Bend in *The Hamlet*, he carries on a profitable business among his fellow soldiers by lending money at
exorbitant rates of interest. He carries on what he calls an
insurance business by betting with them that they will not
be killed in battle. If they live, he keeps the insurance money;
if they die, he keeps it also because there is no one to whom
to return it. When the mutiny takes place, Mr. Harry is
among the British troops in France which are invited to
join it.

Meanwhile, his former Negro companion arrives in Paris
as a lay preacher known as the Rev. Tobe Sutherfield, who is
active in soliciting funds for an organization which will
bring peace to the world through faith rather than force of
arms. He is something of an entrepreneur. Much of the
money which allows him to carry on his reforming enterprise
comes from wealthy old ladies in the United States. Tobe
joins his old friend Harry at the front. Together they join
the Runner in a plan to carry on the work which the Corporal had begun, thereby insuring that the cease-fire will
become a permanent peace. They walk with other unarmed
men across No-Man's Land to meet enemy soldiers, also unarmed, who come to them as brothers. But they are forced
back by a barrage of shellfire directed at them from both
sides. The Negro and Mr. Harry die together. The Runner,
badly wounded, lives on.

Much is made during these episodes of the Masonic
order and its doctrine of love and brotherhood among
men. Mr. Harry had initiated Tobe into the order when
they had been together in the United States. He had escaped from the police in Mississippi because of assistance
from brother Masons. In France he makes everyone in his

company a member. For all of his devious skulduggery, he is a uniter of men. But much is made also of humorous aspects of the former horsethief's experience. Though he is a slick and conscienceless operator, beneath his hardened surface is a capacity for loving, not only a magnificent race-horse but other men as well, for whom he is willing to sacrifice himself. He is the sinner reformed. He is the potential of the Christ in every man. He finally recognizes that the Negro Tobe is in truth his brother, and they die together, joined in the fellowship of death. Of all the characters in A Fable, Mr. Harry, or Mistairy, is the most complex and most successfully realized. He is comic and brave, conniving and dumbly questing, all at the same time, like the complicated simple people of Yoknapatawpha about whom Faulkner wrote most revealingly.

The Corporal's plan for peace fails. The Generals do get the war started again. The Corporal falls before a firing squad, but not before he has had a confrontation face to face with the Marshal who is the Commander in Chief of all the Allied forces. Not only is the old General a symbol of authority; he is also more clearly revealed as the father of the man he must condemn. There is a moment of understanding between the two. Each does what he must do, though one looks toward the past, the other toward the future. Not long after the Corporal's death the Marshal dies also, to be buried with high military honors. But no eternal flame burns over his tomb, nor does his body lie under an Arch of Triumph to symbolize the sacrifice made by a common man for all men.

General Gragnon, commander of the division of which the Corporal's regiment was a part, is also executed. Three American soldiers are given very explicit orders about how he is to be killed. One of them is a Negro named Philip Manigault Beauchamp, who, though not identified as to place of origin, may be thought to be from Yoknapatawpha County—a relative perhaps of Lucas Beauchamp of *Intruder in the Dust* and of Nancy Mannigoe of *Requiem for a Nun*. Because his superiors wish to play down the importance of the mutiny, they order that General Gragnon be shot from the front and by a German weapon, so that it will seem that he died gallantly leading his men to battle and not as a commander disgraced through failure to control his troops. But General Gragnon feels his shame so strongly that he insists on a traitor's death. Just as the fatal shot is fired, he quickly turns so that it enters the back of his head. His executioners then are forced to fill that bullet hole with wax and to shoot him again from the front as they had been ordered. Even death is accompanied by grisly humor.

Everything fits in *A Fable*. Everything that happens is related to everything else that happens, each in its proper place but each a part of a larger plan. Meanings are suggested which are multiple, at one time suggesting the plight of man in a universe over which he has no control, at another time with immense ingenuity paralleling the inspiring story of Passion Week. Almost every principal character is an isolated man, alienated in some sense from his fellows. Many of them are orphans, symbolically or in fact. Some, like the Corporal, are illegitimate and search for a father who can provide them with knowledge of who they really are. At the same time, they are all tangled together in the complicated web of their shared humanity. It is a fable of men, benighted and alone, who seek communion and its promise of salvation. Women stand in background shadows as weeping and sometimes erring ministrants to the travail of men.

Perhaps *A Fable* is too carefully structured, too intricately devised. Its characters may seem too often only to stand for something. Attention is too often averted from the recognition of them as people of flesh and blood and ordinary appetites by temptations to find them overwhelming representatives of abstractions of virtue or vice. What Faulkner attempts to say becomes so abundantly clear so early in the narrative that the unraveling of every strand of interrelated meaning may seem finally only an exercise in ingenuity. If *Intruder in the Dust* is his most regional novel, *A Fable* is his most overtly universal. In it he takes great pains to make it clear that those things which he has been writing about from the beginning are not of the South only, or even of the United States only, but are shared by all mankind. The sin and the guilt and the possibility for redemption belong to men everywhere.

After *A Fable* Faulkner completed the Snopes trilogy with *The Town* in 1957 and *The Mansion* in 1959. Then, in 1962, the year of his death, his last novel, *The Reivers*, again caught up old themes and familiar devices. Aptly subtitled "A Reminiscence," it recounts a story which a grandfather tells to his grandson about what had happened to him many years before, when his own grandfather helped him learn that as a gentleman born he must accept responsibility for whatever he did. Boyhood adventures are affectionately recalled. What had happened to the Sartorises and the Sutpens is briefly told again, picking up and expanding incidents from *Sartoris* and *Absalom, Absalom!* Ike McCaslin, whose own initiation had been detailed in

Go Down, Moses, appears again, an old man now, living quietly in Jefferson. Miss Reba's establishment in Memphis, which had played so prominent a part in *Sanctuary,* is again visited. Boon Hogganbeck, who is partly Chickasaw Indian and who in "The Bear" had finally knifed Old Ben to death, is the boy's admired older companion.

Lucius Priest is the narrating grandfather who tells what had happened many years before, when he was eleven years old. He is a descendant of old Lucius Quintus Carothers McCaslin. His father's mother was a sister of Cass Edmonds, with whom Ike McCaslin had lived as a boy. Uncle Buck and Uncle Buddy, who worried about their father's black descendants who were slaves, were Lucius' great-granduncles. The Priest family's Negro coachman is also descended from the first Lucius, the progenitor of the McCaslin family in Yoknapatawpha County. Though his precise relationship is not revealed, Ned McCaslin, though only a coachman, vauntingly requires awareness that he is by right of blood a member of the family.

The boyhood adventures of Lucius Priest, like those of Huckleberry Finn or of Bayard Sartoris in *The Unvanquished,* are often comic, complicated by conscience, and sometimes slapstick. Lucius' grandfather, also named Lucius but known affectionately as "Boss," is head of the oldest bank in Jefferson. When Colonel Sartoris, President of the second oldest bank, pushes through an ordinance forbidding automobiles to run on the town streets, Boss Priest buys one to challenge his upstart rival, though he agrees with the Colonel that automobiles are an abomination. He intends simply to keep his in his carriage house as a quiet gesture of defiance.

But Boon Hogganbeck, who works in the livery stable owned by Boss's son, the boy Lucius' father, convinces Boss that machines deteriorate when not used. Boon therefore becomes a kind of groom-chauffeur, charged with exercising the automobile, though only on Priest-owned property—an injunction which he finds difficult to observe. Ned McCaslin is naturally jealous of Boon's usurpation of what he considers his right as family coachman. He tries to drive also, with disastrous results. The first high point in young Lucius' boyhood adventures comes when Boon allows him to take the wheel. Like the Faulkner boys in Oxford, he is fascinated by a machine.

When Lucius' parents leave Jefferson to attend the funeral in Louisiana of Mrs. Priest's mother, the boy is supposed to stay with his Edmonds relatives. And now, as in *The Sound and the Fury*, a complicated chain of events stretches forward from the time of a grandmother's death. Instead of doing what his parents intended him to do, Lucius invents an elaborate lie and joins Boon Hogganbeck in a runaway automobile trip to Memphis. They are not far from Jefferson when they discover that Ned McCaslin is with them as a stowaway third passenger. The roads are bad, and the travelers must buy their way across a mud-hole which is continually kept wet by an avaricious countryman who sits beside it with a team of horses he rents at his own price to occupants of mired-down vehicles that need pulling out.

Arriving at Memphis, Boon and Lucius stay with Boon's old friend Miss Reba, in whose establishment Boon's attractive girlfriend Corrie is one of the prostitutes. Ned as a Negro must seek other lodgings, and he does, but in the process he also swaps the automobile for a racehorse misnamed Lightning. One mishap follows another. Lucius battles with another boy who insinuates that Corrie is not all that she should be. Though worsted and wounded in the tussle, he persuades Corrie to lead a better life. The horse is raced, at first with disastrous results, in attempts to win enough money to buy the automobile back. At length, as if by magic, Lucius hits on the secret of how to make Lightning a winner. But the car is returned only when Boss Priest comes to the rescue. Lucius returns to Jefferson to face punishment for his misdeeds.

For all of its surface of comic adventure, *The Reivers* closely follows the pattern of archetypal myths of initiation. The traditional mythical hero is lured away from his hut or castle, as Lucius is lured by Boon. On his journey he meets and must overcome or be overcome by an ominous presence which obstructs his passage, as the countryman by the mudhole obstructs the passage of the runaways from Jefferson. He journeys through a world which is intimate but unfamiliar, like Miss Reba's brothel. He meets and defends or rescues a maiden or discovers a goddess-mother, who can be thought of, together or singly, as Corrie and Miss Reba. The maiden rewards him, as Corrie does when she marries Boon and names their son Lucius Priest Hogganbeck. At the climax of the quest for maturity, he meets and in the face of tremendous obstacles overcomes challenges. His victory is achieved with seemingly magical aid, often with the assistance of seemingly divine intervention, as Lucius on the charger Lightning gallops to miraculous victory aided by a Boss whose name is Priest. Finally, the hero returns, chastened but wiser.

But what happens in *The Reivers* need not be placed against the outlines of familiar myth. The adventures of the runaway trio can stand alone. If Ned is too often casually presented as a storybook Negro, sometimes uppity and usually irresponsible, Boon is set forth more convincingly. Competent but unreliable, he is at the beginning only physically mature. He is a slave to impulse and appetite. His simplicity supplies easy answers to questions of what is right and what is wrong. His errors are innocent, as a child's might be. But Boon is strong and, within limitations, loyal. He means to protect Lucius. When he fails, the failure results from garbled and comic and very human good intentions. His love for Corrie is gruff but sincere. She is a character familiar to almost any reader of fiction, a country girl who is immoral without being really bad, the reformed strumpet who becomes a loyal wife. Her real name, which she conceals because she is ashamed of it, is Everbe Corinthia. Boon will not recognize, though a reader may, its implications of Corinthian art, which is gracefully ornate, and Corinthian morality, which is remembered as given over to luxurious dissipation. Miss Reba, as the "monster" who enslaves her, is again seen as a lovable immoralist, tolerant and generous.

Among these characters who are fleshed out from familiar models, the boy Lucius stands out sturdily. It is his story which is being told, as he remembers it many years later. The others are contributory instruments in the construction of his character. Though Lucius is also a recognizable type, who gets into mischief and must pay for his misdeeds, he nonetheless suggests the kind of boy which almost any man remembers himself to have been. He is foolhardy, he is brave, and beneath the kind of elaborate deceptions in which any boy becomes involved, he is completely honest. Like Tom Sawyer or like Booth Tarkington's Penrod or even, in some measure, like J. D. Salinger's Holden Caulfield, he is incorrigibly resourceful.

But he learns more than any of these. Like Huck Finn, he is willing to accept responsibility for what he has done. The adventures which lead him toward self-knowledge are often hilariously and intricately amusing. The humane comedy of the three novels about Flem Snopes and his ubiquitous relatives and the patient delineation of Ike McCaslin's initiation in *Go Down, Moses* are combined into another parable, which, when it became a motion picture, simplified Faulkner's familiar themes for many thousands of viewers. Their response increased the reputation of *The Reivers* as Faulkner's funniest book.

Courage and Compassion

10

William Faulkner once said that no writer has more than one story to tell. He tries to tell it once, and it does not go right. So he tries it again, with a different set of characters perhaps, or a different setting. Everything that he produces is a fragment. Each flight toward expression finally falls short. *The Sound and the Fury* was started as a short tale, to be told by an idiot, but Benjy's revelation of what happens failed wholly to reveal what had been suggested to Faulkner by his vision of a brave little girl climbing a tree. He then told the same story again, three times more. The result is a dense and difficult novel, wondrously conceived and masterfully executed. Circling ever more closely toward a center, it approaches its theme by indirection, allowing glimpses of motive or meaning, but it fails to snare the total vision.

Truths suggested by vision are elusive. When prisoned by declaration, they become codes which may be useful but which are limiting. Motion when arrested becomes static. Faulkner's achievement is to have created a world in which action, thought, and speculation remain continually fluid. Observation which pauses to view one portion of this world is pushed aside by the rush of other portions which tumble distractingly across the scene. Time and myth and legend and varieties of human error keep the pageant ceaselessly embroiled. "If it aint complicated up enough," Faulkner once said, "it aint true." People like Benjy Compson prefer things to remain in their ordered place. Beyond lies confusion, even terror. That is the territory which Faulkner preferred to explore.

Writers like Ernest Hemingway or Henry James seem to suggest that people are better off when they confine themselves to what they can be sure about. Confronted by the waste land of the modern world, T. S. Eliot submitted himself to the authority of tradition. Faulkner chose to test tradition, to discover whether, like almost any other man-made thing, it might not be deficient. Like Henry David Thoreau, who suggested a second look to men who lead lives of quiet desperation, he reached into the tangle of nature and human nature for fundamental truths. Herman Melville once said that he admired men who dare dive deeply toward truth, even at the risk of their own destruction. Faulkner as a novelist took great risks. Some of his dives were whoppers indeed.

His experiments in ways to tell a story did not always succeed. Some critics have thought that either of the narratives which make up *The Wild Palms* are better when read separately than when a chapter of one alternates with a chapter of the other. The story of Temple Drake in *Sanctuary* overshadows its companion story of Horace Benbow, and Popeye becomes its most memorable male. A *Fable* can seem to be fabulously forced. Each trial at a new technique, however, was an effort to move beyond time-worn ways to quick, new penetration. Faulkner sought innovation, not for its own sake, but to explore toward a truer and more comprehensive view. He abandoned the convention of the novelist-as-narrator or the novelist as a helpful intruder who explains what happens and why it happens. Instead his characters become narrators, each with his own sense of what takes or has taken place. Every reader must enter into the story as mediator. From conflicting or imperfect evidence of people who are usually very sure about what they say, he is led toward insights concerning the human condition.

Joseph Conrad has used this method, though not so consistently nor with such variation in character and tone. In his *The Heart of Darkness* evil looms ominously, deeply rooted and inescapable. No more than do Faulkner's narrators does Conrad's Captain Marlowe know whether everything that he talks about is true. In *Lord Jim* he pieces bits of evidence together gradually, much as Gavin Stevens does in *Knight's Gambit* or *Requiem for a Nun*. The irresistible malevolence which lurks beneath the surface of Conrad's world is self-reflecting, like the beast in the jungle which his friend Henry James supposed could be confined by the circumscribing imposition of form. Relationships among people, James explained, are so infinitely complicated and ultimately chaotic that the novelist in telling about them must contrive a pattern within which they seem to cohere intelligently.

Faulkner is less gloomy than Conrad and less limiting than Henry James. He is suspicious of intelligence which draws restricting boundaries. Those of his characters who do draw such boundaries are so obsessed by what they think is true that what is really true escapes them. Others view the truth distorted by a veil of doubt or suspicion. In *The Sound and the Fury*, because his family's fortunes decline, Mr. Compson supposes all virtue to have disappeared. In *The Hamlet* the sewing-machine salesman Ratliff is sure that Flem Snopes secretly makes love to young Negro customers because he knows that is what all country storekeepers do. Doubt oppresses Joe Christmas in *Light in August*. Certainty imposed by tradition makes the righteous women of Jefferson insist in *The Unvanquished* that Colonel Sartoris marry Drusilla Hawk. Friction created by these opposites supplies much of the drama in Faulkner's fiction.

Both doubt and certainty derive from attitudes toward time. The past impinges on the present in numberless combinations. In *Light in August* Gail Hightower, with little personal experience, is enslaved by legends. Joe Christmas knows little of his ancestry, certainly nothing of legendary glory, but he is warped by experience. Traditional notions of what families should be and how a brother must relate to his sister bewilder Quentin Compson in *Absalom, Absalom!* To Anse Bundren in *As I Lay Dying*, the past is only a time when promises were made. Sometimes time seems best forgotten. It moves noiselessly by Lena Grove, who, as she continues her search for the father of her child, exclaims, "My, my. A body does get around. Here we aint been coming from Alabama but two months, and now it's already Tennessee." Only for idiots like Benjy Compson or Ike Snopes does time not exist. Dilsey makes the best of time, guided by ancient truths which she does not question. Faulkner's later statements, in the address which he gave at Stockholm on receiving the Nobel Prize and in remarks to students in this country and abroad, make it plain that the structure of his belief rested on a foundation of simple but timeless verities. Compassion and courage are chief among them, and respect for nature in all its guises. Man will endure when he discovers these qualities within himself. He has outlived the dinosaur, and he will outlive the atom bomb. However distorted into creeds which regularize and control, these ancient truths alone can lift man's heart. They are more than words. They are common denominators which prove all men brothers.

Crusted over by custom, warped to strange meanings by strange sects, these verities are often difficult to find. One must delve beneath surfaces to discover them even in himself. Brave deeds of ancestors become crutches for crippled men. Love can be used as a convenient word. Compassion can turn inward to become self-pity which is isolating. Courage can become a public pose. People are terrified because of what they imagine to be the inevitable consequences of what they or others who have blundered like them have done. Victory becomes an excuse for retaliation. Defeat writes its own passport to despair. Forgotten are "the problems of the human heart in conflict with itself . . . the old verities and truths of the heart, the old universal truths without which any story is ephemeral and damned."

Faulkner did not come easily to these conclusions. He spoke in Stockholm of a writer's "anguish and travail" as he labors "in the agony and sweat of the human spirit . . .

to create out of the materials of the human spirit something which did not exist before." As he identified and finally made plain this simple and persuasive theme, he became —perhaps as all men must—the captive of his declarations. Much of his later work bristles with determination to inform. In *Go Down, Moses* and *A Fable* he produced patient parables which reveal evil and suggest that something redemptive may be done about it. Few more compelling exposures of man's culpability and promise have appeared in the twentieth century. Faulkner entered boldly into these books and encapsulated himself within the limits of his convictions.

Less certain, he is less present in earlier writings. In *The Sound and the Fury, As I Lay Dying, Light in August,* and *Absalom, Absalom!* he was more often satisfied to present characters who are confused by certainty or doubt, who lack compassion, or misuse courage, but who speak for themselves in a variety of voices. One achievement which sets Faulkner apart from Joseph Conrad or Henry James is the range of his characterization. He caught the tone and attitudes of poor white farmers, sturdy country yeomen, aristocrats in their glory or with glory gone, girls who are lushly amoral and girls who are mean, women who whine and women who are brave or reminiscent, good-hearted madams like Miss Reba and warm-hearted prostitutes like Corrie, brave boys and foolhardy young men, gangsters, bootleggers, petty thieves, murderers, and saints.

Some of them may be found to be stock characters overdrawn, like many of the characters of Charles Dickens, whom Faulkner admired. Only a few are simple. Most of his narrators are too strong-willed to be manipulated into conventional methods of telling a story consecutively, from beginning to end. As people are likely to do, they take it for granted that listeners know what is being talked about. They start at the middle or the end, to speak of consequences of actions, the causes of which are only later disclosed. They reminisce as countrymen do, sometimes laconically, more often drawling at great length, coming leisurely to their point.

Events are likely to seem to them like other events. Parallels are discovered between what happens and what is myth or legend. Because most people are most familiar with the Christian myth, they most easily discover correspondences with it. What they know of folk history or local legend, of classic tragedy or the quest for the Holy Grail, also provides familiar patterns into which contemporary events are fitted. T. S. Eliot once said that all poetry comes from poetry of the past. Faulkner went a further step to suggest that man's interpretation of or excuse for what he does is determined by fables which other men have created. History, that is to say, is a fiction often retold.

The tendency of the human mind to make almost everything seem like something else is so skillfully managed that not only characters but readers also are led toward making such associations. Violence is a reminder of instances of violence in the past. It recalls the implacable, mighty force of nature beside which man's strength seems immeasurably small. Fire and flood, the wild blood coursing through the land, the sound of rushing hooves and the restlessness of mobs, airplanes in flight and automobiles careening at breakneck speed are strategies used by Faulkner to reinforce a sense of urgent movement. One generation passes and another takes its place, continuously to aspire and err. In search for reasons for what he does, man ransacks the past for convenient exemplars.

Faulkner's view has been compared by the French existentialist Jean-Paul Sartre to "that of a man sitting in a convertible looking back. At every moment shadows emerge on his right, and on his left flickering and quavering points of light, which become trees, men and cars only when seen in perspective." The convertible moves, so that it is not where it was. Yet where it was determines where it is. The same old convertible plunges onward, with Faulkner looking continually backward reflecting on the relationship of *Is* to *Was*.

He once explained that the whole of his intention was to capture all of life within a single sentence (within a single word, he said, if that could be done). So elusive is the flow of life that his sentences circle and twist, moving from supposition to fact, from past to present, sinuously evading certainty as they attempt to weave a web in which to catch all meaning. Faulkner's long sentences, his circumlocutions and ruminations, have a hypnotic effect. Readers are lulled to acquiescence to what they do not understand or are compelled toward reveries of their own and to insights which they, no more than Faulkner, can easily explain. Like him, they become overwhelmed by recognition of humanity's long history of anguish, self-torture, and despair, but are heartened also by timeless assurances of the redeeming power of sacrifice, courage, and compassion.

Faulkner's view is an uneasy view, disturbed by contradictions. Though he was not himself a churchman, most of his stories rest on a foundation of Christian virtue. He mined the Bible for analogues of the tales he wished to tell, yet his sharpest satire is directed against people who find scriptural authority for what they do. The necessity for redemption becomes increasingly a theme in his fiction, in which smug piety and self-assured righteousness are bitterly attacked. Negroes are often condescendingly presented as people of quaint antics, yet Dilsey in *The Sound and the Fury* and Lucas Beauchamp in *Intruder in the Dust* are models for emulation. Blackness symbolically represents universal evil, and slavery is a dark stain which disfigures the white man. Pride is an excellent attribute when rightly grounded, but humility is also excellent. Love, when natural, is good. Made self-serving, it becomes destructive.

Outrage at what man has done is balanced by conviction that man can do better. For though Faulkner often spoke of man's tragic fate, his is not the tragic view. His people are human and splendidly absurd, comically belaboring themselves with error. Evil seems certainly to exist, and nature broods in menace or munificence. Humanity is betrayed by humanity. People die, sometimes the victims of themselves, sometimes victims of others. But tragedy is something devised by people like Quentin Compson in *Absalom, Absalom!* as a simple explanation, comforting because it seems to ease a burden.

Faulkner's comic view is more difficult to maintain. It is centered on man, who often means well but does badly. The life which he portrays is complex, and often painful. Man is not redeemed by acts of divine grace. No man can expect special attention from God: God is explained as in the wholesale, not the retail business. Nor do men who are organized by creed necessarily find salvation. Creeds are only man-made formulas. God is not man-made. But every man is "created in the image of God," wrote Faulkner, "so that he shall have the power and the will to choose right from wrong and be able to save himself." Each man must be his own redeemer.

Such emphasis on the responsibility of the individual places Faulkner within a familiar American tradition. He is engaged in what Quentin Anderson has called a retreat from culture, which is a corporate product, the fruit of tradition. Rather like Ralph Waldo Emerson a century before, he relies on personal insight. And Faulkner's protean parables also resemble Nathaniel Hawthorne's fables about adventures of the human heart. It is the heart, Faulkner told a class of young writers at the University of Virginia, "that makes you want to be brave when you are afraid you might be a coward, that wants you to be generous or wants you to be compassionate when you think that maybe you won't." The heart acts impetuously—as Faulkner's characters often do. His quarrel is not, as Herman Melville's has been said to be, with God. His quarrel is with men.

Men have destroyed the great forests. They have desecrated the pleasant places of the earth. The wilderness has disappeared beneath macadam and steel, to remind men of a vanished paradise. Eden is lost because men continue to repeat old error. As an ecologist Faulkner is more denunciatory and far-reaching than even Thoreau. The good land whose spoiling he resents is wilder and more demanding than the humanized landscape around Walden Pond. There are more people in it, created each in the image of nature. They are often violent and uncontrolled. Some are as deceptive as an autumn evening, and some are placid, like the long, quiet, sleepy summer days at Frenchman's Bend. People like Popeye in *Sanctuary* pollute fresh springs. Lena Grove in *Light in August* accepts what nature provides. Ike McCaslin in *Go Down, Moses* realizes that the land is a common heritage, and man a creature of the same shaping force which created the world.

The question of which will last longer, man or nature, is not answered because it does not have to be. For Faulkner, man and the land are conterminous, though man needs nature more than nature needs man. Man's is a puny voice, Faulkner declared, but man has heart and will and determination. He will endure as long as nature endures. Not all people will survive, not necessarily people from Yoknapatawpha, a cursed but burgeoning land, and not necessarily only white people. No person owns any more years than nature allows. But mankind will survive, if only to repeat mistakes which people previously had made. That is its deathless designation.

Its armor is courage and compassion. Strength will avail, and determination, but only when bolstered by pity and love, and by respect for nature, which provides cradle, sustenance, and grave. Life does not die. The human spirit endures, though its creeds and deeds are maliciously subverted for the convenience of people who share in the spirit but refuse to respond to it or who are so scarred by error that even the existence of this spirit remains unnoticed. Man's scrambling mind brings no salvation. The heart coarsened by flesh can be lured by the head to self-serving and self-destroying complexities. In a time more threatened by destruction than Thoreau's time, Faulkner joined the man from Concord, and the man from Nazareth also, by exhorting, "Simplify, simplify!"

But Faulkner may not be a completely reliable guide. He was more an artist than an intellectual. His reading was wide and various, but like that of most people was largely directed by personal predilection. He seems to have liked best those books which reflected his own views or advanced them in directions which seemed attractive. Algernon Swinburne seemed to spring, said Faulkner, "from some tortured undergrowth of my adolescence, like a highway-man, making me his slave." The English poet who liked sound and sweeping rhythms spoke in pagan opposition to convention. "I can not tell to this day," said Faulkner, "exactly to what depths he stirred me." John Keats stirred him perhaps even more deeply. William Butler Yeats and A. E. Housman influenced him. He found a companion voice in T. S. Eliot's plaint against modern sterility and ponderings on the influence of time past on time present.

Among novelists, he moved beyond the sophisticated chatter of Aldous Huxley to Charles Dickens, who was masterful in presenting characters; to Joseph Conrad, whose dark world would be transported to Yoknapatawpha and there lightened by humor; to James Joyce, who had a magician's dexterity with words; and to many more. Read widely, he advised cadet listeners at West Point, read everything, anything, even trash. Faulkner's mind was filled with legendary tales, biblical and classic lore, and native yarns found in Washington Irving or such southeastern humorists as George Washington Harris, whose impious anecdotes about Sut Lovingood he kept on his bedside table.

Beyond this, Faulkner was a good listener and an ex-traordinary mimic. He learned from country neighbors how to tell a tale, lavishly and discursively. A story must flow, Mark Twain once said, "as flows the brook down hills and leafy woodlands, its course changed by every boulder it comes across . . . its surface broken but its course not stayed." To follow such a narrative, a reader must be alert to quick and quizzical changes, to hints concealed by un-derstatement, as the speaker's voice moves leisurely in giant detours, delaying expectation.

American writers have almost always been better at suggesting than explaining. Few have been trained to logical expression, which derives from acquaintance with mankind's great store of knowledge. Since Thoreau was graduated from Harvard in 1827, no one among them of major stature before Ezra Pound and T. S. Eliot completed college—not Walt Whitman, Herman Melville, Emily Dickinson, Mark Twain, Henry James, Stephen Crane, or Ernest Hemingway. This is not the place to argue whether a college education benefits or handicaps an artist, but the lack of it may explain why among Americans there has been an almost universal preference for heart over head. Our writers have been democratic and most often romantic. Their emphasis has been less on authority than on the free man and his sympathetic understanding of what Whitman called men *en masse*. These writers confidently assert faith in possibility for goodness in man and in man's ability finally to recognize truth within himself. America remains a new Eden, threatened by destruction because of willful ingenuity and careless greed, but is still a land of promise.

Faulkner's later patient explanations of what from the beginning he had really meant are less impressive than the inchoate, probing revelations of his writings in the late 1920's and during the 1930's. The oracular voice of the 1950's reveals both more and greatly less than the tantalizing circlings of his earlier period. As he embraced certainty, he abandoned the countervailing efficacy of doubt. Simply, traditionally, and perhaps correctly, he tightened strings to draw elements of his world together, each to its ordered place.

But before he did that, he created the world of Yoknapatawpha. That sprawling countryside filled with people who are ridiculous or pathetic or mean continues to exist. From its traditions and the myths and legends which contributed to them, and from the hapless, well-meaning, or conniving exploits of its inhabitants he created fresh revelations of man's recurring comic plight which is sustained by human error. So various and convincing is this world which is rooted in local and provincial tradition that it expands beyond region or nation to become a timeless image. The problems of Yoknapatawpha are those of the world, odd and baffling and not susceptible to quick solution. Faulkner's achievement is not in providing answers, but in creating a spacious, expansive, and recognizable facsimile in which are embedded ineradicable suggestions of why people act in the strange ways that they do. Once entered, Faulkner's world is perceived as familiar, for each reader recognizes it as his own.

A Selected Bibliography

By Faulkner

1924 *The Marble Faun*
1926 *Soldier's Pay*
1927 *Mosquitoes*
1929 *Sartoris*
1929 *The Sound and the Fury*
1930 *As I Lay Dying*
1931 *Sanctuary*
1932 *Light in August*
1933 *A Green Bough*
1935 *Pylon*
1936 *Absalom, Absalom!*
1938 *The Unvanquished*
1939 *The Wild Palms*

1940 *The Hamlet*
1942 *Go Down, Moses*
1948 *Intruder in the Dust*
1949 *Knight's Gambit*
1950 *Collected Stories of William Faulkner*
1951 *Requiem for a Nun*
1954 *A Fable*
1955 *Big Woods*
1957 *The Town*
1959 *The Mansion*
1962 *The Reivers*

About Faulkner

ADAMS, RICHARD P. *Faulkner: Myth and Motion*. Princeton: Princeton University Press, 1968.

BECK, WARREN. *Man in Motion: Faulkner's Trilogy.* Madison: University of Wisconsin Press, 1961.

BLOTNER, JOSEPH. *Faulkner: A Biography.* New York: Random House, 1973.

BROOKS, CLEANTH. *William Faulkner: The Yoknapatawpha Country.* New Haven: Yale University Press, 1963.

FAULKNER, JOHN. *My Brother Bill: An Affectionate Reminiscence.* New York: Trident Press, 1963; Pocket Books, Inc., 1964.

HOFFMAN, FREDERICK J. *William Faulkner.* New York: The Twayne Press, 1961.

———— and OLGA W. VICKERY, eds. *William Faulkner: Three Decades of Criticism.* East Lansing: Michigan State University Press, 1966.

HOWE, IRVING. *William Faulkner: A Critical Study.* New York: Viking Books, 1951.

MILLGATE, MICHAEL. *The Achievement of William Faulkner.* New York: Random House, 1966.

O'CONNOR, WILLIAM VAN. *The Tangled Fire of William Faulkner.* Minneapolis: University of Minnesota Press, 1954.

————. *William Faulkner.* Minneapolis: University of Minnesota Press, 1959.

SWIGGART, PETER. *The Art of William Faulkner.* Austin: University of Texas Press, 1962.

THOMPSON, LAWRANCE. *William Faulkner: An Introduction and an Interpretation.* New York: Barnes and Noble, Inc., 1963.

TUCK, DOROTHY. *Crowell's Handbook of Faulkner.* New York: Thomas Y. Crowell Company, 1964.

VICKERY, OLGA W. *The Novels of William Faulkner: A Critical Interpretation.* Baton Rouge: Louisiana State University Press, 1964.

VOLPE, EDMUND L. *A Reader's Guide to William Faulkner.* New York: Farrar, Straus and Co., 1964.

WAGGONER, HYATT H. *William Faulkner: From Jefferson to the World.* Lexington: University of Kentucky Press, 1959.

Index

ABOUT THE AUTHOR

Lewis Leary teaches at the University of North Carolina in Chapel Hill, where he is William Rand Kenan, Jr., Professor of English. A graduate of the University of Vermont and Columbia University, where he received his Ph.D. degree, he has also taught literature at the American University in Beirut, the University of Miami, Duke University, and Columbia University, where he was professor of English and chairman of the Department of English and Comparative Literature for many years.

Dr. Leary has long been interested in William Faulkner and has conducted seminars on Faulkner at universities in the United States and abroad. He is the author of a number of critical studies of American writers, including *That Rascal Freneau: A Study in Literary Failure, Washington Irving, John Greenleaf Whittier,* and *Mark Twain.*